RACHID GHANNOUCHI

RELIGION AND GLOBAL POLITICS

Series Editor

John L. Esposito
University Professor and Director
Center for Muslim-Christian Understanding
Georgetown University

The Islamic Leviathan
State Power and Islam in Malaysia and Pakistan
Seyyed Vali Reza Nasr

Rachid Ghannouchi
A Democrat Within Islamism
Azzam S. Tamimi

RACHID GHANNOUCHI

A Democrat Within Islamism

AZZAM S. TAMIMI

OXFORD
UNIVERSITY PRESS

2001

OXFORD
UNIVERSITY PRESS

Oxford   New York

Athens   Auckland   Bangkok   Bogotá   Buenos Aires   Cape Town
Chennai   Dar es Salaam   Delhi   Glorence   Hong Kong   Istanbul   Karachi
Kolkata   Kuala Lumpur   Madrid   Melbourne   Mexico City   Mumbai   Nairobi
Paris   São Paulo   Shanghai   Singapore   Taipei   Tokyo   Toronto   Warsaw

and associated companies in
Berlin   Ibadan

Copyright © 2001 by Azzam S. Tamimi

Published by Oxford University Press, Inc.,
198 Madison Avenue, New York, New York 10016

Oxford is a registered trademark of Oxford University Press

Library of Congress Cataloging-in-Publication Data
Tamimi, Azzam.
Rachid Ghannouchi . a democrat within Islamism / Azzam S. Tamimi
p.   cm.—(Religion and global politics)
Includes bibliographical references and index.
ISBN 0-19-514000-1
1 Ghannashâ, Râshid.   2. Scholars, Muslim—Biography
3. Democracy—Religious aspects—Islam.   4. Islam and secularism—Tunisia.
5. Islam and politics—Tunisia.   6. Tunisia—Politics and government—1987-
I Title. II. Series.
BP80.G27 T36   2001
321.8'092—dc21   00-046519

1 3 5 7 9 8 6 4 2

Printed in the United States of America
on acid-free paper

Preface

It was by virtue of my involvement in Liberty for the Muslim World, a London-based organization concerned with monitoring human rights and democratization in Muslim countries that I developed an interest in pursuing academically the issue of Islam and democracy. Like many Muslims, I had been greatly disappointed with the forcible termination of the democratic process in Algeria and was dismayed by the attempt in some circles to justify the January 1992 military coup as having been inevitable in order to protect democracy from its enemies, the Islamists. I embarked on this work believing democracy to be compatible with Islam and hoping to establish this compatibility by means of academic research.

The idea was to refute the conclusions by some renowned Muslim political writers that Islam and democracy did not work. I also was motivated to pursue this line of research by the democratic experiment in Jordan, where, despite a fully-fledged Islamist participation in the political process, there was still a debate within Islamic movement circles as to whether democracy did, or did not, contradict Islam. This debate had actually been going on in much of the Arab world since the mid-1980s when the breeze of democratization seemed to blow across the region. The most significant development accompanying this trend had been the emergence within political Islam of groups willing to take part in the democratic process and pledging to respect the results of the elections and to play by the rules of the game.

Researching this topic necessitated an exploration of the concept of democracy in Western literature, followed by an investigation of the position of various Islamic schools of thought on the subject. It is no secret that contemporary Islamic revival movements generally dislike ideas that originate in the West, in reaction to Western colonization of much of the Muslim world and out of fear of loss of identity under the hammer of modernization. Writers affiliated with the Sayyid Qutb school, which had the greatest influence on Arab Islamic movements from the mid-1960s through the 1970s to the mid-1980s, had insisted that democracy was an ideology alien to Islam. By the mid-1980s this school started losing ground to another school of thought that maintained that democracy was not an ideology but a set of tools and mechanisms designed to control government power, which they considered to be perfectly compatible with the Islamic concepts of *bay'ah* and *shura*. To be fair, these ideas were not entirely new; they were espoused before by Afghani, Abduh, Kawakibi, Rida, and Malik Bennabi long before the "incompatibility" school took hold.

The focus of my interest shifted slightly in the wake of the international symposium on Power-Sharing Islam, which was organized in London by the Centre for the Study of Democracy (CSD) at the University of Westminster and Liberty for the Muslim World on 20 February 1993. The symposium hosted a number of intellectuals and representatives of Islamic movements. Papers on Islam and democracy, the concept of power-sharing and pluralism, and the experiences of the Islamic movements in Egypt, Jordan, Algeria, Malaysia, Yemen, and Kuwait were submitted.

Drawing on the symposium, I developed an interest in exploring the problems that faced Islamic movements as they participated in the process of democratization. I felt that investigating the attitude of Islamists vis-à-vis such problems would make a more interesting, and at the same time·more challenging, topic of research. The idea was to show that recent democratization experiences in countries such as Jordan, Egypt, Tunisia, Algeria, and Yemen prove that serious obstacles confront the transition to democracy in these countries. As far as I could see, most of these obstacles emanated from outside the Islamic camp, mainly from local authoritarian governments and from global powers seeking to preserve the status quo. There are, however, obstacles emanating from within the Islamic camp itself caused by the emergence of radical trends within the phenomenon of Islamic revival that reject democracy and consider it a heresy imported from the West.

In the meantime I had been in contact with Rachid Ghannouchi, one of the most prominent thinkers in the realm of contemporary Islamic thought and the exiled leader of the Tunisian Islamic movement Ennahda. I developed an interest in Ghannouchi when I met him in London in February 1992, during which time I was asked to translate a paper submitted by him to a conference on Islam and Democracy in North Africa organized at the London School of Economics by its Islamic Society. Thereafter, whenever Ghannouchi was invited to give a talk or present a paper I was asked to interpret his talk or translate his paper. The talks and papers covered issues such as democracy, secularism, civil society, human rights, the nation-state, civil liberties, Islam and the West, the role and future of Islamic movements, Islamic minorities, and the political situation in Tunisia and North Africa.

Rachid Ghannouchi leads a school in modern Islamic political thought that advocates democracy and pluralism. He believes democracy to be a set of mechanisms for guaranteeing the sovereignty of the people and for supplying safety valves against corruption and the hegemonic monopoly of power. While insisting on the compatibility of democracy with Islam, he believes that because of their secular foundations, contemporary forms of liberal democracy may not suit Muslim societies. Ghannouchi's last and most important book, *Al-Hurriyyat al-'Ammah Fid-Dawlah al-Islamiyyah* (Public liberties in the Islamic state), has been an important contribution to the current debate within Islamic circles on the nature, duties, and restraints of government in Islam. Yet, although he has authored ten important books, very little of his thought has so far been made available to readers of English. Little has been written about Ghannouchi in English, and most of what has been written about him by academics happens to be part of a discussion of either the Tunisian Islamic movement or the question of Islam and democracy. Because I have translated many of the talks he has given and the papers he has written for English audiences since he settled in London, I therefore feel something of an authority on his political perspectives. I feel well placed to research the genealogy of his political thought and the way he perceives the process of democratization and the obstacles facing it in the Arab world, especially in the North African region.

This book, which is a treatise in the field of political theory, begins with a biography of the first twenty-five or so years of Ghannouchi's life, depicting his childhood and maturation from the time he was a young boy frequenting school in a remote Tunisian village until he interrupted his postgraduate studies in Paris and returned home. The genealogy of Rachid Ghannouchi's political thought finds its roots in his youth when he was first attracted to Nassirism, then abandoned it for an Ikhwan-Salafi style of religiosity, and finally progressed to an Islamic activism of Tunisian specificity. Several factors contributed to the development of his personality and political thinking. These included the traditional az-Zaytouna school curriculum, the Muslim Brotherhood school of thought, the thought of the Algerian thinker Malik Bennabi, his Islamic movement's interaction with local Tunisian forces, such as those of liberalism and communism, the Iranian revolution, and the Sudanese model of Islamism.

The biographical account leads to an analysis of Ghannouchi's understanding of democracy and his theory of compatibility between democracy and Islam. In this, Ghannouchi is indebted to Malik Bennabi, whose essay on Islam and democracy was Ghannouchi's launching pad and the seed that germinated and gave rise to the lofty work of *Al-Hurriyyat al-'Ammah*. To assess Ghannouchi and to analyze his conception of democracy, it is necessary to reflect on Western democratic theory. It is also necessary to examine some of the core themes of liberal democracy and determine Ghannouchi's position on them. An example of the last point is Ghannouchi's rejection of the widely accepted assumption in the West that secularism is an essential prerequisite of democracy. His argument that democracy is not an ideology, but a tool for electing, checking, and dismissing or replacing a system of government and for protecting the civil liberties and basic rights of citizens, is found to have opponents and supporters both in the West and in the world of Islam.

The same approach is made in the analysis of Ghannouchi's theory that democratization in the Arab world is hindered by secularism, the modern territorial-state, the new world order, and radical trends within Islamism. Ghannouchi's use of the terms *secularism, liberalism, modernity,* and *civil society* is contrasted with Western conceptions of these terms. In analyzing his response to Islamists who reject democracy, his theory of *faragh* (space)—that Islam consists of that which is *dini* (religious) and that which is *siyasi* (political)—is discussed at length. Finally, Ghannouchi's critics are considered. Apart from his political foes and ideological opponents, and notwithstanding his influence and popularity, Ghannouchi is criticized by two groups of Islamists: the first is a traditionalist elite that considers him to be too concessionary to the West; and the second is a class of converts from liberalism or Marxism to Islam, who criticize him for not recognizing, or acknowledging, some of the serious shortcomings of Western democracy and secularization. The book gives consideration to the current debate in and around Ghannouchi about the adequacy, and possible limits, of his comments on secularity.

The overall aim of this book is to introduce to English-speaking audiences a prominent contemporary Islamic thinker, little of whose writings have been translated into English. I have tried to the best of my ability to consider analytically the meaning of Ghannouchi's overall output, which is very prolific; to highlight its key themes; to examine potential inconsistencies within his work; and to try to explain those inconsistencies.

London   A. S. T.
March 2001

Acknowledgments

I am greatly indebted to my *ustadh* and dear friend, Professor John Keane, for his guidance and patience, which made it possible for me to bring this work to completion. The amount of knowledge I have gained since I first met him is invaluable.

I am equally grateful to my dear friend and *ustadh*, Professor John Esposito, for his encouragement, advice, and assistance.

My deepest gratitude is due to my other *ustadh*, Sheikh Rachid Ghannouchi, from whom, and about whom, I have learned a great deal since we met in February 1992.

I wish to thank all those who have helped me during the course of my research. My special thanks go to Professor Abdelwahab Elmessiri, *Ustadh* Munir Shafiq, Dr. Abdelwahab el-Affendi, and Dr. Farid el-Shayyal.

Without the support, encouragement, and loving care of my wife, Rifqah, it would have been impossible to accomplish even a small portion of this work.

Contents

RACHID GHANNOUCHI

1

From Qabis to Paris

In the Village

In a bunker in a small village close to Hamma in the province of Gabès in southeastern Tunisia, Rachid Ghannouchi was born on 22 June 1941. His family, together with several others, had been sheltering from the bombardment of the Axis powers during World War II. It was a time of turmoil, confusion, and imminent transformation.

The tribes of the region had been rebelling against the French colonizers since before the war. By 9 April 1938, the day anti-French demonstrations were organized throughout the country, the tribal uprising had reached the political elite, injecting it with courage and hope after having ignited the people's passion for independence. When France and Britain responded to the German invasion of Poland with a declaration of war on 3 September 1939, French colonial authorities in Tunisia had been struggling to contain a situation that threatened to get out of hand. Hundreds of Tunisians had been arrested and scores of their leaders banished. However, by the end of June 1940 France collapsed and surrendered to the Germans and a new French puppet regime was set up at Vichy. The impact on the Tunisians was enormous. They saw with their own eyes the downfall of a colonial power that to them was arrogant and confident. France, which claimed political, military, and cultural superiority, had been vanquished by Germany, which, being the enemy of Tunisia's enemy, had been seen by many as the new friend of Tunisia. Since then and until the end of the war, Tunisia had come under the control of the pro-German Vichy regime. In spite of mixed feelings among members of the political elite, this was a period of relative relief. Bey Muhammad el-Muncef, who acceded to the throne on 19 June 1942, resisted pressure from both the Axis powers and the Allies to take sides in the war. He identified with the grievances of his people and sought the release of activists detained inside Tunisia or outside it in Algeria or France. His reign witnessed renewed political activism and the return to Tunisia of a number of banished political leaders including Bourguiba, who returned to the country on 7 April 1943. As the Bey was engaged in consultation with the New Desturian Party to form a new cabinet that would have included Bourguiba and Saleh bin Yousef, Allied troops defeated the Germans and conquered Tunis, the capital, on 7 May 1943. On 13 May, the French forced the abdication of Bay el-Muncef in favor of his son Muhammad el-Amein. El-Muncef was initially detained in the south of Algeria, then moved back to Tunis; upon the liberation of France he was banished to southern France where he remained until he died on 1 September 1948.

Following the removal of Bey el-Muncef and for several years after the end of the war, the Tunisians were made to pay for what the French believed was betrayal. Tunisians were collectively accused of supporting the Axis powers in the war and of showing contempt to the French. Indeed, the defeat of France had lifted the spirits of Tunisians, increasing their confidence and self-esteem. There was a rise in attacks on colonial farms and in the rate of desertion from the armed forces. There had also been a marked growth in the size of the anti-colonial armed movement known as the *fallaga*. In what Tunisians believed to be a desire for revenge, the French colonial authorities inflicted collective punishment on the population. Villages were stormed and desecrated under the pretext of searching for remnants of Axis troops; no less than ten thousand Tunisians were rounded up and placed in detention camps and military trials were staged for those accused of collaboration with the Germans.[1] Such were the conditions in Tunisia when Ghannouchi was growing from infancy into childhood.

Ghannouchi grew up in a traditional Muslim community that had not yet been invaded by the features of "modernity," such as modern means of transport and communication and whatever village folks would condemn as imported Western social habits in costume, leisure, and entertainment. The village had no electricity and only very occasionally did mechanized vehicles approach it. Ghannouchi himself rode in a car for the first time at the age of fifteen. The only radio receiver in the village belonged to his uncle from his mother's side, a businessman named al-Bashir. A huge battery that had to be taken to town for recharging powered the radio. Wrapped in tradition and concealed from the outside world, the village had not yet experienced a clash with the Western values that had already had a significant impact on life in towns and cities. If anything undermined tradition in this remote village, it was the burden of history, or what Ghannouchi describes as the remnants of an archaic society that was eroding from within due to internal rather than external factors.[2]

Ghannouchi was the youngest of ten brothers and sisters. His father, Sheikh Muhammad, was one of the few villagers known for having memorized fully the Holy Qur'an. He was not a scholar but was knowledgeable enough to be recognized by the village as an *imam* and a *mufti*. Every Ramadan, the fasting month in the Muslim calendar, villagers would come to Ghannouchi's house, where Sheikh Muhammad would lead them in the *tarawih* prayer, a special prayer performed at night only during the month of Ramadan. Villagers would send their children to Sheikh Muhammad to teach them the Qur'an in the prayer room inside the house in winter and under the palm trees in the field in summer.

Under the instruction and guidance of his father, Ghannouchi learned and memorized the Qur'an, just as his elder brothers did before. He enjoyed living in a stable home. The domestic environment was one of harmony, compassion, and peace despite the fact that his father was married to more than one wife. Ghannouchi's own mother was quite influential; she was the last and youngest of the four wives of Sheikh Muhammad, and she was the most jealous. At the same time, she revered her husband and obeyed him. Concord dominated the relationship between his mother, whom he called *dada*, and his stepmother, Sheikh Muhammad's first and eldest wife, whom he respected, loved, and called *ummı* (my mother). Ghannouchi did not meet his father's two other wives, one of whom died and the other was divorced before he was born.

Economically, the family was neither rich nor poor. Peasants in the village were generally content and felt equal; their society had not yet been plagued with competition and consumerism. There were no destitute families in the village thanks to the prevalent spirit of solidarity. At the same time, those who were rich were happy to share with others and to live modestly like everybody else. Like every other average family in the village, the Ghannouchis rarely ate meat, sometimes only twice a year on *Eid* days. It was customary for those who brought home meat on other than those special occasions to offer some to their neighbors.

Sheikh Muhammad was one of a very few literate people in the village. He was also among the very few who did not believe in offering sacrifices to the *awliya'* (plural of *wali*: a dead saint in folk traditional religiosity). Most villagers adhered to inherited practices believed to be effective in guaranteeing a swift granting of wishes. These included offering a *tays* (billy-goat) to the *jadd*, a local term for *wali*. Nothing, not even poverty or extreme hunger, would be a good enough reason for them to abandon the pledge to dedicate a *tays* to a *jadd*. Sheikh Muhammad would tell his children that such practices were alien to Islam; he would also forbid them from visiting the tombs of *awliya'* and from attending the *mawalid* (plural of *mawlid*: a Sufi custom of celebrating the birthday of a *wali* or that of the Prophet). It was customary for each family to associate itself with a *wali* to whom it would turn for help and whose name its members would invoke to affirm their oaths. Sheikh Muhammad considered such acts to be practices of *shirk* (assigning partners with God), from which he did his best to protect his household.

Sheikh Muhammad once tried to work in trading, but lost his trade and returned to farming. He and his family lived in a large house that was also home to the families of his brothers, Ghannouchi's uncles. They all worked in the field. They would all, men and women, the young and the old, leave for the field early in the morning and return home in the evening exhausted and craving for a meal of *kuskusı*, which they would devour with delight. Such pleasure has long been missed by Ghannouchi, who recalls vividly how the exhaustion from working all day in the field would soon be gone and the nightly "shift" of making baskets from palm leaves would begin. Winter nights were particularly unforgettable. Traditional Tunisian tea would keep them company until midnight and even past it. As they wove the baskets, they would sing together hymns praising God and the Prophet. The singing would uplift their spirits, provide them with energy, and keep them awake.

Until the age of sixteen, Ghannouchi grew up in a large extended family of which his maternal uncle, al-Bashir, was a distinguished member. Al-Bashir had been a great supporter of Arabism and a great admirer of its leader, President Nassir of Egypt. Al-Bashir's house was a regular meeting point, where Ghannouchi would sit together with other members of the family, young and old, to listen attentively to Egyptian radio broadcasts, to Nassir's speeches, and to his uncle's analysis of political events in the country, in the *Mashriq* (Arab East), and worldwide. Of particular interest was al-Bashir's analysis of Nassir's struggle against "Western foes." For Ghannouchi, those evening family meetings were most enjoyable: they were windows through which he saw the world outside the village; they were political alphabets inscribed in his young unquestioning, unsuspecting brain. His uncle would describe Nassir as the *bikbashi* (from the Turkish *binbasi*: an army major), a title Ghannouchi thought was most grandiose and worthy only of a hero like Nassir.

Al-Bashir was also a member of the Bourguiba-led national liberation movement against the French who had been occupying Tunisia since 1881. He had been politically active since the inception of the national movement in the forties. Ghannouchi remembers vividly that at the age of five he saw his mother weeping over the imprisonment of his uncle by the French. Although al-Bashir was imprisoned only for a few months, this was a bitter experience unprecedented in the family and causing it much distress and sorrow. Upon his release, al-Bashir emerged, in the eyes of fellow villagers, as a national hero for whom Ghannouchi had great admiration and respect. When, just before independence, Bourguiba visited Hamma to organize armed resistance against the French, it was al-Bashir and some local leaders who hosted him and made the necessary arrangements for his security. However, after independence, by virtue of Bourguiba's anti-Nassir anti-*Mashriq* disposition, al-Bashir withdrew his support for him. Although henceforth he ceased to be politically active he criticized Bourguiba and his party harshly.

As a child, Ghannouchi witnessed the birth of armed resistance against the French. When he was eleven, in 1952, villagers were mobilized to join the resistance. Hamma had become a resistance stronghold. Its inhabitants were descendants of Bani Hilal, Arab tribes known for their pride and love of chivalry. Less than a year later a battle raged in the mountains overlooking Hamma between the *fallaga* (guerrillas) and the French army. The French killed four of the *fallaga* and threw their bodies in the marketplace for all to see. On his way back home from school, Ghannouchi saw the bodies on the ground. French troops were keeping guard to prevent the removal, and thus the burial, of the "martyrs." The incident had a profound influence on him; it generated within him what he describes as "unlimited hatred" for the French colonizers.

These events coincided with another memorable experience, which occured when Ghannouchi was still at primary school. He came across an article about the atrocities perpetrated by the Zionists in the village of Deir Yassin in Palestine in April 1948. He read how 250 Palestinians, including many women and children, were massacred by Irgun and Stern terrorist gangs under the command of Menachem Begin and Yitzhak Shamir. Both of these men later became prime ministers of the State of Israel. He also read that the objective of this and other carefully designed massacres was to intimidate the rest of the Palestinian population and drive them out of their land prior to declaring the creation of Israel. The depiction of Palestinians being slaughtered or forced out of their homes distressed him enormously. While filling his eyes with tears, the article opened them to an image of the *Mashriq* he had frequently heard his uncle al-Bashir describe. His imaginative mind would fly him to the *Mashriq* on a mission of rescue and support.

In a village that relied entirely on farming, Ghannouchi had to contribute his share to the family's business. In addition to his main task of marketing the produce, he worked with his father in the field. At the age of thirteen, just having finished primary school, his education was interrupted.[3] The school he frequented was part of *an-nizam al-gharbi* (Western system of education), introduced to Tunisia by the French. Ailing Sheikh Muhammad could no longer support the family and his only remaining son at home—young Ghannouchi—had to do his father's work, plowing and harvesting outside the village. His five brothers had already left for the capital city of Tunis. The three very eldest ones, who were his half brothers, left the village in search of work in order to support their two other brothers, Ghannouchi's eldest full brothers, who went to Tunis in pursuit of education. These two had already memorized the Qur'an and their mother insisted that they should go to az-Zaytouna for additional education. This, at the time, was unfamiliar to the village folks. Sheikh Muhammad insisted that having learned the Qur'an they needed not learn any more. He wanted them to stay at home to help him in the field but their mother was persistent. She had always looked up to her brother al-Bashir and wished that her sons would one day become as successful and as knowing of the world as he was. Sheikh Muhammad conceded and allowed his two sons to be the first to leave the village in pursuit of further education. This meant that the family had to work harder, not only to compensate for the loss of their labor but also to send them some money, and food too, to contribute to the cost of their living and education in the capital. Ghannouchi felt burdened by the huge responsibility of being the only male, apart from his father, left at home. He had to take care of his aging parents and of his sisters. But this was not the only reason his father withdrew him from school. Sheikh Muhammad was unhappy with its curriculum, which seemed to clash with his son's domestic Qur'anic education. He became convinced that the French education system undermined the upbringing and training he was keen on providing his son. Signs that young Ghannouchi was being distracted from memorizing the Qur'an had disturbed the old man. This was a crucial turning point in Ghannouchi's life. For had his father not removed him from the Western system of education, who knows what would have become of him?[4]

A year later, Ghannouchi's eldest brother graduated from law school, was appointed as a judge in the nearby town of Gabès, and undertook the task of sponsoring the family.[5] His labor no longer needed, at the age of fourteen Ghannouchi resumed his education in Hamma at a preparatory school that belonged to the az-Zaytouna school system, a network of schools sponsored by *awqaf* (private sector endowment fund) and centrally supervised by the ancient and prestigious religious institute of az-Zaytouna, located in the capital, Tunis. The extensive network, which covered all Tunisian towns, comprised all levels of education: primary, intermediate (preparatory), and secondary. Instead of teaching in French, Arabic was the language of tuition of all subjects. In addition, a special emphasis was placed on Islamic studies.[6]

No longer able to perform farming tasks or maintain the family, two years later Sheikh Muhammad decided to take the family to where his elder son worked and where he could take better care of the family. Having placed the field in the village under the care of relatives, the entire family moved to Gabès. Now aged sixteen, Ghannouchi joined another az-Zaytouna preparatory school. This was the beginning of a new stage in young Ghannouchi's life. It was here where he saw for the first time the effects of Westernization, or what he calls the "features of modernity." In Gabès, as in other provincial towns and cities, Western school uniforms had become the norm. Defiance of Islamic values and of tradition had been on the increase. Contrary to what had been expected, post-independence authorities endorsed and preserved the social and cultural effects of colonialism, including the brothels and taverns opened by the French in every town. While the number of men frequenting these places had been on the increase, very few young men attended prayer in mosques; this was a generation more interested in emulating French conduct than in cherishing tradition.

Ghannouchi's traditional religiosity, which had previously been reinforced by rural society's traditional lifestyle, could now only find support within the confines of his family's new urban residence. In addition, his newly acquired interests—modern literature and soccer—posed yet another challenge to his traditional upbringing. Often, he would escape to a sanctuary in the fields outside town. There, he would climb up the water reservoir overlooking the oasis to read novels that would lift him from the state of anxiety that almost tore him apart, caught as he was between his religious home environment, which pulled him eastward, and a society that was swiftly and unreservedly moving westward. He was especially attracted to the novels of Russian writers such as Leo Tolstoy (1828–1910), author of *War and Peace*, Maxim Gorky (1868–1936), author of *Mother*, and Fyodor Dostoyevsky (1821–1881), author of *Crime and Punishment*. These novels had already been translated and published in Arabic. In addition, Ghannouchi read some of the translated works of Irish writer Bernard Shaw (1856–1950), French author Victor Hugo (1802–1885), and American novelist Ernest Hemingway (1899–1961). The latter's *The Old Man and the Sea* had been one of his favorites. The Arab novelists he read included Najib Mahfuz, Yusuf as-Sibaei, Muhammad Abdelhalim Abdullah, and Colin Suhail. As he read these works he dreamed of becoming a novelist or journalist. At times, he attempted to write some short stories.[7] He was also becoming increasingly fond of soccer, a sport which his father loathed, condemned as a foreign time-wasting game, and ordered him repeatedly to forsake. Usually, his uncle al-Bashir would come to his aid and try to persuade the old man that there was nothing wrong with football. Unlike Ghannouchi's father, a farmer with a conservative outlook, al-Bashir was a trader whose outlook had been illuminated, and attitude moderated, by virtue of his communication with the world of trade and by virtue of having been highly "politicized."[8]

Gradually, due to the pressures of the new environment, and possibly under the added pressure of attaining puberty, Ghannouchi's commitment to traditional religiosity was being eroded. *Salat* (prayer) had become a heavy burden. Against the constant admonition of his father he was tempted to relieve himself of this burden. Traditional religious upbringing was so rigid that it could not stand up to the challenges of the new climate. Out of politeness more than conviction, and perhaps only to appease his father, he pretended that he was still praying and was still learning the Qur'an. By the time he finished preparatory school at Gabès, he had already forgotten much of what he memorized in the village and had stopped praying altogether. This was a gradual process of alienation. Religiosity, including the performance of *salat*, was becoming increasingly insulated from his thinking, his interests, and his concerns. With hindsight he now explains that this happened to him because Islam was never taught to him within a framework of a comprehensive vision of life and the universe, a vision that would have been capable of comprehending, and responding to, changes in life. *Salat* was already part of an expiring ancient world whose legacies, the social underpinnings of which were lost, had been violently swept by Westernization.[9]

At az-Zaytouna

In 1959, at the age of eighteen, Ghannouchi followed the footsteps of his elder brothers and left the village for the capital in pursuit of education at the ancient Arabic-medium az-Zaytouna. The institute was first built as a mosque in the year 698 A.D. by Hassan bin an-Nu'man al-Ghassani whose reign between 690 and 704 A.D. witnessed the consolidation of the Islamic dominion in Tunisia in the wake of the defeat of the Romans in North Africa. The construction of the old az-Zaytouna was completed in 732 A.D. by Abdullah bin al-Habhab. Ziyadatullah bin al-Aghlab, who took over the province in approximately 827 A.D., extended the structure and added several new buildings, completing the project around 840 A.D. [10] It continued to function as a *masjid* (mosque) and *madrasah* (school) until the era of al-Hafsiyun in the thirteenth century when it became a full-fledged university. Teachers were contracted from Andalusia and Sicilia to teach linguistics, literature, jurisprudence, history, philosophy, mathematics, and medicine. In the eighteenth century, the curriculum was revised and only subjects of direct relevance to religious studies were retained. The first attempt to modernize the institution was made in 1842 by Bey Ahmad, who decreed the election of thirty scholars to lecture the students under the supervision of a government-appointed committee that consisted of two senior scholars and two senior judges. The Bey's reformist minister Khairuddin at-Tunisi (1822–1889) formulated a statute to organize the functions and activities of the institute. In 1885, he added to it al-Khalduniyah secondary school, whose purpose was to prepare prospective az-Zaytouna students by equipping them with the knowledge of modern sciences.[11]

The French colonial rule from 1881 to 1956 inflicted considerable damage to az-Zaytouna. The French colonial administration established a parallel French-medium education system, extending from primary to university levels. The resources dedicated to this system were huge and its graduates were given preferences in terms of employment. This was part of an intensive program of Westernization that proceeded until an entire generation was molded as France wished; a generation that led, and imitated, a Western lifestyle in conduct, in administration, and in education.[12] As a result of a combination of neglect and secularization, initiated originally by the French colonial authority and pursued more rigorously afterward by the post-independence "national" authority, az-Zaytouna suffered in the twentieth century the most serious crisis in its history.[13]

It was the fear of losing such a historic monument that prompted Sheikh Muhammad Abduh (1849–1905), who pioneered the modernization of Egypt's al-Azhar—another ancient and very prestigious Islamic university—to visit Tunisia twice just before his death in 1905. There, he toured az-Zaytouna, and met with its scholars and encouraged them to modernize it. To him, modernization meant introducing the Arabic teaching of modern sciences, which had not yet been part of the curriculum. Special committees were set up for this purpose under the supervision of a prominent revivalist scholar, Sheikh Muhammad at-Taher ibn 'Ashoor (1879–1970), author of the voluminous exegesis of the Holy Qur'an known as *At-Tahrir Wat-Tanwir*.

In 1933, az-Zaytouna was proclaimed a university. Teaching in the old building, which was in the design of a mosque, ceased and students were relocated to purpose-built teaching quarters nearby. Since then, the old building has been used only as a mosque. The construction of teaching quarters was possible thanks to the efforts made by teachers and students who collected funds from the public to maintain and modernize the institute. The crisis of az-Zaytouna, however, deepened and culminated in the abolishment, after independence, of its religious education curriculum by a presidential decree issued in 1961.[14] This decision did not affect Ghannouchi nor did it affect any of the students who had already enrolled. The total abolition of religious education was fully accomplished when all students enrolled prior to the said presidential decree had already graduated. The teaching quarters of az-Zaytouna were then taken over by the government and incorporated into the newly established University of Tunisia.

Throughout the years of his study at az-Zaytouna's Ibn Khaldoun Centre in the capital, that is from 1959 to 1962, Ghannouchi was not a particularly strict adherent to Islam.[15] Nevertheless, he was violently traumatized by the conflict between the religious education he received and the thoroughly secularist urban society in which he lived , a legacy of the French colonial rule inherited and consolidated by the regime of President Habib Bourguiba.[16] The term "secularist" here refers not only to a lifestyle that was restrictive of the role of religion in society, but also to one that was Western in appearance and outlook. To Ghannouchi, and to a significant proportion of the traditionally Muslim community of Tunisia, secularization, the process of gradually removing religious influences from public life, was perceived as a colonial design aimed at Westernizing the country prior to integrating it into French culture and politics. The years Ghannouchi spent in the city frequenting az-Zaytouna exposed him to, and made him more aware than ever before of, the identity crisis such secularization had created in his country.[17] Although the French colonizers had already left the country, as far as he could tell Tunisia was still far from being independent. The policies adopted by the post-independence government under the leadership of Bourguiba seemed no different from those adopted by the French colonial authority prior to independence.[18]

An autocrat, President Habib Bourguiba ruled post-independence Tunisia until 1987. In spite of his prominence in the movement for Tunisian independence from France since the 1930s, Bourguiba believed that progress and development were achievable only through the strict emulation of Europe, particularly with regard to social norms. As far as the system of government was concerned, Bourguiba's ruling New Destourian Party followed regional trends set up by Nassir's Egypt and became the Destourian Socialist Party. In the name of promoting national unity, Bourguiba consolidated the power of single party rule, and in the name of modernizing the country he sought to sever all ties with its Islamic past.[19] Although the constitution stated clearly that Islam was the religion of the state, Bourguiba launched his era with a series of reforms that were aimed at eliminating Islamic symbols, restricting religious practice, and replacing what had remained of Islamic laws. The first measure was the standardization of the court system, which meant the effective abrogation of Shari'ah courts. This was achieved by means of a presidential decree issued on 25 September 1956. The abolition of the traditional court system was followed on 1 January 1957 by the publication of Majallat al-Ahwal ash-Shakhsiyah (personal status code), which effectively and immediately did away with all Shari'ah-based family laws, including legislation pertaining to marriage, divorce, and inheritance. In 1961, the president issued a decree removing religious education from the curricula of az-Zaytouna.[20] In addition, Bourguiba ordered the nationalization of the awqaf (endowment) and discouraged religious practices even at the individual level by stripping in public the head-cover of a Tunisian lady and by ordering government workers to break the fast during the fasting month of Ramadan. He himself sought to lead the example of a "modern" person who no longer fasted during the month of Ramadan and who boasted without reservation about his extramarital affairs.[21]

In the final year of his high school education, Ghannouchi studied philosophy and became passionately fond of arguing about theoretical issues. He enjoyed teasing, ridiculing, and discrediting some of his teachers. Apparently, the years he spent studying at az-Zaytouna did not satisfy his needs. Upon graduation, there was nothing attracting him to Islam except some of what he had learned at home from his father. He even felt he was an atheist. This was perhaps a reaction to the school system, to the method employed by his teachers, and to the educational curriculum that prevailed in az-Zaytouna, a curriculum that presented an image of Islam that neither answered his questions nor provided him with any confidence in his faith. The curriculum failed to reflect a contemporary image of Islam. When he entered the lecture hall he felt as if he were entering a history museum. Outside the classroom he found an entirely different world, one that was dominated by a Western lifestyle. It was a world that had nothing to do with Islam. In the lecture hall nothing was mentioned about an Islamic economy, an Islamic state, an Islamic art; and nothing was mentioned about the position of Islam on contemporary issues. All he heard about was what Islamic jurisprudence had to say concerning a runaway servant or a straying camel and such issues that had no association whatsoever with the existing reality. He felt that the contradictory images with which he was being constantly bombarded undermined his commitment to Islam even further. They would have succeeded in obliterating what he had learned earlier from his family had it not been for what he considered to be the depth of the religious education in which he was raised. He could see that the antiquated images of Islam coupled with the pressures of Westernization had their toll on the majority of his schoolmates.[22]

Out of approximately three thousand students studying with Ghannouchi at az-Zaytouna, only three or four students performed *salat* in the small room allocated for prayer within the teaching quarters. The teaching quarters had a courtyard right in the center of the market. Traders could tell it was time for the afternoon prayer when students went out to the courtyard. While traders flocked to the old mosque and performed prayer, students remained in the courtyard, walking, chatting, and smoking. The students' disenchantment with religion, and thus the lack of commitment, was bolstered by az-Zaytouna's extremely backward education curriculum. While life had already been Westernized due to colonial domination and the effect of foreign schools, religious schools remained uncompromisingly adherent to old ways and means effecting no modernization whether to the discourse or to the essence of their education curricula. *Fiqh* (jurisprudence) continued to be taught the way it had been taught centuries ago, discussing problems that no longer existed, "problems that no longer were ours, ignoring the real problems that had been imposed on us by colonialism and that had become the status quo."[23]

Throughout his three years of study at az-Zaytouna, Ghannouchi had never been inside the old mosque. His years of religious education had alienated him ever more and increased his discomfort with religious symbols.[24] Ghannouchi's earlier family upbringing in the village had taught him that religion and life spontaneously intertwined. He learned then that religion had a say in every single aspect of life and acted as a reference point so that actions and sayings were characterized as either *mubah* (permissible) or *muharram* (forbidden). In contrast, urban life, to which he came to be exposed in his adolescent years, had been freed of religious symbols and restraints. Making matters worse, life outside the walls of his school had been transformed into a European style, but religion inside the walls was being portrayed in the image of antiquity. Ghannouchi felt as if he and the young men who studied at az-Zaytouna were making a tour of a history museum that had no relevance to the present. The tour failed to provide them with any guidance and failed to explain to them how to live Islam in a milieu that had already been westernized. To him, that was a somber tour. Compounding the crisis was the fact that most of those who entered religious schools did so not because they sought to learn Islam but because their families wanted them to do so. Others joined because they could not find a place in any other school, or because they were more interested in qualifying for a teaching job than in acquiring knowledge.

French-medium teaching curricula in modern schools were designed to produce Western-minded individuals whose conception of the world, of civilization, and of history emanated from Western culture and not from their own. At the same time, az-Zaytouna curriculum failed, in spite of its supposedly Islamic foundation, to provide students with knowledge in a genuine, albeit modern, Islamic framework. Consequently, an az-Zaytouna graduate would be torn between an extremely backward culture on the one hand and a modern, but alien, culture on the other. He would be torn between a Westernized life he had no option but to be part of and an inadequate Arabic-teaching medium that had very little relevance to what went on outside the school walls.[25]

Nassirism

Intellectually, Ghannouchi grew up as a Nassirist. Nassirism was the ideology of the Arab Socialist Union in Egypt, a form of pan-Arabism attempted by President Nassir of Egypt between 1952 and 1970. Nassir was not originally a socialist. His social project was in essence not much different from that of Hassan al-Banna (1906-1949), who founded the Muslim Brotherhood in Egypt in 1928 of which Nassir became a member. Al-Banna had called for the abolishment of feudalism and for the redistribution of wealth. He was the one who campaigned for the dissolution of political parties, which according to him were corrupt and feudal. Even the Nassirist project of Arab unity was al-Banna's idea. What Nassir had done was to "pull the rug from underneath the Muslim Brotherhood by adopting their own program and suppressing them."[26] In other words, the Muslim Brotherhood seemed to have lost their *raison d'être*. However, it was deemed inappropriate for Nassir's project to be Islamic in character. Socialism seemed the best alternative, especially after Nassir failed to secure Western liberal support. Since the Soviet Union offered to help him implement his development project, it was only expedient to hoist the slogans of socialism and declare opposition to Western imperialism. Whereas initially Nassir's socialism was a mere reaction to what was perceived as Western hostility to his regime, a political maneuver rather than an ideological persuasion, his pro-Soviet policy inevitably left the door wide open for committed socialists who gradually held crucial positions in state institutions. Nassir's power struggle with the Muslim Brotherhood was seized upon in order to promote socialist ideology through the government-controlled media and educational system.

Throughout much of the fifties and the sixties, Nassirism was the fashion that attracted Ghannouchi's generation of Arabized Tunisians, and for good reasons. Soon after the independence of Tunisia, a conflict raged between the Arabists, who sought to preserve Tunisia's Arab identity and bolster its ties with its Arab brethren, and the Westernizers, who believed progress was possible only if Tunisia emulated and strengthened its ties with the West. The conflict was particularly strong in the south of the country where Ghannouchi grew up. Nassirism, which evolved in Egypt in 1952 and promised to achieve Arab unity and liberate Palestine, gave the Arabist trend in Tunisia an ideology and a moral support. The Arabists boasted that in terms of population Egypt was the largest country in the Arab world and that it was, by virtue of its rich culture and "undeniable contribution throughout the history of Islam to the unity and strength of the *Ummah*," the established leader of the Arab-Islamic trend.[27] Hence, the Arabists were not viewed favorably by the authorities in Tunisia. In fact the bitter conflict between Bourguiba and Nassir was, at least partly, due to the fact that the former felt threatened in his own country by the support accorded to the latter by the Arabists in Tunisia. The media in both countries exchanged vicious campaigns. However, in spite of the Tunisian Arabists' support for Nassir, Nassirism had no formal organization in Tunisia; it simply manifested itself as an intellectual trend and as a sentiment.

Following his graduation from high school, Ghannouchi discovered that like many Tunisians with an Arab education he stood no chance of entering a local university. French was the language of tuition in all local universities, and for a student to secure a place he or she would have had to come from a high school whose instruction was in French. Graduates of az-Zaytouna were in effect ostracized and those who were ambitious had no option but to leave home for one of the Arab countries in the *Mashriq* (east) in pursuit of further education. In the employment sector, az-Zaytouna graduates seemed destined to have no future although all the subjects taught at French schools had been incorporated, albeit in Arabic, into az-Zaytouna teaching curriculum. French had become the official language throughout the country and graduates of French-medium schools always stood a better chance of being recruited by both public and private sector employers.

Ghannouchi had only one option: to take up a teaching job at a primary school, which he did for two years. But this was much less than he had hoped to achieve. After all, both of his older brothers, whom he looked up to as models, had accomplished more; the eldest was a judge and the second eldest was a lawyer. Ghannouchi felt it was not appropriate for him to be content with the position of a primary school teacher. Furthermore, he had always dreamed of going to the *Mashrıq*. His heart had long been filled with love and admiration for the Arab *Mashrıq*, which constituted a spiritual refuge for the Tunisian Arabists "in the face of the scorching wind that blew from the West and accomplished its objectives after independence through the instating of Bourguiba and his Francophonic elite."

Ghannouchi increasingly loathed life in Tunisia and kept looking for an opportunity to leave the country. He had been unhappy and restless since his arrival in the capital. The events of the Algerian revolution between 1959 and 1962 had filled his mind and heart with detestation for colonialism and equally for the post-independence authority perceived by him as a continuation of the French rule. He would dream of flying to the *Mashrıq*, especially toward Egypt, which had become the temporary home of Algerian freedom fighters and of the Algerian government in waiting. In addition to Nassir, Ben Bella, who was to become Algeria's first president after independence, was another hero of Arabism. He had an enormous influence on the minds of the young

Arabists of Ghannouchi's generation. As if he needed more charging, Ghannouchi had the opportunity of meeting and helping an Algerian *mujahid* (freedom fighter) by the name of Hussein, who had been wounded in an encounter with the French troops and managed to escape to Tunisia. He sheltered him in his own room, which he shared with another student in a building in the poor district of Mulla Seif. From him he listened to stories of heroism and patriotism. When the revolution accomplished its objectives and the French conceded defeat in Algeria, Ben Bella returned from Egypt to his country via Tunisia. In a speech before a huge Tunisian crowd, including Ghannouchi, he shouted, "*nahnu 'arab, nahnu 'arab*" (we are Arabs, we are Arabs). His words were music to Ghannouchi's ears whose pride and faith in Arabism, and also hatred for Bourguibism, had been further deepened. Having saved some money from his teaching job, he applied for, and obtained, a passport and traveled eastward to Egypt.

In Egypt

Like all Arabized Tunisians who left home for the *Mashriq* in pursuit of moral support and inspiration, Ghannouchi arrived in Egypt bearing a passionate nationalist ideology. For the Tunisian society was divided between two elites: an empowered Westernized elite and an Arabized elite that sought inspiration from the *Mashriq* in its struggle for empowerment. In the *Mashriq* only Nassirism seemed to attract the Arabized Tunisians. It had given them great hopes in restoring Muslim and Arab dignity. But unlike the case in the *Mashriq*, in North Africa Nassirism identified with Islam. North Africans did not differentiate between Islam and Arabism nor did they see a conflict between the two. Ghannouchi and the Arabized of his generation had their imaginations possessed by the *Mashriq* thanks to the influence of those teachers who graduated from universities in countries such as Egypt and Syria and had been active in the ranks of the opposition. It was part of their opposition to the regime in Tunisia to excite their students about life in the *Mashriq*, providing them with great hopes, especially about Nassirism, and encouraging them to go to the East in pursuit of education. In any case, Ghannouchi and Arabized students like him who wanted to study modern sciences such as engineering, medicine, agriculture, pharmacy, or mathematics could only do so in the *Mashriq*. Egypt had been the main attraction, although not all modern sciences had been fully Arabized at its universities.

In Cairo, Ghannouchi met about forty Arabized students who, like him, had come to the East in pursuit of further education in the Egyptian universities. The group, which had arrived in Egypt without permission from the relevant authorities in Tunisia, had been sought by the Tunisian embassy in Cairo; they were considered a potential threat and had to be repatriated. In the beginning, the young men benefited from the traditional hostility between the regimes of Bourguiba and Nassir. They demonstrated across from Nassir's residence until he authorized granting them permission to remain in the country and study at its universities.

In 1964, Ghannouchi enrolled with the Faculty of Agriculture at Cairo University. His choice of agriculture was motivated by the desire to acquire knowledge in this branch of science in order to alleviate the hardship endured by his family and fellow villagers whose agricultural methods were still primitive and laborious. He studied agriculture for three months prior to being forced to quit. Unknown to him and his friends, the regimes in Cairo and Tunis had been engaged in talks aimed at improving relations. Eventually, the talks resulted in reconciling the differences between Nassir and Bourguiba. The rapprochement paved the way for Bourguiba's first visit to the *Mashriq* since independence. In the wake of Bourguiba's trip to Egypt, and upon the request of the Tunisian embassy in Cairo, the Egyptian authorities moved to expel from the country Ghannouchi and his friends whom the Tunisian government referred to as "the fugitives." The incident was the first to shake Ghannouchi's preconceived ideas about Nassirism as a pan-Arab unionist and anti-colonial movement, a movement that derived its ideology from the Arab-Islamic culture. It never occurred to him then that the decision to expel him and his colleagues was taken at the highest level. He thought that perhaps some medium-level official had taken it upon himself to issue the directive out of political courtesy. It was so unbelievable that he tried hard to convince himself that Nassir was "too noble" to be involved in such a trivial matter. Like millions around the Arab world, Ghannouchi was a strong admirer of Nassir, whose long speeches he listened to attentively when he was in Tunisia. Egyptian radio broadcasts throughout the fifties and the sixties created an image of Nassir as the pan-Arab leader whose main project was to liberate the Arab *Ummah* from the shackles of imperialism. His socialist formula was prescribed as the remedy for eliminating poverty and achieving progress and development. Arabs were promised that his armed forces were preparing for the liberation of Palestine.

But to Ghannouchi's great disappointment, the few months he spent in Egypt had exposed him to a different image of Nassirism and of Egypt. He did not find in Egypt what he had always imagined of "ambition for progress, of Arab solidarity, and of unwavering support for the causes of justice and equality." He thought he would find the Egyptians enthusiastically mobilized behind Nassir. But he found a disaffected people who were more preoccupied with the arduous task of earning their living than with upholding the ideals of Nassirism. The songs and the speeches that he, and millions of Arabs around the world, had listened to on the radio and believed in to the extent of idolizing Nassir, were empty slogans, mere propaganda, that did not correspond to any of the realities he saw in the Egyptian streets.[28] The straw that broke the camel's back was his personal experience right from the moment he and his colleagues were reluctantly registered at Cairo University to the moment when they learned of the Egyptian government's plan to extradite them to Tunisia. His short stay in Egypt witnessed the beginning of his disenchantment with Arabism, the ideology that claimed devotion to Arab interests, culture, and aspirations.[29]

Ghannouchi had to flee Egypt when he learned that the Tunisian embassy was intent on tracking him and his colleagues down. The plan was to apprehend them with the assistance of the Egyptian security authorities and put them on a plane bound for Tunis. He thought of escaping to Albania. It is not clear what had attracted him to Albania at the time. He had never met any of its citizens or even anyone who had been there. Perhaps he was influenced by *sawt tirana*, the Arabic transmission of radio Tirana, which he listened to frequently during his Cairo days. Its anti-imperialist rhetoric might have impressed him as did before the anti-imperialist rhetoric of Nassirism. He might have been searching for an alternative following the brief disillusionment with Nassirism. Or he might actually have been approaching, most probably without realizing it at the time, the pinnacle of Nassirism, Marxism. Only in the wake of his disenchantment did he realize that Marxism was the eventual destination of Nassirism. The idea of going to Albania was congruous with Nassirism, which began as passionate nationalism but eventually developed into Marxism. The initial ideological void of Nassirism had to be filled, and the choice of many Arab nationalists was Marxism.[30]

Ghannouchi had sent radio Tirana some of his writings. When his stay in Cairo had to be terminated it occurred to him to go to Albania. Just before reserving a seat on a plane bound for Tirana, he met at the ticketing office a compatriot student, his senior, who advised him not to go to Albania because "it was a closed country." His compatriot explained to him how bad the situation in that totalitarian state was and convinced him to change his destination. He encouraged him to go to Syria instead, and told him there were many friends there who could help him. He also told him that in Syria he could still pursue his education and accomplish his ambition without having to throw himself into the unknown.[31]

In Syria

Once in Syria, Ghannouchi changed his mind and decided to study philosophy instead of agriculture. Perhaps he did so because a large number of Tunisian students had already been studying philosophy and had been doing well; seemingly philosophy was then à la mode. Or perhaps he did so because at high school in Tunisia he was fond of the subject, viciously and cunningly arguing with the teachers of az-Zaytouna over issues pertaining to deity and life after death. At times he was serious, skepticism having crept into his mind under the influence of some philosophical theories. At times he raised questions only to tease or ridicule his az-Zaytouna teachers. He disliked most of them, partly because he came from the country while they were city aristocrats, and partly because of what he observed and loathed of the contradiction between their religious public appearance and the exceedingly Westernized lifestyle they had been leading in private.[32]

In the sixties Syria was passing through a crisis. It was overwhelmed by the effects of ending its thirty-one months of unity with Egypt. In January 1958, Ba'thist officers in Damascus, fearing that internal and external plots might put an end to their dominance, asked Nassir if he would like to forge a union between Syria and Egypt. Nassir gave his assent provided that he would become the leader of the union. The officers agreed and union was proclaimed on 2 February 1958. In the United Arab Republic, the name given to the union, Egypt and Syria were referred to as the Southern and Northern Regions respectively. Soon afterward, Nassir and the Ba'thists, who increasingly loathed Egyptian domination of their country, became estranged from one another, and the union eventually collapsed on 29 September 1961 following a military coup by Ba'thist officers.[33] When Ghannouchi arrived in Damascus the conflict within the Nationalist camp in Syria between the supporters of Nassirist reunification and Ba'th Party separatism was most severe.

The Ba'th Party, where *ba'th* is the Arabic word for "resurrection," was founded by Michel Aflaq and Salahuddin al-Bitar in Damascus in 1940–1941. The constitution of the party, published about a decade later, affirmed its belief that freedom of speech and assembly, of faith and of artistic creativity was sacred. It declared that sovereignty is the property of the people, which is the source of all authority.[34] Ba'th ideology, however, represented an attempt to synthesize a Marxist analysis of society with a pan-Arab nationalist approach to social, economic, and political problems. Theoretically, the Ba'th regarded the regional parties of the various Arab states as no more than branches of a "national" all-Arab structure; in practice, the Syrian and Iraqi branches, which are the most active, have been entirely separate and often at loggerheads with each other. Having been instrumental in creating the short-lived union of Syria and Egypt, the Ba'th Party has since 1963 formed the ruling party in Syria. More recently, and especially since 1970, the party has lost prominence, and power in Syria has been increasingly concentrated in the hands of a minority sect, the Alawites. In Iraq, the Ba'th Party has been dominant since 1968, serving as a cloak for the influence of an officers' junta with a regional and familial power-base.[35]

The Ba'th Party did not impress Ghannouchi. Still seemingly influenced by his former Nassirist background, and in spite of showing signs of disenchantment earlier in Egypt, he identified with the Syrian Nassirists, who campaigned for restoring unity between Egypt and Syria. During the period he spent in Damascus from 1964 to 1968, the Ba'th rule had still been in its early stage and had not yet taken full control. Syria was still in the "liberal age" in the sense that a reasonable margin of freedom, which was to be lost in later years, still existed. Although the country had no parliament at the time, the state had still not imposed itself completely on society. The entire Syrian society was intensely politicized and the Syrians utilized rather well the margin of freedom available to them. Students demonstrated, engaged in open debates, and even clashed on campus over ideological or political differences. The Ba'th started its encroachment on society from the tip of the pyramid downwards by seizing control of the army and the police, leaving the institutions of civil society, such as universities, schools, and mosques—where lectures, debates, and conflicts took place—intact and independent for a while.[36]

Intellectual Debates

At Damascus University, Ghannouchi found himself in the midst of a raging intellectual battle. A fierce conflict had been going on among students belonging to different political trends. The nationalist trend was the most prominent. Conflict within this camp existed between the Nassirists and the Ba'thists. In the meantime, a conflict had been going on between the secularists, who campaigned for the exclusion of religion from public life, and the Islamists, who defended the role of religion as a source of guidance in both the public and private realms. The Islamic trend had been making use of the mosque on campus and was thus considered advantaged. The mosque played a major role; it acted as a center for the distribution of Islamic booklets and leaflets. The *khatib* (mosque orator) was professor Adib Salih, a prominent Islamic intellectual, a leading member of the Ikhwan (Muslim Brotherhood) in Syria, and a senior *Shari'ah* College lecturer at the University of Damascus. At the time he had been publishing a monthly periodical called *Al-Hadarah al-Islamiyah* (Islamic civilization). The magazine was first established by Dr. Mustafa as-Siba'i, the founder of the Ikhwan in Syria who passed away before Ghannouchi arrived in that country. Ghannouchi was so impressed by this prestigious publication (which according to him remains unmatched by any other Islamic publication he has ever come across) that he founded in Tunisia in the 1970s a periodical called Al-Ma'rifah (knowledge or cognizance), which was "intended to emulate Al-Hadarah al-Islamiyah by focusing more on intellectual and less on political questions."[37]

A strong debate had been taking place within the student community over the Israeli occupation of Palestine and its ramifications. The debate focused mainly on how the Arabs could best resist the Zionist project. The Islamists insisted that the liberation of Palestine would only occur when Islam was adopted as a way of life, and therefore participating in an effort undertaken by a non-Islamic regime would be unthinkable. They questioned in particular the legitimacy of jihad under the leadership of the Ba'th Party. Ghannouchi felt inclined to disagree with them and considered their argument to be futile. As the prospect of war loomed in the summer of 1967, he joined demonstrations organized by the nationalists to demand the training and arming of students in order to defend Jerusalem, which was soon lost to the Israelis. The humiliating defeat of the Arabs in the Six-Day War of June 1967 was another tremor that shook the foundations of his Arabist leaning. Damascus itself had been threatened and all the while the masses were being deluded by the Arab nationalist propaganda into believing that the Arabs were victorious.[38]

The attitude toward the West was another important topic of debate. The secularists considered Western progress, whether in the natural or social sciences, the ultimate accomplishment of humanity. They looked up to the West as a model. The Islamists, in contrast, sought to highlight the imperfections of Western civilization, exposing its ills and prognosticating its downfall. The emphasis would be on the spread of atheism and immorality, a term that usually referred to promiscuity and its consequences, including the breakdown of the family, the increase in crime and divorce rates, and the rapid spread of drug and alcohol addiction. The Islamists would stress the necessity of dissociation and full independence from all the faces of Western civilization, especially its "atheist Communist face."[39]

The Islamists would employ in criticizing the West some Western writings such as the work of Alexis Carrel, Man: The Unknown; the work of Oswald Spengler, Decline of the West, and the works of Arnold Toynbee, whose critique of Western civilization impressed them most. The Islamists would in particular seek the authority of Western writings that predicted the collapse of Western civilization to challenge the proponents of secularism within the nationalist trend. They used to refer to the writings of some dissident Communists, such as those of Arthur Kestler (1905–1983), the Hungarian-born British author and journalist. His book The God that Failed, which was first published in English in 1950 documenting his experience, disillusionment, and eventually breaking with Communism, was translated into Arabic and published under the title of Assanam Allathi Hawa, meaning "the idol that fell down." The writings of Milovan Djilas, especially his book The New Order, were popular too. The Yugoslav politician was a lifelong friend of Tito and rose to a high position in the Yugoslav government as a result of his wartime exploits as a partisan. However, he was discredited and imprisoned because of his outspoken criticism of the Communist system as practiced in Yugoslavia.

In the 1960s, the Islamists used such writings as a testimony to the failure of communism. And so were the writings of Dr. Mustafa Mahmud, an Egyptian ex-Marxist medical doctor who found his way back to Islam through contemplating scientific evidence. Of particular interest was Dr. Mahmud's book *Rihlati Min-ash-Shak Ilal-Iman* (My voyage from doubt to belief). The message Islamist students were keen on sending to their opponents was: "This is the model you look up to; listen to what its own people say about it."[40]

European Tour

In June 1965, at the end of the academic year, Ghannouchi decided to explore the Western world. He traveled from Syria to Turkey then to Bulgaria, Yugoslavia, Germany, France, Belgium, and the Netherlands. The tour took seven months. Attendance at the faculty was not compulsory and he felt he needed to see the West. Having had an urge to live in the West and acquaint himself with life there, he moved from one country to another, working here and there to earn his living and cover the expenses of his travel.[41] His decision to travel and tour the West was not unusual. Most Tunisian students did exactly the same. It was customary for those of them who studied in Damascus to spend the summer vacation in Europe. Tunisians generally had a natural affinity to Europe. By virtue of its geographic proximity and cultural influence, Europe was not unfamiliar to them. Students would travel to Europe in summer for tourism as well as for work. There they would usually feel at home and would often come back with good savings and good memories. Ghannouchi seems to have been motivated by the desire—having seen the East—to see the other side of the world, the West.[42]

He worked in Germany for three months as an assistant to a driver at a wholesale store that distributed goods to retailers. In France, he worked in a vineyard, harvesting grapes. In Belgium, he washed dishes at a restaurant and in the Netherlands he worked in a small furniture factory. Throughout the tour, he stayed in youth hostels where he met young people from different parts of the world. The impact of the journey on him was immense.

Upon returning from his European tour, Ghannouchi told his fellow students how shocked he was to see in the West such lost and decadent youth. The splendid image he had depicted in his mind of the West had faded and was replaced by a more realistic image reinforced later on by his readings about the West and about Islam. His observations in the West and the experience of living with Western youth reinforced in his mind the Islamists' perception of the West more than it reinforced the perception of the nationalist camp to which he still belonged. The European tour had in its own way contributed to his migration a year later from Arabism to Islamism.

The Conversion

Although Ghannouchi was not allowed to pursue his studies in Egypt and was eventually expelled from the country, he remained loyal to Nassirism up to the second year of his stay in Damascus. When he first set foot in Syria he met a group of Tunisian students who had already joined al-Ittihad al-Ishtiraki (the Socialist Union). This Nassirist party was the local branch of the Egyptian al-Ittihad al-'Arabi al-Ishtiraki (Arab Socialist Union), which was after the death of Nassir disbanded by President Anwar Sadat, who founded al-Hizb al-Watani (the National Party) instead. Ghannouchi did not join al-Ittihad al-Ishtiraki until after his return from the European tour. He remained a member for about a year during which he went through a transition from a romantic Arabist to a committed ideologue of nationalism. Inside the cells of nationalism, he started learning what nationalist thought was all about.

The writings of Sati' al-Husri were the Arabists' source of inspiration and were studied thoroughly by new recruits. Al-Husri (1879–1968), the first ideologue of Arab nationalism, was born in the Syrian city of Aleppo, was trained as a pedagogue, and occupied various posts in the Ottoman educational system. His writings rebutted attacks by contemporary Muslim critics, for whom Islam was the supreme value, and who considered that the affirmation of a national identity by Muslims constituted a danger to Muslim cohesion and solidarity. His argument was that Arab unity had to precede Islamic unity. Furthermore, he denied that Islam, or any religion, could supply the foundation for a political structure. He affirmed that the individual finds complete fulfillment only in merging himself with the nation and in practicing complete obedience to the state. To him, patriotism and nationalism came before and above all.[43]

Ghannouchi complained that such writings did not provide him with any significant knowledge or with a supply of ammunition useful in the conflict that raged within university debate circles between Islamic and nationalist trends. The foundations of the nationalist ideology were shaken within him as he progressed in the study of philosophy and as a result of the impact left on him by the European tour and the writings he had already read. He felt ill equipped in the fierce discussions he used to have with the members of the Islamic trend. His resistance grew weaker and weaker. He was becoming increasingly convinced that the arguments of the nationalist ideology were brittle. For one, they could not provide him with satisfactory answers to several questions. He asked himself and asked his party associates: "What is Arab nationalism? What is the difference between Nassirism and the Ba'th?" He came to the conclusion that apart from language and history, Arab nationalism was nothing but a set of slogans and passions. The difference between one nationalist party and the other was simply the order in which these slogans were listed. While some chanted freedom-unity-socialism, others chanted socialism-freedom-unity. No clear definitions of such concepts were ever given and no one bothered to investigate their philosophical origins or discuss the proposed strategies for their materialization. So blunt was the manipulation of these concepts that the whole matter had become a joke that he and his friends laughed about.[44]

It was shocking for Ghannouchi to discover that Arabism had a content that was not Arab.[45] It did not take him long to find out that Arab nationalism had its roots in Western political thought. In fact the European influence, through the philosophies of German and French nationalism, was patent in the writings of Husri and of the other ideologues of Arab nationalism.[46] Ghannouchi's confidence in the nationalist ideology was further shaken by the attitude of nationalists toward religion. For in spite of occasional skepticism and confusion, he had never become an atheist and had always been a believer. Before long Ghannouchi started losing faith in the ideology of his nationalist party. In this regard, his disenchantment with Arab nationalism may be attributed to the impression left on him by his Maghreb culture in which the terms "Arab" and "Muslim" were interchangeable, synonymous to be precise. His Syrian experience led him to believe that in the Middle East the concept of Arabism was often opposed to

Islam. He had never felt or ever thought, by virtue of his Maghreb upbringing, that Arabism meant anything other than Islam. However, his presence within the nationalist movement exposed him to a position that clashed with religion: there was an alienation of religion from every activity within the party. He was shocked to discover that the dream he lived for, the dream of Arab nationalism, was an illusion. The Arabism he had known in North Africa did not clash with Islam and was therefore not the Arabism upon which the party he had joined in order to serve the Arab *Ummah* was founded. This was a different Arabism, stripped of its spirit, or rather hostile to its spirit. He felt this was another commodity imported from nineteenth-century European thought and impregnated with the problems and customs of foreign societies that underwent their own unique courses of development.[47]

Ghannouchi soon entered into a debate with other party cadres over the relationship of Arab nationalism to Islam. Whenever a party official was commissioned to have a discussion with him, he would always demand a definition of the position of Islam within the party. He finally concluded that the party had nothing to do with Islam. He wanted to remain in the party, but needed something to convince him to stay there, to convince him that his presence within the party did not contradict his faith or that at least it was not opposed to the basic principle of belief. He would ask: "Is believing in God a condition for joining the party?" The answer was no, this was not a condition. Party members were free to embrace whichever religion they wanted or they could even be irreligious. This turned to be the most crucial moment in his life.

> At that moment, my mind was set on leaving the party, having realized that I had been deceived into thinking that joining the party would serve the Arabism I grew to believe in. I discovered I had been embroiled in a different Arabism the people of North Africa had nothing to do with. For I was, and still am, convinced that Islam is the spirit of this *Ummah*, its maker and the builder of its glory, and is still its only hope for victory and progress. How could it then be so marginalized and transformed into a secondary issue by the nationalist ideology as evident from the gospels of nationalism such as the writings of Sati' al-Husri and some other writings which may even be more hostile to Islam?[48]

Still searching for a camp that could accommodate both his Arabism and Islamic faith, Ghannouchi joined a group of Syrian nationalist students who, after spending hundreds of hours debating the Arab situation and the means of bringing about an Arab renaissance, started having their doubts about the nationalist discourse. They felt they needed to look for an alternative. Initially, they debated among themselves, but then decided to expand the scope of dialogue. They moved from one Islamic study circle to the other acquainting themselves with Islam and its movements. They met with members of various Islamic trends in the Syrian arena including the Ikhwan (Muslim Brotherhood), the group of Sheikh Nassir ad-Din al-Albani, some of the scholars who were active in Damascus such as Sheikh Habannaka, and some elements of Hizb-ut-Tahrir al-Islami (the Islamic Liberation Party). Hizb-ut-Tahrir al-Islami was established in Jerusalem in 1953 by Taqiy-ud-Din an-Nabhani (1909–1977). The party has declared itself to be a political party with Islam as its ideology and the revival of the Islamic *Ummah* as its goal. It seeks to achieve this goal by creating a single Islamic state, erected on the ruins of existing regimes. It is currently banned in most of the Arab countries, but has lately been active in several Western countries among the Muslim youth.[49]

Ghannouchi's tour in search of an alternative to nationalism provided him with an opportunity to meet and learn from several prominent Islamic thinkers in Syria. Adib Salih, Sheikh al-Buti, and Wahba az-Zuhayli were all lecturers at the Shari'ah College at Damascus University. Although Ghannouchi was not registered with the college, he developed an interest in attending, whenever he could, the lectures of these three scholars. He also made the acquaintance of Jawdat Sa'id whom he thought was a very distinguished personality and described as an "active volcano."[50] Sa'id had been a member of the Ikhwan in Syria and was an outspoken critic of the political situation both in Syria and in the Arab region. Later on, he left the Ikhwan and became increasingly influenced by the ideas of Algerian thinker Malik Bennabi. Sa'id's discourse gradually changed, and his focus was no longer on politics but on philosophical and psychological studies, having come to the conclusion that the problem with the Muslims was not political but intellectual. The divorce with nationalism led Ghannouchi to the rediscovery of Islam:

> Eventually, my mind rested assured of the wrongfulness of the nationalist way. While my heart was perfectly reassured of Islam, I realized that what I had been following was not the right Islam but a traditional and primitive version of it. The traditional model was not ideological, nor did it represent a comprehensive system. It was a conventional religious sentiment, a set of traditions, customs, and rituals that fell short of representing a civilization or a way of life. I discovered that I was not a true Muslim and therefore I had to take a decision to re-enter Islam.[51]

Ghannouchi speaks of the night of 15 June 1966 as having been a turning point and a landmark in his life. That was the night he embraced what he called the true Islam.

> That very night I shed two things off me: secular nationalism and traditional Islam. That night I embraced what I believed was the original Islam, Islam as revealed and not as shaped or distorted by history and tradition. That was the night I was overwhelmed by an immense surge of faith, love, and admiration for this religion to which I pledged my life. On that night I was reborn, my heart was filled with the light of God, and my mind with the determination to review and reflect on all that which I had previously conceived.[52]

It was during the third year of his stay in Syria that Ghannouchi divorced the al-Ittihad al-Ishtiraki and moved to the Islamic camp. He boasts of having deserted Nassirism while still at its climax, which is before the 1967 Arab defeat.

In Syria, Ghannouchi had gained no practical Islamic movement experience; he had not joined any group or party and had not even practiced da'wah work (preaching). He was preoccupied with trying to comprehend as much as possible some of what had been written by contemporary Islamic thinkers. During the last two years of his study in Damascus, he read some of the writings of Muhammad Iqbal, Mawdudi, Sayyid Qutb, Muhammad Qutb, al-Banna, as-Siba'i, Malik Bennabi, and an-Nadwi. He attended hadith, tafsir, and fiqh sessions. Where hadith is the study of the sayings and the life of the Prophet; tafsir is the study of the exegesis and causes of revelation of the Qur'an; and fiqh is the study of jurisprudence.

He was invited by more than one organization, including the Ikhwan, to join in but he refrained. Because he intended to return home, and did not know what kind of Islamic activity he would find there upon returning, he deemed it inappropriate for him to commit himself and return to his country with an organizational affiliation. Nevertheless, he had acquainted himself with all sorts of trends, the Ikhwan, the Sufi orders, Hizb-ut-Tahrir al-Islami, and the Salafiyah. The last is the Islamic trend that derives its name from the Arabic root *salaf*, meaning "to precede." A Salafi has been defined as one who draws on the Qur'an and the Sunnah as the only sources for religious rulings. The Salafiyah has taken different forms and expressions owing to changing conditions; however, throughout its different phases it has remained in essence a movement for reform and renewal.[53] The group Ghannouchi encountered in Syria is the latest in a long series of successive groups that claimed to be Salfai. It is known as al-Jama'ah as-Salafiyah or as-Salafiyun. It focuses on matters of creed and morality, such as strict monotheism, divine attributes, purifying Islam from accretions, anti-Sufism, and developing the moral integrity of the individual. For one whole year, Ghannouchi joined the circle of al-Albani, a prominent leader of the as-Salafiyun, whose work in *tahqiq ar-riwayah* (the authentication of narration and the endeavor to cleanse the tradition attributed to the Prophet of fiction) had greatly impressed him.[54]

In France

Immediately after graduation from Damascus University in the summer of 1968, Ghannouchi left Syria for France to pursue his postgraduate studies in philosophy at the Sorbonne. He enrolled for a master's degree in the philosophy of education, and registered under the supervision of Professor Sanders for a dissertation entitled "The Qur'anic Approach to Education."

Ghannouchi had not been back to Tunisia since he left it in 1964. He was afraid that by returning he might risk being prosecuted for leaving the country to go to the *Mashriq* without permission, and could consequently have been banned from leaving again.

At this stage in his life, France seemed the right place to go to. On the one hand, the news from Tunisia was that things were much worse than when he left four years ago. Islam, Ghannouchi was given the impression, had already been uprooted and the whole country had been completely Westernized. He had heard that the *Mufti*, a grand scholar and a highly respected and well-known Islamic personality, had been seen strolling along the beach wearing shorts in the company of his daughter, who wore a bikini. If such was the condition of the *Mufti* (the official expounder of Islamic law), Ghannouchi wondered what the conduct of ordinary people would be. The Syrian scholars he frequently visited in Damascus, especially Sheikh Nassir ad-Din al-Albani, had advised him not to return to Tunisia until circumstances improved.

On the other hand, Paris was still the source of "cultural legitimacy" in Tunisia. In other words, should he hope to be recognized in Tunisia, Ghannouchi needed to obtain an academic qualification from France. It is true he was, like many Arabized students, compelled to travel to the *Mashriq* in pursuit of further education. Nevertheless, if he at all contemplated returning to Tunisia in the future he would have had to "procure commodities saleable in the local Tunisian 'cultural market.'"[55] Furthermore, France was the natural choice for Tunisian students. Britain or Germany would have been an abnormal choice, and going to either would be like going to another planet. Paris was a familiar city, more like a Tunisian backyard; there, one would find a large number of relatives, friends, or fellow villagers. For all these reasons, Paris was his destination.

Scores of Tunisian graduates of the Damascus University had preceded him in going there; for them this was a kind of mandatory "cultural baptism."[56]

When he arrived in France, the student demonstrations that erupted on 3 May 1968 had just finished, though their repercussions had not. There was still so much discussion on campus about the student demands for education reform, demands that were later met and that eventually led to the reorganization of the University of Paris into thirteen independent faculties known as Universités de Paris I à XIII. During the demonstrations, Ghannouchi learned later, the Sorbonne was the scene of serious riots led by militants who openly proclaimed their intention of using the university as a base from which to overthrow the capitalist system.

As a newcomer, Ghannouchi was anxious to settle down and familiarize himself with life in this new "station" before becoming involved in French politics. Of more importance to him at that stage was the need to acquaint himself with the intellectual and social aspects of the life North African students had been leading. He frequented the café shops in Boulevard Saint Michel, then commonly known as the "students road," inside the Latin Quarter. A famous spot for North African students was the restaurant at 15 Boulevard Saint Michel where discussions among students from various trends over political and intellectual issues took place. No Islamic trend existed among the students yet; Tunisian students were either Communists or Arab nationalists, that is, Ba'thists or Nassirists.

Following lengthy discussions, a small nucleus of Tunisian students came into being in early 1969. It included Ahmida Enneifer, Ghannouchi's senior in Syria and a Nassirist who started having doubts about nationalism after arriving in France one year before Ghannouchi. The group also included Ahmed Manai, who was then a postgraduate student and who later (in 1995) authored a book about Tunisian President Ben Ali entitled *Le jardin secret du general BenAli*. For Ghannouchi, this circle constituted another field of activity parallel to the one he frequented at the local mosque, where he became actively engaged with the *tabligh* group.

The Paris community of *tabligh* was founded by a handful of Pakistanis who came to France in 1968 where they recruited a number of *Magharibi* (North African) workers. This was an offshoot of the now global Tablighi Jama'at, which originated in the Indo-Pakistani subcontinent. With followers all over the Muslim world and in parts of the West, Tablighi Jama'at is now one of the most important grassroots Islamic movements in the contemporary Muslim world. It was founded in 1926 by the Sufi scholar Maulana Muhammad Ilyas (1885-1944). According to its followers, the method pursued by the group is still the same as originally designed by its founder, simply to organize units of a number of persons and send them to various villages, or districts, to knock on doors and invite people to the mosque to listen to a *bayan* (statement) delivered after prayer by the unit's *amir* (leader). Those who are recruited are taught the fundamentals of Islam and how to perform its rituals, and are then sent on *tablıgh* missions to recruit others. Tablighi Jama'at is strictly apolitical; not only is it disinterested or unconcerned with politics but it discourages, or even bans, its followers from involvement in political activities.[57]

While the mosque's Tablighi Jama'at environment was void of any discussion, argumentation, or the need for convincing, on-campus discussions among the students covered important current affairs such as the situation in Tunisia, the consequences of the 1968 Paris students demonstrations, and the humiliating 1967 defeat of the Arabs by Israel.

French life in Paris did not have a significant impact on Ghannouchi's thought or conduct. He reckons he must have been lucky to meet the *tabligh* group soon after his arrival: "Living with the *tabligh* community provided me with immunity and protection from fierce winds and added a new dimension to my molding. Never ever before had I had such an experience."[58]

Ghannouchi commenced his *da'wah* activity in a very poor Paris district. His *tabligh* unit used an Algerian trader's house in the district as the center for its *da'wah* activities. Since most of the community consisted of laborers, Ghannouchi was the most qualified among its members to be the *imam* (prayer leader), although he insisted he had no previous *da'wah* experience whatsoever. Together with the members of his *tabligh* group, he pursued the recommended method of the *tabligh*. He would go out to the streets and call on laborers in their houses, in pubs, and in café shops, inviting them to a simple version of Islam that focused mainly on rituals such as *salat* (prayer), *dhikr* (praise of God), *tilawah* (recitation of the Qur'an), and on spiritual and moral aspects such as brotherhood, compassion, generosity, and giving a helping hand to sinners until they repented. "Thanks to the graciousness and persistence of the *du'at* (preachers) many a wretched drunken, who previously abused them, ridiculed them, and even toyed with their beards as they offered assistance to him, was cleansed and transformed into a great *da'iyah* (preacher, or caller to Islam)."

Ghannouchi had sentimentally and practically been assimilated into the oppressed class of *Magharibi* laborers. He lived with them in their destitute quarters and experienced their miserableness and genuineness at the same time. His first ever *da'wah* experience was gained with them, and although he had been a beginner, they introduced him to speak on their behalf. In the districts of Belle Ville, Drancy, and Nanterre, his Islamic culture descended from its philosophical tower to the standard and practical daily concerns of this vanquished and uprooted group. It was here that he learned the art of oration and was transformed from a teacher of philosophy into a cultured Islamist, into a *da'iyah*. The simplicity and humbleness of the *tabligh* community, together with its emphasis on the spiritual and moral aspect of Islam, had a lasting influence on his personality.

In France, students like Ghannouchi, who had no scholarships and whose families were poor, endured severe hardships trying to make a living. Most of them worked as night guards at hotels and factories. Night guarding was the most convenient job one could hope for because it required very little, if any, physical effort, and a student could study while on duty and could in most cases have several hours of sleep. Ghannouchi had not been so fortunate. Although he badly needed such a job, he did not get one. Instead he took up a variety of other jobs, especially in cleaning and in the distribution of commercial publicity materials. The latter entailed wandering for several hours distributing publications to households, sometimes in severe cold weather and in heavy rain. What had been a source of distress and torment for him was that the distribution supervisor was a "wretched Frenchman" who did not hesitate to instruct workers to distribute little material and dispose of the rest in the River Seine.

Accommodation was a big problem for him. During his stay in Paris he had to shift from one lodging to another. Campuses were restricted to students who had scholarships. At times, he had no alternative but to sneak in with one such student and spend the night in his room. This meant at times waiting for several hours in the cold or in the rain until the host student returned to his room. Eating was another problem. He was strict in observing *halal* food requirements and during those days no *halal* food facilities were readily available. The pressures of the French libertine atmosphere were another problem. He once wrote in his diary that he felt as if he were a citadel in the midst of a raging storm.

> The one year I spent in Paris was the hardest and most trying in my entire life. The test was tough and I was rather anxious that I might fail. The mere thought of failing, even for once, was terrifying. I could not imagine how much, had I fallen, I would have despised myself and how hypocritical it would have been of me to stand up afterward and admonish others. Praise be to Allah who protected me until the ordeal was over.

The Parisian social environment contradicted the Islamic values he believed in, especially with regard to the relations between the sexes. Whereas in Islam marriage is the sole framework within which a man and a woman can establish a sexual relationship, there seemed to be no restriction whatsoever in the lifestyle he saw in Paris. For him, the shift from Damascus, whose society was still quite conservative, to Paris was enormous. Furthermore, although there were many Tunisian students in Paris, very few of them observed Islamic teachings. On campus, Muslim students conducted themselves in the Parisian style. A student who did not have a girlfriend was considered abnormal or a dimwit.

To escape from such an environment, Ghannouchi frequented a club of Catholic students in the vicinity of the Sorbonne. He felt more comfortable in its conservative surrounding. Male and female students at the club conducted themselves decently and had a serious attitude toward life. Ghannouchi visited the club's library, spent some time in its café, and occasionally joined the group discussions or the sightseeing trips organized by its members. He felt this was a good opportunity for him. Firstly, he interacted with the French people themselves, learning more about them and improving his communication skills in French; secondly, he engaged in dialogue about Islam with the Catholic students; and thirdly, he enjoyed the wholesome, or what he describes as the "clean, seduction-free and acceptable" atmosphere of the club. Out of curiosity, Ghannouchi attended mass at the Catholic church. He wanted to learn about Catholic worship and explore its impact on the psyche. His impression was that there was little substance in it. This was a form of traditional religiosity much more inferior, in his assessment, than the traditional religiosity he grew to rebel against in his own country. As far as he could tell, Catholic worship rituals consisted of no more than hymns and songs that might have had some influence on the soul but none on the mind.[59]

Although the period he spent in Paris was not long, it was for him a bitter experience of estrangement. Islam was completely alien. The Muslim community was lost, and there was only one mosque, the Paris Central Mosque, which was established during the 1940s as a reward for the thousands of North African troops who took part in the liberation of France from Nazi occupation. The mosque was under the control of a man of Algerian origin called Hamza Abu Bakr. The Parisian Muslim community did not have much respect for Abu Bakr who, at least from the Algerian point of view, was considered a traitor for deputizing for the Sahara in the French National Assembly during the French colonial era.[60] Ghannouchi did not like Abu Bakr because he prevented him from organizing any activity inside the mosque. Abu Bakr relied on well-built black Saharan aides whose task was to intimidate and even beat whomever he instructed them to discipline. Disciplinary measures included detention in the cellar underneath the mosque. Because of his active participation in the Association des etudiants islamique en France, which comprised a small group of university students who occasionally met inside the mosque, Ghannouchi was perceived as a threat and was warned that he would be punished.

The Islamic society was headed by an Iranian student through whom Ghannouchi became acquainted with the thoughts of Mehdi Bazargan, some of whose writings had already been translated from French to Arabic. A prominent Iranian modernist and reformer, Bazargan (1907–1995) was one of the major voices of Islamic opposition in both the pre- and post-revolutionary eras in Iran. He played an active role in the revolutions that toppled the Shah when Khomeyni sent him to organize the oil workers' strike in mid-1978. In February 1979, Khomeyni appointed him the first prime minister of the provisional government, but he resigned in November, complaining that he was being rendered powerless by a multitude of power centers.[61] The fact that the Islamic Society was headed by the only Iranian student in the society impressed Ghannouchi. This student was a staunch Ja'fari, that is a follower of the main Shiite school of jurisprudence known as al-Ja'fariyah, which derives its name from Abu Ja'far Muhammad al-Baqir and Ja'far as-Sadiq, the fifth and sixth of the twelve Imams of Shiism.[62] For Ghannouchi, the arrangement reflected a high degree of tolerance, for no one objected to the Shiism of the Iranian student or considered it an impediment to his election as head of a society the rest of whose members were all Sunnis.

Eventually, Abu Bakr threw the students out of the mosque, forcing them to retreat to a rented accommodation in the Latin Quarter, which they turned into a center for the society, of which Ghannouchi had become the general secretary. The society organized a seminar every Saturday evening that used to be attended by fifteen to twenty students. Dr. Muhammad Hamidullah, who was then in his sixties, would deliver a fifteen to twentyminute talk about a specific Islamic issue followed by a question and answer session. Considered one of the most prominent scholars of Islam, Dr. Hamidullah has translated the Qur'an into French and has authored a two-volume biography of the Prophet, *Le prophet du l'Islam*. He has written a number of other books including *Majmu'at al-Watha'iq as-Siyasiyah Lil'ahd an Nabawi wal-Khilafah ar-Rashidah* (The set of Political Documents During the Era of the Prophet and the Rightly Guided Caliphate).

In addition to the debates that went on among students in the Latin Quarter's café shops, the Tunisian left had been witnessing a noticeable increase in its strength and influence. The leftists managed to convene a series of big meetings at the *mutualité* hall to denounce the policies of President Bourguiba and call for a revolution against his regime. In the same hall, Ghannouchi attended a rally in support of the Palestinian resistance movement, which had just begun. He was impressed by a speech given by French historian Vincent Monteuil, who later embraced Islam and called himself Mansur. According to Ghannouchi, Monteuil's speech in support of the Palestinian cause infuriated the supporters of Israel in France.[63]

Returning Home

Ghannouchi had just started preparing his thesis for the master's degree on the philosophy of education in Islam when his elder brother, al-Mukhtar, came to take him back home. Al-Mukhtar had heard that his younger brother had been active with the *tabligh* community. Some Tunisian workers, who happened to come from the south and knew the Ghannouchis well, saw young Ghannouchi roaming Paris while preaching Islam and wearing a long beard and a Pakistani-style cap. When some of them returned home for the holidays, they told his family. Shocked and dismayed, the family could not believe that youthful Ghannouchi, who left the country in modern appearance and was expected to return even more modern, had become a wandering *shaykh*. Fearing that he might have gone astray, they sent their eldest on a rescue mission. At the time Islamic conduct was viewed as some kind of an idiocy. The renunciation by an educated young man of the libertarian lifestyle, especially in Paris, in favor of adherence to the teachings of Islam was cause for ridicule and astonishment, so much so that insanity would be suspected. Ghannouchi's brother, who was a senior judge, came to Paris with the story of the serious illness of his mother, whom Ghannouchi had not seen for three years. He had seen her only once since he first left Tunisia when she traveled to Tripoli in Libya in the summer of 1966 for the sole purpose of seeing her youngest son. The mother's illness was dramatized for no reason other than to convince Ghannouchi to halt his "idiotic" activity.

The rule within the *tabligh* group was such that new recruits were expected to make a four month pilgrimage to Pakistan, and in the case of a "cultured" recruit like Ghannouchi it would have been seven months, where he would have undergone initiation and would have been fully indoctrinated.

Ghannouchi's brother appeared out of the blue just as he was preparing to take the *tabligh* pilgrimage to Pakistan. He left with his brother for Tunisia thinking he was going to see his mother and come back to France within a month, and so he left his belongings in Paris. He still took seriously the advice given to him by al-Albani, namely that he should not return to Tunisia where Islam had been uprooted. At the same time he was anxious to finish his master's degree without which he stood very little chance of being offered decent employment back home.

Ghannouchi accompanied his brother, travelling by land through Spain. In the city of Córdoba they visited the grand mosque and toured with great distress the relics of the Islamic civilization. The visit affected the brothers immensely. Ghannouchi wept bitterly and so did his brother, in spite of his noncommitment to Islam at the time. Ghannouchi's elder brother had at a young age memorized the Qur'an but became less religious as he grew up. He eventually stopped praying altogether, and that was, according to Ghannouchi, due to the influence of the secular atmosphere of the 1950s and 1960s. But after that somber tour of al-Andalus (Andalusia, in southern Spain) he returned to prayer and had, until he passed away, been a practicing Muslim and an absolute supporter of his younger brother's family and of the Islamic movement he later founded.[64]

Inside the mosque, Ghannouchi walked toward the *mihrab* (prayer niche) to perform *salat*. A priest intervened to stop him, but as Ghannouchi raged in anger and was prepared to fight him, the priest let him pray.

In the company of his elder brother, Ghannouchi traveled through Algeria where he met Malik Bennabi for the first time. Ghannouchi had longed to meet him after having heard so much about him and having read some of his books. He had been impressed with Bennabi's great skill of social and historical analysis, and had wanted to listen to him directly. As Ghannouchi sat before him, he was overwhelmed by the notion that he was sitting in the company of Ibn Khaldoun's successor.

Malik Bennabi was born in the Algerian town of Constantine in 1905. From a young age he had shown special interest in comparative cultural and political analysis. However, he finished his undergraduate studies in Paris in 1935 and graduated as an electrical engineer. He remained in Paris until 1956 where he published several works including *The Qur'anic Phenomenon, The Conditions of Civilization, The Direction of the Islamic World,* and *The Afro-Asian Concept.* Then he moved to Cairo where his books were translated into Arabic and where he established links with the Algerian students studying in the city. In 1963, he returned to his home country, where he was appointed director of higher education. It was there that he published *The Algerian Horizons, Diary of a Witness of This Century, The Problem of Ideas in the Muslim World,* and *The Muslim in the World of Economics.* In 1967, Bennabi resigned his government job and preoccupied himself until his death in the last day of October 1973 with intellectual activities, the most prominent of which was the series of seminars he organized annually in Algiers, and which attracted students from across the Arab Maghreb.[65]

Bennabi attracted Ghannouchi to his Islamic philosophy, which he judged as stemming from "scientifically" analyzing reality and then conducting dialogue between such analysis of reality and the religious text. This, in his opinion, was different from what had been accepted in Islamic thought as the norm, as he had been reading in the works of Mawdudi and Qutb, where a vision of reality is derived solely from the text.[66]

Ghannouchi's wish to meet Bennabi was granted unexpectedly, and the unplanned turns in his life enabled him to meet Bennabi not only once but several times as shall be seen in the following chapter. After their meeting, Ghannouchi was to become not only a major player in Tunisian politics but also one of the most prominent figures in contemporary Islamic political thought. The next chapter will explore, mainly on the basis of interviews conducted with him, the development of his political thought from the moment he returned home in late 1969 until he was forced into exile in the late 1980s.

2

The Journey to Democracy

The seventies were the decade in which Ghannouchi's political thought developed. The ten years from 1970 to 1980 were to witness the undoing of some of his earlier persuasions and the making of new ones. A number of influences, sometimes working concurrently and sometimes consecutively, combined to transform Ghannouchi into an Islamic democrat. This chapter will seek to explore these influences and explain the manner in which they contributed to Ghannouchi's intellectual transformation.

Change of Plans

After visiting his family in the south of Tunisia, and on his way back to Paris to pursue his studies, Ghannouchi decided to pay a visit to the az-Zaytouna mosque, his first visit ever to this ancient shrine. Until then, he was still determined to heed the advice of al-Albani, namely not to settle in Tunisia because it had become un-Islamic. To his great astonishment, inside the mosque he saw a study circle comprised of a *shaykh* surrounded by scores of persons, mainly children and old people. Among them, he saw a young man whom he had never met before but to whom he was attracted because his presence inside the mosque, or of anyone his age, seemed odd. Ghannouchi approached the young man, asked him his name, and appealed for an explanation. Why would a young man want to be in the mosque?, Ghannouchi asked. It wasn't surprising to see old people in the mosque, but children and young men were a surprise. It was not true then that Islam had been uprooted. After few exchanges, Ghannouchi accompanied the young man to another mosque in the neighborhood, where he was introduced to a circle run by a five-member Tabligh community established one year earlier by a Pakistani mission. The group included Abdel Fattah Moro, who had been a student of law and who later was to co-found *Harakat al-Ittijah al-Islami*–the Islamic Tendency Movement (MTI)–with Ghannouchi in 1981. Moro was to become MTI's secretary general and Ghannouchi its president.

What Ghannouchi had seen represented for him a glimpse of hope; perhaps an Islamic future awaited Tunisia. This was for him a sufficient reason to abandon his plan of returning to Paris, to forget about the master's degree, and even to forget about the personal belongings he left behind. For the second time, Ghannouchi's destination changed because of an unexpected encounter. The first time, of course, was when his destination to Albania was diverted toward Syria upon the advice of a fellow student.

He joined the Tabligh group and participated in its activity. Soon afterward, still in 1970, Ghannouchi became the leader of a "clandestine" organization known as al-Jama'ah al-Islamiyah (the Islamic Group) whose founding members were drawn from the Tabligh cell. Although al-Jama'ah remained a secret organization because of the ban on all such activities by Tunisia's single-party regime, its members used as a platform a government-sponsored institution called the Qur'anic Preservation Society (QPS).

For a number of years henceforth, Ghannouchi and some of the members of al-Jama'ah traveled every year to meet Malik Bennabi in Algeria, where they were given an exclusive audience and were lectured on philosophical and political issues. The most memorable of these meetings were the annual Islamic Thought Seminars held in 1970, 1971, and 1972. Ghannouchi and his colleagues Sheikh Abdel Fattah Moro, Fadhel Beldi, Salih bin Abdullah, and Ahmida Enneifer were anxious not to miss any of these functions.[1]

Malik Bennabi, whom Ghannouchi hails as "a pillar of Islamic thought and a revivalist of Ibn Khaldoun's Islamic rationalism,"[2] had a profound influence on the Tunisian Islamic group. Ghannouchi conceives of Islamic rationalism as the dualism of reason and revelation as sources of knowledge.[3] Harmony is assumed to exist between the two sources. Through the adoption of revelation as a funadmental to which reason must refer in a process of interpretation, any contradiction between the two is rendered illusory, erroneous, fictitious, and liable to be eliminated.[4] Rationality in the Islamic theory, according to him, meets with Greek and modern Western philosophies on the level of recognizing the existence of an objective reality, "which reason is capable of discerning if it is properly employed," but parts company with them in that "it rejects the principle of reason's independence of knowledge as a whole."

> Both revelation and reason remain vital and efficient in the evolution of reality, so long as they remain intimate and interactive with it. With separation, reason expatiates in the deserts of abstraction, while legislation stagnates and corrodes. This dialogue between reason and revelation on the one hand, and revelation and reality on the other, is essential to the life of both reason and religion. Revelation's relation to reason is like that of the eye to light—as expressed by Abu Hamid al-Ghazali. Neither may exist without the other. Such is Islamic rationality; it has as its foundation stone the principle of recognition of the dualism of reason and revelation and the insistence upon the need of each for the other, for mutual rejuvenation.[5]

Having read Sayyid Qutb during his student years in both Syria and France, and having been to some extent influenced by his thought during that initial period of self-searching, Ghannouchi listened attentively to Bennabi as he strongly criticized Qutb. Bennabi had been unhappy with Qutb for having alluded in an article to him, without mentioning his name, as an Algerian writer on Islam who believes that Islam is one thing and civilization is another. Bennabi was clearly offended by Qutb's remark, which he thought was demeaning. His critique of Qutb was the first in a series of experiences that shook Ghannouchi's confidence in the Mashariqi thought. Bennabi seemed to have deeper knowledge and better understanding of civilization than Qutb. Bennabi believed that whereas civilization was the transformation of any good idea into a reality, Islam was a set of guidelines, a way of life, or a project that creates a civilization only when put into practice, when its adherents carry it and move through the world positively influencing man, material, and time. Therefore, a Muslim may be uncivilized just as a non-Muslim may be civilized.[6] In contrast, Qutb insisted that civility is a synonym of Islam, and that a Muslim is civilized while a non-Muslim is not. Contrasting the two arguments, Ghannouchi concluded that Qutb's theory would inevitably lead to takfir (that is charging someone with unbelief). He grew increasingly convinced that Qutb must have borrowed the belief of the al-Khawarij that a person is not a Muslim unless he or she is sinless and must have applied it to the question of civility. Hence his belief that a person is not a Muslim unless he is perfectly civilized; therefore all those backward Muslims must be infidels.[7] Al-Khwarrij (plural of khariji, meaning exiter) is the term used to describe the first religio-political dissenting group in the history of Islam. They came into existence as a consequence of the great fitnah (sedition) between 656 and 661 A.D. The founders were recruits in the army of the fourth caliph 'Ali ibn Abi Talib. They soon turned against him upon his acceptance of arbitration to resolve the conflict between him and his opponent Mu'awiyah who later founded the Ommiad dynasty. Al-Khawarij ended up declaring both 'Ali and Mu'awiyah and every one else in their respective camps apostates. The main distinctive feature of their ideology is that a Muslim who commits a kabirah (major sin) is an apostate from Islam. Muslims who do not join them in their belief are too considered apostates.

The influence of Bennabi was to be reflected in Ghannouchi's own definition of civilization:

By the civilization of a given people we mean the provision of at least the necessary level of social guarantees: food, housing, clothing, education, and security, in addition to a specific level of intellectual and spiritual consciousness. If we were to distinguish between civilized man and uncivilized man, or what Bennabi refers to as the pre-civilization man, it suffices to look at the direction in which the activities of each of these two human models proceed. Both of them initiate activity aimed at self-preservation: food, drink, sex, and accommodation. But whereas the backward one restricts such activity to what we may call "the circle of self-preservation," the civilized one—even though he too exerts an effort within the same circle to self-preserve—is superior in two ways. First, the instinctive self-preserving activity is not steered nor checked by desires as in the case of the uncivilized. The civilized one is subdued to an idea or a value or a principle. In his case desires are checked by a principle or an idea, and are therefore influential only within the circle drawn for them. Hence, not everything that fulfils the desire, or anything that is within the reach of the living being, should be sought after; nor should every edible thing be eaten; nor should anything that fulfills the sexual desire be practiced. For a civilized person there are the good and the evil, the halal (permissible) and the haram (forbidden), and there is that which undermines the chastity, the honor, the pride, and the faith. The second thing that distinguishes civilization man from pre-civilization, or backward, man is that even though the civilized exerts an activity within the circles of self-preservation, he is not its prisoner. He surpasses it to another horizon, the horizon of values, ideals, ideas, and principles. This he considers to be the horizon that befits him, the horizon for which he was created. A civilized man considers his activity within the circle of self-preservation not an end in itself, but a necessary ladder to ascend to the second horizon. Whenever it becomes clear to him that his activity within the circle of self-preservation is accomplished only at the expense of what he believes in of ideals, ideas, and principles, civilization man does not hesitate to sacrifice life that is in conflict with what he cherishes of values and principles. Principled men are the cream of the human race; they are the lamps that illuminate the roads when issues are confused and when darkness prevails.[8]

The sessions with Bennabi had been very useful for Ghannouchi, who upon his return home from Paris bore the thought of the *salafi* school. This thought was apolitical and concentrated mainly on matters pertaining to 'aqidah (creed) and mazhar (appearance), such as the shape of a man's *lihyah* (beard) or the length of his *thawb* (garb), a thought that was more in line with the Tabligh approach to Islam. Bennabi's thought helped Ghannouchi discover that his earlier *salafi* orientation did not suit the Tunisian situation. Not only did it fall short of providing a comprehensive view of life, but also it could not cope with what he gradually discovered to be a unique Tunisian environment that was the product of a profound process of modernization and a legacy of well-established traditions in jurisprudence, dogmatic theology, and practice. This is what Ghannouchi calls *al-khususiyah at-tunisiyah* (Tunisian specificity). It was Bennabi who boosted Ghannouchi's confidence, and that of his colleagues, in their country's future and encouraged them to proceed forward with their Islamic activity. Once it was remarked by a participant in Bennabi's annual Islamic Thought Seminar that Tunisia had already been Westernized and that it no longer constituted an Islamic civilizational center, and that Algeria was suited to inherit its position thanks to its revolution and the progress it had been making in the cause of Arabization. Bennabi responded by explaining that grand centers in the history of civilizations are neither born in days nor do they die in days. He insisted that Algeria could never take Tunisia's place.[9]

The Philosophy Curriculum

Settling down in his country, Ghannouchi took up a job teaching philosophy to high school finalists. This turned out to be a very important subject for which six hours a week had been allocated. Students were anxious to do well in philosophy because the marks obtained in the final exam would be multiplied by six, and therefore a high score would enhance the position of students aspiring to proceed to university. Teaching this course challenged Ghannouchi, especially because the curriculum was designed in such a way that it focused primarily on the materialistic aspect of Western philosophy as represented in Marxism, Freudianism, Darwinism, and existentialism. The author of the curriculum was a leftist, whom Ghannouchi suspected was closely associated with French Marxists. Ghannouchi reckoned that the aim of teaching such a purposively designed philosophy curriculum to high school students was to transform students into militant Marxists, skeptical about all moral and humanistic values, skeptical about faith and all absolutes apart from the materialistic absolute. In this way, students would be molded into individuals fond of Western revolutions and models and suspicious of Islam and its history. The end product would be citizens disrespectful of Islam, rebellious against it, and even enemies of it.[10]

While on the job, Ghannouchi published an article entitled "Barnamij al-Falsafah Wa Jil ad-Daya'" (The philosophy curriculum and the generation of loss) in a leading Tunisian daily newspaper. In his article, he held the philosophy curriculum responsible for "the loss of an entire generation in Tunisia, the loss of national identity as a result of confusion and disorientation." He warned that in the absence of a clear definition of a Tunisian cultural identity, the philosophy lesson did not only fail to provide solutions to the problems Tunisians encountered, but also constituted an element of sabotage, destruction, and disorientation of both individual and society. His assessment was that the philosophy lessons were damaging in two ways. On the one hand, they offered contradictory answers to the problems faced by the pupils, who were still unable to choose between such answers because they lacked the cultural standard on the basis of which a choice could be made. On the other hand, they offered the pupils answers to problems that were not theirs, but that were the product of other societies that had cultures and circumstances completely different from those of Tunisia. The societies from which the answers to local problems were borrowed had their own values and customs, and had their own conceptions of the universe and its purpose and of man and his destiny.[11]

He observed that by focusing solely on Western philosophy, the philosophy lessons addressed primarily the psychological and sociological problems of Western societies and offered a set of solutions that were reflective of the social and religious upheavals and particular situations experienced by these societies. In his article, Ghannouchi sought to demonstrate that by emphasizing Marx, Freud, and Sartre, the philosophy curriculum served to discredit religion. He pinpointed for example the historical analysis offered by Marx, an analysis that only dealt with the phases Western societies had been through. The evidence, according to Ghannouchi, was that no mention of Islamic societies is to be found anywhere in Marx's analysis.

On the basis of his understanding of Marx, Ghannouchi sought to explain that Marx's theory that economics was the basic factor that governed everything including religion, morality, and politics emanated from his analysis of a phenomenon exclusive to the European experience. The questions Ghannouchi raised in his critique of the philosophy curriculum included:

> How could Marx's theory be considered a universal law applicable, as suggested by the school curriculum in Tunisia, to the history of humanity? How could Marx's theory that religion is people's opium and a barrier hindering social revolution against capitalism be considered a general rule applicable to every religion while such perception is the product of the particular experience of European societies, an experience marred by the collaboration of the Church with feudal lords and their collective endeavor to dissuade the people from rebelling against oppression?

Ghannouchi then applied the same line of questioning to other Western philosophers. He asked: "How could Freud's theory, that whatever befalls humans of psychological disorders is sexually related, be considered a scientific theory when it was largely a reflection of the state of mind of an oppressed Jew in a majority Christian society that debased sexual desire?"

Irrespective of whether the Jewishness of Sigmund Freud (1856-1939) had, or had not, anything to do with his theories, they continue to stir controversy and misgiving. In Islamic circles, Freud's theories are condemned for promoting immorality and libertinism. Furthermore, his analysis is said not to apply to Muslims simply because sexual desire, in the Islamic context, is recognized as a natural instinct whose fulfillment, provided it takes place in marriage, is desirable and is considered an act of worship.

With regard to Sartre, Ghannouchi asked: "How could Sartre's view of moral values and of freedom be viewed as a universal theory without tying it to a specific historical phase in the development of Western society, whose moral values had been crushed, whose spiritual bonds had been weakened, and whose judgement of life, as a consequence of vanishing ideals, is that it is fruitless and is a source of anxiety and weariness?"

Ghannouchi had one explanation for the way in which the philosophy curriculum was designed: "A conspiracy is being hatched against the *Ummah*, or else whose interest is served by the process of transmuting this generation, uprooting it from its cultural habitat, and severing the ties between it and its surroundings, leaving it astray, not knowing to what community it belongs or which culture to identify with, which ideals to look up to or which values to refer to?"

Nevertheless, Ghannouchi stressed that he did not object entirely to teaching these philosophies to high school students. What he meant to criticize was teaching them to students who had not first been equipped with what he called the skills of critical analysis.

> We want the students to be taught what is right and what is wrong in these philosophies with an emphasis that they were developed for different cultures and in dissimilar circumstances. In order to protect our children from loss and from cultural subordination to the colonialists, and if we must teach them Descartes, Marx, Durkheim, Sartre, and Darwin, we should teach them at the same time that we have our own culture on the basis of which we ought to devise our own solutions for our own problems.

Concluding his article, Ghannouchi proposed that instead of teaching students two separate subjects, the first called *al-falsafah al-gharbiyah* (Western philosophy) and the other *al-firaq al-islamiyah* (Islamic sects), one subject that teaches all ideas, both Islamic and non-Islamic, should be taught but from an Islamic perspective. "We either issue from a distinct identity, or personality, through which we view the world and deal with it, or we emanate, theoretically, from a void while in reality we take Western thought to be the point of departure or frame of reference."

Refinement

Providing a profound critique of the philosophy curriculum was Ghannouchi's way of promoting Islam as a better alternative; it was his means of communicating the Islamic idea to the youth with whom he interacted. This was his preoccupation during much of the 1970s in the classroom, in out-of-school seminars, in articles, and in lectures.

Ghannouchi admits that, initially, his critique was radical; it rejected almost everything that came from the West. However, at a later stage, and as a result of interacting with other forces in Tunisian society, especially the Marxists, his critique became more moderate and refined. As part of the development of his discourse, he no longer rejected completely the notion that the economic factor influenced the conduct of humans. He started focusing on the concept of social justice, on Islam's declared war against poverty, on siding with the oppressed. Once refuted at the very foundations, Marxism was incorporated into his analysis as an element.[12]

The outcome of the new critical analysis was still to reject the notion that Western concepts were absolutes but not to reject them altogether. They remain possible, albeit partial, explanations of human conduct and of human history. Henceforth, Ghannouchi's discourse stressed that the life of a Muslim is influenced, like the life of any other human being, by factors that cannot and should not be ignored, including sexual, economic, and social factors.[13] He started reading the Qur'an with a new insight. He began to discover that, in the Qur'anic discourse, the economy is an essential dimension. *Zakat*, the payment by the rich of money to the poor, is the third most important of Islam's five pillars. Furthermore, the first battle fought by the Prophet's companions after his death was motivated by an economic consideration, namely the abstention of the *muratddun* (renegades) from paying the *Zakat* under the pretext that it was a tax payable only to the Prophet during his life. He began to realize that a comprehensive reading of Islam would lead one to conclude that economic, political, sexual, and social factors had already been sufficiently emphasized in the Qur'an, and therefore denying the effect such factors have on people's lives, as he used to do, was a mistake. The new approach helped him to see the significance of the fact that an entire Qur'anic chapter, *Surat Yusuf* (Chapter twelve), was dedicated from beginning to end to the narration of a love story. This story, he discovered, ended with the triumph of noble values against lust but without denying the existence of the latter. Instead of ignoring such lust, Islam, through the Holy Qur'an and the Sunnah of the Prophet, provided humans with guidelines to help them fulfil their sexual desires in a manner conducive to the development and preservation of the human race. He was fascinated by the fact that the Qur'an refers explicitly to, and discusses at length, such sensitive issues as love, puberty, menstruation, marriage, and sexual intercourse.[14]

The new approach to critical analysis marked a shift in Ghannouchi's intellectual development from the attitude of absolute rejection of Western philosophy, which was perceived as having no element of truth whatsoever and assumed to be entirely false, to the attitude of what he calls *ar-rafd an-nisbi* (relative rejection) or *at-tafa'ul al-mawdu'i* (objective interaction). This was the direction in which the nascent Islamic movement of Tunisia moved. The transition reaped two fruits. On the one hand, it prepared the ground for establishing a sound relationship with the leftists within the Tunisian trade unionist movement. On the other hand, it enabled the Islamists to extract from the Western thought analytical tools not incompatible with Islam and useful in dealing with crucial and pressing issues such as the questions of governance, civil liberties, the rights of workers, and the rights of women.[15]

Ghannouchi could by then see that much of the Islamic analysis of the Western thought had been based on the reaction of Islamists to what was perceived as a Western threat to their own culture. He lamented that whereas Arab secularists accepted Western thought in totality and treated it as if it were a set of absolutes, the Islamists rejected everything that came from the West. He suggested instead that the more appropriate manner in dealing with the West would be to invoke the Qur'anic verse: "Let not the hatred of others to you make you swerve to wrong and depart from justice. Be just, that is next to piety."[16] Justice to him, as understood from this verse, meant interacting positively. He came to realize that it was justice that made it possible for Ibn Rushd (Averroes) and other Muslim philosophers to interact with Greek thought, taking from it that which they believed to be compatible with Islam and rejecting that which they believed was incompatible.[17]

The Ikhwan Connection

Upon returning to Tunisia from France, Ghannouchi conceived an Ikhwan-Mawdudi thought, although the only practical *da'wah* experience he had was a Tablighi one.[18] His Ikhwan line of thinking was acquired through reading the literature written by Ikhwan ideologues, such as the group's founder Hassan al-Banna and its other prominent thinkers including Sayyid Qutb, Abdel-Qadir 'Awdah, Muhammad al-Ghazali, and Yusuf al-Qaradawi.

Using the platform of al-Jama'ah al-Islamiyah, Ghannouchi pursued for three years the method of the Tabligh community. In 1973, the government, alarmed by the emergent Islamic trend, intervened and outlawed al-Jama'ah's activity, at which point Ghannouchi realized the need to reconsider his group's methodology. He thought that perhaps such an open activity of the Tabligh did not suit Tunisia under the prevalent circumstances. The approach, he wondered, might have worked more successfully in an open environment such as that of India or Pakistan or even Western Europe. The reason why it did not seem to suit Tunisia lay in the nature of Tunisia's political system. The extremely autocratic Tunisian regime adopted and sought to impose on society a radical but peculiar mode of secularization. The regime was not content with restricting religious practice to the private sphere, but oscillated between the desire to eliminate religion altogether and the tendency to monopolize it, interpreting it and even speaking in its name. For purely practical considerations, Ghannouchi felt compelled to reorganize his group so as to include in addition to what he calls "an open public educating process" a clandestine organizational structure. By then, the number of fully-fledged members had reached forty, and that was the moment the group decided to hold its very first conference at which Ghannouchi was elected leader. It was then too that the need was felt for learning from the experience of the Ikhwan, in both Egypt and Syria.[19]

Al-Ikhwan al-Muslimun (The Muslim Brothers or Muslim Brotherhood as it is commonly called in English literature) was founded in 1928 in Egypt by Hassan al-Banna (1906-1949) with the declared objective of reforming society on Islamic foundations. Soon afterward, variants and offshoots emerged in various parts of the Arab world. The Ikhwan of Syria was officially founded in 1944 by Dr. Mustafa as-Siba'i, who had earlier met al-Banna in Egypt.[20]

Ghannouchi had already known some of the ideas of the Ikhwan. His contact with the Ikhwan organization in Syria during his undergraduate years provided him with an insight about the way it functioned. As he stood at the threshold of a new phase in his Islamic activism, he felt that he and his group needed to acquaint themselves more deeply with the experience of the Ikhwan in Egypt. Of particular interest to them was the period that preceded the persecution and banning of the group by the Nassir government in the mid-1950s and then once more in the mid-1960s. Although the Ikhwan movement had not been solely responsible for generating the phenomenon of the *sahwah* (Islamic awakening) in the late 1960s and early 1970s in the Arab world, Ghannouchi recognized that it was the literature and experience of the Ikhwan that had the greatest influence in shaping the thinking and attitude throughout the 1970s of millions of young Muslims around the world. His group of Tunisian Islamists, who passionately sought to re-identify with the long-deserted Qur'anic teachings and values, was no exception.

Al-Banna's diagnosis of the causes of the crisis and his prescription for salvation influenced Ghannouchi just as it did in the case of other emerging Islamic leaders across the region. Ghannouchi was particularly impressed by al-Banna's declaration that:

> Just as political aggression had its effect in arousing nationalist feelings, so has social aggression had its effect in reviving the Islamic ideology. Voices have been raised in every land, demanding a return to Islam, an understanding of its precepts, and an application of its rules. The day must soon come when the walls of this materialistic civilization will come down upon the heads of its inhabitants. Then their hearts and souls will burn with a spiritual hunger, but they will find no sustenance, no healing, no remedy, except in the teachings of this Noble Book.[21]

Of interest to Ghannouchi too was al-Banna's admonition to his followers that they should always bear in mind that they had two fundamental goals. The first goal is "to free the Islamic homeland from all foreign influence." The second goal is "to establish an Islamic state that acts according to the precepts of Islam, applies its social code, advocates its principles, and propagates its mission to all of mankind." Al-Banna warned that as long as this state remains absent every Muslim is sinning, and is responsible before God for his failure and slackness to establish it. He wanted his followers to accomplish the above two goals "in the Nile Valley and the Arab world, and in every land that Allah has blessed with the Islamic creed." The ultimate objective was to unite all Muslims within one Islamic state.[22]

For Ghannouchi, the Ikhwan was a liberation movement that seemed at the time a model, a source of inspiration. Not only was he impressed by the two ambitious goals, but also more importantly by what al-Banna referred to as "Our Special Aims." "Apart from these two aims," al-Banna explained, "we have some specific aims. If they are not accomplished our society cannot become wholly Islamic." Al-Banna's passionate appeal to his "brothers" to consider the effects of oppressive policies and colonial designs on Egyptian society sounded familiar to the emerging Islamic movement of Tunisia. Ghannouchi did initially think that Tunisia and Egypt were not much different, and therefore what worked for Egypt should work for Tunisia. The echoes of al-Banna's address to his brethren in Egypt reverberated in Tunisia:

> Recall that more than 60 percent of Egyptians live at a subhuman level. Only through the most arduous toil do they get enough to eat. Egypt is threatened by murderous famines and is exposed to many economic problems of which only Allah knows the outcome. Recall too that there are more than 320 foreign companies in Egypt, monopolizing all public utilities and all important facilities in every sector of the country; the wheels of commerce, industry, and all economic institutions are in the hands of profiteering foreigners; and our wealth in land is being transferred with lightning speed from our hands to those of others. Recall also that, out of the entire civilized world, Egypt is subject to the most diseases, plagues, and illness; over 90 percent of the Egyptian people are threatened by physical infirmity, the loss of some sensory perception, and a variety of sicknesses and ailments. Egypt is still backward, with no more than one-fifth of the population possessing any form of education, and of these more than one hundred thousand have never gone further than the primary school level. Recall that crime has doubled in Egypt, and that it is increasing at an alarming rate to the point that there are more people coming out of prisons than out of schools; that up to the present time Egypt has been unable to properly outfit a single army division.[23]

Of particular relevance to Ghannouchi's cause was al-Banna's reminder to his fol-lowers that these symptoms and phenomena were not exclusive to Egypt; they could be observed in many other Islamic countries. Wherever they were, he stressed, members of the Ikhwan should endeavor to reform education, to fight poverty, ignorance, dis-ease, and crime, and to create an exemplary society deserving to be associated with the Islamic *Shari'ah*. To achieve these objectives, al-Banna suggested that the approach of the Ikhwan would have to be founded on three things: profound faith, proper organiza-tion, and continuous labor.[24]

Local Heritage

In the beginning, Ghannouchi's thought was a reflection of the reformist thought that came from the *Mashriq*, mainly from Egypt. It was not the product of a local religious tradition and had still not established roots at home. However, it did not take him long to appreciate that there was in his own country an Islamic Tunisian legacy, a rich heri-tage, on the ground of which he felt it was necessary to stand. The task of reconnecting with this legacy had to go through the gates of Tunisia's most prestigious institute, az-Zaytouna. It was at az-Zaytouna where he himself did much of his pre-university studies, and it was there that he saw the drastic effects of neutralizing one of the most influential institutions in Tunisian history. Having embarked on a mission of reform, of particular interest to him was the role played by az-Zaytouna during the past two centuries. He dis-covered that the scholars of az-Zaytouna played a significant role in the modernization endeavor that preceded the colonial era. Long before the French colonized Tunisia and imposed on it what Ghannouchi calls "pseudo-modernization," az-Zaytouna's moderniza-tion project emanated from the desire to benefit from the modern sciences and modern systems of administration while maintaining the country's Islamic cultural identity.

It was out of az-Zaytouna that the mid-nineteenth century reform movement in Tu-nisia emerged calling for the modernization of education, administration, and govern-ment. One of its main demands was the restriction of the powers of government. This led to the formulation of the 1864 constitution, believed to be the first of its kind in the Muslim world in that it restrained government and introduced what was known in the Ottoman caliphate as *tanzimat*, a form of administrative policy. The reform movement was led by Khairuddin at-Tunisi, prime minister and author of a book entitled *Aqwam al-Masalik Fi Ma'rifat Ahwal al-Mamalik* (The most straight path to learning the condi-tions of states). The book was practically a collection of contributions made by az-Zaytouna scholars. For despite his zeal and enthusiasm, at-Tunisi was not an Islamic scholar him-self but a shrewd politician and an economist. In any case, his book provided a general plan for reform.[25]

Ghannouchi deemed it essential for him and his group to be perceived as the inheri-tors or true followers of the nineteenth-century Tunisian reform movement. Firstly, it was necessary for him that his ideas did not appear exotic, but indigenous and deeply rooted in a legacy the Tunisians respected. Secondly, at a time when the government in Tunisia sought to restrict his group's activity and when he and his followers interacted more vigorously with their adversaries, it was necessary for him to establish a resem-blance between the activity upon which he and his group had embarked and at-Tunisi's project of reform. Thirdly, and having gone thus far, it was necessary for him to stress that neither at-Tunisi nor any of the Islamic scholars of his time had intended to cast doubt on Islam or introduce changes to it. He felt the need to stress that those pioneers of reform sought only to understand Islam better and explore new means and methods to implement it, relying on the explanations and interpretations of both classic and contemporary scholars. For his own purposes, it was necessary to illustrate that the group's endeavor to borrow from the West was legitimate. Three established rules provided legitimacy for such an endeavor: the rule that "wisdom is a believer's long-cherished objective," the rule that "religion has been revealed for the benefit of humanity," and the rule that "*Shari'ah* is fully compatible with the vital interests of the human community."[26]

Ghannouchi was particularly impressed by the example of as-Sadiqiyah school, which he often alludes to. The school was established by at-Tunisi for the purpose of teaching modern arts and sciences within an Islamic framework. The purpose of the school, according to the founding declaration, was:

> To teach the Qur'an, writing, and useful knowledge, that is, juridical sciences, foreign languages, and the rational sciences that might be of use to Muslims being at the same time not contrary to the faith. The professors must inculcate in the students love of the faith by showing them its beauties and excellence, in telling them the deeds of the Prophet, the miracles accomplished by him, and the virtues of the holy men.[27]

At-Tunisi's reform endeavor, in Ghannouchi's assessment, was an Islamic project aimed at learning and borrowing from Western civilization without conceding the country's Arab-Islamic identity. Hence, the mission of the new Islamic movement Ghannouchi and his colleagues had set up was to pursue the same endeavor, namely to reform the country through the adoption of modern tools and techniques but within an Islamic framework.

As part of his mission to reconnect with the Tunisian Islamic legacy, Ghannouchi returned to az-Zaytouna in search of his roots. This was when he started, for the first time ever, studying the writings of Tunisian Islamic thinkers. All of his previous readings, that is since his conversion in Syria, were—apart from the writings of Bennabi—of books written by thinkers from the *Mashriq*. This was the literature that paved his way to Islam, but failed to enlighten him about the *Magharibi* Islamic heritage and particularly about Tunisia's experience of Islamic modernization. The first Islamic Tunisian book he read was authored by Ibn 'Ashoor, one of the most prominent figures of Tunisian Islamic thought and author of two important works, *At-Tahrir Wat-Tanwir* and *Maqasid Ash-Shari'ah*.[28]

Tunisian Specificity

By the mid-1970s, Ghannouchi's thought and that of his emerging Islamic movement had acquired a specific Tunisian character that was the product of the interaction of three main components.[29]

The first component is what he himself calls *at-tadayyun at-taqlidi at-tunisi* (the traditional Tunisian religiosity), which is comprised of three elements: the Maliki school of jurisprudence, the *al-Ash'ariyah* doctrine of theology, and Sufism.[30] The triad is the outcome of a long history of exchange, interaction, and conflict. According to Ghannouchi, what is so peculiar about this combination is its relevance to the predominance of taqlıd (imitation) and shortage of ijtihad (innovative thinking) during what he describes as the era of stagnation in the history of Tunisia. He sees the exclusive adoption of the Maliki school of fiqh (jurisprudence) as a sign of rigidity and intolerance, and consequently a restriction of ijtihad. The adoption of the al-Ash'ariyah doctrine of theology, in his analysis, compounded the crisis, because the doctrine tends toward al-Jabriyah (fatalism). The founder of the doctrine, Abu al-Hasan al-Ash'ari (873-941), had previously been a member of al-Mu'tazilah, which held that persons intuitively are self-conscious of their capacity to make choices and that this conscious awareness and intention will make persons responsible for the outcome of their acts. Al-Ash'ari deserted al-M'utazilah and rejected its doctrine in favor of the doctrine of al-kasb, which he himself formulated to the effect that human powers are derived by acquisition from God.[31] Although the al-Ash'arıyah doctrine was initially formulated so as to adopt a balanced position between the fatalism of al-Jabriyah and the free will of al-M'utazilah, and although it eventually gained more support among Sunni theologians, Ghannouchi is of the opinion that it was more inclined toward fatalism than free will. With the addition of Sufism to the combination, the political implication of the triad, Ghannouchi observes, serves to consolidate authoritarian systems of governance. While the al-Ash'arıyah doctrine lays the foundation for fatalism, and consequently the stupefaction of the people, Sufism legitimizes the unquestionable submission by the follower to his master.[32]

Initially, Ghannouchi decided to resist this combination and combat al-Jabriyah and taqlıd. His priority was to assert that man is responsible for his actions, and therefore change is within human means. As part of this endeavor, he chose for his master's degree at the Tunisian University the topic of "al-Qadar 'Inda Ibn Taymiyah" (Destiny in the thought of Ibn Taymiyah). As it turned out, Ghannouchi was the first researcher in contemporary Tunisia to write a treatise on Ibn Taymiyah (1263-1328), a very influential Islamic scholar whose writings had been banned in az-Zaytouna because of his criticism of both fatalism and Sufism. Ghannouchi's strategy was aimed at shaking the cultural foundations upon which authoritarianism rested in Tunisia. If change was ever to be effected, fatalism had to be replaced by the doctrine of free will, taqlıd had to be replaced by ijtihad, and the blind following of Sufism had to be replaced by an attitude based on equality, freedom of choice, and the de-sanctification of Sufi figures.[33]

However, it did not take long for Ghannouchi to reconsider his confrontational strategy. In the second half of the 1970s, his group's friction with the regime became more frequent and priorities had to be set right. On the one hand, the rebellion against the cultural triad seemed futile. Ghannouchi discovered that society was too resistant, it just could not be molded the way he wished. On the other hand, as the regime intensified its war against the expanding Islamic movement, the last thing Ghannouchi wanted was to open new war fronts. His choice was to make peace with the guardians of religious traditions, az-Zaytouna scholars, and leaders of Sufi orders. His priority was to dedicate all the resources of his group in the struggle within the political arena. Undoubtedly, this was a concession, a price that had to be paid for political activism. Ghannouchi himself admits that one of the serious repercussions of political activism is that it places constraints on the endeavor to effect intellectual and theological reform.[34]

The second component of Tunisian specificity, as conceived by Ghannouchi, is the *salafi* religiosity, of the type he embraced initially following the example of the *Mashariqi* Islamic thought to which he was exposed during his years of study in Syria. This component in turn is comprised of four elements. The first is the rejection of doctrinal or jurisprudential *taqlid* (imitation) and the call for a return to *al-masadir* (the original sources), that is the Qur'an, the Sunnah, and the experience of the first three generations of Muslims. The second is the political and social thought of the Ikhwan, which is based on stressing the comprehensiveness of Islam, establishing the principle that *hakimiyah* (sovereignty) is the exclusive prerogative of God, and declaring existing regimes to be un-Islamic and consequently launching a struggle to change them. The third is the Ikhwan's educational and training program, which focuses on the nurturing of *taqwa* (piety), *tawakkul* (having faith in God), *dhikr* (praising and glorifying God), *jihad*, collective work, *ukhuwah* (brotherhood), *zuhd* (asceticism), and strict adherence to the Sunnah. The fourth is the Ikhwan's intellectual program, which tends to over-emphasize the doctrinal and moral aspects at the expense of the political and social aspects. Ghannouchi is critical of this particular element, which in his opinion has been overwhelmed by the tendency to judge situations and people against a doctrinal scale. As a result, people are divided into two categories, that of the brothers and that of the adversaries.[35]

The third component is what Ghannouchi calls *at-tadayyun al-'aqlani* (rational religiosity). This form of religiosity has been described as rational because of its appeal to intelligent judgment and reasoning in the process of understanding religious doctrines and interpreting the holy text. Because of the influence of the *salafi*-Ikhwan religiosity earlier on, rational religiosity did not express itself clearly until the second half of the 1970s.[36] This is the period when Ghannouchi and his group started interacting and communicating with other political and intellectual groups in the Tunisian arena. At this stage too, writings by former members of the Ikhwan in Egypt, which were critical of the Ikhwan, had started reaching the Islamists of Tunisia. Among the most influential of such writings were those of Dr. Fat-hi Osman, whose critique created interest and stirred controversy within Ghannouchi's group about the validity of the Ikhwan's ideology and methodology. The critique of the Ikhwan also reached Tunisia through the *Al-Muslim al-Mu'asir* (The contemporary Muslim) magazine, which used to be published in Kuwait.[39]

In addition to discussing the critique of the Ikhwan, the debate within Ghannouchi's group included an endeavor to revive what was referred to as *at-turath al-islami al-'aqlani* (the Islamic legacy of rationality). The need was felt, as part of the attempt to counter the *at-tadayyun at-taqlidi at-tunisi* (traditional Tunisian religiosity), to restore respect for the *al-Mu'tazilah* approach to interpreting the Islamic text. Based on the belief that human reason harmonizes with revelation, the *al-Mu'tazilah* approach was deemed more conducive to the group's objective of shaking the foundations of *taqlid*. Thenceforth, Ghannouchi's group embarked on a process of *'aqlana* (rationalization), defined by Ghannouchi as the endeavor by a Muslim "to be in perpetual dynamism with his reality." It means, in other words, giving reality due consideration in the planning of any action because an action governed solely by a given interpretation of sacred text would be a futile task. With *'aqlana*, planning becomes the fruit of a balance between the human value and the text on one the hand and this human value and reality on the other.[38]

The Split

However, the strategy of *'aqlana* soon backfired. Some members of Ghannouchi's group wanted to pursue it further while others were apprehensive that it might eventually lead to undermining the revelation itself. A new trend had emerged calling for the restoration of respect and recognition for the political opposition groups in Islamic history such as the Kharijites and the Shiites that is for factions which opposed the Salafis and the Sunnites in general.[39] The *'aqlaniyun* (rationalists) adopted a severe critique of the Ikhwan, which they started portraying as a major obstacle hindering the progress toward an Islamic renaissance. They also sought to restore respect for the reformist school, whose prominent figures such as Tahtawi, al-Afghani, Abduh, al-Kawakibi, and Qasim Amin had been discredited in some of the writings of the Ikhwan. In addition, they were more inclined toward what Ghannouchi calls *alfahm almaqasidi* (the purposive cognition) than toward *alfahm annassi* (the textual cognition) of Islam. They called for the interpretation of the texts in light of *almaqasid* (the purposes), such as *'adl* (justice), *tawhid* (monotheism), *hurriyah* (liberty), and *insaniyah* (humanism). In this way, *nusus* (pl. of *nass*, that is text) of *al-hadith* (the sayings of the prophet) are accepted or dismissed not in accordance with the criteria set by the scholars of *al-hadith*, but on the basis of their compliance with the *maqasid* (purposes) of *Shari'ah*. The rationalists, who later on became known as *al-yasar al-islami* (the Islamic left), wanted also to restore recognition of the West, especially its socialist or leftist component, as a source of what they deemed a greatly needed expertise. Hence, they sought to counter the influence of the *salafi-*Ikhwan thought, which perceived the West more as a decaying materialistic civilization. In contrast to the Ikhwan-promoted religiosity, which adopted an ideological scale by which people were divided into the categories of *mu'min* (believer) and *kafir* (infidel), the rationalists, who considered such categorization to be naive and uninformed of real conflicts in the world, promoted a categorization based on political and social criteria. Their categorization divided the people into *watani* (patriot) and *kha'in* (traitor), or *thawri* (revolutionary) and *raj'i* (reactionary), or *fallah* (peasant) and *iqta'i* (feudal lord). Hence, a person may be a Muslim but an *kha'in* and may be a Marxist but a *watani*.[40]

The rationalists' critique of the Ikhwan targeted in particular the thought of Sayyid Qutb, whose theory of *jahiliyah* (barbarity) called for *mufasalah* (alienation and departure) from blasphemous society by the community of believers, which he considered to be the *Ummah*. Qutb had suggested that apart from this small community of believers, or *jama'ah*, there was nothing Islamic about society, and therefore the *jama'ah* was responsible for standing out in distinction and then working for the transformation of society by expanding its own power base. Addressing the community of believers, he declared:

> We must free ourselves from the clutches of *jahili* society, *jahili* concepts, *jahili* traditions, and *jahili* leadership. Our mission is not to compromise with the practices of *jahili* society, nor can we be loyal to it. *Jahili* society, because of its *jahili* characteristics, is not worthy to be compromised with. Our aim is first to change ourselves so that we may later change the society. Our foremost objective is to change the practices of this society. Our aim is to change the *jahili* system at its very roots—this system which is fundamentally at variance with Islam and which, with the help of force and oppression, is keeping us from living the sort of life which is demanded by our Creator. Our first step will be to raise

ourselves above the *jahili* society and all its values and concepts. We will not change our own values and concepts either more or less to make a bargain with this *jahili* society. Never! It and we are on different roads, and if we take even one step in its company, we will lose our goal entirely and lose our way as well.[41]

Qutb spoke of a bitter, strenuous, prolonged struggle to free the natural order from man-made shackles and establish it over and above other orders.[42] For this, he called for preparing "ourselves for quite a long time to be fit for this unrelaxing task" by means of exalting "ourselves to the level of true religion."[43]

Ghannouchi did not entirely disagree with the rationalists' critique of Qutb, whose conception of *jahiliyah* and *hakimiyah* he did not accept. Nor did he disagree with them on the need to restore respect for the reformist school of the nineteenth and early twentieth centuries. However, he did not condone their skeptical attitude toward the sacred text, nor did he accept the extension of their critique to the entire *salafi*-Ikhwan school. But above all he disliked their suggestion that the *al-burguibiyah* (Bourguibism, referring to the reforms introduced by President Bourguiba) was an extension of the Tunisian reformist school of Khairuddin at-Tunisi and at-Tahir al-Haddad.[44]

The debate within al-Jama'ah al-Islamiyah erupted into disagreement and resulted in splitting it. What caused the split, from Ghannouchi's point of view, was the perception that the *al-yasar al-islami* group had gone too far when it raised the question of the relationship between the text and reason and called into question the position of *Shari'ah*. The dispute was augmented by the rationalists' call for making a distinction between, on the one hand, *'ibadat* (rituals) and *akhlaqiyat* (ethics), both of which they considered to be immutable or absolute, and on the other hand, every thing else, which they categorized as mutable. This was entirely unacceptable to Ghannouchi and the bulk of his al-Jama'ah al-Islamiyah, especially that the group of *al-yasar al-islami* was being perceived as approaching Bourguibism itself.

Consequently, the Islamic leftists deserted Ghannouchi's movement and became increasingly isolated and marginalized. While in fact they called themselves *at-taqaddumiyun al-islamiyun* (The Progressive Islamists), they borrowed the term *al-yasar al-islami* (the Islamic Left) from a publication edited in Egypt by Hasan Hanafi. *Al-yasar al-islami* became the name by which they were better known throughout the region because they divided Muslim intellectuals into two categories: the first comprising those who are *taqaddumi* (progressive), *yasari* (leftist), and *mustaqbali* (futurist); and the second comprising those who are *raj'i* (reactionary), *yamini* (rightist), and *madawi* (living in the past).[45] A leading member of the Progressive Islamists was Ahmida Enneifer, one of the founders, together with Ghannouchi, of the al-Jama'ah al-Islamiyah in 1970. He was later to become the religious adviser to Education Minister Ash-Sharfi, who was known for his strong opposition to the Islamic movement and who, according to Ghannouchi, undertook the task of eliminating what had remained of religious elements in the education curricula through the strategy of *tajfif al-yanabi'* (drying the fountainheads).[46]

Enneifer contests Ghannouchi's analysis of the reasons for the split. From his point of view, the main cause of the split was the disagreement over the relationship with, or the position toward, the Ikhwan. In 1975, he traveled to Egypt, where he met with a number of senior Ikhwan members. He left Egypt with the impression that the Ikhwan were a mere deception.[47] Not only did their doctrine seem unconvincing to him, but also he was bitter about their patronizing attitude. Enneifer concluded from his visit that the Ikhwan corresponded more to legend than to anything else. Their methodology appeared to him to be totally obsolete and decided it could if copied in his country only lead to disaster. Disillusioned with the Ikhwan, he called for a "Tunisian Islam." In a series of articles published in Al-Ma'rifah, he sharply criticized Al-Banna and warned against the re-employment of his ideology, which he insisted was not in step with the real problems of society. When the editor censored a paragraph on Al-Banna in one of these articles, Enneifer protested and eventually withdrew from the publication. But in addition he was very critical of what he perceived as an outright refusal by Ghannouchi and his followers to recognize any positive aspects of the Bourguiba project of modernization.[45]

Ghannouchi maintains, however, that the split was not simply over matters of policy. He insists that it had to do with the rationalists' position vis-à-vis the sacred text. While accepting that the exercise of self-criticism was necessary, he maintains that this has to be within the bounds of the Islamic scripture, which remains an ultimate frame of reference. "Had we rebelled against this frame of reference, nothing would have been left for us to refer to for guidance. Modernity, whether Tunisian or Western, has to be viewed through the Islamic [sacred] Text; stringent controls have to be maintained."[49]

Ghannouchi admits, however, that his group did initially resist acknowledging the influence of Westernization on society and adopted a rejectionist position toward the Westernized segments of society. Furthermore, they rejected Bourguibism in totality and could only see its negative aspects. In favor of what they had imported from the Mashriq, they also rejected the Tunisian traditional style of religiosity. Hence, they ended up clashing with the society as a whole. They clashed with the Westernized elite, particularly with the communists whom they considered to be among the most Westernized; they clashed with the traditional society represented in the shuyukh (pl. of shaykh, that is, scholar) of the az-Zaytouna; and they were at odds with the regime. Ghannouchi realized by the mid-1970s that such a clash was bound to produce one of two results. The Islamists would either succeed in transforming the entire society by imposing on it their own ideas, and he knew this was not possible in the foreseeable future; or they would interact with society through a process of "give and take" or "marriage and reconciliation."[50]

In spite of the split, Ghannouchi could still see a positive side to this dramatic development. The emergent debate was very useful in that it helped him and his colleagues regain what he calls "our consciousness" and in that it established the tradition of self-criticism that helped them question the imported thought instead of merely dealing with it from the position of unconditional acceptance.[51] Unknown in Islamic circles before, the tradition of self-criticism gave birth to a debate that, while leading to the dissension of the rationalists, gave rise—at a time when the membership of al-Jama'ah al-Islamiyah had considerably increased—to demands for muhasaba (accountability) and ma'sasah (institutionalization). It also paved the way for interacting with the democratic thought, for discovering new dimensions in the conflict between the state and society and within society, and for bridging the gap between the Islamic movement and the trade unionist movement.

It has been argued that Ghannouchi's intellectual maturity was as much a reflection of the political development of the Tunisian Islamic Movement as the latter was of the former.[59] From the mid-1970s to the early 1980s five main factors directly influenced Ghannouchi's thought and the development of his movement's political standing. These were the liberal democratic current that emerged in Tunisia in the second half of the 1970s; the 1978 violent confrontation between the trade unions and the government; the clash and interaction on campus with the leftists; the Iranian revolution; and the socio-political thought of the Islamic movement in Sudan.[52]

Democratic Breeze

In the mid-1970s, a movement advocating democracy in Tunisia emerged from within the secularist camp. Ahmad al-Mestiri, a former leading member of the ruling Destourian Party and an ex-minister, led the founders of the movement. He had dissented together with a group of former officials from the party and started criticizing the regime for its autocracy and suppression of freedom of speech. The movement set up an independent newspaper, Ar-Ra'y, which defended the cause of political pluralism and civil liberties. Prior to this development the issue of democratization and terms such as political pluralism and civil liberties had never been raised whether by the Islamists or the secularists in Tunisia. Ghannouchi was quick to respond. He initiated contact with the leaders of the new political movement, the democratic trend as he refers to it. This was the beginning of his march along the path of democracy.[54] Undoubtedly, the debate within al-Jama'ah al-Islamiyah had prepared him and his colleagues for the new era of opening up and communicating with other political trends.

Ghannouchi believes that his earlier education and training may have prepared him for espousing the cause of democracy. He attributes his inclination toward democracy to two factors. The first is his philosophical background, or what he calls "my philosophical molding." For him, the philosophy lesson was a theater not for dogmatic indoctrination, but for free philosophical debate, for disputation, and for controversy. In other words, Ghannouchi benefited from having had a non-dogmatic training, one that exposed him to a variety of schools of thought. His open-minded approach enabled him for example to test Arab nationalism, only to discover that it was no more than a combination of dogma and irrelevant sentimental slogans: unity, liberty, and socialism. The second factor was his non-partisan approach to Islamic thought. From the time of his conversion from nationalism to Islam in Damascus in 1966 until his return to Tunisia in 1970, he chose not to join any Islamic organization. Instead, he communicated, and maintained good relations, with all the Islamic groups he came across. He read and studied the writings of classical and contemporary thinkers, including the ideologues of contemporary movements. His decision to remain free of organizational constraints throughout the period of educating himself in Islam had prepared him to accept the notion of pluralism.

Prior to establishing contact with the democratic trend, Ghannouchi and his group were still concerned primarily with combating Marxism. Their strategy was based on the thought received from the Mashriq through the writings of Sayyid Qutb for whom conflict existed between haq (truth) and batil (falsehood), or between iman (belief) and kufr (disbelief), or between Islam and jahiliyah. The interaction with the secularist democrats made Ghannouchi realize that conflict can take other than a purely ideological form. In addition to ideological considerations, there were important political considerations. He could by then see that in his country there was a major conflict between a single-party regime led by a dictator who tightly controlled all aspects of life in the country, and those who struggled for a democratic system of government, for political pluralism, and for freedom of speech.

The communication with the democrats could not have come at a better time. The demands for *muhasaba* and *ma'sasah* by some members of al-Jama'ah al-Islamiyah were given a boost by the democratic touch. Charges that the leadership of the group was autocratic and that it had so far failed to transform the group into an institution and to formulate a constitution prompted Ghannouchi to convene a general conference. Prior to the conference a constitution was drafted and circulated among members for discussion. The conference, known as *al-mu'tamar at-ta'sisi* (the founding conference), was held in 1979. The draft constitution was adopted, and the conference elected for the first time *majlis ash-shura* (*shura* council), *al-maktab at-tanfidhi* (executive bureau), and the regional representatives of al-Jama'ah. Ghannouchi was elected its *ra'is* (president).

At this point, Ghannouchi seemed certain his *Mashariqi* thinking needed thorough revision. One of its main deficiencies, according to him, had been its disregard for the struggle by Arab political thinkers against despotism since the dawn of modern Arab renaissance about two centuries ago. The *Mashariqi* thinking, he observed, had no interest in early reformist discussion of the concept of democracy, which had, notably outside the ranks of the *Mashariqi* Islamic movement, been debated intensely, and had developed under the influence of a variety of social and political factors.[55]

Nineteenth-century Islamic political thinkers, who were clearly influenced by European liberal democratic thought, tried to establish a resemblance between democracy and the Islamic concept of *shura*. Faced with a crisis of government augmented by autocracy and corruption, they sought to legitimize the borrowing of those aspects of the Western model they believed were compatible with Islam and capable of resolving the political crisis at home.

The discussion of democracy in the Arab Islamic literature can be traced back to Rifa'ah Tahtawi (1801–1873). He was the first Islamic scholar to campaign for interacting with the European civilization with the objective of borrowing from it that which does not conflict with the established values and principles of the Islamic *Shari'ah*.[56] Shortly following his return to Cairo from Paris, Tahtawi, the father of Egyptian democracy,[57] published in 1834 his first book, *Takhlis al-Ibriz Ila Talkhis Bariz*. The book summarized his observations of the manners and customs of the modern French.[58] In it he praised the concept of democracy as he saw it in France and as he witnessed its defense and reassertion through the 1830 revolution against King Charles X.[59] Tahtawi tried to show that the democratic concept he was explaining to his readers was compatible with Islam. He compared political pluralism to forms of ideological and jurisprudential pluralism that existed in the Islamic experience:

> Religious freedom is the freedom of belief, of opinion and of sect, provided it does not contradict the fundamentals of religion. An example would be the theological opinions of the Al-Asha'irah and the Al-Matiridiyah; another would be the opinions of leading jurists within the doctrine of the branches. For by following any one of these schools, a human feels secure. The same would apply to the freedom of political practice and opinion by leading administrators, who endeavor to interpret and apply rules and provisions in accordance with the laws of their own countries. Kings and ministers are licensed in the realm of politics to pursue various routes that in the end serve one purpose: good administration and justice.[60]

An important landmark in Arab democratic thought was the contribution of Khairuddin at-Tunisi (1810-1899), leader of the nineteenth-century reform movement in Tunisia and author of *Aqwam al-Masalik Fi Ma'rifat Ahwal al-Mamalik*. The main preoccupation of the book is tackling the question of political reform in the Arab world. While appealing to politicians and scholars of his time to seek all possible means in order to improve the status of the community and develop its civility, at-Tunisi warned the general Muslim public against shunning the experiences of other nations on the basis of the misconception that all the writings, inventions, experiences, and attitudes of non-Muslims should simply be rejected or disregarded. He further called for an end to absolutist rule, which he blamed for the oppression of nations and the destruction of civilizations.[61] Khairuddin at-Tunisi believed that "kindling the *Ummah*'s potential liberty through the adoption of sound administrative procedures, and enabling it to have a say in political affairs, would put it on a faster track toward civilization, would limit the rule of despotism, and would stop the influx of European civilization that is sweeping every thing along its path."[62]

In his search for the causes of decline in the Muslim world, Jamal ad-Din al-Afghani (1838-1897) diagnosed that it was due to the absence of *'adl* (justice) and *shura* (council) and non-adherence by the government to the constitution.[63] One of his main demands was that the people should be allowed to assume their political and social role by participating in governing through *shura* and elections.[64] Al-Afghani attributed the decline to despotism, which is the reason why thinkers in the Muslim countries of the *Mashriq* could not enlighten the public about the essence and virtues of republican government.

> For those governed by the republican government, it is a source of happiness and pride. Those governed by a republican form of government alone deserve to be called human; for a true human being is only subdued by a true law that is based on the foundations of justice and that is designed to govern man's moves, actions, transactions, and relations with others in a manner that elevates him to the pinnacle of true happiness.[65]

To al-Afghani, a republican government is a "restricted government," a government that is accountable to the public, and that is thus the antithesis of the absolutist one. It is a government that consults the governed, relieves them of the burdens laid upon them by despotic governments, and lifts them from the state of decay to the first level of perfection.[66]

Muhammad Abduh (1849-1905) believed that Islam's relationship with the modern age was the most crucial issue Islamic communities needed to address. In an attempt to reconcile Islamic ideas with Western ones, he suggested that *maslaha* (interest) in Islamic thought corresponded to *manfa'ah* (utility) in the Western thought. Similarly, he equated *shura* with democracy and *ijma'* with consensus. Addressing the question of authority, Abduh denied the existence of a theocracy in Islam and insisted that the authority of the *hakim* (governor) or that of the *qadi* (judge) or that of the *mufti* was civil. He demanded strongly that *ijtihad* should be revived because "emerging priorities and problems, which are new to Islamic thought, need to be addressed."[67] He was a proponent of the parliamentary system. He defended pluralism and refuted the claims that it would undermine the unity of the *Ummah*. He argued that the European nations were not divided by it. "The reason," he concluded, "is that their objective is the same. What varies is only the method they pursue toward accomplishing it."[68]

Abdurrahman al-Kawakibi (1849–1903) wrote two books on the subject, *Taba'i' al-Istibdad* (Traits of despotism) and *Umm-ul-Qura* (The mother of villages). The first is dedicated to defining despotism and explaining the various forms it may take, with much of the discussion focused on political despotism. The relationship between religion and despotism and what he calls the "inseparable tie" between politics and religion are discussed. While stressing that Islam as a religion is not responsible for the forms of despotic government that emerged and reigned in its name, al-Kawakibi concluded that "God, the omniwise, has intended nations to be responsible for the actions of those whom they choose to be governed by. When a nation fails in its duty, God causes it to be subdued by another nation that will govern it, just as happens in a court of law when a minor or an incompetent is put under the care of a curator. When, on the other hand, a nation matures and appreciates the value of liberty, it will restore its might, and this is only fair."[69] The entire book is an attempt to explain the reasons why the Muslim *Ummah* had declined and had become an easy prey for nineteenth-century colonial powers. Like al-Afghani and Abduh, al-Kawakibi attributed the success of the Western nations to the adoption of logical and well-practiced rules that had become social duties in these advanced nations. He observed that these nations were not harmed by what appeared to be a division into parties and groups, because such a division was only over the methods of applying the rules and not over the rules themselves.[70]

In his other book, al-Kawakibi constructed a series of dialogues involving fictional characters, which he described as thinkers, each belonging to a known town in the Muslim world. He imagined that these prominent figures were summoned to a conference organized in *Umm-ul-Qura* (Mecca) during the *hajj* (pilgrimage) season to discuss the causes of decline of the Muslim *Ummah*. One character, al-Baligh al-Qudsi, says: "It seems to me that the cause of tepidity is the change in the nature of Islamic politics. It was parliamentary and socialist, that is perfectly democratic. But due to the escalation of internal feuds, after the *al-Khulafa' ar-Rashidun* (the Four Rightly-Guided Caliphs) it was transformed into a monarchy restrained by the basic rules of *Shari'ah*, and then it became almost completely absolute." Ar-Rumi, another character, comments: "The calamity has been our loss of liberty." The conferees finally agree that progress is linked to accountability while regress is linked to despotism.[71]

Muhammad Rashid Rida (1865–1935) believed that the cause of the *Ummah*'s backwardness was the loss by the Muslims of the truth of their religion. Bad political rulers, he explained, had encouraged this. True Islam, he added, involves two things, acceptance of *tawhid* (the creed of monotheism) and *shura* (council) in matters of state. But despotic rulers, he lamented, have tried to make Muslims forget the second by encouraging them to abandon the first.[72] He stressed that the greatest lesson the people of the Orient can learn from the Europeans is to know what government should be like.[73] In his book *Al-Khilafah* (The caliphate) he emphasized that Islam is guidance, mercy, and socio-civic policy. About the last, which he seems to use as a synonym for politics, he says:

> As for the socio-civic policy, Islam has laid its foundations and set forth its rules, and has sanctioned the exertion of opinion and the pursuit of *ijtihad* in matters related to it because it changes with time and place and develops as architecture and all other aspects of knowledge develop. Its foundations include the principles that authority belongs to the *Ummah*, that decision-making is through *shura*, that government is a form of republic, that the ruler should not be favored in a court of law to the layman—for he is only em-

ployed to implement *Shari'ah* and the will of the people, and that the purpose of this policy is to preserve religion and serve the interests of the public.[74]

Workers' Revolt

Part of Ghannouchi's strategy was to re-establish a bridge between the pioneers of Islamic democratic discourse and his generation. As democracy was rapidly becoming the primary concern of political opposition trends within Tunisia, including his own, he felt it was necessary to revive the legacy of nineteenth-century Islamic thinkers that had been obscured by the proliferation across the Arab region of the anti-democracy *Mashariqi* thought of Qutb.

As they communicated with the Tunisian democrats, Ghannouchi and his group pursued their ideological struggle along two fronts. They challenged the Marxists, mainly on campus, and criticized the Westernization policy of the government of President Bourguiba. The transformation in the outlook and methodology of the Islamic group coincided with the 1978 workers' uprising. The general strike called by the Workers Union on 26 January 1978 had spilled over and paralyzed the entire country. Massive demonstrations swept the streets of Tunisia. Workers, students, and impoverished citizens shouted slogans against the regime, which ordered the army to confront them. It is estimated that between four hundred and five hundred civilians were killed during the clashes with the army. The impact of this development on the Islamic movement, which played no part in the uprising, was immense. Ghannouchi recalls:

> The workers' revolt, which was the apex of the leftist activism in Tunisia, had awakened us from our slumber and had alerted us to the importance, and to the social and economic ramifications, of the problems the workers had been complaining of. Prior to that moment, we had been preoccupied with the issues of *da'wah* and *tabligh* and with pure intellectual debate. We used to criticize the regime only lightly, having still been influenced by the Ikhwan. The ideological question was the main problem for us, and the communists were our prime enemy, whether in the university or in the trade unions. Although Bourguiba was also an enemy, he was not in our perception the primary enemy.[75]

By virtue of such a passive attitude on the part of the Islamists, Tunisian Marxists propagated what they believed to be an incontestable fact, that the ruling party had encouraged the emergence of the Islamic movement in order to undermine the left. Ghannouchi acknowledges that his Islamic group did, undoubtedly, contribute to the weakening of the left. But he discounts as absurd any suggestion that the Islamic phenomenon was the creation of the regime. He argues further that had it been so, the regime should have been in a position to get rid of it when and if it wanted to. He does not deny, though, that the regime might have sought to benefit, or might have indeed benefited, from the emergence of Islamism in weakening the left. However, he points out that there is a big difference between saying that the regime benefited and saying that it is the one that planned or welcomed, or had a role in, the emergence of the Islamic current. He denies that his group had, at any time, any ties with the ruling party or with the state.

> The state was overconfident that it had successfully eradicated Islamic activism in Tunisia. Such overconfidence was expressed by Dr. Abdelbaqi al-Hirmasi, who stressed in a paper published in 1969 that modernity in Tunisia had been so profound and extensive

that it would no longer be possible for the Islamic current to re-emerge. It was God's Will that the Islamic current re-emerged in that very same year. Having had the illusion that it had accomplished the secularization process, which was carried out in the name of modernization, the regime believed the state was eventually free from any Islamic influence on its policies in economics, administration, arts, or legislation. The regime had the conviction that it was no longer obliged to flatter Islam, or make it any concessions, or even take it into account.

The Tunisian government's self-assurance and unawareness of the growing Islamic current might have been bolstered by the fact that the Islamists had not at the beginning been focusing on what the regime would have considered sensitive issues. They focused mainly on criticizing the intellectual foundations of what Ghannouchi calls "the materialist philosophy and its most flagrant image—Marxism." While they did not directly criticize the state, it was the leftists who stood in the forefront confronting the regime and criticizing its economic and social policies. Until 1978, the government believed that the people's passion for Islam was successfully extinguished; it rested assured that the religious rituals practiced by some young men were insignificant, and that the existence of groups of worshippers in the mosques was a remnant of the phenomenon of backwardness and underdevelopment. Clearly, the regime was wrong in its assessment of the Islamic trend. The crackdown on the Workers Union led eventually to the weakening of the Marxists and the boosting of the Islamists, whose movement rapidly attracted a large following. No sooner had the regime muzzled the leftist opposition than an Islamic one spoke.

The Left

As they engaged the communists on campus, Islamist students realized that their own tools were limited and that what they had to offer fell short of what was required. The communists raised issues, such as the conflict between imperialism and national liberation movements and the class conflict within society, that the Islamic students could not by virtue of the nature of their training address. The affiliates of the Islamic current did not think such issues were of significance until they were perplexed by the 1978 workers' revolt. Stunned by the uprising, they wondered how such a massive popular demonstration of discontent could take place without their participation or foreknowledge. It was only then that the Islamists became aware of their neglect of the social question, the plight of the poor, and of another conflict that had been taking place in society. Ghannouchi is unequivocal about the impact the left had on him and on the members of his movement. "It was thanks to the left that we realized that the socioeconomic conflict was no less important than the ideological conflict, that is between communism and Islam. It was the left that opened our eyes to the conflict between the exploited, destitute, and impoverished majority and a small minority that in collaboration with the state exploited the entire population."

As he focused on the socio-economic dimension, Ghannouchi endeavored to show that Islam supported the poor and the oppressed and opposed extravagance and exploitation. He turned to the Islamic text, re-reading it with a new insight, highlighting those parts of it that supported the oppressed. He started seeing other aspects of the conflict that *Mashariqi* thought stopped short of addressing. Earlier, his contact with the democrats alerted him to a political aspect, which reflected a conflict between authoritarianism and the masses that aspired for freedom and justice. Now, he could see a social aspect that reflected, locally, a conflict between the "exploited poor and the exploiting rich" and, globally, a conflict between "world capitalism and the poor nations." The interaction with both the democrats and the Marxists happened as Ghannouchi and his followers engaged in a process of revision and criticism of the intellectual models they imported from Pakistan and Egypt, those models which saw only a single dimension of the conflict, the ideological one.

Ghannouchi encouraged the members of his group to join the trade unionist movement. The strategy was no longer to engage the communists on ideological grounds, but to defend the rights of the workers.

> We realized that God did not create us for the purpose of opposing the communists, but in order to accomplish the objectives of Islam, which may agree in part with communism as it may agree in part with any other ideology. One of Islam's fundamental objectives is to establish justice in the world. The value of justice is the greatest value in Islam, and Just is one of the attributes of God. How could we then have embroiled ourselves in opposing those, even if they were Marxists, who struggled for securing the interests of the poor and the oppressed? Learning from the examples set by the Prophet, we decided that defending justice should be our foremost priority.

The Islamists started calling for strikes, both in the university and within the trade unionist movement, in support of the struggle of the workers. In the aftermath of the severe blow the regime dealt to the Workers Union in January 1978, mosques in Tunisia turned into sanctuaries for those rebellious against the state. For the first time in Tunisia's modern history, social and political issues were raised and discussed inside the mosques, which were transformed from mere places of worship to intellectual platforms for political and cultural debate. In this way, the issues that had until then been restricted to the elite, were communicated to the general public, of course after having been impregnated with an Islamic character. In schools and universities, the Islamic current seemed to be doing well. Large crowds of students took part every year in the rallies organized by the Islamic movement to commemorate the anniversary of the January 1978 events.

On 1 May 1980, the Tunisian Islamic movement celebrated, for the first time, the Workers' Day. The movement organized a rally in a mosque attended by a crowd of about five thousand. Ghannouchi seized that opportunity to tell the huge crowd how Islam provided guarantees for protecting and rewarding labor. An issue of relevance to the Tunisian situation was the ownership of agrarian property and the rights of farm workers. Addressing the subject from an Islamic perspective, Ghannouchi spoke a language the Islamists in Tunisia had never been heard speaking before. He told his audience: "The ownership of agrarian property is social in nature. The function of such ownership is to serve the community, and therefore those who have been given the right to ownership may lose it. The *Ummah* has the right to strip it of them if they fail to dedicate it in the service of the community."[76]

In his speech, Ghannouchi explained that all the land in Tunisia, as well as in much of the Arab region, was a land of conquest, and therefore the absolute right of ownership belonged to the *Ummah* as a whole. He highlighted the principle of the association between ownership and work, stressing that the only party that had a right to reap the fruits of the land was the worker. Hence, all transactions that accorded a non-working owner a right to the fruits of the land, including leasing the property, were null and void, for the only way to benefit from the land would be to cultivate it. He stressed that this principle derives from the four foundations upon which Islamic economy is based. The first is the doctrine of *tawhid* (monotheism), a concept that entails the rejection of all forms of deities that enslave humans, whether such forms are in the image of an idol or a despotic political authority or a capitalist monopoly. The second is the doctrine that everything in this world belongs to God, that all resources are His, and that humans as an *Ummah* are His vicegerents. Thus, the *Ummah* as a whole is responsible for dispensing resources and serving justice. The third foundation is the doctrine that humans are resurrected after death. Hence, accumulating wealth in this life can be conducive to a good life in the Hereafter only if this wealth is dedicated to the benefit of the community. Finally comes the concept of *ukhuwwah* (brotherhood). This concept is supposed to act as a preventive measure against exploitation of fellow humans and at the same time to encourage those "who have" to share with those "who have not." These foundations, he concluded, are bolstered continuously through the implementation of a set of fundamental measures. The most important of these is *Zakat*, a compulsory share of the wealth the rich are ordered to pay to the poor, either directly or through social welfare programs run by the state or by the community.[77]

The Iranian Revolution

Ghannouchi's emphasis on socio-economic issues could not have taken place at a better time. As his movement was becoming a credible agency for voicing public grievances, the Iranian Islamic revolution succeeded in removing the shah and installing a cleric, Khomeyni, on his throne. Not only did the revolution boost the popularity of Islam in Tunisia, but it also had an immense effect on the Tunisian Islamic movement. It turned to be a significant contributor to the development of Ghannouchi's political thought and of his group's maturation. Ghannouchi acknowledges this fact and recalls:

> As we readied to accept the notion that conflicts other than the ideological existed along the political and social fronts, the Iranian revolution came to give us a new set of Islamic discourses. It enabled us to Islamize some leftist social concepts and to accommodate the social conflict within an Islamic context. While the communists insisted that Marxism had discovered the nature of conflict within society, and that it was alone capable of offering the solution through the class conflict argument and the triumph of socialism against capitalism, we saw in the Iranian revolution a turbaned *shaykh* (cleric) commanding the revolution of the oppressed against a despotic agent of imperialism and against a rotten capitalist class.[75]

In January 1979, after twelve months of popular uprisings, a coalition of Iranian opposition forces under the spiritual leadership of Ayatollah Ruhollah Khomeyni (1902–1989), who had still been in exile in France, toppled the American-supported regime of Muhammad Reza Shah Pahlavi. For people throughout the Islamic world, the Iranian revolution was very inspiring. It demonstrated that opposition forces organized in the name of Islam could overthrow a Western-influenced secular regime.

For Ghannouchi, the most important intellectual contribution of the Iranian revolution was the way in which it presented the conflict between the poor and the rich. He
saw in its discourse a re-presentation of the class conflict within an Islamic framework
and using Islamic terminology. It was the notion of an Islamic revolution against *taghut*
(a false god; or a symbol of tyranny and oppression) that drew his attention. In addition, the Iranian revolution played its part in shaking what had remained of the foundations of the *Mashariqi* thought. This thought was based mainly on Sayyid Qutb's
interpretation of three Qur'anic verses: "If any do fail to judge by what Allah has revealed, they are unbelievers" (5: 44); "If any do fail to judge by what Allah has revealed,
they are wrong-doers" (5: 45); and "If any do fail to judge by what Allah has revealed,
they are those who rebel" (5: 47). Qutb's interpretation led to the conclusion that governments in the Muslim countries, and even societies that were content with them, were
unbelieving. His paradigm recognized only black and white, belief and unbelief, Muslim and non-Muslim. Ghannouchi found that the Iranian revolution provided Muslims with a new paradigm based on the interpretation of Qur'anic verse, "And We wished
to be Gracious to those who were being oppressed in the land, to make them leaders
and make them heirs. To establish a firm place for them in the land, and to show Pharaoh,
Haman, and their troops what they were dreading from them" (28: 5).

The Iranian revolution opened Ghannouchi's eyes to see in this Qur'anic verse a
key, a remedy, and a light. It provided him with an Islamic guideline in the question of
social conflict. He discovered that Islam recognized the existence of a conflict between
the oppressed and the tyrant, and that Islam stands in favor of the former against the
latter. He started seeing in Islam a revolution for the liberation of the world's oppressed.
He could by then proclaim with confidence that prophets were sent for no other reason
than to support the oppressed against the tyrant. He felt as if this verse was never before read by any Islamic thinker and as if Khomeyni was the first to discover it.[79]

Initially, Ghannouchi and his fellow Islamists, who had still been under the influence of some *Mashariqi* thought, kept their distance thinking that this was above all a
Shiite revolution of no relevance to them as Sunnis. But as he saw the magnitude of the
event, it was no longer possible for him and his colleagues to remain indifferent.[80] Passions for the Iranian revolution intensified and Khomeyni's pictures started appearing
in the Tunisian Islamic movement's publications. The Tunisian Islamic intellectual
discourse had become permeated with revolutionary remarks in support of the workers,
of the trade unions, and of the poor, and with strong attacks on extravagance and sharp
criticism of the Tunisian government's foreign policy. Ghannouchi recalls:

> Henceforth, our criticism of the state was no longer just religious or moral as in the past.
> It had become more profound. The rift between the regime and us had grown wider.
> From our point of view, the state identified with domestic and external oppressors; our
> own strategic choice was to identify with the oppressed. The state was for dictatorship
> and we were now for democracy. The Iranian revolution had come at the right time to
> provide us with Islamic analytical tools for conflicts our traditional cultural discourse could
> not deal with.[81]

Tunisia had no Shiites, and most of its citizens had hardly ever known anything
about the differences between Shiism and Sunnism. Hence, it did not take long before
the Iranian revolution was perceived not as Shiite but simply as Islamic. This was not

the case in Shiite-populated parts of the Arab world where many Sunnis were reluctant to support the revolution. In an article published in *Al-Ma'rifah*, Ghannouchi endeavored to educate his readers about the nature of the Iranian revolution, and to answer questions raised by some puzzled readers about who was behind it and what its objectives were. He wrote:

> Answering such questions requires knowing a number of facts. The first is that the Iranians are an ancient Muslim people, and they embrace the Shiite Ja'fari denomination that is characteristically different from the Sunnis in that the *imam* enjoys significant moral influence, is awarded full obedience, and has the power of disposing with the *khums*.[82] The second fact is that Iran possesses a huge petroleum reserve and is the second largest oil exporting country. The third is that Iran occupies an important strategic location that gives it the benefit of being the largest barrier precluding the Russian expansion in the direction of the Middle East. The fourth is that the West, formerly Britain and lately the United States of America, has been anxious to control this country through the Pahlavi family. The services of the Pahlavi regime to the colonialist powers have enabled them to achieve a number of goals. The first is the mutilation of the Islamic identity of the Iranian people through the dissemination via the education system, the media, and the arts of immoral behavior, such as promiscuity, gambling, and alcohol drinking. The second goal is to impoverish the Iranian people in spite of the enormous natural resources they possess for the purpose of keeping them constantly preoccupied with earning their bread while the shah and his family live lavishly. The third goal is to squander the wealth of the *Ummah* in the purchase of weapons from America.[83]

One may imagine that such an analysis would, to a certain degree, apply to Tunisia, and therefore by writing such an article about the Iranian revolution not only did Ghannouchi express support for it but also appealed to the Tunisians to strike a comparison. Alluding to the situation in Tunisia, he explained that circumstances of domestic oppression and foreign influence in Iran led to the eruption of a revolution that sought to implement the Islamic agenda. The first goal on this agenda was to combat despotism and repression. The second goal was to eliminate vast class distinctions and whatever is associated with them of extravagance and injustice. The third goal was to combat political subordination to world imperialism so that Iran could become an independent Islamic state governed by an Islamic system. The fourth and final goal was to liberate the Iranian society from the immoral colonial culture that considers pleasure to be the object of living.[84]

At the time, Ghannouchi was particularly impressed with Khomeyni's success in uniting behind him all political trends within Iran. Such unity, he thought, was possible because "all political trends sought real national independence, freedom, and justice." The same, he expected, would be possible elsewhere in the Muslim world "because Islam has become the ideology of the oppressed people."[85] In his article, Ghannouchi strongly criticized the Islamists elsewhere in the Sunni world for not coming forth and expressing support and solidarity for the Iranian revolution, which according to him "set a precedent in the ongoing conflict between the forces of *taghut* and the forces of *taharrur* (liberation)."[86]

Many Sunnis as well as Shiites would certainly disagree with Ghannouchi, for to them there are many more differences between the two denominations than just those mentioned by Ghannouchi in his article. Most probably Ghannouchi knew little about the ongoing debate at the time of the revolution concerning Shiism in the regions of direct Sunni-Shiite friction, especially in Iran itself, in Iraq, in parts of the Arabian Peninsula, in Lebanon and in Pakistan. Like Ghannouchi, Sunnis in regions not inhabited by Shiites were more, and sometime unreservedly, sympathetic toward the revolution than those who co-existed with Shiites. Such Sunnis do not carry the burden of the historical legacy of the political dispute that took place more than fourteen centuries ago and that caused the first major split within the *Ummah*. The ramifications of that ancient incident continue to influence the political thinking of many Muslims today.

Ghannouchi's enthusiasm for the Iranian revolution led him to regard Khomeyni as a *mujaddid*, one that belongs to the rank of leading Islamic reformers whose mission, according to a Prophetic tradition, is to revive or renew the faith and practice of the Muslim *Ummah*.[87] According to Ghannouchi, three such persons existed in the twentieth century. Al-Banna, Mawdudi, and Khomeyni are found by him to share a number of common features.[88] The first is *ash-shumuliyah*, in that they conceive of Islam as a comprehensive way of life. The second is *al-wataniyah*, in that they give priority to national issues including political, social, and economic reform. The third is *al-istiqlaliyah*, in that they seek to liberate their people from Western cultural and political influences without excluding the possibility of benefiting from the West. The fourth is *as-salafiyah*, in that they relate to the *usul* (fundamentals or roots) of Islam from which they obtain guidance. The fifth is *at-tawakkul*, in that their programs include an element of trust and confidence in God's help and support. The sixth is *ash-sha'biyah*, in that they appeal to the people and emanate from them. The seventh is *at-tanzim*, in that their movements function by means of organized networks of members and supporters.[89]

In spite of his support for the Iranian revolution, Ghannouchi maintains that his movement, while having benefited from the revolution's social dimensions, chose not to emulate its methodology.[90] The Iranians, who hoped that Muslims elsewhere in the Muslim world would follow their example, had anticipated that Ghannouchi in particular, who showed so much enthusiasm for the revolution, would lead in his country a revolutionary change following the example of the Iranian experiment. But Ghannouchi thought of the Iranian revolution as just another experiment from which lessons could be drawn. Just as he rejected the material philosophy of Marxism but incorporated into his thought and into the methodology of his movement some of its social dimensions, he adopted a similar position toward the Iranian revolution. He rejected it as a model for reform but benefited from some of its aspects in formulating a strategy for the gradual reformation and development of the Tunisian Islamic society.[91]

The Sudanese Experience

As the critique of the *Mashariqi* Islamic thought intensified, Ghannouchi paid a visit to Sudan in 1979 to acquaint himself with the Islamic movement there. He was stunned to see a completely different model to the ones described in the Pakistani and Egyptian literature of the *Mashariqi* Islamic thought. The most striking aspect of this model was the attitude toward women. In its preliminary stage, the Islamic movement in Tunisia was influenced in the question of women by the *Mashariqi* discourse, which was highly critical of the status of women in the West and which highlighted the dangers posed by such a status to family life and to the entire society. Such literature reacted to the extensive participation of women in political and social activities by condemning their mixing with the society of men and insisting that their role should be restricted to the home as wives and mothers. In Tunisia, the movement had to stand up to Bourguiba in his war against Islamic values and had to challenge his claim that he was the emancipator of women. In the meantime Ghannouchi developed a discourse that focused on attacking Bourguiba's attitude toward polygamy, considered by his government to be a criminal act, although adultery was not considered so, and that also criticized the introduction of mixed education. In the beginning, the Tunisian Islamic movement was not very enthusiastic about the education of girls. If at all necessary, it was felt that educating females should be minimal just to make them literate and provide them with a modest level of education. The preference was to get them married at a young age and protect them from the dangers of an increasingly promiscuous society.[92]

In the Sudanese model, Ghannouchi noticed that women participated fully in the political and social programs of the Islamic movement. During his visit, he observed that male and female members of the movement communicated comfortably. The women attended meetings, participated in discussions, voiced their opinions in public, and not only seemed to have equal rights but were also equally responsible. Of special significance was a Nile cruise organized by Dr. Hassan Turabi, leader of the Sudanese Islamic Movement, in honor of visiting Tunisian guests Ghannouchi and Sheikh Muhammad Salih Enneifer, a prominent Tunisian. The guests sat in the boat surrounded by male and female students who, in the words of Ghannouchi, innocently and spontaneously shared responsibilities and participated equally in giving talks, asking questions, reading poems, telling jokes, and preparing and serving food.[93]

Back in Tunisia in 1980, Ghannouchi delivered a speech that was published later in his book Al-Mar'ah al-Muslimah Fi Tunis (Muslim woman in Tunisia) under the title "Al-Mar'ah Fil-Haraka al-Islamiyah" (The woman in the Islamic movement). In the article, he strongly criticized his movement's previous position on women and called for a review in the direction of affirming the principle of equality between the sexes and the necessity of actively involving women in all political and social activities. He pointed out that this necessitated lifting any restrictions on the education of women, who should be encouraged to attain the highest levels possible of education. He stressed the need for training and developing Islamic women leaders, who "would set the example in embodying the values of Islam and whose contribution in the pursuit of a comprehensive Islamic renaissance would be invaluable." He deemed this to be essential in order to challenge the secularist women leaders of the Bourguiba era. His remarks reflected a radical change of position, especially as he stressed that "the innocent mixing of men and women is not prohibited" and that "polygamy is not an Islamic duty, and therefore Muslims should not make too big an issue out of it."[94]

Although his criticism of the traditional position on women issues stirred controversy within the ranks of his group, it led to improving the relationship between Tunisian women and the Islamic movement to the extent that within less than a year the number of women members more than doubled.[95] One important development in this regard occurred when, and upon the encouragement of Ghannouchi, two women attended for the first time a meeting of the movement's central committee. A male member of the committee took the floor to protest against the attendance of the two women, demanding that such an action should have been preceded by a *fatwa*. He insisted that a commission should have been created to give an authoritative judgment on female participation at the level of political authority. One of the attending women, a teacher by the name of Afifa Makhlouf, contested the man's claim. She argued that if men thought they had the right to set up a commission to judge the legality of women's participation in political life, why shouldn't women set up a commission to pass the same judgment on the political role of men? In her opinion Islam was revealed as guidance for men as well as for women and therefore she saw no reason why a commission was needed so as to authorize or forbid the political action of one or the other of the two sexes. After Afifa's intervention, the problem of women's participation was resolved once and for all, and was no longer a subject of debate.[96]

The fruits of this development were to be reaped by the movement later on, when a large proportion of women voted for the movement in the 1989 elections. The enhancement in female support is said to have been induced by the movement's announcement in July 1988 that it had accepted the Personal Affairs Code, which it had earlier opposed, as a sound framework for organizing the affairs of the family. Ghannouchi refutes the claim by some political writers that the members of his group would be shocked to hear him state that the law forbidding polygamy was an *ijtihad*.[97] He maintains that when he did make that statement in 1988, that is after the removal of Bourguiba from power, none of his fellow Islamists within the movement protested.[98]

Until about 1984, Ghannouchi strongly opposed the Personal Affairs Code and denounced the anti-polygamy law. But as the Ben Ali regime, which replaced that of Bourguiba in 1987, announced it was intent on democratizing the system, opposition to the code was becoming an obstacle hindering the official recognition of the MTI. Marxists and other opponents of the Islamic trend sought to prevent the legalization of MTI under the pretext that it opposed the code, which they deemed to be a great national accomplishment.[99] Ghannouchi's position, which was unanimously adopted by his movement, was that polygamy is not a religious duty, and therefore as a *mubah* (permissible matter) it can be restricted under certain circumstances. Ghannouchi denies claims by his critics that this was a purely tactical move. He insists that although the new position was politically beneficial, it was not an aberration from the mainstream of Islamic thinking but "was based on a *qa'idah fiqhiyah* (jurisprudential rule)."[100]

Going Public

The Tunisian authorities had become increasingly alarmed by the expansion of the Islamic phenomenon and decided to monitor its activists more closely. In December 1980, two leading members of the Islamic movement were arrested on suspicion of forming an unlicensed organization. One of them had in his possession a briefcase that contained documents suggesting that he was a member of a secret organization headed by Ghannouchi. The documents included the 1979 Founding Manifesto, which had still not been made public. The detainees were afterward released, but Ghannouchi suspected that the government was now preparing to crack down on his group, and thus suggested that it was time the movement went public. He believed that going public would embarrass the authorities and frustrate any plans to repress them. Some of his colleagues disagreed. They were of the opinion that going public might be construed by the government as an act of defiance and that the government might therefore go ahead with its plan to crack down on the movement anyway. To preempt any action by the government, the leadership of the movement dissolved itself and handed over responsibilities to the leaders of the student movement who had not yet been known to the authorities.

Two important developments ensued in the few months that followed. Internally, the debate between those who wanted to go public and those who were opposed to such a move was settled in referendum, the first of its kind to be conducted by the movement since its establishment, in which all members participated. Ghannouchi argued convincingly that since the government already knew about the movement there was no point in keeping the public uninformed. Furthermore, by going public the movement would be forced to develop and implement its political and social programs, which thus far remained theoretical and untested. Seventy per cent of the members voted in favor of going public. In the meantime, the government of President Bourguiba headed by Prime Minister Muhammad Mzali announced on 4 April 1981 its intention to allow the formation, and permit the activity, of political parties in prelude to calling for parliamentary elections.[101] On 9 April 1981 the movement's elected Shura Council met and endorsed the result of the referendum. In a press conference on 6 June 1981, Ghannouchi announced the formation of the Islamic Tendency Movement (MTI) and released its Founding Manifesto, which became its statute.[102]

Authored by Ghannouchi, the manifesto expressed the movement's commitment to democratic process, including pluralism and the sharing and alternation of power, and stated that the democratic process should exclude no one, not even communists, and affirmed that the electoral process was the source of legitimacy.[103] The Iranians were dismayed by this declaration and denounced the Tunisian Islamists, accusing them of having been influenced by false Western values. The move was surprising for the Iranians because it was at the climax of the Tunisian group's enthusiasm for the Iranian revolution that an application for registering the movement as a political party was made. Ghannouchi responded by announcing that although he and his movement supported the Iranian revolution and considered it to be a great revolution, they did not see it as a model.

We were dismayed by the Iranian reaction. We thought the Iranians had no right to act as if they were curators in charge of other Muslims. It was wrong for them to consider their model the only acceptable model of change. As far as we were concerned, the methods of change were unlimited, and therefore each Islamic movement was at liberty to look for the method of change that suited its circumstances. We started having misgivings about the intentions of the Iranians, and we had reservations regarding what we saw as their tendency to oversimplify the global conflict, restricting it to a conflict with the Americans, whom they called the arch-Satan. Numerous dimensions existed in the global conflict, and thus it would be naive to exclude all the other dimensions in favor of only one. We saw that it did Islam no harm benefiting from "the other," espousing and incorporating into our thought and strategy what we deemed useful and valuable such as the idea of democracy. Furthermore, we rejected the Iranian idea of "exporting the revolution" and refused to accept that there was one single Islamic approach to change and reform. As far as we are concerned the door of *ijtihad* remains open and no one has the right to shut it. There is neither church nor a pope in Islam that claims possession of the key to the Heavens.[104]

From Totalitarianism to Pluralism

The founding of MTI was a crucial turning point in the life of Ghannouchi and in the history of his Islamic movement. Henceforth, he openly pledged his full commitment to democracy "as a system of government and as a method of change."[105] At the time, such a stand was still unacceptable to many Islamic movements, which, like the Iranians, considered the MTI declaration either a recognition of the ruling regime and the legitimacy of an "un-Islamic" state, or an imitation of the West. Ghannouchi recalls:

> We were criticized in the *Mashriq* where not a single Islamic party, particularly in the Arab countries, had yet expressed clearly such democratic tendencies. The Tunisian Islamic movement continued to be criticized although before too long all the other movements within the mainstream current of Islamism proceeded in the same direction, though in small doses. Whenever pressed by reality, they took a dose of the medication our movement took in one go in 1981.[106]

In the early 1980s, Ghannouchi had an argument in Cairo with Omar at-Tilmisani, the then *murshid* (leader) of the Muslim Brotherhood, whom he describes as "pious and venerable in character, moderate in thoughts and firm in standing." He sums his experience as follows:

> With the prickly mood of a North African, I stood arguing with at-Tilmisani over the question of political pluralism, insisting that the Ikhwan should submit an application to be recognized as a political party, and that they should consider forging alliances with other opposition parties. But the *murshid* considered the suggestion to be nonsense and out of the question. He argued that the Ikhwan were a party above the parties and a group above the groups. He even insisted they were bigger than a mere party, and hence how could they be allied with those secularist or corrupt groups?[107]

Three years later, Ghannouchi was relieved to hear the news of an alliance the Ikhwan in Egypt had forged with al-Wafd Party. It was rather surprising for him, because only a short while earlier their official standing had still been an absolute rejection of political pluralism.

Compulsory Contemplation

Less than two months after celebrating May Day in 1981, and soon after the official proclamation of the MTI, the regime decided to step in and curtail the growth of the Islamic movement. On the seventeenth day of the fasting month of Ramadan, 17 July 1981, the leaders of MTI and five hundred of its members were arrested. It is ironic that when the movement was still secretive the government took no measures against it. However, when it responded to the promise of liberalization by going public and submitting an application for recognition as a political party punishment was inflicted upon it.

Ghannouchi was imprisoned from 1981 to 1984. For him this was a period of contemplation and reflection. The past ten years, or so, had been hectic and eventful. Inside his prison cell, he reflected on the accomplishments of his movement. Despite its young age, the Tunisian Islamic Movement managed to reconnect with the roots of Islamic renaissance as expressed in the thoughts of its pioneers: at-Tunisi, Tahtawi, ath-

Tha'alibi, al-Fasi, al-Afghani, and Abduh. Like these pioneers, who were not greatly appreciated by the more *salafi* thought of the *Mashriq*, Ghannouchi agonized over the state of backwardness the Muslims were in. The way forward "was to revive and comple-ment the work of these leading thinkers, and to borrow, as at-Tunisi once put it, from the West a substance that would revive the Muslims." However, the real challenge was how to realize the gains of Western progress without sacrificing Islam, how to challenge the claim of the Westernized elite in his country that the fruits of Western "progress" could only be reaped by doing away with Islam. Such a task, he thought, required an enormous amount of collective effort on the part of contemporary Islamic thinkers and Islamic movements worldwide. The objective would be to realize, within the framework of a modern Islamic *ijtihad*, the gains Westerners had accomplished and then seek to surpass them. The concern of the Muslims, therefore, should no longer be how to re-sist modernity nor how to destroy the accomplishments of the Western mind. No longer perceiving them to be in conflict with Islam, the real challenge, he thought, was to find ways and means for incorporating such accomplishments, and then excelling them, without undermining the foundations of Islam or the independence and identity of Muslims.[108]

In prison, Ghannouchi memorized the Holy Qur'an and studied with eagerness a number of classical works in the field of *tafsir* (exegesis of the Qur'an) and *fiqh* (juris-prudence). He read Ibn Taymiyah, al-Ghazali, Ibn Rushd, Ibn Hazm, az-Zamakhshari, al-Qarafi, Ibn 'Ashoor, and a number of more contemporary authors including the Iraqi Shiite philosopher Baqir as-Sadr. He even developed an interest in learning English.

Ghannouchi and his imprisoned colleagues decided to make the best possible use of their time. In addition to learning the Qur'an and studying Islamic literature, they embarked on a three-stage project named *jihad silmi* (peaceful *jihad*). The first stage involved a thorough assessment of the Tunisian society, past and present. To achieve this, Ghannouchi started in 1983 working on the draft of a treatise that he entitled "Al-Mujtama' at-Tunisi: Tahlil Hadari" (Tunisian society: A civilizational analysis). The analysis, as he stated in his introduction to the treatise, was part of the effort made to respond to "the most important challenge facing our movement, society, and *Ummah*."[109] The challenge was "to reflect on the path of the movement and the situation of society so as to reinforce positive elements and avoid negative ones, to clarify the image of the aspired civilizational alternative and to determine the short-term objectives and the means of accomplishing them."[110] Diagnosing the Tunisian reality, Ghannouchi traced the roots of current problems to pre-colonialism, specifically to the time when at-Tunisi's pio-neering reform project was thwarted under pressure from the French. Despotism, Westernization and mismanagement in the post-independence era were blamed for the severe economic and identity crises that afflicted the country.

The document provides a detailed analysis of Tunisian geographic, demographic, historical, and cultural specificity and of the factors that contributed to the espousal of a unique model of traditional religiosity by the Tunisian people. An attempt was made to explain the ways in which post-independence political, educational, social, and eco-nomic policies led to the popular uprisings of 1978 and 1984. Exploring the factors that made Tunisia vulnerable to foreign intervention, Ghannouchi reflected on Islamic history and highlighted the causes of the Islamic civilization's decline. Such decline in his opinion started on the day the *shura*-based government of the first Islamic state model was toppled and replaced by an authoritarian model that sought to justify itself in the name of religion. The pre-colonial situation in Tunisia was in his analysis far from wholesome and there was an urgent need for reform. A reform from within was being attempted and could have blossomed had it not been for French intervention. The failure of independence to accomplish the aspired hopes of the people of Tunisia was attributed to the adoption by the post-independence single-party government of policies in politics, education, and economics dominated by the practice of despotism, opportunism, favoritism, selectivity, and experimentation once with radical socialism and once with radical liberalism.[111]

It is evident from this sizeable piece of work that Ghannouchi had access in prison to a fair amount of information on the past and current state of Tunisian economy, demography, education, health, industry, commerce, and agriculture. Under the reign of President Bourguiba, prisoners were permitted to bring in books if the prison library, which Ghannouchi describes as broad, did not satisfy their needs.[112] The treatise was subsequently distributed among MTI members so as to collect their comments and suggestions as to how it could be developed further.

The second part of the project was to involve a characterization of a model modern Islamic society. Ghannouchi's book Al-Hurriyat al-'Ammah Fid-Dawlah al-Islamiyyah (Public liberties in the Islamic state), which will be discussed in the next chapter, was intended to serve this purpose. The third stage was to involve a contemplation of the methodology of change. A number of attempts were made later in the history of the movement to evaluate the approach adopted to effect change and to reform the state and society. Ghannouchi wrote several articles on this subject prior to his imprisonment and wrote several others after his release.[113] However, the official position of the movement on the methodology of change was expressed for the first time in the MTI manifesto of 1981 and was reiterated in the Ennahda manifesto of 1988.

3

The Question of Democracy

In the privacy of his prison cell, from June 1980 to August 1984, Ghannouchi had ample time to reflect on his past. The past twenty years had taken him through significant stages of maturation. They saw his migration from a North African model of Arabism to a *Mashariqi* form of Islamism and eventually to a specifically Tunisian, or *Magharibi*, form of Islamism. The last combined what he deemed to be the best aspects of the various experiences to which he had been exposed and excluded those aspects he deemed irrelevant to his Tunisian environment. The amplitude of time behind the prison walls, and the moderate conditions and reasonable treatment afforded to him—following the cessation of torture and painful flogging during the initial period of interrogation—seemed a gift from the heavens. Despite the limitedness of space, this was a golden opportunity for him to research a topic of great importance, the question of public liberties, and there was no better way to do this in the given circumstances than to write a book.

He regarded the agony of his first imprisonment to be an offer of destiny because it uprooted him from the tumult of recurring daily problems, and hurled him into a state of incessant work to respond to the challenge.[1] He spent two full years in hectic work to absorb all that he could lay a hand on of relevant references. In spite of his incarceration, he was allowed—thanks to the sympathy and tolerance exhibited by some of the prison guards—to bring in the books and references he requested. He undertook a number of projects, one of which was to study a translation of a book on women by Roger Garaudy, which inspired him—together with his recent experience in Sudan—to write a treatise on women's rights and on the status of women inside the Islamic movement. Garaudy's book in Arabic bore the title of *Fi-Sabil Irtiqa' al-Mar'ah* (In the cause of the progress of the woman).[2] But the more important projects had been his translation of a booklet authored by Malik Bennabi entitled *Al-Islam Wad-Dimuqratiyah* (Islam and democracy), and starting the project of writing his most important work, *Al-Hurriyat al-'Ammah Fid-Dawlah al-Islamiyyah* (Public liberties in the Islamic state). Some of Ghannouchi's writings while serving his prison sentence, including his translation of Bennabi's treatise,[3] were published under the pseudonym of Mu'adh as-Sabir. Publications bearing this pseudonym included a booklet on Palestine entitled *Al-Qadiyah al-*

Falastinyah 'Ala Muftaraq Tariq (The Palestinian issue at a crossroads) and an article critical of the Iranian regime under Khomeyni.[4]

The latter was Ghannouchi's first published criticism of the Iranians. It came in response to a vicious attack on the MTI by the Iranians. The attack was launched in a bulletin published by the Iranian Revolutionary Guard against a number of Islamic movements in the Arab world, including the Muslim Brotherhood in Egypt and the MTI in Tunisia, accusing them of being counter-revolutionaries and lackeys of the West. In his article, Ghannouchi criticized the Iranians on two levels. He criticized them for portraying themselves as if they were the possessors of absolute truth, as if they alone understood the message of Islam, and as if their revolution was the only legitimate method of change. The Iranians, he stressed, failed to see that their understanding was only one of several possible interpretations and their revolution was only one of several possible models of reform. On the second level, he criticized the Iranian foreign policy, which "reflected an extreme oversimplification of international relations" by declaring the United States of America the arch-Satan and the only enemy. The world, in Ghannouchi's opinion, could not, nor should it, be divided into friends and enemies; it is far more complex than the Iranians thought. "The Iranians, who had no hesitation to establish links with the Marxist regime in South Yemen or with the Polisario Front in the Moroccan Sahara just because they were anti-American, seemed naive."[5]

Bennabi

The booklet Ghannouchi translated in prison into Arabic was the text of a lecture delivered in French by Bennabi at the *Magharibi* Students Club in Paris in 1960. Titled "Democracy in Islam," the lecture is indicative of the fact that the *Magharibi* thought vis-à-vis the question of democracy had been well ahead of that of the *Mashariqi* thought. The 1950s and the 1960s witnessed Sayyid Qutb theorizing for the rejection of democracy. Throughout the 1970s, his ideas were being embraced by thousands of Islamic activists in the *Mashriq*. In the meantime, a different school of thought was developing in the Arab Maghreb drawing from the nineteenth-century reform movement of Khairuddin at-Tunisi and the ideas of Abduh (who had twice visited Tunis and had associates there), Bin Badis, ath-Tha'alibi, at-Taher al-Haddad, Allal al-Fasi, and others.

Bennabi's approach to addressing the question of the relationship between Islam and democracy shows that a lively debate on the issue had been in progress in the early 1960s within the ranks of North African students in Paris. It is possible that Ghannouchi was inspired by the renewed debate in his own country in the late 1970s to study Bennabi's talk and translate it into Arabic to make it available to the Arabized Islamists within his movement. It is also possible that he wanted the ideas of Bennabi to reach the Islamists in the *Mashriq* who had been critical of the Tunisian Islamic movement's declared commitment to democracy.

Bennabi's treatise began with the question "is there democracy in Islam?" In search of an answer, he pointed out that defining the concepts "Islam" and "democracy" in a conventional manner would lead to the conclusion that with respect to time and location the connection between the two is nonexistent. But what does one mean by democracy and what does one mean by Islam? In the case of the latter, Bennabi affirmed that the origin of the word Islam is well-known: it is a Qur'anic word with a known Arabic root and a meaning elucidated by the Prophet in a famous *hadith* in which he answered the question "What is Islam?"[6] As for the word *dimuqratiyah* (Arabic for democracy), Bennabi observed that this is clearly not Arabic and that it must have entered the Arabic vocabulary sometime in history unknown to most, if not all, those who use it or refer to it. "Nor is known with absolute certainty the moment of its birth in its own original language, although we know that it is originally Greek, perhaps dating back to Pericles, around the year 430 B.C."[7] To assert this point, Bennabi cited the historian Thucydides according to whom Pericles is reported to have made a famous funeral speech in which he said

> Our constitution is called a democracy because power is in the hands not of a minority but the whole people. When it is a question of settling private disputes, everyone is equal before the law; when it is a question of putting one person before another in positions of public responsibility, what counts is not membership of a particular class, but the actual ability which the man possesses. No one, so long as he has it in him to be of service to the state, is kept in political obscurity because of poverty.

Bennabi explained that democracy, which is compounded of two Greek words, means in the most simplistic of all meanings the rule of the people, or the rule of the masses, or "what we may call today in brief analytical expression the rule of man." In contrast, Islam means to worship Allah alone and to perform *salat* (prayer), pay *zakat* (alms), observe *siyam* (fasting), and perform *hajj* (pilgrimage). As such, the concepts Islam and democracy, with regard to time and place, seem unconnected.

Having defined in the simplest terms possible the two concepts, Bennabi asked whether some sort of a comparison can be made between democracy, which is a political concept that establishes the authority of man within a specific social system, and Islam, which is a metaphysical concept that establishes the subordination of man to the authority of God within a given social system. "What the given definitions seem to yield is a contradiction, an incompatibility of some sort, similar to the slogans raised by the French Revolution during its struggle against the church: 'We want neither a Lord nor a master.'"

Such seeming tension between Islam and democracy, or contradiction to use Bennabi's word, would be expected to widen the gap between the two concepts, and as such any comparison would be rather difficult. But this difficulty in his opinion is the outcome not of the reality purported by either concept but of the manner in which we choose to express such reality. For instance, he explained, democracy is expressed through the linguistic meaning given by a lexicon that has been associated with the legacy of the French Revolution. What should be done, he suggested, is to redefine democracy without associating it with any other concept including Islam itself. In other words, Bennabi sought to deconstruct the concept of democracy and reconstruct it in isolation from its historical connotations using terms unlimited to the linguistic derivative and free from any ideological implication.

To do just this, he suggested, democracy ought to be considered from three aspects: democracy as an attitude toward the ego, democracy as an attitude toward the other, and democracy as the combination of the socio-political conditions necessary for the formation and development of such attitudes in the individual. These three aspects, he continued, encompass the subjective and objective requirements of democracy. These are the psychological propensities upon which the democratic attitude is established and the assets upon which the democratic system in any society depends. For democracy can never be accomplished as a political reality unless its conditions are fulfilled in the character building of the individual and in the norms and traditions of the country. In other words, the democratic attitude is bound by conditions without which it can never be achieved. Bennabi explained:

> These conditions—contrary to the depiction of the romantic philosophy of the era of Jean-Jacques Rousseau—are not created by nature, nor are they the requisites of natural law. They are the upshot of a specific culture, the crowning of the movement of the humanities and a new appreciation of the value of man, his appreciation of himself and his appreciation of the others. The democratic attitude is the product of this movement over the centuries and of this twin appraisal of the value of man.

The democratic attitude in Europe was, according to Bennabi, the outcome of the Reformation and the Renaissance. This is its correct historical meaning, and therefore it cannot simply be severed from the history of Europe so as to be applied to other nations. However, whether in Europe or elsewhere, the general rule with regard to the nature of the democratic attitude is that it is the outcome of a specific social reality. In psychological terms it is the middle position between two ends that are opposed to each other; the end that expresses the psyche and feeling of the oppressed slave on the one hand and the end that expresses the psyche and feeling of the oppressing master on the other. Free man, or new man, in whom the values and conditions of democracy are embodied, is the positive coordinate that is the sum of two negatives that individually negate all such values and conditions: the negative of servitude and the negative of enslavement.

Bennabi appealed to the history of humanity where, he suggested, numerous examples of the evolution of a democratic attitude that resisted both servitude and enslavement existed. The debate between Moses, the liberator of the oppressed, and Pharaoh, the oppressor, is one example. Pharaoh's attitude is not one of negating the ego but of negating the other; it is a negation of the democratic attitude. The same scenario is repeated in almost every culture, from the very ancient to the very modern. As Bennabi suggested:

> We must consider any project aimed at founding a democracy an educational enterprise for the whole community, a comprehensive program that encompasses psychological, ethical, social, and political aspects. For democracy is not—as is superficially understood in the common usage, that is within the limits of its etymology—a mere political process. Nor is it simply a process whereby powers are handed over to the masses, to a people whose sovereignty is recognized by a specific statement in the constitution. But it is the generation of an attitude, and of objective and subjective responses and standards, that collectively lay the foundations upon which democracy, prior to being stated in any constitution, stands in the conscience of the people. The constitution is usually nothing but the formal outcome of the democratic enterprise once transformed into a political reality indicated by a text inspired by customs and traditions, and dictated by an attitude generated in a given circumstance. Such a text would have no meaning if not underpinned by the customs and traditions that inspired it or, in other words, the historical justifications that necessitated it. Hence is the naiveté of the constitutional imports borrowed today by some governments in developing African and Asian states that seek to establish a new

order in their countries in emulation of the deep-rooted democracies. Such borrowing may be necessary at times, but it is definitely not enough on its own if not accompanied by appropriate measures to spread and establish what is being borrowed in the psyche of the borrowing country's population.

Still not providing a definition of democracy apart from considering it to be an attitude, Bennabi went on to address the question of whether or not democracy, as an attitude, exists within Islam. He argued that this is dependent on the provision of what he earlier referred to as the general conditions of the democratic attitude. For a better understanding of this issue he suggested answering the following questions: Does Islam provide and guarantee these objective and subjective conditions, in the sense that it creates an attitude toward the "ego" and the "other" compatible with the democratic attitude? And does it create the appropriate social circumstances for the development of such an attitude? Does Islam truly reduce the quantity and intensity of the negative motives and of the anti-democratic tendencies that characterize the conduct of the oppressed and the conduct of the oppressor?

Bennabi stressed that the answer to the question "is there democracy in Islam?" is not necessarily obtainable from a given rule of *fiqh* (jurisprudence) deduced from the Sunnah or the Qur'an, but is obtainable from a comprehensive understanding of the essence of Islam. According to him, Islam should be viewed as a democratic enterprise through which the position of a Muslim in the encompassing society is seen clearly. What matters most in the process is that a Muslim's temporal activity is conditioned by the general principles of Islam. An Islamic model of democracy would not be restricted to endowing man with political or social rights, but would endow him with a value that surpasses every political or social value, a value proclaimed in Qur'anic verse number 70, chapter 17: "We have honored the children of Adam." Bennabi concluded: "This verse was revealed as if to lay the foundations for a democratic model that is superior to every other model, where the divine element within man is taken into consideration and not just the human or social aspects as in the other models. Thus, a kind of sanctity is endowed upon man raising his value above whatever value other models may give to him."

Bennabi's objective was to show that Islam has its own way of inspiring a democratic attitude, by providing man, by virtue of a divine honor bestowed upon him, with a legitimate reason to resist both servitude and enslavement. Citing examples from Islamic text and early history to prove this point, Bennabi established what he called an organic link between Islam and democracy. What follows in his treatise is a discussion of "how" and "when" an Islamic democracy is realized and whether such a democracy is capable of achieving what "*laicist* democracy" has guaranteed of individual rights, political rights, and social securities. To begin, he stressed the need to distinguish between what Islam has the potential to offer and the prevalent state of the contemporary Muslims. "Democracy exists within Islam, not during the era when Islamic traditions petrify and lose their brilliancy such as nowadays, but during the era of their making and when society is developing, such as during the first forty years of Islamic history."

In other words, the first forty years of Islamic history witnessed the founding of an Islamic democratic system that on the basis of a Qur'anic theoretical foundation made tangible accomplishments represented in guarantees of individual rights and in the restrictions imposed on rulers and the sources of legitimating their authority. Bennabi observed that fundamental individual rights such as the right to freedom of belief and expression, the right to work and freedom of movement, and the right to privacy were established and sanctified. As a further measure to bolster what he suggested may be described as political democratic rights, social democratic rights were established in the form of economic principles such as the imposition of zakat (alms) and the forbidding of riba (usury), maysir (gambling), and all other practices conducive to monopoly. "The Islamic democratic enterprise in the economic sphere is established on general principles aimed at the distribution of wealth so that it does not remain exclusively in the hands of the few."

Bennabi acknowledged the fact that this system of democracy did not last long because of the Ommiad coup against al-Khilafah ar-Rashidah (the Rightly Guided Caliphate). However, he pointed out that although the "tyrant" re-emerged in the image of the despotic ruler, the "slave" did not re-emerge so long as Muslim individuals held fast to the Islamic spirit. Hence is his optimism that: "At this moment in history, the Muslim countries stand at the threshold of democratic transition and there are signs that there will be a democratic renaissance. However, any attempt at establishing a democracy must begin with instilling a new appraisal of man in the conscience of the Muslim so that he does not fall into the pit of servitude or enslavement."

A Movement in Exile

Having translated Bennabi's "Ad-Dimuqratiyah Fil-Islam," Ghannouchi decided to write a book on liberties, which was completed after his release from prison. In the introduction to his book, he wrote:

> When some ideas on the subject had ripened together with some thoughts and options concerning the standing thorny problems, which constitute the subject matter of this book, a political détente ensued thanks to the "Bread Revolution" of 1984. I was released leaving behind the life of contemplation and writing to plunge into the leadership of the movement, facing up to an extensive campaign of malicious propaganda aimed at discrediting Islam and casting doubt on its ability to organize life.[8]

Soon after his release from prison, Ghannouchi perceived a concentrated endeavor to undermine the guarantees that Islam provided to safeguard public and individual liberties and to protect the rights of political and religious minorities and the rights of women. He saw an attempt to deny Islam's "great capacity and ability to face up to oppression." One of the hot issues debated was the question of apostasy and its relevance to individual and political freedoms. Another quite related issue was democracy. Ghannouchi complained that an extremely distorted image of Islam was being presented by its opponents "who portrayed it as if it were a threat that posed a serious challenge to modern civilization and to the public and personal liberties of the people. Islam was so unfairly portrayed as if it were an obstacle hindering the progress of Muslims by denying them their basic rights." In contrast, he noticed that Western democracy was being portrayed as an ideal, a perfect and sole model of an advanced and progressive civilization, and hence it stood forth as an acute antagonist to Islam.

But as he set out to defend Islam, he discovered that much distortion had also been made about the nature of Western civilization, and most importantly about the concept of democracy. Although less than a century earlier democracy had been highly spoken of by Islamic reformists, it seemed now that it had become the exclusive demand of the secularists. Within the Islamic camp democracy was still shunned as an alien product of the colonial West, which had nothing good to offer to the Muslims. This issue became the overwhelming topic that took Ghannouchi into its grip after his release. The Islamic movement in Tunisia had been going through a transition from the stage of preaching Islamic values, in response to what it considered to be a domineering alien culture, to the stage of responding to the concerns of Tunisian society in particular and Arab society in general. This was the time when, as Ghannouchi put it, the presentation of unequivocal answers to the challenges facing Islamic thought in a country like Tunisia, where Westernization had been most profound, had become an indispensable epistemological necessity for the Tunisian Islamic Movement.

Appreciating that the task ahead of him was not facile, Ghannouchi felt the necessity of acquainting himself anew with contemporary Islamic thought, with the gist of relevant Western thinking, and with reality and its requirements. He wrote:

> Consequently, I was obliged to remove myself once more from the tide of everyday life and devote it to a fresh task. So I blew the dust off the prison manuscripts. This would not have been easy had it not been for the compelling circumstances during which I was advised to disappear for the whole summer of 1986 after it had become apparent that there was a strong determination on the part of the regime to eradicate the Islamic movement. It was a valuable opportunity, which I tended to think was my last chance, for the formulation of my thoughts, convictions, and experiences with regard to the major problems facing Islamic thought, which so often deprived me of the sweetness of slumber. No sooner had I collected the orchard fruits and the twigs started shedding their leaves than I, as well, had freed myself of my load and concluded the irksome task of formulation. A wave of genuine exultation and pleasure swept over me. It was really a moment of accomplishment that made it easy for me to look death in the face. So I quit my sanctuary and utter solitude in full confidence, feeling as though I had accomplished something that would immortalize me.

But no sooner had he finished working on his book than he was once again arrested and sent to detention. In August 1987, Ghannouchi and eight-nine other leading members of the Mouvement de la Tendence Islamique (MTI) were brought to trial before the state security court, accused of inciting violence and seeking to change the nature of the state. All but fourteen of the defendants were convicted. The majority were sentenced to prison terms of between two and twenty years; two of those sentenced to death were executed; other death sentences, including Ghannouchi's, were commuted to terms of life imprisonment with hard labor. President Bourguiba was not impressed. He ordered a retrial insisting on a death sentence for Ghannouchi. But on 7 November 1987, Bourguiba was toppled in a bloodless coup. The new president, Zine El Abidine Ben Ali, who had been appointed prime minister in October, and had previously served as minister of the interior, came to power in an atmosphere of mounting crisis. In the months prior to President Bourguiba's removal more than three thousand MTI supporters had been detained. The new president ordered their release, and Ghannouchi walked free. "I walked out of my dungeon with a new momentum and fresh zeal. I returned to the book, which had originally been intended as a dissertation for a doctorate degree at the Faculty of *Shari'ah*, once more searching for the right circumstances to submit it to the university in Tunis."

He was encouraged by the declaration made by the new president that "our people deserve an advanced and institutionalized political life, truly based on the plurality of parties and mass organizations. . . . We shall see that the law is correctly enforced in a way that will proscribe any kind of iniquity or injustice."[9] Indeed, the initial period of President Ben Ali's era saw a commitment to the creation of a multi-party system. Under Law No. 88-32 of 1988, governing the formation and activities of political parties, six opposition parties were registered in addition to the ruling *Rassemblement Constitutionnel Democratique* (RCD). But the law prohibited the establishment of political parties on confessional, ethnic, racial, or regional bases.

In an attempt to gain recognition under the new law, the MTI changed its name in December 1988 to Hizb al-Nahdah (the Renaissance Party, written in English as Ennahda), dropping the reference to Islam from its title. Prior to the legislative election of April 1989, Ennahda submitted its application to be registered as a political party. By the time of the vote, it had not received the necessary recognition. Nevertheless, Ennahda supporters ran more or less openly as independents competing for 129 of the 141 available parliamentary seats. Ennahda-backed independents emerged as the largest opposition force, winning 14.5 percent of the national vote and as much as 30 percent in some urban centers, including Tunis.[10] The combined total vote of all the opposition parties recognized under Law No. 88-32 amounted to less than 5 percent. Ennahda's emergence as the only credible electoral competitor ever to challenge the ruling party's monopoly of power gave the Tunisian government a self-interested motive for discouraging its free participation in the political process. On 6 June 1989 Ennahda's application to form a political party was rejected, leaving its supporters liable to prosecution on grounds of membership in an illegal organization, an offense punishable by up to five years' imprisonment. Despite Ennahda's impressive showing at the polls, none of its candidates were returned to parliament. In fact, all of the seats in parliament were awarded to candidates from the ruling RCD.

It would emerge later that Ennahda had committed the biggest mistake in its history. Ghannouchi was anxious to avoid provoking the regime. He knew there were red lines not to be crossed. He actually sent a letter to President Ben Ali assuring him that all his movement aspired for was no more than ten seats in parliament. All the movement seemed to hope and plan for was an official recognition that would confer legal protection on its members, activities, and institutions. Hence, the objectives declared during the election campaign by its members were quite modest. However, what took Ghannouchi and the movement by surprise was what Ghannouchi describes as "the people's tempestuous craving for change."[11] Equally surprising for Ennahda was the extent to which secularist political groups lacked popular support. Ghannouchi recalls, "The people astonished us. They had so much confidence in us, much more than we had been prepared for, much more than local and international circumstances would permit."[12]

The popular support for the movement dazzled its leaders. In the midst of the excitement all was forgotten about the local, regional, or international balance of powers that were not to be upset. Members pressed for full-fledged participation. This seemed to them a golden opportunity. Many of them now realize with hindsight that it was a fatal mistake to respond to the thirst of the people for change by standing for the election in as many constituencies as possible. They provoked the regime, which felt truly threatened. Had the movement not done so, Ghannouchi now thinks, it might have been able to avert the disastrous consequences.[13]

The elections, which were supposed to mark the beginning of a new era of national reconciliation, turned out to be the end of what Ghannouchi refers to as "a rather short wedding party." Hopes in the democracy introduced by Tunisia's new ruler were quickly dispersed. In May 1989, Ghannouchi traveled into voluntary exile in London, where he has remained ever since. "All our concessions became of no avail. Not even the relinquishment of the very name of our movement helped. Nor was of any avail the flexibility and moderation that we forced on ourselves to avoid a return to confrontation and to spare our country's resources so that they may not be used except for the purpose of development and in confronting the colossal challenges facing our nation."[14]

Ghannouchi seemed to take the entire organization with him into exile. His departure was to be followed by a series of measures by the regime of President Ben Ali aimed at discrediting and crushing Ennahda once and for all. In April 1990, a prominent figure in Ennahda, Professor Moncef ben Salem, was arrested following publication of an interview with an Algerian magazine in which he criticized the human rights situation in Tunisia. In May 1990, he was sentenced to three years. In January 1991, Ghannouchi's deputy, lawyer Abdel Fattah Moro, fell victim to a government-sponsored defamation campaign that brought an end to his career. In February 1991, an arson attack on the ruling party's offices in the Bab Souika district was seized upon by the government as proof of the violent and anti-democratic nature of Ennahda. Although the movement had officially repudiated the attack, and although the authorities could not prove the movement's involvement, sensational reports in the government-controlled press were used by the government to split the leadership of Ennahda. Shortly afterward, three leading figures, Abdel Fattah Moro, Fadhel Beldi, and Benaissa Demni, announced that they were freezing their membership of Ennahda because of its use of violence. The official campaign to marginalize and discredit Ennahda culminated in a press conference held by Interior Minister Abdallah Kallal on 22 May 1991 in which he accused Ennahda of plotting to seize power in Tunisia in order to declare a religious theocratic state. Thousands of Ennahda members were arrested. At least seven of them died in custody in circumstances strongly suggesting that their deaths were caused by torture.[15] Ennahda members who escaped imprisonment were forced underground or into exile. Many of them have sought refuge in Western Europe. Since then, Ennahda has been a movement in exile.

By his self-imposed exile, Ghannouchi might have hoped to dedicate himself to what he felt he was more suited for, to the domain of thought and *da'wah*, rather than that of politics and organization. He might, as a leader, have felt responsible for what had happened to the movement and might have wanted to leave the task of pursuing the struggle to somebody else. But Ennahda members insisted there was a much greater benefit for the movement in his dedicating a greater part of his time and effort to the leadership of the movement. They insisted that in view of the special circumstances experienced by their movement and their country, Ghannouchi was obliged to remain in the field where he was most needed.[16]

What is so unique about Ennahda within Islamic circles is its democratic institution. It has, since its founding conference in 1979, been governed by a constitution that distributes power and determines relations among its four main offices: the president, the executive committee, the *shura* council, and the general assembly. The first three are elected once every three years. Since 1979, ten leaders have occupied the position of president; most of them are currently in prison. According to Ghannouchi, Ennahda does not approve of eternal leaders who exist above criticism and election, and the relationship between the president and the movement's members is unlike that which exists between a Sufi *shaykh* and his disciples. During the movement's last conference in 1995, the difference between the first and second candidates for the presidency was only a small number of votes. Ghannouchi, the first candidate, won no more than 52 percent of votes. As for the mechanism of running Ennahda, the general assembly, which meets every three years, calls to account the leadership that served during the previous term, discusses and endorses a proposed plan for the forthcoming three-year term, and elects a new president and a new *shura* council. Until the 1995 conference, the constitution stated that the president was responsible for appointing his cabinet, the executive committee. Till then, he was not required to obtain endorsement of his appointees from the *shura* council. This provision was amended in the last conference, and now the president is required to obtain the council's endorsement of his cabinet.

Al-Hurriyat al-'Ammah

It was in his exile in London that Ghannouchi finally had the opportunity to return to his book and finish it. Published by the renowned Centre of Arab Unity Studies in Beirut in 1993, *Al-Hurriyat al-'Ammah Fid-Dawlah al-Islamiyyah* (Public liberties in the Islamic state) is considered one of the most important references in contemporary Islamic political thought. Divided into three main sections, the book consists of an introduction, six chapters, a conclusion, and seven appendices.

The first section of Ghannouchi's *Al-Hurriyat* consists of two chapters; the first is a brief five-page discussion of the concept of freedom in the West. At the outset, Ghannouchi defines what he means by the term "West." In this context, it is "this material philosophy and what springs out of it of relations based on power, utilitarianism, and hedonism, and of an international order based on oppressing the weak, plundering their resources, and destroying their cultures. It does not mean the Western people as a whole, because these are the first victims of this philosophy, of these values, of these systems, and of these oppressive multi-national companies."

In this chapter, Ghannouchi paves the way for his forthcoming discussion of the Islamic concept of freedom by criticizing the West for failing to live up to its declarations in the field of freedom and human rights. He chooses not to engage in any philosophical discussion of the concept of freedom because "this is not the field for it and because discussing the essence of freedom in an attempt to prove its existence usually ends with negating it altogether." Referring to Kant's *Critique de la raison pure* and Ibn Khaldoun's *Al-Muqaddimah,* Ghannouchi expresses support for what he calls their advocacy of "restricting reason to the world of phenomena." The other reason why he avoids a philosophical discussion of the concept is that discussions on the question of freedom have shifted to more visible fields—such as ethics, law, and politics—after having departed the field of metaphysics. The focus has increasingly been on the relationship between man and political, social, and economic institutions, that is on the rights of man. "Liberties, in the plural, rather than the philosophical concept of "freedom" is what everyone now talks about."

Ghannouchi recognizes that the struggle for liberties in the West has led to the incorporation into state constitutions of the rights of man and to the promulgation of various world declarations on human rights. However, he sees a major flaw arising from "the lack of guarantees that see the equitable and universal implementation of these rights." He subscribes to the critique that the Western conception is "formal or negative" in the sense that it endows an individual with theoretical authority but no real power to realize his rights or shield himself against despotism. "It is true that an individual has in theory the right to think, speak, or travel the way he wishes. But how can he accomplish all of this if culture, wealth, and power are monopolized by a limited group of citizens who are supposed in theory to be his equals?"

Ghannouchi is of the opinion that the conflict between the bourgeoisie (the class of small property-owners) on the one side and the feudal lords and the church on the other played a fundamental role in creating the circumstances that led to the birth of various human rights declarations and bills of citizen rights.

> The bourgeoisie found it convenient to defend a concept of human rights based on the nature of man that is free from the authority of a king, a clergyman, or a deity. It was also of convenience in the process of eradicating the influence of the church to advocate the nation-state where citizenship would be founded on no relation with religion if not on antagonism to it. Of interest was also the elimination of all the restrictions imposed on industry and commerce by the old aristocracy.

One may be tempted to conclude that Ghannouchi seems influenced—perhaps by virtue of being a Tunisian—more by the French than any other European experience. His remarks are reverberations of de Tocqueville, who wrote to his friend Beaumont, in 1828, describing the rise of the bourgeoisie at the expense of the feudal aristocracy and the serfs: "It gained everything which the two other orders lost, for it approached more than they did the natural condition of the human race. . . . After all, a reasonable equality is the only condition natural to man, since the [European] peoples have approached it from such different starting points and moving along such different paths."[17]

The disenchantment with religion that accompanied the birth of civil rights might have been more characteristic of the French Restoration period when, according to de Tocqueville, an alliance was forged between aristocracy and the church. De Tocqueville's description of the developments that led to such a state of affairs is reverberated in Ghannouchi's elucidation throughout his book, and in various papers and lectures, of the position of religion in nineteenth-century European political thought. In 1821, de Tocqueville wrote to an English friend:

> The nation was, or rather believed itself to be, governed by priests and saw their influence everywhere. Then what is called the Voltairean spirit was reborn, that is to say, the attitude of systematic hostility and mockery not only of the ministers of religion but of religion itself, Christianity in all its forms . . . Caricatures, theatres, and songs were dominated by bitter satires against the clergy and took on an inconceivable violence.[18]

The Concept of Freedom

Without going into the details of the Western theories on the concept of freedom, but seemingly alluding to the notion of "negative" freedom, Ghannouchi criticizes the definition of freedom as the freedom from external compulsion, a notion that, according to him, "confirms the negative mechanical nature of individual freedoms."[19] In what may be construed as sympathy for the notion of "positive" freedom, he argues that restrictions on free will are not always external; some may be subjective—whether ascribed to the power of self-motivation or desire, or to the lack of consciousness or knowledge.

In Western political thought a distinction is drawn between a negative and a positive notion of freedom. The liberal definition of freedom is normally couched in the former, in terms of "freedom from" rather than "freedom to." Negative freedom is the condition in which one is not compelled, not restricted, not interfered with, and not pressurized. A man is normally said to be free to the degree to which no man or body of men interferes with his activity. According to Isaiah Berlin, freedom in this sense is defined as an area of non-interference, and the wider the area of non-interference, the wider is man's freedom.[20] Political philosophers have disagreed over how wide this area could or should be. Locke, Adam Smith, and Mill believed that social harmony and progress were compatible with reserving a large area for private life over which neither the state nor any other authority must be allowed to trespass. Hobbes, in contrast, argued that if men were to be prevented from destroying one another and making social life a jungle or a wilderness, greater safeguards must be instituted to keep them in their places. While both sides agreed that some portion of human existence must remain independent of the sphere of social control, that a minimum area of personal freedom must be preserved, the debate continues over what this minimum must be.[21]

The positive notion of freedom is said to derive from the wish on the part of the individual to be his own master. It is the wish of a man that his decisions depend on himself, not on external forces of whatever kind. It is the desire to liberate oneself from a dominating self that may, on the one hand, be identified with reason, with a "high nature," with the self which calculates and aims at what will satisfy it in the long run, with the "ideal" or "autonomous self." It may on the other hand be identified with irrational impulse, uncontrolled desires, with a "lower nature" concerned with the pursuit of immediate pleasure, with the "empirical" or "heteronomous" self. This conception of freedom suggests that man is divided against himself. His personality is split into two: the transcendent, dominant controller, and the empirical bundle of desires and passions to be disciplined and brought to heel. Historically, the desire to be self-directed has taken two forms: the first, that of self-abnegation in order to attain independence; the second, that of self-realization, or total self-identification with a specific principle or ideal in order to attain the selfsame end.

The dominant liberal view, which defines freedom exclusively in terms of the independence of the individual from interference by others, has been said to rely simply on an opportunity concept. In other words, being free is a matter of what one can do, of what it is open to one to do, whether or not one does anything to exercise these options. Advocates of the positive notion of freedom challenge this view. They believe that freedom resides, at least in part, in collective control over the common life. In the latter case, freedom involves essentially the exercising of control over one's life. Accordingly, one is free only to the extent that one has effectively determined oneself and the same of one's life. Instead of being an opportunity concept, positive freedom is said to be an exercise concept.[21]

Arguing against the notion of negative freedom, Ghannouchi suggests that compulsion may assume various shapes, which may be so subtle, cunning, and disguised that the victim is unaware of it. This, he explains, is the form of compulsion the state and capitalist institutions in the West exercise by virtue of their influence on the media, education, and entertainment. Subsequently the influence is exercised on the minds of the public whose choices may be manipulated in a manner that would guarantee the monopoly of power by certain political or financial institutions.[22] It would not be erroneous to conclude that Ghannouchi might be inclined to favor positive freedom, but in its original Kantian form rather than the extreme form that leads to legitimating despotism as articulated by Fichte and Comte. Kantian freedom is the ability to realize oneself in autonomous choices, choices that will always contain an act of rational obedience toward the moral law. According to Kant, when the individual has entirely abandoned his wild, lawless freedom, to find it again, unimpaired, in a state of dependence according to law, that alone is true freedom, for this dependence is the work of the individual's own will acting as a lawgiver.[23] In its self-directing, self-realizing exercise, the Kantian notion of freedom may be said to compare well with what Ghannouchi calls "the Islamic concept of freedom," where servitude to God alone is the road to freedom.[24]

Ghannouchi's discussion of the Western concept of freedom may seem reductive. He himself admits so, as explained earlier, maintaining that it is not his objective to indulge himself in such detailed discussion. His objective throughout Al-Hurriyat's first chapter is not to provide his Arab readers with an outline of Western thought regarding the concept of freedom. Rather his aim is to lay the foundation for Al-Hurriyat's main theme, namely that whatever the West has to offer, it is to be assessed and sieved using an Islamic set of standards, or frame of reference.

Islamic Concept of Freedom

Ghannouchi seeks to establish 'aqidah (Islamic faith) not only as the source—as far as Muslims are concerned—but also as a more sound foundation for the concepts of both freedom and human rights. Islamic 'aqidah, Ghannouchi explains, is founded in the belief in one transcendental god, who, despite his closeness and immense influence on his creatures, is unlike anything He created. As such, Islam does not tolerate the notion of immanentism, which justifies for a state, a church, a ruler, or a cleric the claim of having or representing absolute divine authority. In other words, belief in one transcendental, yet near, god inspires the rejection of despotism. 'Aqidah provides a source of legal authority that is supreme and above all else, governor and governed, and that thus imparts confidence and a sense of equality and intimacy to believers.[25]

Ghannouchi's starting point in defining this concept is a plea for conceiving of Islam as a comprehensive revolution against idols and despots and a liberation movement aimed at emancipating man from all kinds of servitude except to God. It would follow in light of this that freedom is not simply a permission or license but an *amanah* (trust), that is a responsibility and consciousness of and commitment and dedication to the truth.[26] Citing a number of Islamic thinkers on the topic, including 'Allal al-Fasi of Morocco, Hassan Turabi of Sudan, Malik Bennabi of Algeria, and Muhammad Iqbal of Pakistan, he notes that the concept of freedom has been elucidated by these thinkers as a legal grant and not a natural right. They share in common the belief that man would not have obtained his freedom had it not been for the Revelation and that man was not born free but to be free. Freedom, in this sense, is a process of strife and toil by way of servitude to God. The more man becomes faithful in servitude to God the freer he becomes from all other deities and the higher he ascends in the scale of human excellence.[27]

The legislative implications of the Islamic concept of freedom have been addressed by Islamic jurists throughout the history of jurisprudence to the effect of establishing and refining a legal framework for man's freedom, or, as Ghannouchi put it, for his duties.[28] Ghannouchi credits Ash-Shatibi (d. 1388) for elaborating this framework in his book Al-Muwafaqat, which sets out the objective of Shari'ah (Islamic law) as being the realization of the main interests of humanity. These interests are classified into daruriyat (essential needs), hajiyat (important, but not essential needs), and tahsiniyat (ameliorative needs). The first class consists of guarantees necessary for the protection of faith, life, reason, progeny, and wealth. The idea is that Islam, as a religion, was revealed for the purpose of guaranteeing and preserving man's essentials needs. The guarantees provided by Islam for accomplishing this end constitute the general framework of human rights, including the right to choose a faith, the right to life, the right to education, the right to free expression, the right to have a family, and the right to own property.[29]

Ghannouchi sees that the first and most important human right guaranteed by Islam is the freedom of belief, which he defines as the individual's right to choose his faith away from any compulsion. He explains that by virtue of being a God-given right, freedom of choice is sanctified and guaranteed by Islamic Shari'ah. The golden rule in this matter, he points out, is Qur'anic verse 256 of Chapter 2: "No compulsion in region."[30] It is from this rule that the rights of non-Muslims in an Islamic state derive legitimacy. Ghannouchi addresses this topic in detail in his earlier book, Huquq al-Muwatanah, Huquq Ghayr al-Muslimin Fil-Mujtama' al-Islami, first published in Tunis in 1989. An English translation titled The Right to Nationality Status of Non-Muslim Citizens in a Muslim Nation was published in 1990 by the Islamic Foundation of America.

Citing the hadith of the prophet "Humans are as equal as the teeth of the comb," Ghannouchi asserts that Muslim leaders must face the rather complex problem of the relations between Muslims and non-Muslims within Islamic states and in the world at large. He warns that this issue is loaded with fallacies and baseless arguments, which have projected Islam as a menace that denies people their basic human rights of freedom, justice, and the pursuit of happiness. "The issue is sometimes dealt with in terms of secularity versus religiosity. The underlying assumption is that only a secular state, that separates state and religion, can guarantee these freedoms."[31]

Citizenship Rights

Ghannouchi's The Right to Nationality begins with a brief outline of the essential components comprising the principles of justice, equity, security, and community and the protection granted to non-Muslims in a Muslim state as rights ordained by divine law. He affirms that when the term *dar-ul-Islam* is used it connotes one nationality for those residing in it, Muslims and non-Muslims, and for all of whom the fundamental rights are guaranteed by the Qur'an, the Sunnah, and Islamic jurisprudence. The first of these rights is equality, which is positive and comprehensive regardless of race, ethnic origin, color, social status, or creed. The second right is freedom, which encompasses freedom of thought and freedom of belief including the right of non-Muslims in a Muslim state to build churches, temples, monasteries, synagogues, and so on. The third right is the freedom of movement including the right to establish schools and religious institutions.[32]

However, he talks of two categories of citizenship in the Islamic state: *muwatanah 'ammah*, which may be translated into "unqualified" citizenship, and *muwatanah khassah*, which may be translated into "qualified" citizenship.[33] Such categorization in his opinion is the fruit of freedom of choice. He explains that although a person who resides in an Islamic state has, irrespective of his or her religion or race, an absolute right to a decent living, he or she has the freedom to choose between embracing or rejecting the objectives and principles underpinning the state. When a person chooses to embrace Islam, he or she becomes a Muslim citizen not discriminated from the rest of the Muslim members of society save for distinctions of personal talent or professional qualifications. When a person chooses not to embrace Islam, then he or she would have to express loyalty to the state and recognize its legitimacy—in order to acquire the right to citizenship. By doing so, he or she pledges not to engage in any activity that may be construed as threatening to the state's order.[34] In the latter case, citizenship is qualified, and such qualification is only lifted when the concerned person embraces Islam. While enjoying full freedom in personal matters, that is those pertaining to faith, food, drink, and marriage, a non-Muslim citizen may be denied some of the rights guaranteed to Muslim citizens such as the right to occupy senior positions in the state that may be considered of significant bearing on its identity.[35]

Ghannouchi notes that scholars and thinkers continue to disagree, except with regard to the position of head of state, on which senior positions, or which public functions, should be denied to non-Muslim citizens in an Islamic state. There are those, like Said Hawwa, who are of the opinion that non-Muslim citizens should not be part of the state administration, a position described by Ghannouchi as too extreme.[36] Hawwa is of the opinion that:

> The people of the *dhimmah* (Christian, Jewish, and other non-Muslim citizens of the Islamic state) have no right to any of the functions of the state. They have no right to participate in the *shura*, they have no right to domination, and they have no right to elect the leaders of the Islamic state. Muslims may, if they so will, employ them out of necessity in some state functions provided they do not rule over the Muslims because one of the stipulations of the *dhimmah* contract is that they be subservient to the believers, and subservience entails not being in the forefront.[37]

Other scholars, Ghannouchi adds, are of the opinion that *dhimmis* have the right to participate in elections at all levels and may be nominated for any position apart from that of the head of state, and may therefore be members of nationally or locally elected councils.[38] Ghannouchi also refers to a modern Sudanese *ijtihad* that grants Christian-majority provinces in Sudan the right to opt for a legal system other than *Shari'ah* in order to organize their affairs.[39] Although he is in favor of minimizing the difference between *muwatanah 'ammah* and *muwatanah khassah*, he is keen to point out that nowhere in the past or the present "do we know of a state whose constitution is void of such similar restrictions." The purpose of these restrictions, according to him, is "to safeguard the state, or to protect the freedom of citizens as well as the right of the majority to impart on public life a color of their choosing."[40]

Riddah: Apostasy or Sedition

Any discussion of the freedom of faith in Islam must raise the question of *riddah* (apostasy). In classical literature, *riddah* is defined as "the voluntary and conscious reversion to *kufr* (disbelief) after having embraced Islam by means of denying any of its fundamentals whether in matters of *'aqidah* (faith), *Shari'ah* (law), or *sha'irah* (rite)." An example of the first would be the denial of Deity or Prophethood, of the second the licensing of prohibitions, and of the third the negation of obligations.[41] In his treatment of this concept, Ghannouchi discusses in detail the opinions of two Muslim schools of jurisprudence. The first school, to which most classical jurists belong, considers *riddah* a religious offense punishable by death. The second, to which Ghannouchi subscribes, considers *riddah* a political offense unrelated to the Islamic guarantee of a person's right to freedom of faith. So, *riddah* in this case is not equivalent to apostasy but to sedition. In other words, it is an act of mutiny or treason, an offense punishable within the framework of the authority's responsibility for preserving the community and maintaining law and order. This school is still a minority, and apart from a few classical scholars most of its advocates are nineteenth- and twentieth-century jurists and thinkers.[42] The position adopted by Ghannouchi on this issue, as well as on the rights of non-Muslims and on women's rights, has not made him or his thought welcome in certain parts of the Arab world, especially in the Arabian Peninsula, where the *salafi* school of thought is predominant. Nor, of course, do his ideas meet the expectations of liberals who, in a modern nation-state, would object to the inclusion of creed in the definition of citizenship rights.

In addition to freedom of faith, from which freedoms of thought and expression emanate, Ghannouchi talks of economic and social rights. While the right of an individual to own property is guaranteed in Islam, he points out that this is not considered a natural right, as in international conventions or declarations, because in the end everything belongs to God. Therefore, all that pertains to ownership, such as the methods of acquiring and disposing of property, should take place in accordance with the rules of *Shari'ah*. He is of the opinion that until the advent of colonialism in the nineteenth century, ownership in the Muslim countries—throughout Islamic history—was never established on "the Germanic model cited by Marx as the typical model of ownership in the European civilization. Nor was individual ownership considered an absolute right to the extent that a property owner would be free to dispose of his property as he wished: selling it, or passing it to inheritors, or even destroying it as stated in Roman Law." Ghannouchi's view is that the right to ownership is inseparable from the concept of *khilafah* (vicegerency). "Ownership is a fruit of man's function as God's vicegerent on Earth."[43]

Notwithstanding the above, Ghannouchi insists that not only is an individual's right to ownership guaranteed in Islam, but also it has an important role to play. Power is distributed among the members of society by virtue of their shared ownership of the resources. This, Ghannouchi maintains, imparts on political freedom and *shura* a social import. In the Islamic model the aim is to make ownership as accessible as possible to every member of the community. Without explaining how this can be achieved in reality, and whether it was the case at any time in history, Ghannouchi considers this a superior model in comparison with the two known Western models: "the socialist, in which individuals are denied the right to ownership altogether and where the state owns every thing, and the capitalist, in which property is in the hands of the very few, who consequently monopolize power."[44]

The difficulty is never with enumerating the sublime principles of Islam, such as the prohibition of usury, monopoly, extravagance, and so on, and the imposition of *zakat*. Rather, the difficulty is in envisaging how such principles can be translated into modern Islamic economics. Although, understandably, this task is beyond Ghannouchi, who is not an economist, his discussion of economic rights is strained by the absence of a depiction of any actual Islamic model.

As for social rights, Ghannouchi states that these are taken to mean "the needs of an individual in his livelihood of social and health-care." Such rights, he maintains, have not been of interest to Western constitutions and human rights declarations until recently, and only as "a reaction to pressure from 'socialist theories' and trade unions and to banish the ghost of the Marxist revolution." In contrast, he insists, they have been well established in the Islamic tradition since the inception of Islam.[45]

Once more, Ghannouchi makes no distinction here between theory and practice. Apart from reference to the early community of Madina and the list of guarantees enshrined in the constitution of the Islamic Republic of Iran, he writes more about values inherent in Islam than a model of a social-care or health-care system. Nevertheless, since most important social rights stipulated by modern constitutions in the West are the right to work, the right to medical care, and the right to social security, Ghannouchi endeavors to root these rights in the teachings of Islam. By so doing he hopes to show that Islam supports these rights and would want to see them guaranteed for individuals in a Muslim society. But he gives no example nor does he propose any mechanism as to how these rights are to be institutionalized. His treatment of this issue may, however, be understood as endorsement of the mechanisms employed in the countries, especially in the West, that have enshrined these rights in their constitutions or human rights commitments.

Democracy's Islamic Roots?

The second section of Ghannouchi's *Al-Hurriyat al-'Ammah Fid-Dawlah al-Islamiyyah* deals with political rights and liberties. The section begins with a couple of definitions.

> The phrase "political rights and liberties" in constitutional terminology means that the *Ummah* is the source of authorities, and is the possessor of supreme sovereignty in matters of governance in that it chooses the government, monitors its performance, calls it to account, power-shares with it, and dismisses it. Political liberties are a set of mandatory rights recognized by the state as belonging to the citizens. They are: the right to partici-

pate in governance by pressuring and influencing the government via direct or indirect elections and the right to information, assembly, political party formation, and trade union organization.[46]

These principles, Ghannouchi points out, form together the general edifice of the liberal democratic system prior to having been developed further in the aftermath of World War II, when the talk of rights and liberties had become inseparable from the talk of democracy. It is for this reason that he attempts in chapter three of Al-Hurriyat to introduce to his readers the concept of democracy.

In his book, as well as in his papers and talks on democracy, Ghannouchi's objective is to stress, firstly, that democracy is by no means as simple as some people hold it to be. "Even though it offers some conceptions on freedom and suggests mechanisms for applying them and for establishing consensus in a nation-state, and that it could as a whole be described as 'not bad,' yet democracy cannot surpass being one of many possibilities." Secondly, Islam does not contradict democracy but rather shares with it several common features that constitute a firm foundation for a common ground where benefits are exchanged, mutual interests are realized, and a formula for coexistence is achieved.[47]

The second statement is still disputed by some "liberal" thinkers who cannot accept the notion of a marriage between democracy and religion. However, this is by no means a universal position. An increasing number of thinkers do recognize that Islam preaches equality, justice, and human dignity. These are ideals that have played a role in developments as diverse as the Christian Reformation of the sixteenth century, the American and French revolutions of the eighteenth century, and even the "liberation theology" of the twentieth century. Islam, it has been observed, is not lacking in tenants and practices that are compatible with democracy and pluralism. Among these are the traditions of ijtihad, ijma' (consensus), and shura (council).[48] In general usage, the Arabic word ijtihad denotes the utmost effort, physical or mental, expended in a particular activity. In its technical legal connotation, it denotes the thorough exertion of the jurist's mental faculty in finding a solution for a case of law. In the context of Islamic legal theory, the Arabic term ijma' denotes the agreement of a generation of mujtahidin (pl. of mujtahid, a scholar qualified to form opinions on religious matters) concerning a particular issue that has arisen since the death of the Prophet.

Ghannouchi perceives of democracy as being the upshot of a far-reaching historical evolution. To him, it is by no means an artificial edifice erected by theorists, or jurists, or political thinkers. Most of its rules are derived from those prevalent in medieval Europe; from human civilizational legacies which all underwent gradual historical growth until they provided the foundation of a new system. He argues that the Europeans benefited from the Islamic civilization in creating profoundly enlightened conceptions of social values whose fruit was the emergence of liberal democracy. "Europe's contacts with the world of Islam created a psychological shock, which awakened Europe from the slumber of feudalism, from the failure of ecclesiastical religion, and from the dictatorship of aristocracy."[49]

Several other contemporary Islamic thinkers share the opinion that "democracy" has Islamic roots. Dr. Tawfiq Ash-Shawi's book Fiqh Ash-Shura Wal-Istisharah begins with an assertion that democracy is a European version of Islam's shura. He explains that past Muslim rulers who seized power other than through the means of *shura* in the wake of the Guided Caliphate era had suspended the practice of *shura* in selecting the ruler. The suspension continued until modern times when other nations excelled the Muslims in respecting the freedom of expression and in guaranteeing political liberties. The European nations succeeded in establishing a *shura*-based system of government they call democracy. In other words, "when the tree of *shura* withered in the land of Islam for lack of maintenance, its seeds landed, that is during the Renaissance, in the lands of the Europeans where the tree of democracy grew and blossomed."[50]

Ghannouchi is very much in favor of this line of thinking, which has been lent support by another prominent Islamic thinker, Hassan Turabi, who stresses the Islamic origin of the modern democratic thinking and traces it back to the contract of *bay'ah*, or homage. Turabi argues that in the primitive age of direct democracy, some political practices were known. These only found their way to constitutional thinking toward the end of the Middle Ages, when European thought discovered a constitutional principle to express the theoretical foundation for democracy. The Europeans derived the origin of this democratic theory from their contacts with the Islamic political *fiqh* (jurisprudence). The essence of democracy, or the government of the people, emanated from Islamic political *fiqh* early on when the Muslims accepted the Almighty Allah as their Lord and recognized the supremacy of His Law, *Shari'ah*. The Muslims knew they were equal and that they were Allah's *khalifah* (vicegerent) on earth. Whatever the overwhelming majority within the community of believers decided on the basis of their belief in the supremacy of *Shari'ah* would not have been different from what any one single individual or any small group of believers chose. Consensus was the legitimate source of earthly power, which in agreement with the people's belief submitted to *Shari'ah*. Political relations were founded on a covenant between the community of believers and the *wulat* (rulers). The delegation of power to *wulat-ul-amr* (those holding office) was based on the contract of political *bay'ah*. Such is its name in the Qur'an, in the Sunnah, and in *fiqh*. Various contracts in the transactions within society were analogous to the contract of *bay'* (selling and buying), the most familiar of all contracts. This concept, according to Turabi, did perhaps find its way to the West in just the same way as Islamic concepts in theology, politics, natural sciences, and social sciences found their way to European thought.[51]

Understanding Democracy

Ghannouchi's approach to the question of democracy is in the first place an attempt to understand the Western concept of liberal democracy in prelude to suggesting that an Islamic model of democracy is possible. He suggests that it would be impossible to understand liberal democracy without invoking the European Enlightenment, which sparked the revolution against the old epoch and its symbols. He finds it only natural for a civilization fettered by the authority of the divine right of kings to make its target the emancipation of man from despotism. It did so by proclaiming the equality of men so as to eliminate privileges, by espousing liberalism so as to reassert the value of man in the face of the church and feudal institutions, by declaring the people to be the source of sovereignty instead of the king, by establishing pluralism on the relics of autocracy, and by the separation of powers to prevent centralization and despotism. The most important principles that constitute the essence of liberal democracy are, therefore, the sovereignty of the people, elections, the separation of powers, and public liberties. In total, the objective of all of these is to empower the ruled and equip them with pressure tools so as to stand up to the rulers and influence their decisions.[52]

Ghannouchi adopts Bennabi's definition of the essence of democracy as an educational enterprise for the whole nation. It has psychological, ethical, and socio-economic aspects and is neither a mere process of transferring authority to the people nor a mere declaration that a certain nation has by way of a constitution become sovereign. Having been so impressed by Bennabi as to call him the grandson of Ibn Khaldoun, Ghannouchi is keen to describe in detail the process by which Bennabi traced the roots of what he referred to as the democratic attitude.[53]

As Ghannouchi sees it, the democratic system is made up of form and essence. On the one hand, form is represented in recognizing the people's sovereignty, which is exercised through a number of "constitutional techniques." These may vary from one system to the other in detail but agree on the principles of equality, election, separation of powers, political pluralism, freedom of expression, and freedom of assembly, and the right of the majority to rule and of the minority to oppose. The essence of the democratic system on the other hand is the acknowledgement of the dignity of man. Accordingly, man is entitled to earn a number of rights that protect his dignity and guarantee his right to participate in the administration of public affairs, while maintaining the ability to pressure and influence the governors, and at the same time enjoying security against repression and despotism.[54]

Although here Ghannouchi uses the expression "people's sovereignty" he is found in the same chapter to talk about sovereignty as one of two pillars upon which the "Western state model" is founded. It is clear, as shall be seen later, that he uses the term sovereignty to talk about two different things. While no further elucidation of what he means by the "people's sovereignty" is given, it would not be unreasonable to suggest that he probably means the "power of the people" to participate in government and to see that government is conducted in the public interest. By equality he must mean political equality, which in electoral democracy is said to be achieved if a number of conditions are met. The first of these conditions is that all adult citizens must be entitled to stand for election regardless of race, color, sex, or religion. Secondly, all citizens must possess the right to vote; in other words, there should be universal adult suffrage. Thirdly, no one must possess more than a single vote; each should have an equal voice at election time. Finally, all votes must be of equal value, a principle that can only be achieved if electoral constituencies are of equal size.[55]

The principles of "separation of powers" and "political pluralism" are discussed by Ghannouchi in detail in Al-Hurriyat's sixth chapter, entitled "The Fundamental Principles for Resisting Despotism in the Islamic State." With regard to the first, Ghannouchi explains that the "separation of powers" is one of the guarantees suggested by Western political thinkers to curb despotism. Elucidated by the Englishman Locke and then by the Frenchman Montesquieu, the concept was quite popular during the era of the struggle against despotism in recent history.[56] Following Montesquieu, the three powers normally considered to be separable in the exercise of government are the legislature, the executive branch, and the judiciary. The first of these powers formulates policy and enacts it as law, the second carries policy into action, and the third applies the law according to rules of procedural justice and resolves disputes. In order to limit power, Montesquieu thought, the three powers he had identified must be separated as much as possible and balanced against each other.

Ghannouchi offers a brief account of the American model, the Swiss Federation model, the English parliamentary model, the Soviet Marxist model, and the French Fifth Republic model to show the wide variation in the application of the separation of powers and the advantages and disadvantages of each model. He himself supports a separation of powers of some sort as a safeguard against despotism. For this reason he enters into a lengthy discussion of the various opinions of contemporary Islamic thinkers regarding the principle of the separation of powers within an envisaged model of an Islamic political order. He concludes that this matter has been decisively settled neither by religious text nor by contemporary political theories in favor of one or the other of the opinions that seek to establish and organize power relations within an Islamic state. Nevertheless, the most appropriate constitutional principle, in his judgment, is that of cooperation among different state institutions. But since the power of legislation is invested in the Book, the Sunnah, and the councils of scholars who undertake to interpret the text and come up with *ijtihad*, the function of fundamental legislation is not only completely independent of the "state" but also overriding. And since all members of the Muslim community, including the head of state and his assistants, submit completely to the authority of the judiciary, the Islamic "state" (and here too he means government) is essentially executive in nature.

Similarly, Ghannouchi opens the discussion of the principle of political pluralism with a review of both the Western liberal and the Western Marxist conceptions of political pluralism. In the first case, the distribution of political power through several institutions that limit one another's action is seen not as an inevitable "evil" but as a necessary "good" to prevent the monopoly of power and establish a balance between the ruled and the ruler. In the second case, which Ghannouchi refers to as "the Marxist democracies of the Soviet Union and its likes," pluralism is detested as a process of class division, which Marxism had come to abolish. Then Ghannouchi embarks on a detailed discussion of the position of Islamic political thought and contemporary Islamic movements and parties on the question of political pluralism, dividing them into two schools, one that accepts the idea and one that rejects it. His own position is one of support for the founding of a modern Islamic political order within which parties with different *ijtihad* in political action form and compete for the confidence of the *Ummah* in order to serve its interests. The premise from which he emanates is that *shura*, and for that matter concepts such as *al-amr bil-ma'ruf wan-nahy 'anil-munkar* (enjoining good and forbidding evil), represent an essential foundation for the establishment of an Islamic system of government. Consequently, political pluralism might be the most appropriate framework for training and empowering citizens to shoulder their responsibilities in the public domain. Although the concept of political pluralism is quite new and is, evidently, found nowhere in classical Islamic literature, he points out that traditional Islamic society knew various forms of pluralism. He dates the oldest form of pluralism back to the battle of Siffin (657 A.D.) between the followers of Ali, the fourth Rightly Guided Caliph, and those of Mu'awiyah, the founder of the Ommiad Dynasty. That was the conflict that prepared the ground for the emergence of three political trends, the Shiites, the Kharijites, and the Sunnites, each struggling for power to enforce their vision and interpretation of text and history. While these trends or groups coexisted, they were always suspicious of each other and the ambition of each of them had always been to seize power. The decline of *ijtihad* and the consolidation of despotism are blamed for the failure of classical Muslim schools of jurisprudence to devise mechanisms by which such political trends could have consolidated *shura* and contested for power peacefully rather than through cabal and violence.

A Minimal Definition of Democracy

Ghannouchi's conception of democracy seems quite in line with the model of democracy many contemporary political writers in the West have come to identify with. According to Macpherson, the liberal model of democracy is based on a number of basic stipulations. The first of these is that government and legislatures are chosen directly or indirectly by periodic elections with universal equal franchise, the voters' choice being normally a choice between political parties. The second is that there is a sufficient degree of civil liberties (freedom of speech, publication, and association, and freedom from arbitrary arrest and imprisonment) to make the right to choose effective. The third is that there is formal equality before the law. The fourth is that there is some protection for minorities. The fifth is that there is general acceptance of a principle of maximum individual freedom consistent with equal freedom for others.[57] Democracy is understood as a system of procedural rules, which specify who is authorized to make collective decisions and through which procedures such decisions are to be made. It comprises procedures for arriving at collective decisions in a way that secures the fullest possible participation of interested parties including equal and universal adult suffrage; majority rule and guarantees of minority rights, which ensure that collective decisions are approved by a substantial number of those expected to make them; the rule of law; and constitutional guarantees of freedom of assembly and expression and other liberties, which help guarantee that those expected to decide or to elect those who decide can choose among real alternatives. Democracy in a sense is a method of preventing those who govern from permanently appropriating power for their own ends.[58] Or put slightly differently, modern political democracy is a system of governance in which rulers are held accountable for their actions in the public realm by citizens, acting indirectly through the competition and cooperation of their elected representatives.[59]

Ghannouchi's ideal system of governance is one that recognizes the dignity of man and adopts a package of organizational and educational mechanisms. The purpose would be to protect man's dignity, provide a set of guarantees necessary to prevent despotism, and create the right climate for the blossoming of man's potentials so as to achieve progress and to participate responsibly in the process of deciding his own destiny. It is the system in which the political, economic, and cultural gaps between the "ruled" and the "ruler" diminish until they disappear altogether. It is the system in which, at the legal level, the ruler becomes truly the servant of his people and no more than an ordinary member of the community.[60] This, he suggests, might have been the ideal democracy, that is the ideal of full political and social participation rather than representation, the ideal where the governed become governor so as to realize their aspired aims and objectives. If such is the ideal, it would follow that the size of popular participation in public affairs is a measure of the extent to which any given regime is democratic, and the higher the level of participation the closer the regime is to the democratic ideal.[61]

Notwithstanding the above remarks, there is no evidence, whether in *Al-Hurriyat* or in other works authored by Ghannouchi, that he is interested in, or perhaps aware of, the current debate in Western thinking between what has been referred to as elite and participatory models of democracy, or between anti-normative realism and normative idealism.[62] The core of the theory of elite democracy has been Joseph Schumpeter's claim that "the democratic method is that institutional arrangement for arriving at political decisions in which individuals acquire the power to decide via a competitive struggle for the people's vote."[63] Accordingly, democracy is defined not as a kind of society or a set of moral ends or even a principle of legitimacy, but rather a method for choosing political leaders and organizing governments. In this model the role of voters is neither to generate issues nor to choose policies. It is the leaders (political parties) who aggregate interests and decide which are to become politically salient, and it is them who select issues and structure public opinion. Voters are consumers and parties are entrepreneurs offering alternative packages or personnel; it is they who create demand, bowing to consumer sovereignty only with regard to the yes/no decision by the voters about who among the pre-selected candidates will be their representatives. In other words, this model reduces the normative meaning of democracy to a set of minimums modeled on a conception of bargaining, competition, access, and accountability derived more from the market than from earlier models of citizenship. In this model, secret ballot, civil rights, alternation, regular elections, and party competition are central to every modern conception of democracy.[64]

In contrast, the participatory model of democracy is based on active participation in ruling and in being ruled (that is in the exercise of power) and also in public will and opinion formation. Democracy in this sense allows all citizens, and not only the elite, to acquire a democratic political culture. The advocates of this model criticize the elite model for sacrificing in the name of realism what has always been taken to be the core of the conception of democracy, namely, the citizenship principle. They insist that without public spaces for the active participation of the citizenry in ruling and being ruled, without a decisive narrowing of the gap between rulers and ruled, to the point of its abolition, polities are democratic in name only.[65] Macpherson has suggested a possible third alternative where the two seemingly irreconcilable models, or what he refers to as "senses," may merge. In this case, democracy is not merely a mechanism for choosing and authorizing governments but as well a quality pervading the whole life and operation of a national or smaller community, a whole set of reciprocal relations between the people who make up the nation or community.[66]

Inadequacies of Western Democracy

In order to assess the accomplishment of the democratic system as developed in the Western experience against the democratic ideal, Ghannouchi finds it necessary to trace the roots of the concept "democracy." He points out that the definition of democracy as the rule of the people presumes the equal participation of all individuals, within a given society, in government. Not only is this practically impossible because a large number of under-age or "unqualified" individuals do not enjoy equal rights in the democratic process, but also because no fixed measures exist to determine those who are entitled to such rights. Citing the example of ancient Athens, he reminds readers that eligible citizens did not exceed 20,000 out of a population of 320,000. Slaves, women, and aliens were excluded. Then moving to more recent times, Ghannouchi points out that throughout Europe for a long time only male property owners were permitted to vote. In Britain, for instance, women above the age of thirty voted for the first time after World War I in 1918, and since 1929 women the age of twenty-one have been entitled to vote. French women were allowed to vote in 1945 and Swiss women in 1971. He also points out that although theoretically individuals are supposed to have equal voting powers, the overwhelming majority of the population in any Western democratic country are influenced and manipulated by an extremely influential minority of business interests, media tycoons, and pressure groups.[67] This makes the definition of democracy as the rule of the people by the people for the people a dream. Democracy as practiced in the West today is not the rule of the people, nor is it self-government, but a "multi-party" system of governance exercised by an elite of political leaders, and in which some form of dialogue takes place among the representatives of various pressure and interest groups. Democracy in practice is nothing more than the rule of the elite in the name of the people.[68] Ghannouchi is not alone in thinking so. It is widely recognized that the modern model of democracy is far from the democratic ideal, and is very different from the classical Greek model. Government in today's democracy is left in the hands of a class of professional politicians; the public does not govern but only participates in the process of selecting the government.[69]

Nevertheless, Ghannouchi believes this is no good reason to shun democracy. Citing examples of the criticism voiced by the proponents of participatory democracy, or those whom he describes as "the antagonists of traditional democratic theory who cast doubt on the authenticity of democratic representation," Ghannouchi asserts that no matter how limited may be the embodiment of the democratic ideals in real life be, democratic government strikes a reasonable balance between public opinion and pressure groups although, admittedly, the balance is tilted in many instances in favor of the latter.[70]

This is not where the problem with the Western model of democracy lies. The real problem, as seen by Ghannouchi, is that so long as the sphere of popular participation, no matter how extended it may be, remains restricted to the national boundaries, liberal democracy has the potential to smack of nationalism and even racism. The privileges of the democratic system, including liberties and rights, do not go beyond the citizens of the nation concerned. "It is no wonder that the most admirable democracies in modern times, those of Britain and France, have been among the most brutal colonial powers of modern history."[71] Ghannouchi's view is shared by some other Islamic thinkers who observe that successful Western democracies with stable civil societies have been brutal colonial powers. Where democracy did not succeed, they argue, no imperial powers emerged.[72] Ghannouchi takes this further to suggest that because Western democracies have been founded to a large extent on utilitarian ideas, or what he calls "the values of hedonism and power," only force can check their lust for hegemony.

As a consequence, a society run by a Western democratic system of government is shattered and confused. Greed, deception, and brutality prevail in the absence of the influence of an absolute value that transcends the will of man. No security for the weak is realized whether the weak is a minority within the same society, where the will of the majority is divine, or another nation prevented by the lack of power from challenging stronger adversaries. Eventually, the weak has no choice but to succumb or perish according to the Darwinian rule of the survival of the fittest. The will of the victor is the ultimate truth.[73]

The problem, as he sees it, is not really with the ideal, or even the mechanics, of democracy, but with some aspects of the philosophy in which this ideal, or for that matter its variants, is nurtured. While expressing admiration for the democratic ideal, as well as for democratic procedures, Ghannouchi seeks to show that democracy is not a mere mechanical process that takes place in isolation from a world-view of some sort. Liberal democracy is influenced and steered by Western philosophies, such as those of Darwin, Hegel, and Nietzsche, that provide justification for and legitimation of the attitude of the powerful against the weak. He cites as examples the oppression of the blacks and the Indian tribes in America, the North African immigrants in France, the Palestinians in occupied Palestine, and the Muslims in the Balkans. In each of these cases, oppression takes place with the direct or indirect involvement of a liberal democratic government. Democratic governments, or regimes supported by democratic governments, are in many parts of the world embroiled in the perpetration of atrocities and even genocide to exterminate entire communities. Such practices, Ghannouchi affirms, are testimonies that speak of the inhumane side of Western democracy and that tarnish its face. "Although democracy has established political equality and removed traditional aristocratic privileges in the West, it has gradually led to the re-emergence of absolute inequality in economic terms. It has, thus, produced a new form of aristocracy based on capitalism and monopoly of economic power that in turn influences political parties, the media, and public opinion."

Ghannouchi is particularly critical of the foreign policies of Western democracies, seen as reflective of a double standard.

> Some of the oldest democracies, such as Britain and France, had ministries for the colonies. The same democracies, in which homosexuality, fornication, gambling, abortion, and birth control have been legalized, impose unfair conditions on weaker nations and show no sympathy whatsoever despite the miserable conditions endured by them. The existence of no less than one quarter of humanity in absolute poverty—as a result of which scores of millions perish every year—is a damning testimony to the failure of modern democracy, to the inadequacy of its legal mechanisms and intellectual foundations for cultivating a humanistic attitude and awarding human dignity a position in the list of priorities higher than prosperity and national glory for whose accomplishment billions of dollars are spent by Western democracies. In light of this tragedy, the accomplishments of modern democracy dwarf and diminish. The tools of modern democracy have undoubtedly provided liberties and rights for Western humans and have come up with guarantees to prevent injustice. But what about other humans in a world that by virtue of technological progress and thanks to the communications revolution can no longer afford to be divided? In such a new reality, shouldn't an act of aggression—not only against another community but also against any single human being—be regarded as an act of aggression against the entire humanity and a threat to its security and stability?

In spite of condemning the Western model of democracy for being inadequate, or heavily flawed, Ghannouchi insists that "it is still a thousand times better than despotism that is grinding the masses in some of the Arab countries where the state has been turned into a highly sophisticated machine of repression." This may be construed as a sign of incoherence in Ghannouchi's thought. But if one were to assess his motives of such a discourse, he might not be so incoherent after all. On the one hand, his book *Al-Hurriyat* is laden with political messages to authoritarian regimes in the Middle East and North Africa, to the secularists in his own country and elsewhere in the Arab region, and to affiliates of the Islamic movement both at home and around the world. His book is not a pure work of academia although it was originally designed as a Ph.D. thesis. On the other hand, he seeks to prepare the ground for launching his model of Islamic democracy, most appropriately on the ruins of liberal democracy. Hence is his oscillation between acclaiming the ideal and denouncing the real.

Ghannouchi is also aware of the problem that the term "democracy" has become so flexible that it encompasses some of the most contradictory regimes. Indeed, the twentieth century has seen, in various parts of the world, liberals, socialists, conservatives, anarchists, fascists, nationalists, and now Islamists all claiming their ideas to be democratic, and each seeking to preach true democracy. He affirms that it is simply not possible to judge the democratic nature of a given regime by merely accepting its claim of affiliation to the democratic club. The real nature of a political system should, in his opinion, be investigated by checking the circumstances of its birth and development, and by looking into the values, traditions, philosophies, and the works of art and literature prevalent among its adherents regarding their conception of man and nature. The individual and collective conducts that emanate from such values and philosophies in dealing with the "other" both internally and externally should be called to account.

> For it is not democratic ornaments that matter, nor being a signatory to declarations such as those pertaining to the sovereignty of the people or to human rights, nor even the existence of parliaments and parties or the holding of elections. Such democratic decor has been adopted by some of the most dictatorial regimes in countries where enormous injustices and numerous violations, such as the occupation of other people's land by force, exploitation, and rampant corruption, including bribery and fraud, continue to be legitimated in the name of democracy.

Democracy versus Autocracy

Ghannouchi's critical analysis of liberal democracy is aimed at showing that the root of the malady lies not so much in the mechanisms or institutions of democracy. That is to say not in elections, parliament, and majority rule, pluralism, or press freedom. Rather it lies in the philosophies underpinning a world-view that "drives a wedge between the soul and the body, one that ultimately declares war against God and does everything possible in order to replace Him by man." Human calamities are, therefore, not due to the democratic system or its known mechanisms, which can function successfully and produce a suitable formula to organize the relationship between the governor and the governed. It would seem only prudent to benefit from the procedural aspect of liberal democracy and discard the philosophy underlining it. "For once democratic procedures are firmly established, they have the might to transfer legitimacy from an autocrat such as Louis XIV or any other such dictator who might proclaim 'I am the party' or 'I am the state' to an institution of governance that emanates from, and respects, the will of the people."

But for a democratic regime to succeed in curbing despotism and prevent what Ghannouchi calls modern slavery, it would have to be founded on sound philosophies and noble humanistic values that recognize the spiritual and ethical dimensions of man. If man's humanity is to be preserved, his constant need for, or his inability to do without, his Creator should be recognized. With reference to Bennabi's treatise on Islam and democracy, Ghannouchi asserts that for an ideal model of democracy to be accomplished, a philosophy that recognizes the dignity of man, and protects him from falling into the pits of hegemony and servitude, is an essential prerequisite. As far as he is concerned, such sound philosophy can only be found in Islam. However, in the absence of a fully developed Islamic democratic model, and until such model is put into practice, he has no hesitation to recommend the Western democratic model as a starting point. This perhaps is an example of Ghannouchi's frequent tendency to conduct himself more like a politician than a philosopher. Taking into consideration the current struggle against authoritarianism in various parts of the Muslim region, including his own country, Tunisia, a Western model of liberal democracy would undoubtedly be a better option. For in spite of its "broken promises" liberal democracy remains a "reasonable" system of government whereby the right of the people to self-determination within the democratic state is recognized and respected.

> The flaws inherent in the liberal democratic system should never be used as a pretext for rejecting it, for there is no alternative out there to democracy except dictatorship. An incomplete freedom is always better than no freedom at all, and to be governed by an imperfect democratic order is better than being governed by a despotic order that is the whims and desires of a tyrant.

Notwithstanding his criticism of liberal democracy, not only does Ghannouchi deem it the best available option, but he actually sees in it an excellent mechanism for the realization of the Islamic concept of *shura*. Hence is his implicit criticism of nondemocratic regimes in the Arab World that claim to derive their legitimacy from Islam. He warns Muslims that they should categorically reject the *fatawa* (pl. of *fatwa*: legal opinion) that are issued by "despotic minority regimes who have been so disrespectful of their people." At the same time he condemns as hypocritical Muslim regimes that prohibit elections under the pretext that holding elections would constitute an imitation of the West and an innovation that is rejected by Islam.

It is not unusual for Ghannouchi, especially when giving press interviews or when addressing a non-academic audience, to speak of liberal democracy in the most favorable terms raising few, if any, of the aforementioned objections to the philosophy underpinning it. He does so usually when he speaks as the leader of Ennahda, that is as a politician whose most immediate concern is to draw attention to, and perhaps lobby support for, his movement's struggle against authoritarianism. Some observers may see this as a source of tension in his discourse. It has indeed been a point frequently raised by his critics as shall be discussed in the final chapter. In an article published in *The Observer*, Ghannouchi wrote: "If by democracy is meant the liberal model of government prevailing in the West, a system under which the people freely choose their rep-resentatives and leaders, in which there is an alternation of power and in which civil liberties and human rights are guaranteed, Muslims will find nothing in their religion to prevent them from applying democracy."[74]

Ghannouchi's enthusiasm and commitment to democracy is beyond suspicion. The seeming tension in his discourse on democracy can easily be resolved by taking into consideration the fact that when he talks about democracy he sometimes does so with only its procedural aspect in mind. At other times, and that is when he is quite critical of it, he speaks of the philosophies underpinning it. It is the former that he has in mind when he warns "it would not be in the interest of Muslims to imagine an incom-patibility between democracy and Islam."[75]

Ghannouchi's theory of compatibility between Islam and democracy stems from the assumption that government in Islam embodies a civilian authority whose political conduct is answerable to the public. It would follow that there would be no place for theocracy in Islam because policy-makers could, and ought to, be opposed or criticized by individuals or groups if their policy-making were thought to be ill-advised or mis-guided. Stemming from the concept of al-amr bil-ma'ruf wan-nahy 'anil-munkar (enjoin-ing good and forbidding evil) is the conviction that standing up to the authorities when they go wrong, or endeavoring to correct them, is one of the most important duties in Islam. Muslims are enjoined by their religion to have recourse to shura as a principle for governing relations between the political authority and the people. It would, there-fore, be advisable for today's Muslims to find in democracy the appropriate instruments (elections, parliamentary system, separation of powers, etc.) to institutionalize and imple-ment shura. The implementation of this fundamental Islamic principle at the level of the state has been suspended, or at least limited, for many centuries. In order to pro-mote the democratic idea in a milieu that has at times been extremely hostile to it, Ghannouchi argues that even from a pragmatic point of view, and to serve its own in-terests, the Islamic movement should advocate democracy because the only other alter-native would be dictatorship. He stressed that having become the main opposition group in most Arab societies and consequently the main target of persecution and repression by dictatorial regimes, the Islamic movement stands to benefit most from democracy. On the one hand, democracy represents the hope of salvation and deliverance from exclusion and persecution. On the other, it represents a peaceful means of empower-ment because the Islamic movement represents the majority whereas despotic govern-ment represents the minority. But above all "democracy is needed for its worth. It is the set of mechanisms that Muslims can greatly benefit from today in order to re-establish their own modern shura-based system of government."[76]

Foundations of Islamic Democracy

It is this shura-based system of government for which the rest of Ghannouchi's Al-Hurriyat is dedicated. Chapter four of the book is a detailed description of what he calls the basic principles of Islamic government. His method in discussing the concept and the funda-mentals of state and government in Islam is to invoke the opinions of classical as well as contemporary Islamic scholars, thinkers, and movement leaders and then sum up, emphasizing the opinion he deems to carry more weight. More recently, Ghannouchi has written a number of papers and addressed academic and political conferences in several European countries on the question of state and government in Islam. I have translated much of this material into English. So far as these papers or lectures convey the gist of what he has written in chapter four of *Al-Hurriyat* they may, in the course of this discussion, be referred to instead.

The Islamic system of government, which Ghannouchi advocates and proclaims to be the ultimate project of the modern Islamic revivalist movement, is said by him to be characteristically bound by a set of divine guidelines. It is a system that is aimed at achieving justice and peace in the world. The philosophy behind this is that Islam is God's final Word to humanity, and is therefore, by necessity, a comprehensive and global message of mercy and justice to all mankind. An important component of this message is the body of laws known as *Shari'ah*. Ghannouchi explains that *Shari'ah*, which he sometimes defines as a set of broad guidelines as opposed to a body of laws, is entirely fair and merciful, having been revealed by God for the purpose of serving and guarding the interests of humanity.[77] As such, *Shari'ah* transcends the limits of time and place. This is the underpinning of *'ilm usul al-fiqh* (the science of the fundamentals), founded by Imam Ash-Shafi'i (d. 819), and *'ilm al-maqasid* (the science of purposes), founded by Imam Ash-Shatibi (d. 1388). Both of these sciences are of crucial importance to Ghannouchi in his endeavor to find within *Shari'ah* itself the precepts of an Islamic democratic system of governance. This is crucial simply because no political theory can be considered Islamic if formulated outside the domain of *Shari'ah*. It would simply be illegitimate from an Islamic point of view.

Ghannouchi has relied on, and greatly benefited from Imama Ash-Shatibi's theory of *al-masalih* (pl. of *maslahah*, exigency, requirement or interest).[78] Ghannouchi's fascination with Ash-Shatibi's theory lies in what he sees as its applicability to various aspects of *Shari'ah*, which according to Ash-Shatibi serves to protect five major exigencies: faith, life, mind, progeny, and property. Drawing on Ash-Shatibi, Ghannouchi refers to guidelines and regulations the objective of which is the maintenance of basic human interests and protecting them from infringement or corruption. "These guidelines and regulations together form a framework, which is spacious enough to comprise all known fundamental rights such as the right to life, to freedom of choice, to education, to owning property, and to participate in public life, and in the establishment of a just system of government."[79]

Concept of the State

Before discussing the Islamic concept of state, Ghannouchi provides the readers of, *Al-Hurriyat* with a description of what he calls the "Western concept of state." What is clearly of interest for him here is not a historical account of how the modern state came to being, but rather an investigation of its characteristic features. He begins by asking: "If the Islamic state is inspired by divine revelation, then what is it that inspires the modern Western state?" Since the Western state is said to be a state of law, it is with law that Ghannouchi chooses to begin his analysis.[80]

On the basis of what he refers to as anthropological evidence, he points out that no community of humans has ever been void of some kind of deities to whom community members showed some degree of submission. It was out of this submission to a Supreme Being that the concept of "law" evolved. The divine will referred to frequently by clerics had been the essence of law and the source of its respect. The very early foundations of law had been the same as those of religion. In religious societies law evolved out of religion and was identified with it to the extent that the clergy were themselves the law-makers. The transformation, in many civilizations, of religion into an institution that monopolizes the interpretation of religious texts, and that speaks in the name of God, had tempted monarchs to exploit the expanding influence of the religious institution so as to bestow sanctity on their own authorities. Gradually, the will of a monarch had become the Will of God, and the rule of law had become confused with the will of the ruler, who from then on had no hesitation to proclaim "I am the state, I am the shadow of God on earth." In what amounted to a race for power and influence, clergymen claimed that they alone spoke for religion. The result was catastrophic for both religion and politics. Such was the very foundation of despotism.

Ghannouchi finds it unsurprising that for two centuries political revolutions in the West focused on liberating the law from the grips of clerics and monarchs in order to effect a transition from autocratic rule to the rule of law. Their ultimate objective was to strip from monarchs the sovereignty and hegemony they claimed to have acquired directly from God. They sought to limit the powers of kings and clerics, and to transfer such sovereignty to the people, or to their representatives. The transfer from autocracy to the rule of law is the essence of the modern Western state for which it is deservedly described as the state of law. This democratic state, Ghannouchi explains, is founded on two main pillars: legitimacy and sovereignty, where legitimacy is the adherence of the authority to a law that is made in accordance with a recognized procedure and that is valid irrespective of the number or identity of the rulers. In such a state, the conduct of government is subject to fixed and firm rules, which citizens not only expect the government to observe but also have the right to complain against any violations of the same before an independent panel of judges. In other words, not only does the government have to refrain from any act that violates the established legal system, but also it has necessarily to respect "the basic values and sublime objectives of society." It has furthermore to do its best in order to serve the people so as to guarantee their voluntary acceptance of the regime, its legislation, and its justice system.

Sovereignty, in contrast, is said by Ghannouchi to mean that the state is the supreme authority above which no authority exists, especially in the field of legislation. It is an authority that rules over all and surmounts all. Sovereignty is the property of the ruling authority, whether in the image of a person or an institution, which possesses the legislative power in society. By virtue of its empowerment, and enjoying the capacity to make or change legislation, this authority emerges as the supreme legislator to whom all other authorities submit. In the Middle Ages, he maintains, the pope exercised this supreme authority in his capacity as Christ's deputy. Long before that, Constantine's will was the power of the law. Then the modern state emerged as the inheritor of such sovereignty.

As Ghannouchi sees it, the modern state possesses the supreme legislative in two ways. The first is by virtue of the absence of any higher authority. The second is because its authority is undisputed. So, whereas the state's sovereignty in the internal sphere is absolute, its sovereignty in the external sphere means total independence in conducting relations with other nations. This, he observes, would include the right to declare war and even annex the territories seized from a defeated enemy. Furthermore, the concept of sovereignty is a legal one. It is intended to bestow legitimacy on law, which itself is the product of the sovereign, whether a person or an institution.

In his assessment, the state in the Western conception is the beginning and the end of everything; it is sovereign above all and is required to justify its decisions to no other party. In spite of the historic accomplishments associated with it (including upholding the rule of law, checking rulers' conduct, recognizing people's rights, guaranteeing the freedom of expression, and establishing a separation of powers), the Western concept of the state is tarnished. It is this very conception, in Ghannouchi's opinion, which led to devastating wars, to the persecution of the weak by the strong, to the rise of fascist, Nazi, and Proletariat dictatorships, and to providing a justification for tyranny and colonialism. Furthermore, the principles of legitimacy (which he defines as the submission of the state to the law) and sovereignty (which he defines as the belief that the state's legislative authority is supreme) leave many problems unresolved. The fundamental problem is how to curb the willful desire of man to dominate others and exploit their basic need to be part of an organized community. He sees no satisfactory solution to this problem within the framework of the Western concept of the state. In fact, Ghannouchi echoes a problem that has preoccupied political thinkers over the ages. For if a state is sovereign when its rulers owe allegiance to no superior power and are themselves supreme within the local legal order,[81] and if a government is legitimate when the majority of those governed by it believe that it has authority and that it properly should have that authority,[82] then not only are we dealing with concepts that are a matter of degree but whose establishment depends very much on the sources of empowerment, which in turn are subject to a number of factors that may vary not only from one environment to another but also from culture to culture. It is here, perhaps, where a fundamental difference exists between the Islamic and liberal conceptions of both sovereignty and legitimacy.

An Islamic Concept of the State

In his discussion of the Islamic concept of state, Ghannouchi begins with the elementary supposition that for humans to live in decency and security, they need to be part of a community. A community in turn requires some form of an authority to organize relations and administer justice among individual members. When an authority derives its laws and regulations from *Shari'ah* it is said to be Islamic.[83] By authority, Ghannouchi presumably means government. Nevertheless, a reader of Ghannouchi might easily notice that his usage of the terms "state" and "government" is not consistent, and on several occasions the term "state" means government. The likely explanation for this discrepancy is the high degree of overlap between the two terms in Islamic literature. This issue will be discussed in more detail in chapter six.

For Ghannouchi, Islam is a complete and comprehensive way of life that encompasses economic, social, spiritual, moral, political, diplomatic, and penal aspects. It comprises some detailed laws and regulations that outline specific measures regarding social welfare, the distribution of wealth and inheritance, the organization of family relations, the establishment of justice, *shura* and equality, the protection of right and truth, the prevention of falsehood and evil, and affording support to the weak and the oppressed. Clearly, the concepts of right, truth, falsehood, and evil to which Ghannouchi refers are defined in accordance with Islamic values, though incidentally he regards them to be universal values toward which humans are inclined by instinct. Foremost among these values are the principles of monotheism, justice, and equality:

> The Islamic state's function is to accomplish Islam's objective of creating a "community" that dedicates itself for the establishment of good and justice and for combating evil and oppression. For fourteen centuries, Islam's relationship with the state was never severed; that is since the Prophet—peace be upon him—established the first state in Madina and until the emergence of the secular state in modern times as a product of Western colonialism. It was the Western colonizers who used force to replace *Shari'ah* law by Western law in the Lausanne Treaty. This was only possible with the collaboration of an elite, including people like Bourguiba and Ataturk, that viewed Islam just as a secular Christian would view his religion, considering it to be an obstacle that hinders progress and development.[89]

Ghannouchi acknowledges that numerous studies have been made to either prove or disprove concepts such as the Islamic state, the Islamic economy, Islamic education, Islamic international policy, and human rights in Islam.[85] In fact, questioning the very existence of the concept of state in Islam by Muslim writers, such as Ali Abd-ur-Raziq (1888–1966),[86] started after the official collapse of the Ottoman caliphate in 1924. Since then, Islamic political writers have tended to indulge in the painstaking task of proving that such a concept had been in existence.[87] In the meantime, and amid a growing popular support for an Islam-based social order, Islamic groups and parties have emerged throughout the Muslim world for the purpose of reinstating the *khilafah* (caliphate). The determination of these various groups to struggle for the reestablishment of an Islamic state is cited by Ghannouchi as an indication that it constitutes an integral part of Islam as they understand it.[88]

In support of the theory that an Islamic concept of state does exist, Ghannouchi argues that by virtue of the unique multi-dimensional nature of Islam, being a faith, a code of conduct, and a set of guidelines for a system of government, a state is an essential requirement. For without it an Islamic way of life cannot be fully established. He further argues that the failure to set up such a state inevitably undermines religion itself, whose laws remain ineffective and whose objectives remain unaccomplished.[89]

Ghannouchi substantiates his argument with what he describes as an irrefutable proof from history. It took the emerging Muslim community in Mecca only thirteen years to establish an Islamic state in Madina. The first Islamic state comprised all the required criteria, namely a people, a territory, a government, and a law.[90] It lasted fourteen centuries and only collapsed when Muslims relaxed their commitment to Islam, thus granting foreign intervention an opportunity to deal a fatal blow to their political order.[91] He explains that the Islamic mission during the time of the Prophet passed through two stages. There was no state in the Meccan stage, where the Islamic community lacked authority and had no sovereignty over the land. Meccan leaders felt threatened by the new religion, which promised justice, equality, and the abolition of all forms of discrimination whether on the basis of color, race, or wealth. When it became apparent that Mecca did not qualify as a base for his state, the Prophet started searching in earnest for an alternative location to set up his base. He met in the eleventh year of his mission with a delegation from Yathrib, the pre-Islamic name of Madina. The delegation consisted of twelve men and women, who embraced Islam and pledged allegiance to the Prophet. This was known as the first *bay'ah* (homage contract) of 'Aqaba (the name of the location where the meeting took place). In the following year, a larger delegation comprised of seventy-three men and women arrived from Yathrib. The delegates met the Prophet and concluded with him what is known as the second *bay'ah* of 'Aqaba, proclaimed the most important contract in the history of Islam because it laid the foundations for the Islamic state in Madina. The Prophet was promised by the delegation that once in Madina he would be protected and defended by its people as much as they would protect and defend their own wealth and kin. Upon his arrival in the first capital of Islam, the Prophet was received as head of state.[92]

A clear distinction is made here between the first contract and the second. The first, Ghannouchi explains, was a recognition that Muhammad was a prophet, an acceptance of Islam as a religion. The second, however, recognized Muhammad as a political leader and pledged to support him in building the state. The Prophet is, therefore, said to have long preceded European Renaissance thinkers in establishing the Islamic state and society on a contract to which all groups within and around Madina were by free choice signatories. Several Arab and Jewish tribes lived in and around the city. It had also become home for the *al-muhajirun*, the immigrants, who fled persecution and oppression in Mecca. The Prophet, in his capacity as the political leader and head of state, drew a constitution known as the *Sahifah* (document), which organized relations among the various components of the new community. The articles of the constitution can be summarized as follows:

- Islam is the source of law and order, and each sect, or distinct religious community, maintains the right to administer the personal affairs of its own members;
- All groups recognize the Prophet as the head of state;
- All groups pledge to take part in defending the state and be loyal to it, and the state pledges to administer justice and protect the rights of groups and individuals;
- Tribal and blood-related preferences or concessions are repealed, and the community of Madina is one single *Ummah*, Arabs and non-Arabs, Muslims and non-Muslims.[93]

It would seem that Ghannouchi's definition of the state is compatible with the idea of the state in international law: an association of persons, living in a determinate part of the earth's surface, legally organized and personified, and associated for their own government. In the example given above, the association of persons comprised the Muslims, both those who came from Mecca and those who embraced Islam in Madina, and the Jews and the pagans whose tribes and rights were stated in the *Sahifah*. The part of earth was the province of Madina, which had well recognized borders. The legal instrument was the *Sahifah*, which amounted to a constitution that organized relations and determined the rights and duties of community members or "citizens" of the state. The government was headed by the Prophet.[94] However, what was peculiar about this very first model of the Islamic state is that it was a city state and was not distinguishable from the *Ummah*. The differentiation of the *Ummah* into state and civil society, according to Ghannouchi, started following the death of the Prophet. The territory under Muslim rule started expanding and the population increased very rapidly. As a safety valve against absolutism, power was divided between the caliph and society. This theory will be discussed in more detail in chapter seven.

For a system of government to be Islamic, it would have to be founded on a set of fundamental principles, which Ghannouchi maintains characterized the first model of Islamic government, which lasted until about the middle of the first century of Islamic history. These are the very same principles upon which, he suggests, a modern Islamic democracy would have to be founded.[95]

Vicegerency

The first of these fundamental principles is the belief that man is God's vicegerent on earth. It is the belief that humans have been honored by their Creator and gifted with the faculties of the mind and will power. Everything else in the universe has been created for the purpose of serving them and achieving their happiness. The divine honor bestowed on them confers upon them rights that no one else has the right to deny or violate. Humans, in their capacity as vicegerents of their Creator, are expected to defend their God-given rights and struggle to preserve them.[96] It is here where Ghannouchi finds a fundamental difference between the Islamic world-view and that of the Western civilization. It is the difference of maintaining, as opposed to severing, the link between man and God. The Islamic vision is based on the belief that divine revelation has been intended to serve the interest of humanity, and that the most pertinent interest of all is the administration of justice. This is illustrated in statements such as that of Ibn Al-Fahim whom Ghannouchi quotes as saying: "The subject matter of *Shari'ah*-based policy is justice, although no provision in respect of it was revealed. This is so because God has sent His Messengers and revealed His Books in order to administer fairly the affairs of the people. This is the justice on which the heavens and earth are based and according to which if the signs of truth become apparent and its face is revealed, in whatever way possible, then it is there that God's law and religion are to be found." He also quotes Ibn as-Salah as saying: "*Shari'ah*-based policy is defined as every measure that directs people nearest to rightness and furthest from corruption, even if such policy was not prescribed by a revelation nor was a revelation made in respect of it. The way that leads to justice is the way of religion."[97]

In contrast, Western political thought, Ghannouchi observes, is the fruit of rationalist philosophy and the principles of natural law.

> It is also the product of the grinding war, which took place in the West between reason and religion. It is the product of the conflict between two antagonists. There was on the one hand the struggle for freedom, self-determination, and the right to enjoy the goodness of this world on the basis of the centrality of man in the universe and the absolute ability of reason to understand and explain the universe and to organize life. On the other hand, there was the church and its despotic authority, which it exercised for many centuries of darkness, backwardness, and oppression. Reason and science eventually won the war. As a result the people recovered their rights and rid themselves of the church's control over man's mind and conscience and over the organization of life. In the end, natural law replaced God's revelation as the philosophical basis for legislation.[98]

Freedom and Responsibility

Pointing to the wisdom of choosing Arabia as the birthplace of Islam, Ghannouchi explains that no other place at the time could have guaranteed the people's freedom of choice, and thus the establishment and spread of the new religion. While absolute governing systems existed in neighboring regions, where ancient civilizations existed, no absolute authority controlled the Hijaz province in Arabia.[99]

Stressing that the concept of freedom in Islam is a fundamental one, Ghannouchi cites agreement among authoritative Muslim jurists that there is no responsibility without sanity and freedom.[100] Not only has this concept contributed to the progress of Muslims, who built a great civilization, but it had a considerable impact on Western thought as well. Ghannouchi subscribes to the theory that through direct contact with the Muslims in the Arab East during the days of the crusaders, as well as in Spain and southern Italy, the Europeans were fascinated by the lifestyle of the Muslims. Compared to the medieval European lifestyle, the Muslims had freedom, dignity, and motivation. This influence contributed to the revival of the spirit of rebellion against the theocratic shackles imposed on the European mind, conscience, and social conduct, and was the spark that ignited the Renaissance.[101]

Together with reason and will, the right to freedom of choice is a basic requirement of vicegerency. But Ghannouchi points out that freedom of choice is referred to in the Islamic text mostly in the negative, that is by way of forbidding compulsion. The Qur'an clearly states: "There is no compulsion in religion" (2:256); "As for thee, wilt thou force men to become believers?" (10:99); and "Thou art not in authority over their conscience"(88:22).[102]

Because of the great influence belief has on all aspects of individual and collective behavior, freedom of faith, and what it entails in terms of freedom of thought and expression, is the basis of freedoms and rights in Islam. If man does really have the freedom of faith and if compulsion is forbidden, even unimaginable, then compulsion in everything below that is forbidden *a fortiori*. Compulsion in marriage, in work, in associating, or in choosing where to live is prohibited. The fundamental element is that man is free and constricting his freedom is an exception.[103]

With reference to the Universal Declaration of Human Rights, which states that humans are born free and equal in dignity and rights, Ghannouchi maintains that this principle is originally Islamic. A similar, but stronger, phrase is attributed to 'Umar ibn al-Khattab, the second of the four Rightly Guided Caliphs who succeeded the Prophet as heads of state. He is quoted as saying: "How could you enslave people when they were born free?" It is reported that he said so in support of an Egyptian Copt citizen of the Muslim state, reprimanding Amr ibn Al-'Aas, a well-known army commander and a companion of the Prophet, whose son humiliated the Copt's son. The caliph judged that the Copt had the right to *qisas* (judicial remedy). In doing so, Omar emphasized his citizens' right to dignity and to equality before the law irrespective of differences in creed.[104]

However, God-given freedom to man in the Islamic conception is not supposed to be absolute permissiveness nor is it supposed to be a heedless and spontaneous thrust to fulfil desires. It is primarily a responsibility and a realization. It is one's responsibility toward one's conscience, Creator, and fellow humans. For in addition to bearing within him an aspect of the spirit of God, man has inherent within him desires and ambitions that could lead him to misery and hardship in this life and in the Hereafter if he did not subdue them by means of a divine guidance. While Islam clearly affirms man's status, freedom, and enormous abilities, it underlines his weaknesses. For this purpose, Ghannouchi affirms, God sent messengers who urged humans to respond to their Lord's call warning them against the repercussions of being tempted to rebel against their Creator under the pretext of asserting their independence. "A free man, who is truly God's vicegerent, is he who worships God by contemplating the wonders of His creation in the heavens and the earth and in himself and who exploits the resources made available to him in this universe, enjoys its bounties, and meets the needs of his body, soul, and society in a balanced manner without excessiveness."[105]

Justice

Justice in Arabic is 'adalah or 'adl from the root 'adala, which means to be balanced, to engage in acts that are framed by an awareness, born of the pursuit of reason over passion. The opposite of 'adalah is zulm (injustice or oppression) from the root zalama, which means to do wrong or evil, to ill-treat or oppress, to harm or commit an outrage or to darken. An Islamic political order is supposed to prohibit all forms of injustice. Not only is injustice considered a grave sin, an atrocious crime, and a cause for decline and destruction, but it is considered to be an aggression against God Himself.[106] Islam's main mission is the administration of justice and the elimination of all forms of oppression. One of the main tasks of the community of believers is to deter injustice and support the wronged. Ghannouchi subscribes to the Islamic school of thought that advocates that Islam only permits the use of force in self-defense when all other means of deterring aggression have failed. This conviction is based on the Qur'anic verse: "Fight in the Cause of Allah those who fight you, but do not transgress limits, for Allah loves not transgressors" (2:190). Stressing that Islam prescribes fighting to deter aggression and endorses the principle of self-defense and the combating of tyranny,[107] Ghannouchi quotes Ali Belhaj, the imprisoned leader of the Islamic Salvation Front in Algeria, as saying: "An example of such aggression and tyranny is the oppression of Muslims who work peacefully for promoting the message of Islam and for establishing its law. The victims of abuse and aggression have every right to defend themselves. Islam is a religion of peace, but not a religion of capitulation and subjugation to tyrants."[108]

In accordance with the concept of al-amr bil-ma'ruf wan-nahy 'anil-munkar (enjoining good and forbidding evil), Ghannouchi regards it the responsibility of each member of the Muslim community to participate in the task of deterring injustice. "This is what prompted a great scholar such as Ibn Taymiyah to conclude that God may support a just state even if it were non-Muslim and may bring defeat unto the unjust state even if it were Muslim."[109]

Legitimacy

According to Ghannouchi, an Islamic state derives legitimacy from two sources: an-nass, defined by him as the combination of the Qur'an and the Sunnah (Prophet's sayings and actions); and *shura*.[110] The *an-nass*, expressed also as the full acceptance of and compliance with the commands and rules of the *Shari'ah*, is the supreme authority from which an Islamic system of government derives its philosophy, values, legislation, and ends.[111] *Shura*, which is frequently translated as council or consultation, is the second source of legitimacy.

Shari'ah

An-nass, or divine revelation, represented in the Qur'an and the Sunnah, constitutes what Ghannouchi calls the document of vicegerency, or in more modern terms the power of attorney by virtue of which authority is acquired and the affairs of the human community are managed.[112] It is within the framework of divine revelation that *ijtihad* and innovative thinking take place. While the scripture perpetuates the existence of Islamic society, *shura* is the mechanism by virtue of which society materializes and develops. Ghannouchi makes a clear distinction between the authority of *Shari'ah* (rule of Islamic law), whose supremacy as the source of legitimacy is unquestionable, and *fiqh* (jurisprudence), *fikr* (thought), and *tafsir* (interpretation), which are tools or mechanisms that collectively make up the process of translating divine principles into practical measures. All forms of comprehension and interpretation lie within the realm of *ijtihad*, and can therefore be accepted or rejected by the *Ummah*. In other words, the applicability of an *ijtihad* always depends on its acceptability. This once more confirms that no theocratic authority exists in Islam, and that no one can claim to have the sole right to interpret religious texts or to speak in the name of the Heavens or to be God's shadow on earth.[113]

The authority of *Shari'ah* is supposed to surpass any other authority in the Muslim society. Consequently, an Islamic state can best be described as a state of law. By virtue of its divine origin, law in an Islamic state acquires sanctity not conferred upon it in any other state, and this has a significant implication for the concept of sovereignty. Ghannouchi contends that the concept of sovereignty widely adopted in Western political thought, and defined as "the supreme, irresistible, absolute, and uncontrolled authority," is rather vague with regard to determining the sovereign in the case of the modern Western state. Nevertheless, the definition of the concept perfectly applies to the status of *Shari'ah* in the Islamic state with regard to its supremacy, sanctity, absolute neutrality, and perfect knowledge of its source. Unlike the "sovereign" in liberal democracy, assuming it to be the parliament, whose decisions bear within them the source of their legitimacy as well as immunity to objection, *Shari'ah* is immune from abuse so long as interpreting it is not monopolized by a political body or power. The adoption of what he describes as "catastrophic decisions" by parliaments and the frequent subjugation of members of parliament to what he calls "pressures" and/or "allurements" are some of the failures of the Western tradition. These failures are consequent to granting absolute powers to legislators who in turn assume the role of God.[114] Clearly, he means to suggest that an Islamic model of democracy would avoid such failures because of the restricting role played by *Shari'ah*.

Shura

The second source of legitimacy in an Islamic state is *shura*. Simply translated, *shura* means council or consultation. However, to Ghannouchi it means much more. At its highest level it is the principle that the power of interpreting the text is not to be monopolized by any one particular person or institution; interpretation is the prerogative of the entire *Ummah*, the vicegerent of God. The *Ummah* collectively and unitedly deputizes for God in implementing His law, the *Shari'ah*, and is therefore held responsible by Him and is accountable to Him. The *Ummah* can be defined as an *'aqidah* (faith) embodied in a *jama'ah* (community) of humans. In order to facilitate the proper and smooth implementation of *Shari'ah*, the *Ummah* establishes a *dawlah* (state), whose *hukumah* (government) is accountable to it. The *Ummah* should, ideally, have the power to set up, advise, direct, and dismiss the *hakim* (governor). The powers delegated by the *Ummah* to the *hukumah* are limited, just enough to empower it to carry out the set of tasks pertaining to the implementation of certain aspects of *Shari'ah*. This in modern terms, Ghannouchi suggests, may be equated to the task of law enforcement. Apart from that, the *Ummah* retains its responsibility *of al-amr bil-ma'ruf wan-nahy 'anil-munkar* (to enjoin good and forbid evil) and to establish the institutions necessary for serving the community and defending its interests. In other words, the *Ummah* does not retire once a *hukumah* is appointed; the *hukumah* only takes charge of tasks that individuals and groups are incapable of carrying out. Hence is the assertion that the Islamic political order is neither theocratic nor totalitarian. It is not theocratic because the *Ummah* is responsible. It is not totalitarian because not only does the *Ummah* concede very little power to the *hukumah* but also because sovereignty, within the framework of the supremacy of the *an-nass*, lies with the *Ummah* and not with the *dawlah*.[115]

The usage of the terms *dawlah* (state) and *hukumah* (government) exhibit a high degree of overlapping, not only in Ghannouchi's writings but in most modern Islamic literature. The reason for this phenomenon is probably the fact that both terms in their modern connotations are quite new. *Dawlah* is derived from a root word that means to rotate, alternate, or take turns. Whereas its Turkish derivative, *devlet*, strictly means state and its Persian derivative, *dawlat*, sometimes refers to government, in modern Arabic the term corresponds to the modern concept of the state. *Hukumah* as government is a nineteenth-century neologism adopted as Muslims became increasingly aware of and interested in European forms of government. As in European usage, *hukumah* is now understood as the group of individuals who exercise the authority of the state. In classical Arabic usage, *hukumah* had the broad sense of adjudication; it referred to the dispensation of justice. Government in the narrow sense was referred to as *wilayah* (from the primary meaning of closeness to something, hence administration or government). In traditional Islamic juristic writings, the state does not itself exist as a corporate institution with legal personality; governmental institutions are shown to be legitimate because they implement *Shari'ah* and not because they are authorized by a state possessed of its own legal authority.[116] The distinction between the two terms is more problematic for Islamic thinkers and writers because such a distinction in contemporary Arabic thought reflects the political and legal secularization undergone by post-colonial Western-type territorial states.

According to Ghannouchi it is the *Ummah*, being the vicegerent of God, that is awarded supreme authority and is assigned the task of establishing justice and combating oppression and corruption. He suggests that the *Ummah* exercise *shura* at two levels.

1. At the legislative level, the *Ummah* participates effectively in enacting the necessary bylaws and regulations for applying or accommodating revealed divine guidelines

to changing circumstances. Some divine laws assume the form of broad guidelines that provide the Muslim *Ummah* with a comfortable margin for interpretation without undermining the integrity or losing the essence of the revealed text.[117] In fact, not all the laws which form the subject matter of conventional Muslim jurisprudence *(fiqh)* rest on injunctions expressed in clear-cut terms of command and prohibition in the Qur'an and the Sunnah. By far the larger part of *fiqh* rulings is the outcome of various deductive methods of reasoning, among which *qiyas* (deduction through analogy) figures most prominently.[118] *Shari'ah* refrains deliberately from providing detailed regulations for the entire manifold changing requirements of social existence. The need for continuous temporal legislation is, therefore, self-evident. In an Islamic state, this legislation would relate to the many problems of administration not touched upon by *Shari'ah* at all, as well as the problems with regard to which *Shari'ah* has provided general principles but no detailed laws. In either instance it is up to the *Ummah* to evolve the relevant detailed legislation through an exercise of independent reasoning *(ijtihad)* in consonance with the spirit of Islamic law and the best interests of the *Ummah*.[119]

The most notable advantage of exercising what Ghannouchi refers to as private and public *shura*, is that the *Ummah* stands on a common ground of unity and consensus and is protected from straying. However, he points out that Islam has not outlined a specific formula for the public's involvement in running the affairs of the *Ummah*. By leaving this open, Islam renders it possible for the Muslim intellect to endeavor to deduce diverse legislative formulae and benefit from human experiences, such as in the election of the members of *ahl-ul-hal wal-'aqd*, the traditional Islamic equivalent of the elected representatives of the people in modern parliaments. The representation of the *Ummah* can be further consolidated by the creation of an institution, or institutions, whose members are elected from among senior judges and scholars. The function of such an institution would be to act as a constitutional control over parliament in order to guarantee its adherence to the Islamic constitution, which stipulates that all legislative and executive bodies must abide by *Shari'ah*. This is comparable in Western systems to the constitutional control exercised by a supreme court or equivalent institution.[120]

The *Ummah* exercises its legislative authority within the framework of *Shari'ah* in various forms including deputizing, as explained above, and direct *shura* by means of plebiscites to settle vital issues such as pacts, and electing the head of state and the members of the *shura* council. These forms also include individual *ijtihad* as well as collective *ijtihad* by groups, universities, mosques, the media, and specialized institutions. Such practice provides the *Ummah* with ample space for deliberation, making choices, and asserting preferences.[121]

2. At the political level, the *imamah* (leadership) is a contract between the *Ummah* and the ruler by virtue of which the latter pledges to implement the law and administer the affairs of the former. No ruler is legitimate without having been commissioned or contracted to do the job by the *Ummah*, to whom the ruler is accountable. Ghannouchi notes here that only the Shiites differed from the rest of the Muslims in assigning the *imamah* to Ali and eleven of his descendants. In doing so, they completely wrote off the practice of *shura*. However, he does recognize that in modern times the Shiites have developed a new *ijtihad* that has brought them much closer to the rest of the Muslims, reinstating *shura* as an integral element of the Islamic system of governance. This is obviously a reference to the reforms introduced by Khomeyni and his successors to Shiite

political thought and the practical measures taken in Iran to consolidate the practice of *shura*. The adoption by the modern Shiite state in Iran of the mechanisms of Western liberal democracy is seen as an example of inevitable transformation. While the idea of setting up an elected parliament and an elected council of senior scholars is Islamic in essence, the methods and means have come from the Western tradition. By employing such methods and benefiting from the experiences of liberal democracy, contemporary Muslims can develop the concept of *shura*, at the political level, to produce Islamic forms of democratic practice.[122]

Conclusion

Ghannouchi conceives of democracy as a political system that derives legitimacy from the public and that accords the ruled the right to choose, audit and, when necessary, replace the ruler by means of mechanisms that may vary from one democratic regime to another. However, all such democratic models share in common the mechanism of free election. For him, democracy establishes the principle of the alternation of power through the ballot box, guarantees a number of basic liberties for the public, such as the freedom of expression and the freedom of forming political parties, and protects the independence of the judiciary. Democracy is a mechanism that guarantees the sovereignty of the people over the ruling regime and that accomplishes a number of important values that shield the public against injustice and despotism.[123]

Ghannouchi's main interest has been to stress the need for democracy, to prove its compatibility with Islam, and to analyze the obstacles hindering its success in the Arab region. He acknowledges, however, that democracy is blemished by "broken promises." In so doing, he echoes the concerns of some Western authorities on democracy. Bobbio, for instance, spoke of the "broken promises" in terms of the gap that exists between the ideal of democracy as it was conceived by its founding fathers and the reality of democracy as it exists today.[124] For Bobbio, the broken promises include "the survival of invisible power, the persistence of oligarchies, the suppression of mediating bodies, the renewed vigor in the representation of particular interests, the break-down of participation, and the failure to educate citizens (or to educate them properly)." The most serious of these, especially with specific reference to Italy, is "the presence (and robust constitution) of invisible power which survives alongside visible power." Since one of democracy's defining characteristics is the "visibility" or transparency of power, Bobbio considers "the continued existence of oligarchies or of elites in power" to be incompatible with democratic ideals.[125] However, some of these broken promises, according to Bobbio, could not objectively be kept and were thus illusions from the outset. Some others were not so much promises as misplaced hopes, or simply have come up against unforeseen obstacles.

Ghannouchi adds to these broken promises a major failure in the attitude of democratic governments in the West toward other countries. He sees a major problem in the fact that the privileges of the democratic system, including liberties and rights, are exclusive; they are not extended to those who live beyond the borders of the nation concerned.[126]

Ghannouchi hopes that an Islamic model of democracy, once devised, will fill this gap. Nevertheless, he is not oblivious of the fact that the "ideal" may never be accomplished in reality.

According to our faith, an ideal is only accomplishable in the Hereafter. In this world, what matters is that we quest for the ideal. What also matters is that no contradiction is created between the ideal and reality, because such a condition in the eyes of Islam would be hypocrisy. What we believe in, as Muslims, is that we are expected by God to make every possible effort in order to pursue the ideal. This is only possible in as much as human resources permit, and these are limited.

As for the mechanisms devised by Western democracy, Ghannouchi believes that they are good and can be improved. According to him, the real problem with Western democracy lies not in these mechanisms but in the fuel that feeds them. It lies in the materialist philosophy that eventually transformed these mechanisms, through the role played by finance and the media, into ploys, ultimately producing choices that represent not the people but influential financial and political centers.

The Islamic contribution would, according to Ghannouchi, be primarily in the form of a code of ethics, a transcendent morality that seems to have no place in today's democratic practice. It is deficiency in such transcendental morality, he warns, that ultimately turns democracy into "rule of the people by the rich and powerful for the interest of the rich and the powerful." He cites the example of elections in the United States, where money, the media, and lobbies play the most crucial role in deciding not only who wins the election but also who runs for office. What Islam provides is not only a set of values for self-discipline and for the refinement of human conduct but also a set of restrictions to combat monopoly and a set of safeguards to protect public opinion.

He is optimistic that by assimilating the Western democratic system, Islam can, for the benefit of humanity, preserve the positive aspects of democracy. This, he suggests, can be achieved by transforming the Islamic principle of *shura*, which implies involving the *Ummah* in government, from a mere admonition, or a set of general principles, to a proper governing institution. This, he envisages, should be similar to what the Western "mind" did with Muslim discoveries in geometry and algebra, developing them "so marvelously into visible technologies; a feature of the Western genius and scientific revolution."

Ghannouchi conceives of civilization as a continuum. Therefore, the progress achieved by any phase in this continuum, whether Greek, Islamic, or European, belongs to the entire humanity. It is upon this consideration that he argues that just as it would be so naive, if not insane, to reject modern industrial technologies just because they were made in the West, it would be insane to reject important Western accomplishments in the field of government and administration. By benefiting from these accomplishments the Muslims will be able to activate, or institutionalize, Islamic political values, such as *shura*, *bay'ah*, *ijma'*, and *al-amr bil-ma'ruf wan-nahy 'anil-munkar*, whose purpose is to establish justice and achieve human happiness.[127]

Like industrial mechanisms, democratic mechanisms should be regarded as universal human accomplishments that can function in diverse cultural climates and can coexist with different intellectual backgrounds. These mechanisms are not to be confused with Western ideologies, such as secularism, nationalism, capitalism, and power-hungry utilitarianism, which eventually lead to the marginalization of religion and the deification of man. These are values within which the Western model of democracy evolved. But they are not absolute prerequisites for the realization of people's sovereignty or for establishing equality among citizens. Nor are they essential conditions for forming a government that is truly representative of the people. Nor are they in themselves guarantees for the continuation of the democratic process. Furthermore, none of the democratic mechanisms, in his assessment, is incompatible with the values of Islam. He argues to the contrary: democratic mechanisms have proven to be the best means for Islamic values to be transformed from a set of lofty ideals to practical solutions applicable to living realities. Similarly, and for optimum viability, the democratic system will find no better values, and no better philosophy, than those offered by Islam.[128]

Ghannouchi hopes that an Islamic model of democracy will arise out of the marriage between democratic tools and Islamic values. This, he is convinced, is not impossible. "The democratic system has worked within the framework of Christian values giving rise to Christian democracies and within the framework of socialist philosophy giving rise to socialist democracies. Why on earth should it not function within the framework of Islamic values to produce an Islamic democracy"?[129]

However, democracy has its enemies, both domestically and internationally, and numerous obstacles hinder its progress. The remaining chapters will deal with what Ghannouchi regards to be the main obstacles facing a transition to democracy in the Arab world, and particularly in the Maghreb region.

4

Secularism

Adherence to democracy, and what it entails of pluralism and the alternation of power through the ballot box, has been Ghannouchi's slogan since he set up *Harakat al-Ittijah al-Islami* (Islamic Tendency Movement, the MTI), in 1981.[1] By the time this explicitly Islamic platform was replaced—in the hope of qualifying for registering as a political party—by Ennahda in 1988, he was glad to see that peaceful means of change through democracy were becoming acceptable to an increasing number of Islamic movements elsewhere in the Arab region.

> In spite of the enormity of the international campaign against what is called fundamentalism or political Islam, which some Jewish, Arab, and Western circles have—for different ends—nominated as the new threat following the collapse of communism, and in spite of the efforts made to associate Islam with terrorism and with detestation of civil rights, democracy, and the West, a tendency within the Islamic current, which an observer's eye cannot miss, and which today attracts the largest section of the Islamic current, is persistently searching for opportunities to work within the framework of law, through society's formal institutions such as parties, associations, and trade syndicates, employing the tools of democratic action through debate, negotiation, election, and accepting the verdict of the ballot box, freedom of expression, and the alternation of power.[2]

He was by then confident that whenever such opportunities of participation in political action were made available to the Islamic current (another way of describing Islamic movements), the Islamic current proved a high degree of respectability, moderation, and responsibility.[3] Ghannouchi cites as examples of ongoing processes in which Islamic movements have taken part those of Jordan, Yemen, Kuwait, Lebanon, and Morocco.[4] He cites as examples of experiments aborted so far those of Iraq, Sudan, Tunisia, and Algeria.[5] The abortion of some of these experiments, especially in his own country in 1989 and in neighboring Algeria in 1992, has not eroded his optimism that one day local, regional, and global changes will take place in favor of democracy. It is only a matter of time for him. Authoritarian regimes, he stresses, have no future. "They are extremely brittle and will eventually decompose."[6] In addition to the political and economic crises, which have subsequently created legitimacy crises in various parts of the Arab world, Ghannouchi's optimism derives from the successes achieved by the Islamists in the cancelled elections of Algeria and Tunisia and in the elections held in Jordan, Kuwait, and Yemen. He sees in these successes a clear indication that if democracy were permitted to develop and take its course in the Arab region, Islam would rule because nothing today has the aptitude to compete with it.[7]

Little work, if any, has been done on transition to democracy in the Arab region.[8] Recent work on transition to, and consolidation of, democracy has focused mainly on three regions: Southern Europe, the southern cone of South America, and post-communist Europe. According to the criteria set by Linz and Stepan, no real transition to democracy has been taking place in the Middle East and North Africa, and that is possibly why this region has been excluded from this field of research so far.

A democratic transition is said to be complete "when sufficient agreement has been reached about political procedures to produce an elected government, when a government comes to power that is the direct result of a free and popular vote, when this government de facto has the authority to generate new policies, and when the executive, legislative, and judicial power generated by the new democracy does not have to share power with other bodies de jure."[9] Some of the encouraging signs of reform witnessed in the late 1980s and early 1990s in some Arab countries fall short of fulfilling these criteria; at best they may only be said to show signs of liberalization. This liberalization is said to entail a mix of policy and social changes such as less censorship of the media, somewhat greater space for the organization of autonomous working-class activities, the introduction of some legal safeguards for individuals, the releasing of political prisoners, the return of exiles, perhaps measures for improving the distribution of income, and toleration of opposition. Democratization, in contrast, is said to entail liberalization but is a wider and more specifically political concept. It requires open contestation over the right to win control of the government, and this in turn requires free competitive elections the results of which determine who governs.[10]

In their work, Linz and Stepan have been primarily concerned with analyzing the conditions and practices that lead to the breakdown of authoritarian regimes, to the process of transition from authoritarian to democratic regimes, and especially to the political dynamics of the consolidation of post-authoritarian democracies. They have come to the conclusion that democracies need five interacting arenas to become consolidated: a lively civil society, relatively autonomous political society, rule of law, a usable state, and economic society.[11] At least one or two of these arenas are found to be missing in any given Arab country. In almost every Arab country, the rule of law is non-existent.

Ghannouchi is of the opinion that serious obstacles hinder transition to democracy, or democratization, in the Arab world, and particularly in North Africa. Democratization to him means "transformation from authoritarian systems of government to democratic systems of government where open contestation over the right to win control of the government through free competitive elections takes place in an atmosphere of respect for basic human rights and the freedom of speech and assembly."[12] He sees that secularization, the territorial state, and intervention by foreign powers are the main obstacles.[13] The foreign powers Ghannouchi refers to constitute what is now known as the new world order that "endeavors to preserve a status quo it deems best suited for serving its interests."[14]

Of the three obstacles, Ghannouchi considers the government-enforced policy of secularization, also referred to by him as "modernization," to be the most formidable. Nevertheless, he recognizes that some obstacles emanate from within the Islamic camp itself. These are represented mainly in the results of the extremist thinking and the overzealous attitude of radical elements within the Islamic movement. He states, however, that such obstacles do not emanate from Islam itself, but are the product of a climate of repression. They are therefore surmountable provided an environment of political freedom prevails. He cites for instance the transformation undertaken by some of the most radical Islamic trends, such as the Salafis in Kuwait and the Gamaat in Egypt, when they were allowed to operate publicly and take part in the democratic process. In both cases, and in spite of their known extremist views, the supposedly radical Islamists chose to struggle for their ideological and political convictions from within the system. They agreed to play the "game" according to the rules set by their own adversaries.[15]

This chapter will discuss Ghannouchi's theory that while transition to democracy in the West was not obstructed by secularization, in the Arab world, the same process produced the exact opposite: dictatorships evolved, and oppression instead of justice, repression instead of freedom, and bankruptcy instead of development prevailed.[16] Such was the outcome of secularization in the Arab world because traditional society, which Ghannouchi equates with civil society and considers to be a precondition for democracy, was destroyed.[17]

The terms *secularism* and *secularization* are not encountered anywhere in Ghannouchi's published works, including *Al-Hurriyat*. He has developed the idea that secularism has been detrimental to traditional society in papers written since he moved to London in 1992.[18] It is noticeable that Ghannouchi uses the term secularization with some laxity. He often uses the terms modernization and Westernization as if they were synonyms, not only of each other, but also of secularization. In his earlier writings, the term Westernization is used in the same context as secularization is used in more recent writings.[19]

Secularism and Secularization

Secularism, which in Arabic is *'ilmaniyah* (from *'ilm*, science) or *'alamaniyah* (from *'alam*, world), is according to Ghannouchi best defined as *dunyawiyah*:[20] that which is worldly, mundane, or temporal. It is a term, he explains, that came to the Muslim world together with other related terms—such as modernity, Westernization, and modernization—within the context of colonialism. While secularism is understood to mean liberating the political from the authority of the religious, all these terms have been used in different contexts to describe the marginalization of Islam, or its exclusion from the process of restructuring society during both the colonial and the post-independence periods.[21] Secularization in the Arab region, and especially in North Africa, has entailed severing society's cultural roots; its objective has been to effect a complete break with the past.[22] Ghannouchi says little more about the origin or the meaning of these terms except to stress that in North Africa they relate more to the French experience, in which—more than anywhere else in the Western world—modernity entailed a break with the past.[23] Undoubtedly, secularism, and for that matter what Ghannouchi considers to be its related terms, are not simple concepts, nor are they without controversy.

In the English literature on secularism and secularization, political theorists and historians agree at least on one fundamental observation, namely that "secularism" is a Christian product. Apart from that it has been defined in a variety of ways. On the one hand it is said to be a reaction or a protest movement.[24] On the other hand, it is said to be a doctrine or an ideology.[25] Its eventual objectives have ranged between denying God and eliminating religion altogether and simply restricting religion to the private sphere and recognizing the existence of a "god" that has no say in people's worldly, or secular, affairs. In any case, the concept cannot be comprehended unless viewed within the context of Europe's evolution and its Christian reform movement. Long before the Renaissance, and deep into the Middle Ages, the term "secular" was used to describe functions that were extra-ecclesiastical, though sanctioned and requested by the religious establishment itself. This was either for practical reasons, because priests could not or did not perform such functions, or out of the necessity of introducing reforms to the institution itself in response to changes in social or political circumstances. In order to survive in the first centuries of its existence, Christianity had to posit the principle of the separation of faith and the city; a separation that ran parallel with the distinction between the world and the body. Christ's injunction of "render unto Caesar"—which became extremely important in St. Paul's writing—added a political dimension to Christianity and the already dual nature of Christ.[26] In the course of religious revival, reform movements, which sought to purge Christianity of cultural, traditional, or superstitious accretions, had an almost explicit secularizing impact. Reform movements such as the Renaissance, humanism, Lutheranism, Calvinism, deism, and unitarianism were all secularizing forces within Christianity, purging faith and practice of immanentist conceptions of deity, progressively applying the canons of reason to doctrine, and reducing mystical, miraculous, sacramental, and sacerdotal claims. In the process, religious institutions ceased to be central in society and religious consciousness diminished.[27]

Coined by George Jacob Holyoake (1817–1906), the term secularism described a nineteenth-century movement that was expressly intended to provide a certain theory of life and conduct without reference to a deity or a future life, thus proposing to fulfil a function of religion, apart from religious associations. Politically, it sprang from the turmoil that preceded the passing of the Reform Bill in 1832.[28] Secularism, whose essential principle is assumed to be seeking for human improvement by material means alone, arose and developed at a period when the relations of science and religion (in Europe) were beginning to be regarded as those of sharp opposition. It proclaims the independence of "secular" truth, arguing that secular knowledge is founded upon the experience of this life and can be maintained and tested by reason at work in experience. It conceives that, just as mathematics, physics, and chemistry are "secular" sciences, so it would be possible on the same lines to establish a secular theory of the conduct and welfare of life, and to add the instruction of the conscience to instruction in the sciences, in a similar manner and on similar conditions.[29] In its mildest forms, secularism deals with the known world interpreted by experience and neither offers nor forbids any opinion regarding another life. It follows, at least theoretically, that unless dogma actively interfered with human happiness, secularism was content to leave it to flourish or perish as it may.[30]

However, through its course, secularism has been intermingled with atheism. Charles Bradlaugh (1833–1891), an associate of Holyoake, considered that secularism was bound to contest theistic belief and that material progress was impossible so long as "superstition" so powerfully manifested itself. Some believe that, in this matter, Bradlaugh acted more consistently than Holyoake did and that his action is confirmed by the fact that secularism was most vigorous when linked with anti-religious views. This position is further bolstered by the assumption that the attempt to ignore, rather than deny, religion is impractical because religion embraces both secular and spiritual concerns. It is argued also that it would be an impossible proposition to maintain that there is a God, but that He does not concern material existence. The assumption that a secularism that does not include a definitely anti-religious theory is bound to fail is believed to have pushed in the direction of complete denial of God.[31]

The intellectual revolution of the nineteenth century, symbolized by the contributions of Freud, Marx, and Nietzsche, involved an advocacy of atheistic thought that effected a significant change in the interpretation of man in the world.[32] It has been argued that even though all traces of the eschatological view were not eradicated in this secular thought, and even though teleological thought remained at the heart of certain "materialist" views of the world and society, the suppression of the ultimate divine basis of things produced a fundamental break, a reversal which meant that, henceforward, it was at the heart of secular thought that the "disenchantment of the world" took place via the agency of critical thought.[33]

The French equivalent of secularism, *laicisme*, has a much more radical connotation than the English term. If the latter is a crystallization of Holyoake's idea, the former may be considered an application of Bradlaugh's concept of secularism. *Laicisme* is conceived of as a doctrine of complete freedom from, and non-interference by, religion. It involves the belief that functions performed erstwhile by a priesthood ought to be transferred to the laity, especially functions of judicial and educational kind.[34] In France, *laicisme* accomplished, though not completely until early this century, the constitutional separation of church and state. Religious instruction in state schools was abolished in 1882 and replaced by general ethical instruction.[35] Its extreme form involves anti-clericalism and the advocacy of *Kulturkampf* against the church. The term *Kulturkampf* refers to the repressive political movement against the Roman Catholic Church, instigated in 1871 by Bismarck, with the intention of wresting all educational and cultural institutions from the church, and conferring them instead upon the state.[36] In Turkey, it was regarded by Kemalism an essential part of the process whereby modern political institutions could be constructed.[37] Tunisia and Algeria are two Arab North African countries where *laicisme* is advocated or adopted with varying intensities.

Although Ghannouchi is critical of secularism as a whole, he maintains that in the Western tradition secularism is not only justifiable but has had positive aspects. It is justifiable in the West due to the nature of the Christian religion. He is insistent on distinguishing between Western secularism and the secularism that evolved, and has been advocated, in the Arab and Muslim countries. The latter form of secularism is neither justifiable nor constructive. He sees the rise of secularism in the West as having been associated with the need by reformists, especially during the Renaissance, to free their societies from the constraints imposed on them by the church. "There might have been genuine intellectual, psychological, and historical justifications for the rebellion against the religious establishment, a rebellion, then, deemed essential for the emancipation of man and the progress of society."[38]

Ghannouchi subscribes to the view that Christianity in medieval Europe was responsible for the emergence and success of secularism in the West.

> It recognized the division of life into what belonged to God and what belonged to Caesar, it lacked a system for legislation and regulation of mundane affairs, and it had for many centuries been associated with despotic regimes and with oppressive theocracies. Furthermore, medieval Christianity entertained the existence of a special class of people, the priests, who claimed to be God's representatives on earth, interpreting what they alleged was His Word and using their religious powers to deprive members of the community of their basic rights. In other words, the Christian theocratic establishment constituted a major obstacle hindering progress and development, and consequently hindering democracy. In contrast, the rise of secularism in the Muslim world occurred in completely different circumstances.[39]

It is indeed a historical fact that until the beginning of the nineteenth century, and specifically until just before Napoleon invaded Egypt in 1798, the entire Arab region was Islamic in norms, laws, values, and traditions. It was during the Western colonial era (inaugurated by the French campaign that paved the colonial path before other European imperialist powers) that the Arab region witnessed gradual intellectual, social, and political changes. These had primarily been the result of the impression left by the modes of thought and conduct brought to the area by Western colonialists.[40]

The Origins of Arab Secularism

Ghannouchi believes that it was not until the middle of the nineteenth century that Europe began to have a tangible cultural impact on the Arab region.[41] It was then that secularism entered the intellectual debate in the Arab world, and it was thenceforth that a new cultural model was being introduced quietly by enthusiasts and admirers of the West. In addition, the authorities of colonialism played a significant role in imposing secularization. Together, these endeavors put forward a new set of standards alien to the Islamic standards upon which local culture was based. Although European colonial powers, such as France and Britain, were intruding enemies that had their imperialist ambitions in the Muslim world, an elite composed mainly of Western-educated intellectuals admired them for their scientific and cultural progress.

The early Arab debate on secularism centered mainly on the relationship between religion and the state, and on the means of accomplishing the successes Europe had been able to achieve in science, technology, and governance. For this reason, it has been suggested, the term "secularism" was translated to a term pronounced either as *'ilmaniyah*, a word derived from *'ilm*, the Arabic word for science or knowledge, or pronounced as *'alamaniyah*, a word derived from *'alam*, the Arabic word for world or universe. Ghannouchi suggests that the translation of the term secularism to any other word, such as *la diniyah*, which implies the exclusion or marginalization of religion, would have been met with outright rejection by the Muslims. It was therefore necessary to introduce it through a term that implied knowledge and success, which Islam not only encouraged but also demanded.[42]

Nevertheless, the meaning of *'ilmaniyah* or *'alamaniyah* in the Arabic literature is no less varied and confused than it is in the Western literature. In his four-volume encyclo-

pedia on secularism, Elmessiri lists eighteen different definitions of "secularism" collected from modern Arabic literature. That is why in his approach to the study of secularism, Elmessiri distinguishes between secularism as a concept, secularism as a movement, and secularism as a paradigm or sequence.[43] He argues that as a concept, the
definition varies from one dictionary to the other and from one writer to the other. The
concept becomes more ambiguous when applied to a non-Christian culture, especially
when applied to Islam. As a movement, he suggests, secularism is best understood if
regarded as arising out of, and passing with, the conditions of its time. And as a paradigm, it is best thought of as a continuously unfolding sequence. Thus the nineteenth-
century definitions may seem irrelevant to today's reality. He further explains that this
sequence unfolds gradually with relevance to time and place, and therefore the meaning
of the concept does not only change from one place to the other but from one historic
moment to the other.[44]

Apart from associating Arab secularism with European colonialism, Ghannouchi's
writings do not provide a detailed account of its roots and subsequent development.
Although such treatment would have been reinforcing for his argument that secularism
is alien and irrelevant to Muslim renaissance, it is likely that he has not, at least so far,
felt the need to do so. Most of his discourse refers to the impact of secularization on
society and politics, specifically in Tunisia but more generally in the Arab region as a
whole. Nevertheless, it would seem that historical evidence is on Ghannouchi's side in
his claim of the colonial origin of Arab secularism. One can easily trace the rise and
reinforcement of secularism to colonial influence and subsequently to the post-independence territorial-state, which Ghannouchi maintains, as shall be discussed in chapter
six, is a product, or extension, of the colonial project.

The decline of the Islamic civilization had prompted a number of Arab intellectuals,
some of whom had already been exposed to European culture and had been impressed by
the accomplishments of Europe, to call for radical reform. As a consequence of the intellectual debate aroused within the Arab world by the European Renaissance, conflicts were
initiated between *din* (religion) and *'aql* (reason), between *asalah* (nobility) and *mu'asarah*
(modernity), *din* and *dawlah* (state), and *din* and *'ilm* (science or knowledge). Two trends
were initially distinguishable among the intellectuals engaged in the debate; one Islamic
and the other Christian. The leaders of the Islamic trend believed that modernization and
progress should be sought but without relinquishing the accomplishments of the Islamic
civilization. Their objective was to create an Islamic renaissance that could deliver the Arabs
from the state of backwardness while protecting them from the European colonial campaign that had been taking place since Napoleon set foot in Egypt.[45]

Rifa'ah Tahtawi (1801–1873) was the first to campaign for interacting with the European civilization with the objective of borrowing from it that which does not conflict with
the established values and principles of the Islamic *Shari'ah*. He criticized those who opposed the idea of taking knowledge from Europe saying: "Such people are deluded; for
civilizations are turns and phases. These sciences were once Islamic when we were at the
apex of our civilization. Europe took them from us and developed them further. It is now
our duty to learn from them just as they learned from our ancestors."[46]

Other nineteenth-century Islamic reformists, also referred to as Muslim modernists,
including Khairuddin at-Tunisi (1810–1899), Jamal ad-Din al-Afghani (1838–1897),
Abdurrahman al-Kawakibi (1854–1902), Muhammad Abduh (1849–1905), and Abdel

Hamid Bin Badis (1889-1940), followed the model of Tahtawi in stressing that Muslims could benefit from European successes without undermining Islamic values or culture.[47]

The Christian trend consisted of a group of Christian Arabs, some of whom had received their education at the Syrian Protestant College and then settled down in Egypt. The group included Shibli Shumayyil (1850-1917), Farah Antun (1874-1922), Georgie Zaidan (1861-1914), Ya'qub Suruf (1852-1917), Salama Musa (1887-1958), and Nicola Haddad (1878-1954).[48] *Al-Muqtataf* and *Al-Hilal*, founded respectively in 1876 and 1892, were two bulletins published and edited by writers and thinkers belonging to this group, which endeavored to propagate such ideas as the love of country and fellow countrymen should transcend all other social ties, even those of religion.[49]

Through their superfluous writings, these thinkers succeeded in consolidating the foundations of secularism in the Arab world. Praising the liberal thought of France and England during the eighteenth and nineteenth centuries and condemning the hegemony of traditions over the human mind, they stressed that reason should set the standard for human conduct. For modernization to take place, they demanded that only traditions that were compatible with this objective should remain.[50] The main aim of these intellectuals was to lay down the presuppositions of a secular state in which Muslims and Christians could participate on a footing of complete equality.[51]

The next generation of thinkers, mostly Muslim followers of Abduh, branched into two conflicting schools of thought. Some, like Muhammad Rashid Rida, pursued a *salafi* (traditional Islamic) course. Others, like Qasim Amin (1865-1908) and Ahmad Lutfi as-Sayyid (1872-1963), began—having been influenced by the Christian pioneers of the secularist school of thought—to work out the principles of a secular society in which Islam was honored but was no longer the guide of law and policy. Seeking to reconcile secularist ideas with Islam, they went so far as to develop Abduh's emphasis on the legitimacy of social change into a *de facto* division between the two realms, that of religion and that of society, each with its norms.[52]

Although Ghannouchi says little about the history of the rise of Arab secularism, he criticizes its pioneers for having founded the principles of their thought on the erroneous assumption that for Muslims to progress, Islam should, just like Christianity, be restricted to the spiritual, or private, sphere of life. Furthermore, he accuses them of misrepresenting Islam, portraying it as if it had a spiritual authority, or a clergy, that hindered scientific discovery and prohibited freedom of thought, and that should therefore be prevented from interfering in temporal matters. He suggests that the assumptions about Islam's conflict with reason or with science were merely extrapolations from the Euro-Christian context. The presupposition that Islam and Christianity adopted identical positions on questions such as the freedom of thought and the emancipation of the mind would inevitably lead to the conclusion that as Europe rid itself of the influence of religion as a prelude to progress, the Arabs needed to constrain Islam.[53]

The Arab version of secularism, in Ghannouchi's assessment, has been a declaration of war against Islam. Islam loses its essence if marginalized or restricted to a private sphere. It is meant to shape and influence the lives of Muslims. Its values and principles are aimed at liberating mankind and at establishing justice and equality. For this reason, he stresses, Islam encourages research and innovation and guarantees the freedoms of thought, expression, and worship. Therefore, secularism is entirely unnecessary in the Muslim world. Muslims can achieve progress and development without having to erect a wall between their religious values and their livelihood.[54] The term progress, which in Arabic is *taqaddum* from the root *qadama* (to move forward), is used by Ghannouchi to mean scientific and technological accomplishments, whereas development, which in Arabic is *tanmiyah* from the root *nama* (to grow), refers to economic success. Like nineteenth-century Muslim modernists, Ghannouchi insists that the scientific and technological underpinnings of the modern Western civilization are reducible to categories of knowledge and practice that Muslims can learn and benefit from without having to give up their cultural identity.[55]

Secularism in the Arab Maghreb

The model of secularism that emerged in the Arab Maghreb is considered by Ghannouchi to be one of the most radical forms of secularism. It has been of particular interest to him because his Ennahda Party, and prior to that its precursor the MTI, has been in conflict with an autocratic regime known for espousing an extreme form of secularism, which Ghannouchi maintains is more radical than Kemalism itself. Ruling elites in both Algeria and Morocco have espoused similar models of secularism since independence. Ghannouchi observes that what is common to the secularist elites of the Arab Maghreb is that they are all graduates of the French school of thought. It is a school that has absolute confidence in reason, in the human being as the center of the universe, and in science as the ultimate solution to human problems. Notwithstanding this clear cultural background, North African secular elites have not pursued the model of their Western inspirers. Nor have they even emulated the Turkish model. In both of these models a relative separation is established between religion and the state. Thus, the state withdraws from the spiritual sphere, leaving it to the religious establishment to cater to.[56]

Ghannouchi points out that the constitutions of the Arab Maghreb countries state clearly that "Islam is the religion of the state." One would, accordingly, expect these states not to be strictly secularist, in the sense that state and religion are separate. But they are not. Whereas in classical theocracies the religious establishment is in control of the state, it is the state, which is run by a secularist elite in every single one of these cases, that monopolizes religion and controls its institutions.

> *Imams* (prayer leaders) in mosques are appointed by the state, which administers their affairs and may even dictate to them what to say and what not to say during the Friday sermons. A dual role is played by the head of state; on the one hand he is *amir-ul-mu'minin* (leader of the faithful) and *hami hima-d-din* (protector of the sanctuary of religion), who orders the establishment of a special department for issuing *fatwa*, or religious judgment, and the formation of special councils for Islamic *da'wah* (preaching); and on the other he is the apostle of modernization.

Nationalizing Religion

Pseudo-secularism is what Ghannouchi prefers to call this model of secularism; it is a counterfeit that takes from Western secularism its most negative aspect and discards the positive aspect. The proponents of pseudo-secularism believe that modernizing society should not be restricted to propagating knowledge and science, but should also include reshaping society according to the manner in which they envisage the French model, a model that advocates a break with the past. But instead of establishing a separation between what is mundane and what is religious, or merely marginalizing the role of religion in society, pseudo-secularists seek to impose full control over the institutions and symbols of religion. They even monopolize the right to reinterpret religion. In other words, the Arab Maghreb version of secularism has been turned by its advocates into some form of a "church" that, Ghannouchi believes, is not much different in essence from the church in medieval Europe. He cites examples from his own country. The Tunisian head of state acts as if he were a *mujtahid* (an authoritative scholar) and in so doing he sees no need for the testimony of experts. Former President Bourguiba went so far as to call upon his people to follow his example by not observing the fast during the month of Ramadan. He issued a *fatwa* ordering state employees to break the fast. In one of his speeches he ridiculed the belief in the existence of Paradise and Hell in the life after death; he also denied the miracles of the prophets. He closed down the well-known Islamic university of az-Zaytounah and decreed the prohibition of *hijab* (women's Islamic code of dress). Both he and his wife made a point of appearing in public wearing swimsuits and he openly boasted that he had extra-marital relationships. Furthermore, he imposed restrictions on the number of citizens allowed to perform pilgrimage. Worst of all, he nationalized the endowments of religious institutions. Upon his instructions, one of his judges condemned a senior scholar of Islam for the "crime of interpreting the Qur'an in a manner that contradicted the interpretation of his Excellency the President."

While considering the Tunisian regime to be the most radically secularist regime in the region, Ghannouchi stresses that other regimes in the area, which might not have reached the same level of defiance, are not in essence much different. They share in common a policy of nationalizing religion and its institutions. While employing religion as a source of legitimacy, they grant themselves the right to dispose with it as if it were their own private property. They even monopolize the right to speak in its name and to interpret it the way they deem fit in order to fulfil the mission of "modernizing" the state. Not a single state in the Arab Maghreb region has permitted the establishment of any religious institution that is independent of the state. None of them has ever hesitated to describe as obscurantism any interpretation of religion that is different from their own, so as to justify repressing it and excluding those who subscribe to it. Society in the Arab Maghreb, Ghannouchi laments, is not the source of authority but its field of action. He explains that two methods have been used in this regard. The first is the invention, in imitation of the Western experience, of a national identity that is considered to be superior to any other identity such as Arabism or Islam. The second is to reform, in a Stalinist fashion, the people's mindsets, so as to "become sound and compatible with the modern life, and to uproot obscurantism."

Modernization: Process of Hegemony, Not Liberation

Despite the common features, Ghannouchi distinguishes the Moroccan model from the Algerian and Tunisian models. The Moroccan model is said to differ slightly with regard to the role religion is permitted to play in society. This, in his assessment, is prompted by the monarch's need to assert an authority that derives legitimacy from religion itself.

In contrast to Western secular states, the modern state in the Arab Maghreb does not recognize power sharing. It permits neither equitable distribution of wealth nor genuine representation of the will of the people. The secular state in North Africa has been no more than a tool delegated, as if by design, by the former colonizer to an elite that has been entrusted to take care of the colonizer's interests and to reproduce its relations and values. It is justified and defended at times in the name of secularism and modernity, and at times in the name of noble universal values such as democracy and human rights. In this way authority, wealth, and culture remain the property of a minority elite while the majority of the population is excluded or marginalized.

As mentioned earlier, Ghannouchi tends to use the terms secularization, modernization, and Westernization as synonyms in spite of the fact that historically and conceptually they are not the same. It is not that he is unaware of this fact. In the North African context he sees these terms as implying one thing, namely "a process of attempting to impose on the region, by way of controlling its inhabitants and monopolizing its resources, values that are incompatible with its own."[57] This overlap between the terms secularism and modernity is not unique to Ghannouchi, but is frequently encountered in contemporary Arabic literature. Secularism is spoken of as an inevitable product of modernity, and the accomplishment of modernization is unimaginable without secularization. Ghannouchi understands both secularization and modernization to mean, in the Arab context, the process of Westernizing the Arab region. In his assessment the process is not accomplished by borrowing development and progress from the West "but by pledging the Arab region indefinitely to Western hegemony while decorating public life with aspects of Western lifestyles that are not only dispensable and irrelevant to progress but also contravening of Islamic fundamentals."[58]

Modernity

As with secularism, the manner in which the term modernity is applied in the Arab world only highlights the problem of concepts that are arbitrarily taken out of their historical contexts to be transplanted in an entirely inhospitable terrain. Modernity is a complex phenomenon. It is said to refer to modes of social life or organization that emerged in Europe from about the seventeenth century onward and that subsequently became more or less world-wide in their influence.[59] However, its roots go deep in European history. In many respects, especially with regard to the foundations of its philosophical claims, modernity is a Christian European phenomenon rooted in three monumental (Christian-inspired) events: the "discovery of the new world," the Renaissance, and the Reformation.[60]

Modernity is described as the diffusion of the products of rational activity—scientific, technological, and administrative—and is said to imply the increasing differentiation of the various sectors of social life—politics, the economy, family life, religion, and, in particular, art.[61]

The most powerful Western conception of modernity, and the one which has had the most profound effects, asserted above all that rationalization required the destruction of traditional social bonds, feelings, customs, and beliefs, and that the agent of modernization was neither a particular category nor social class, but reason itself and the historical necessity that was paving the way for its triumph.[62] In this sense, modernity is a post-traditional order that institutionalizes the principle of radical doubt and insists that all knowledge takes the form of hypothesis: claims which may very well be true, but which are in principle always open to revision and may have at some point to be abandoned.[63] The idea of modernity makes science, rather than God, central to society and at best relegates religious beliefs to the inner realm of private life. Therefore, according to Touraine, it is impossible to describe as "modern" a society that tries primarily to organize and to act in accordance with a divine revelation or a national essence.[64] Rationalization is seen as the sole principle behind the organization of personal and collective life, and it is associated with the theme of secularization or, in other words, with a refusal to define ultimate ends.[65]

The secularization of Western culture, as a consequence of the process of disenchantment, which led in Europe to a disintegration of religious world-views, was simultaneous with the development of modern societies. Cumulative and mutually reinforcing processes have been identified with the emergence of modern societies, which no longer remained restricted to Europe. These include the formation of capital and the mobilization of resources, the development of the forces of production and the increase in the productivity of labor, the establishment of centralized political power and the formation of national identities, the proliferation of rights of political participation, of urban forms of life, and of formal schooling, and the secularization of values and norms.[66]

In recent times, modernity has become a global phenomenon. Giddens resembles it to a juggernaut, a runaway engine of enormous power which humans can drive to some extent but which also threatens to rush out of their control and which could rend itself asunder.[67] According to him, modernity's dynamism emanates from three interconnected sources. The first is the separation of time and space, in a manner that provides means of precise temporal and spatial zoning. The second is the development of disembedding mechanisms that "lift out" social activity from localized contexts, reorganizing social relations across time-space distances. The third is the reflexive appropriation of knowledge, to the effect of rolling social life away from the fixities of tradition. The emergence of the nation-state is seen as the fruit of the first source; symbolic tokens, notably money, and expert systems, which remove social relations from the immediacies of context, of the second. Symbolic tokens and expert systems involve trust that operates in environments of risk, in which varying levels of security can be achieved. Reflexivity means that social practices are constantly examined and reformed in the light of incoming information about those very practices, thus constitutively altering their character.[68]

Modernity is said to have four basic institutional dimensions. The first is capitalism, a system of commodity production centered upon the relation between private ownership of capital and property-less wage labor. The second is industrialism, the use of inanimate sources of material power in the production of goods, coupled to the central role of machinery in the production process. The third is surveillance, the supervision of activities of subject populations in the political sphere. The fourth is control of the means of violence. The four dimensions are interrelated. Capitalism involves the insulation of the economic from the political against the backdrop of competitive labor and product markets while surveillance is fundamental to the nation-state, whose successful monopoly of the means of violence is said to rest upon the secular maintenance of new codes of criminal law. Direct relations exist, on the one hand, between military power and industrialism and, on the other, between industrialism and capitalism.[69]

The complexity of modernity is that as a project, it developed through time, sometimes as a contradictory process, with an indistinct and arbitrary beginning point. Its different components, such as the capitalist economy and the nation-state, did not occur simultaneously. Both Marx and Weber were of the opinion that the territorial state was first put into place before capitalist market economies began to grow. However, as a concept, as a theoretical term, modernity has a more distinct, nonetheless quite complicated, history. The term did not appear until the nineteenth century, when many social scientists, philosophers, and political economists began to talk about "the age we are in" as modern. In other words, the term modernity has a history that is not identical to the history of what is considered to be the main components of the project modernity, capitalist market economies, territorial states, and separation of church and state.

By virtue of the disembeddedness and reflexivity of the project's institutional dimensions, it is said to be inherently globalizing. Globalization is defined as "the intensification of world-wide social relations which link distant localities in such a way that local happenings are shaped by events occurring many miles away and vice versa."[70] Hence, all states, societies, and individuals, whether they like it or not, today live in the world of modernity and are influenced positively as well as negatively, to varying degrees, by its consequences.[71] Is modernity then inevitable?

Pseudo-Modernity

Ghannouchi is of the opinion that a modernity-modernization package was brought by the colonialists to the Arab region and was then adopted by the national governments that succeeded them. It was a package carefully designed to impose foreign hegemony on Arab and Islamic societies, especially in the Maghreb, denying them the beneficial aspects of modernity that brought about political and economic successes in the West.[72] He maintains that secular elites in Arab societies, "who claim to be the missionaries of modernity," have inherited the role of the colonialists and have inherited their thoughts as well as their means and methods of dealing with the masses, which they view as primitive and backward.

> In the absence of democratic institutions and under the influence of power intoxication, the Westernized elite have become so corrupt that they ended having a relationship with the masses very similar to the one that existed between the ruling white minority and the black majority in South Africa. The exception is that in the South African case the white minority was more independent of Western influence. As the lust for power vanquished the desire for genuine modernization, the state was transformed into a machine of total repression, especially as the people increasingly moved toward Islam to reassert their identity and shield themselves from the state.[73]

This state of pseudo-modernity, as Ghannouchi calls it, has taken over the remaining institutions of civil society. Mosques, endowments, courts, religious schools, trade unions, parties, charities, and the press have all been seized. He cites the example of

Tunisia where, as part of the war against backwardness, the state took control of the economy too. The remarks made by Bourguiba in this regard stand witness to the nature of this pseudo-modernity state.

> The era of the independence of national organizations is over. There is no more room for the party to stand as an independent unit, nor for the General Laborers Union to stand as an independent unit, nor for the National Union of Farmers to stand as an independent unit, nor for the Union of Industry and Commerce to stand as an independent unit, nor for the General Union of Students to stand as an independent unit. Tunisians, whether they are in the General Laborers Union, or in the National Union of Farmers, or in the Union of Industry and Commerce, or in the General Union of Students, are above all members of the National Constitutional Party.[74]

Ghannouchi argues that throughout much of the Arab world, with varying degrees, the modernization pursued by the ruling elites was based on nationalizing society and containing it within the elitist state and containing the state within the party and the party within the person of the leader. The primary concern of the modern Arab state has been to maintain its hegemony on the society and on its educational, judicial, cultural, economic, and vocational institutions. An important target of state hegemony has understandably been the army and the police. These, Ghannouchi explains, were the first state institutions to be modernized or "transformed into repressive apparatuses." The emerging oligarchies needed to shield themselves and protect their interests from the general public. They also needed to legitimize their monopoly of power. The powers granted to both departments increased as the first signs of social rebellion surfaced. Today, Ghannouchi notes, prisons of the "pseudo-modernity" state have become homes, not of criminals, but of writers, artists, intellectuals, athletes, and all sorts of talented people, whether Islamists, nationalists, leftists, or otherwise. "Their crime is that they dream of democracy."

Ghannouchi holds the West morally responsible for creating and maintaining, in the name of promoting modernity, undemocratic secularist regimes in Northern Africa. He wonders whether the West would pride itself of having accomplished a modernity that has ended in police states that "legitimize repression in the name of democracy and human rights and in the name of defending civil society against an alleged obscurant fundamentalist onslaught." For this reason, Ghannouchi maintains that the conflict between the Islamists and the regime in Tunisia is not between fundamentalism and modernity as propagated by the authorities there. Nor is it a conflict between democracy and religious extremism. "We wish it were. For had it been fundamentally a civilizational conflict, it would have been possible to search for common denominators."[75]

But if pseudo-modernity is objectionable, would genuine modernity be acceptable? Ghannouchi's position is that it would be acceptable provided it emanated from within, that is in response to local needs and in conformity with local culture and value systems. He strongly believes that no Muslim would reject modernization in as far as it means employing modern tools, procedures, or mechanisms in managing politics or in running the economy. As for his own group's convictions, he is keen to stress that Tunisian Islamists value human dignity and civil liberties, accept that the popular will is the source of political legitimacy, and believe in pluralism and in the alternation of power through free elections. Nevertheless, he acknowledges that conflict between the

Islamic culture and some aspects of the incoming Western culture may exist, whether in Tunisia or in other parts of the Arab or Muslim world. Perhaps it is these points of conflict that provide existing regimes with the opportunity to claim, in pursuit of Western support and protection, that they represent the forces of modernity that are engaged in conflict with the forces of reaction and obscurantism. But are they really the representatives of true modernity? Ghannouchi answers, citing the example of what he describes as the most infamous pretender of modernity in modern Arab history: "Bourguiba was not a modernizer except in as much as he was anti-religion and in as much as he was infatuated with the French and American models of industrial and scientific progress. But as far as governance was concerned, he resembled more the kings of medieval Europe, or the defunct rulers of Eastern Europe, than the liberal democratic systems of the West."[76]

What Ghannouchi seeks to explain is that contrary to what the official media in his own country and in its neighboring states propagate, the conflict between governments and Islamic movements has no relevance whatsoever to what may exist between Islam and modernity of points of disagreement.

> The conflict is not a religious one. Nor is it even a conflict between religion and the Western concept of secularism. It is a political conflict between the oppressor and the oppressed, between a people that has been struggling for its freedom and dignity, for power sharing as well as resource-sharing, and an absolute corrupt ruler who has turned the state into a tool for repression. Like snakes, despotic rulers keep changing their skins. In the past Bourguiba practiced repression in the name of national unity, while Nassir did it in the name of liberating Palestine and uniting the Arabs. Today, it is practiced in the name of democracy, human rights, defending civil society, and making peace with Israel. But slogans do not alter the fact that the nature of the conflict is merely political. It is about legitimacy and whom it belongs to. It is about the nature of government, about the choice between autocracy and democracy.[77]

Ghannouchi's quest is a very important one, and his role in this regard is invaluable. As shall be discussed in more detail in chapter six, some Western writers and politicians, motivated by their hostility to Islam or by their own national interests, have campaigned for unconditional Western support for despotic regimes in the Arab world. Their pretext is that these regimes wage war on behalf of modernity and Western civilization against Islamic fundamentalism, which is seen as a serious threat. Ghannouchi's endeavor to dispel this illusion is unlikely, on its own, to influence policy makers in Western capitals. However, he hopes that, together with other efforts, it will contribute to creating a condition of awareness and to promoting a better understanding within Western public opinion, and particularly within intellectual ranks, of reality in the Arab region.

A Century of Modernization

More than a century of modernization has produced disastrous results; the most terrible of all, according to Ghannouchi, has been undermining the cultural identity of the people. He cites as an example the measures adopted against Arabic. Modernization in the Arab Maghreb countries was accompanied by a persistent campaign to replace Arabic, the symbol of identity and the official language of Islam, by French. So far, all the

Arabization projects executed in the three countries of the Arab Maghreb to repair the damage done over the years have failed. The new generation is torn between the two languages, neither of which is commanded well. In addition, a series of measures was adopted in order to undermine the traditional institutions of civil society, an issue that will be discussed in more detail in the next chapter.

In the era of modernization, Ghannouchi charges, economic institutions have been taken over by the ruling elite and the state has been transformed into a family of interests, more like the Mafia. The gap between the ruling elite and the rest of society has grown. Increasingly less people are involved in decision making or in benefiting from the policies of government. Democracy, as a set of mechanisms for the proper administration of society and as a formula for power sharing, has been rejected and only a decorative form of "democracy" may be permitted mostly in response to pressure from an embarrassed West. The circle of repression has been on the increase. The number of political prisoners has been on the rise. In response to state repression, at least two of the three countries have witnessed the eruption of extreme forms of violence which, Ghannouchi predicts, is only likely to persist and escalate so long as the root of the problem is not addressed.[78]

Violence, both overt and covert, is the means by which the state's mission of modernization is accomplished.[79] The extent to which a state relies on violence is dependent on the degree of its legitimacy. Nowhere in the Arab world, let alone in the Arab Maghreb, has the state been founded on democratic legitimacy. In Algeria and Tunisia, a single party, the National Liberation Front (FLN) in the former and the Constitutional Party in the latter, ruled alone for nearly a quarter of a century, deriving legitimacy from the struggle for liberation and independence. In Morocco, however, a cocktail of liberation legacy, religion, and a small dose of democracy constitutes the source of legitimacy. Over the years, the failure of the modernization process in fulfilling the basic needs of the people diminished the war of liberation legacy as a source of legitimacy. Economic hardship prompted a rise in public protests and in demands for justice and democracy. The state's response has been a mixture of repression and containment. In every case some kind of a strictly controlled form of pluralism has been permitted.[80]

In Algeria, and under mounting pressure in the wake of the popular uprising in 1988, the state had no option but to concede to the will of the people and opt for pluralization. The objective was to give the state a chance to regain control and then withdraw its concessions. The popular impact was much greater than expected, and the containment plan ended in failure. This is the testimony of former Algerian Prime Minister Dr. Abelhamid al-Ibrahimi:

> The elitist, oppressive, Westernized, and corrupt state reacted exposing its true nature as an imperial legacy and a remnant of colonialism in the land of Islam. A comparison between the methods used in the Algeria of 1992 to suppress the people, who have been marginalized by a fake and backward version of modernity, with the methods pursued by the French occupation authorities in pre-independence Algeria would show clearly the resemblance and the linkage between the colonial state and the subordinate state and between the old and the new liberation revolutions.[81]

Pointing to the resemblance in attitude, and asserting the connection between the Algerian secularists and their French counterparts, Ghannouchi quotes a Le monde editor as expressing bafflement at the success of the Islamists in the Algerian elections by asking "Will the army save democracy in Algeria?".[82] He also quotes a senior French official as expressing similar concerns. "In a statement aimed at calming the fears of the dismayed French people and dissipating their anxieties in the wake of the Algerian volcanic eruption, French politician Michael Jobar proclaimed with confidence: 'The Algerian army has not spoken yet.'"[83]

The army in Algeria eventually did speak. Just a few days before the second round of elections was due to be held, the military took over, suspended the democratic process, cancelled the first round of elections, sent the victors and their supporters to desert concentration camps, and set fire to the entire country. Ghannouchi is highly critical of the Western response to the cancellation of elections in Algeria.

> What matters in the Western political rationale is the outcome. Ethics and human rights are referred to only when needed. Values become a necessity if they bring to power those "liberals" who resemble their counterparts in Eastern Europe. These same values are shunned if they result in bringing to power the genuine and sincere children of the land, and in putting an end to minority regimes that are the legacy of the colonial era.[84]

The Western official indifference to the war against democracy is attributed by Islamists to the fact that Islamists are the victims. As has been the case in Algeria, they are repressed under the pretext of saving democracy from them. Alleging that if the Islamists were permitted to gain power through the ballot box they would put an end to democracy, the purported supporters of secularism justify for themselves undermining what they set forth to protect, and justify in that cause violating every single human right. In the meantime, their Western friends remain silent. Ghannouchi seizes upon this to echo a question that has been asked many times before: "Is it fair to turn a blind eye when the secularists break the law in the present and condemn the Islamists for the mere supposition that they might break the law in the future"?[85]

He cites the example of Algeria, which is a repeat of what happened before in his own country, to prove that when the democratic choice of the people is not in favor of the secularist elite, undemocratic measures become acceptable. These may include emergency laws, government-appointed parliamentarians, and forged elections. It is not uncommon in the Arab countries that the ruling party can gain up to 98 percent and the only presidential candidate may win no less than 99.99 percent of the votes. As a precautionary measure, any competitors, who may not necessarily be fundamentalists, as in the Tunisian case, are sent to prison.[86]

Ghannouchi supposes that North African secularist regimes are in real dilemma. On the one hand, their programs of development and modernization have proven to be a total failure and their records of human rights are so "shameful" that they have been condemned by every single human rights organization in the Western hemisphere. On the other hand, they face a serious challenge posed to them by Islamic movements that demand justice, democracy, and independence. What makes things worse, from his point of view, is that the repression resorted to by these regimes "whose legitimacy has been eroded by corruption and bankruptcy" is not restricted to Islamists. Ghannouchi believes that Islamists have not been targeted because of their ideology, although admittedly repressing them causes less problems at the international level, and may even be profitable in some ways.[87]

Linguistic Illusions

Ghannouchi makes a point of distinguishing between Western and Arab experiences with secularism. He acknowledges the accomplishments of secularization in the Western tradition and points out that the political model which has been governing in Tunisia and other similar places in the Arab world since independence does not resemble the Western liberal model except in its rebellion against religion and in its libertinism. In all other aspects, as far as he is concerned, the model identifies more with fascist and communist models.[88] Western secularism led to the emancipation of the mind from the authority of religion, and emancipated both religion and society from the authority of the church. In contrast, secularism in the modern Arab experience resulted in pledging religion, society, and the mind to the hegemony of a new church, the state of the secular elite, or what he refers to as "the state of secular autocracy." In the Western experience, secularism accomplished scientific progress, industrial revolution, and democratic government. Secularism in the Arab experience has destroyed society and turned it into an easy prey to a corrupt elite that very much resembles the Mafia in Italy or the white minority in the defunct apartheid regime of South Africa.[89] Secularism in North Africa is a church of the same type against which the West rebelled. In this regard, he cautions against falling for linguistic illusions:

> Sometimes, language overwhelms us with a world of illusions, and causes the West to sympathize with its secular "children" who are now claiming to lead the Muslim world toward modernity. These are the illusions of the language and not the realities of the Muslim world. The Muslim world is governed by pre-modernity European-style regimes from the age of theocracy and authoritarian monarchy. Such regimes certainly do not belong to the age of democracy, freedom, and people's sovereignty, and people's right to self-determination.[90]

The linguistic illusions Ghannouchi warns against have been recognized as a serious impediment to fruitful communication between Muslims and Westerners. John Keane refers to this very problem saying: "Language as we know is not simply a matter of transporting meanings to others in a non-problematic way as if words are like digital impulses; language itself shapes meanings and it is therefore also about power and politics. Words sometimes and often act as roadblocks between individuals, groups, whole societies, and indeed civilizations; words get in the way of mutual understanding and reinterpretation."[91]

A shocking example of what Ghannouchi terms "secular theocracy" in Tunisia is the indictment forwarded by the state's attorney general when he demanded the execution of Sheikh Rahmouni in 1962. The indictment read: "The defendant has permitted himself to have an understanding of the Qur'an contrary to the understanding of his Excellency the President." Ghannouchi cites a number of other examples including a reference to a meeting of *imams* (mosque prayer leaders) on the twenty-ninth day of the fasting month of Ramadan in March 1992, when Tunisian President Ben Ali addressed the congregation saying: "The State has sole responsibility for religion." In another incident, the Tunisian minister of religious affairs took it upon himself to issue a *fatwa* declaring Ennahda (Renaissance Party) godless. It is in the shade of this secular theocracy, Ghannouchi relates, that mosques are considered to be the property of the state and their *imams* fully accountable to its authority. They are appointed by the state and can be punished or fired if they fail to carry out the instructions of the prime minister.[92]

Nevertheless, Ghannouchi recognizes that not all models of secularization in the Muslim world are equally bad. He considers the Turkish model, for instance, to be milder; that is in spite of the fact that some Arab Maghreb governments claim to emulate it. In the Turkish experience, some room has been left for religious freedom, and society has retained many of its religious institutions, which remain relatively independent. In Tunisia, however, "the 'pope' is represented in the person of the president, whether Ben Ali or Bourguiba, who proclaims 'I am the representative of Islam and no one has the right to speak in the name of Islam but me.'"[93]

Just as he distinguishes between Western and Arab secularism, Ghannouchi does the same with modernity. He affirms that the Muslims need "genuine" modernity as much as anybody else does. To him genuine modernity entails the emancipation of humans and securing their right to freedom of choice; the generation of scientific and technological progress; and the establishment of a democratic system and reasserting the sovereignty of the people. However, he qualifies this by the need to approach modernity through "our own door, and not through the door of France or America or Russia." This, he explains, is the difference between the Islamic approach to modernity and that of the Westernized elite in the Muslim countries.

> The problem is not really with modernity or with science or even with secularism. The problem lies with false modernity, which is the deconstruction of the institutions of traditional society. This process was started by the colonial invaders who came to the Muslims promising them industrial progress and a deliverance from backwardness if they rebelled against Islam, the whole of Islam, both its *Shari'ah* and *'aqidah* components.[94]

For Ghannouchi, false modernity manifested itself in the deconstruction of Islamic society and rebuilding it on non-religious foundations, not in terms of a separation between religion and state, but totally excluding religion from all aspects of public life.[95] In other words, modernity in the Arab case has not implied the adoption of scientific methods and industrialization, but a process of radical secularization whose main concern is to struggle against Islam and its heritage.

Modernity and secularism, as understood by Ghannouchi, are not inevitably linked. As far as he can see, only the French and Marxist models assume an absolute linkage between the two. This is another example of how different definitions lead to different conclusions. Ghannouchi is aware of this, and is keen on starting with a clear definition. In this regard he refers to a discussion that took place once between him and Muhammad Arkoun on the relationship between Islam and secularism. Ghannouchi asked Arkoun to define secularism. We are told that Arkoun said it meant giving the mind the right to search with no restrictions or in other words granting reason absolute authority to search without obstruction. Ghannouchi responded by saying that this particular concept is perfectly compatible with Islam. He said: "Islam places no restrictions on the mind. The Qur'an clearly encourages believers to explore, think, and search. The first thing believers have to reason and be convinced about is faith, which—as important as it is—is not acceptable through compulsion or imitation. Islamic doctrines do not speak of areas where thinking, reasoning, or searching is restricted."[96]

However, secularism as defined by Arkoun is not the secularism spoken of by its adherents in the Arab world. Ghannouchi explained to him that the model of secularism preached in the Arab world has only been conducive to despotism. To its Arab devotees, it has meant in practice absolute control of the entire nation, of its resources, of its religion, and of the conscience of its subjects in the name of democracy, modernity, and sometimes even in the name of Islam itself.[97] As for the values of true modernity, Ghannouchi believes that many of them are perfectly compatible with Islam. "Once the Muslims are given a chance to comprehend the values of Western modernity, such as democracy and human rights, they will search within Islam for a place for them. They will implant them, nurse them, and cherish them just as the Westerners did before when they implanted such values in a much less fertile soil."[98]

In his treatment of secularism, Ghannouchi's main concern has been to focus on the impact of secularization on the Arab region, and to show that contrary to the situation in the Western world, it has, especially in North Africa, been associated with authoritarianism and lack of respect for human rights. The following chapter will discuss Ghannouchi's theory that secularism is detrimental to civil society, not only in the Arab world but in the West, too.

5

Civil Society

Tunisian Society

Rachid Ghannouchi maintains that as part of the Islamic *Ummah*, Tunisia acquired a profound civil sentiment from Islam. He explains that in Tunisia, like in most other parts of the Muslim world, traditional Islamic society was subjected to mutilation first at the hands of the colonialists and then at the hand of the modern territorial state. It is true, he concedes, that the period of ideal Islamic rule, during which the scripture and the will of the people were superior to the will of the ruler and during which power rotated in accordance with the people's choice, did not last long. It is also true, he adds, that imperial models that combined old and new forms of government and theocracy with democracy soon afterward replaced the Prophet's model of government. However, he stresses, the authority of the ruler never exceeded the executive sphere, and legislation remained the sole responsibility of the scholars. The same applied to society's judicial, educational, and cultural institutions. These, together with a large number of independent public institutions, were funded by *awqaf* (endowment trust), which in turn relied on *zakat* and *sadaqa* (alms). In this way, society preserved a high degree of independence from the state.[1] In addition to Ghannouchi, this opinion is now held by a number of contemporary Islamic thinkers. They include Dr. Salim El-Awwa in *On the Political System of the Islamic State* (1980), Dr. Tawfiq Ash-Shawi in *Fiqh Ash-Shura Wal-Istisharah* (1992), and Munir Shafiq in *Al-Islam Wa Muwajahat ad-Dawalah al-Hadithah* (1992).

Ghannouchi argues that Tunisian civil society remained invariably vivid and intact from the Islamic conquest in the late seventh century until independence in 1956, notwithstanding the fact that danger started creeping in with the advent of French colonialism in 1881. The colonizers embarked on a "modernization" campaign that was met with great resistance by the Tunisian public. For instance, until the French took over, all properties in the pre-colonial era were privately owned. Property was owned by tribes, by families, or by the *awqaf*. Education, at all levels, was available free of charge and was independent of the government. An individual citizen sought protection in his tribe, his family, his Sufi denomination, or his professional association. The colonialists started undermining the country's cultural edifice with the consequence of undermining the values of compassion, cooperation, and fraternity in favor of materialistic and individualistic incentives. A considerable proportion of public properties was seized, and the local market—which was based on the principle of self-sufficiency—was linked to the French and European markets. Formal cultural, judicial, political, and social institutions were set up to compete with and undermine local *ahli* institutions. Despite all of this part of civil society remained intact though weakened. Mosques and most schools remained independent. According to Ghannouchi, things became worse after independence.

> The profound roots of traditional civil society, with its values and civil structure, managed to generate a resistance movement that struggled against the occupier and confronted its plan to destroy civil society. However, the secular trend, which was created and sustained within the parallel educational institutions that were founded by the colonizer, succeeded in infiltrating the resistance movement and in controlling it.

The independence achieved from the French was not, Ghannouchi stresses, a victory. Instead, it turned to be a resumption of the process of destruction. It turned to be an intensive campaign to culturally annex Tunisia to France as fast as possible. Whereas the French failed in their bid to undermine Tunisian Islamic heritage, their successors, the Tunisian nationalists, in the name of modernity, succeeded. Westernization, which Ghannouchi defines as the process of stripping society of its cultural identity, continued ever more vigorously through the "propagation of self-debasing values and institutionalizing admiration for the colonizer, which meant blindly imitating it, considering it to be the model for civilizational progress." But while doing so, the modern post-independence state made every effort to avoid copying the Western values of freedom, rule of law, and democracy. The government of independence had become an oppressive autocracy. In order for the process of "subordination and destruction" to be complete, it was necessary to destroy the Islamic cultural foundation and the civil institutions of society. Tribal and public endowment properties were completely seized in order to destroy the tribal sector, and Bedouins were forced to urbanize. The system of education was Westernized and under the pretext of the emancipation of women, a campaign was launched to encourage relinquishing family values. Women were told their freedom lay in adopting a Western lifestyle and their true value in their economic contribution. Through the control of educational and economic institutions, the post-colonial government succeeded in undermining society in favor of state power.

> It did not take long for the people to realize the failure of the modern state model. Society felt the danger such a state model posed to its integrity and viability. A popular uprising against dictatorship and pseudo-modernization ensued. It was initially leftist, in pursuit of justice; then became liberal, in pursuit of democracy; and in the final stage it became Islamic, in pursuit of an Islamic cultural identity, a common ground on which all those who struggle for justice, democracy, and development in Tunisia can stand.

This, Ghannouchi stresses, has been the declared mission of his Tunisian Islamic Movement, "an endeavor that is aimed at reviving the Islamic spirit so as to constitute a foundation for the reconstruction of civil society." In pursuit of this goal, his movement supported and joined the workers and student unions and sought to restore the role of the mosque as a center of cultural and educational activities. Convinced that the conflict in Tunisia is in reality between freedom-lovers and tyrannical rulers, between those who defend society and those who defend hegemony, Ghannouchi led his movement along the painful path of reconstructing civil society. This turned to be a task for which he and his followers had to pay dearly, some with their lives and the rest with imprisonment or banishment.

> The Islamic Movement has succeeded in breathing a new life in civil society by tilting the balance in favor of the people's state rather than the state's people. This, and the potential threat it poses to the ruling autocracy, prompted the police state to intervene with all forms of repression and persecution, and with staging an election in which the president and his party won 99.99 percent of the votes.

Ghannouchi holds Arab secularists, who have been in power since independence, responsible for the destruction of traditional civil society. He cites as an example the measures adopted by former Tunisian President Bourguiba. Prior to his coming to power, and in spite of the French colonial policy of modernization, or more precisely Westernization, 80 per cent of Tunisia's educational institutions belonged to the private sector and were financed by the independent *awqaf* (endowment) establishment. About one-third of the country's agricultural land belonged to the *awqaf*. Nationalization was to become the tool of modernization and, as Ghannouchi puts it, "the axe that hacked what had remained of civil society." Institutions such as the students association, the laborers association, and religious and educational societies were nationalized too. The entire society became the property of the one and only party, the ruling party, which ultimately expressed only the wishes and the will of the leader.[2] Such mutilation led to severe destruction of political life not uncommon to most of the former colonies of the Western democratic world.[3]

Ghannouchi's theory is that prior to the colonial era, the Islamic society had never been governed by a hegemonic totalitarian state and had never lost its identity. It was vivid, dynamic, and self-reviving. Secured by a "comprehensive" social order, society was self-sufficient by virtue of its economic, cultural, and social activities and thanks to the independence of its "civic" institutions. It was the process of pseudo-secularization, or pseudo-modernization, that destroyed traditional civil society and failed to build a modern one capable of supporting a viable democratic process.

> The process of modernization, whether during the colonial era or after independence, failed to produce a democratic state or a modern civil society. Although both were hoisted as slogans during this process, the outcome had been the birth of autocratic hegemonic "secularist" dictatorships that used the state as a tool to undermine the edifice of society and to exploit its resources for the benefit of a ruling oligarchy. More than a century of modernization, during both periods, accomplished none of the declared promises of modernity: scientific and industrial progress, development, social integration, democracy, and the reconstruction of civil society.[4]

Civil Society

Like democracy and secularism, the term civil society is an intruder to Islamic political thought. Few Islamic thinkers have paid attention to the term or have addressed the concept. However, in an attempt to re-assess the early Islamic political experience and redefine its terms so as to accommodate modern political theories, some Islamic political writers have applied the term "civil society" to the Madina community set up by the Prophet soon following his migration from Mecca to Yathrib. The pre-Islamic community is likened to the state of nature while the new contractual arrangement in Madina is said to resemble the social contract. Proponents of this theory argue that the individualism of the state of nature, having been replaced by the acceptance of Islam by a community of Muslims, soon gave way to an organic conception of the community, the *Ummah*.[5]

This in a sense is similar in meaning to the term civil society as used until the middle of the eighteenth century by European political thinkers. It described a type of political association, which places its members under the influence of its laws and thereby ensures peaceful order and good government. The term formed part of an old European tradition traceable to Aristotle, for whom civil is that society, the *polis*, which contains and dominates all others. In this old European tradition, civil society was coterminous with the state. Civil society and the state were interchangeable terms. To be a member of a civil society was to be a citizen—a member of the state—and, thus, obligated to act in accordance with its laws and without engaging in acts harmful to other citizens.[6] One may contrast this with the concepts of *Ummah* and *dawlah*; these two, according to Ghannouchi, were also interchangeable at least until the end of the Rightly Guided Caliphate in 661 A.D.

Not only is the use of the term civil society so recent, although some Muslim and Arab political thinkers do point out that Ibn Khaldoun (1332-1406) had used the term "civil policy" to describe the condition whereby every member of society (citizen) contributes personally and morally to the total sum of civil power, which counters that of the state. But it is the product of, and is associated with, the European experience, and particularly its liberal-democratic tradition.[7] It is perhaps on this ground that Ernest Gellner strongly argues against the applicability of the concept of "civil society" to what he considers to be its two contrasts: the successful (Islamic) and unsuccessful (Marxist) *Ummahs* (societies).[8]

In the European tradition the concept has been through several transformations. As mentioned above, until the middle of the eighteenth century, the term civil society described a type of political association that through law ensured peaceful order and good government. Until then, civil society and the state were interchangeable terms.[9] As of approximately 1750, a new trend, originating in the Anglo-American world and seeing the two terms as different entities, started spreading. The growth of independent "societies" within civil society was being recognized as strategically important in order to guard against the authoritarian potential of the sovereign, centralized constitutional state that stood over its subjects.[10] John Keane distinguishes four overlapping phases in the development of the concept of civil society between 1750 and 1850. The first is illustrated by the works of Adam Ferguson (1723-1816), who perceived the state and civil society to be identical. The second is illustrated by the ideas of Thomas Paine (1737-1809), who called for restricting the power of the state in favor of civil society, and who deemed the state a necessary evil and civil society an unqualified good. The third is illustrated by the works of Hegel (1770-1831), who countered Paine's enthusiasm for civil society. Hegel viewed civil society as a self-crippling entity in constant need of state supervision and control. The fourth phase is illustrated by the works of de Tocqueville (1805-1859), who argued against the Hegelian view and urged the importance of protecting and renewing a pluralistic, self-organizing civil society independent of the state.[11] Before the end of the nineteenth century, interest in the topic of civil society fell into obscurity and disappeared almost without trace to resurface more than a century later[12] and become a shining emblem, to use the words of Ernest Gellner.[13] According to Keane, the language of civil society and the state began in Japan in the 1960s, and it subsequently played a leading role in theoretical and political debates in both halves of Europe, throughout Latin and North America, the Islamic countries, and parts of south and east Asia.[14]

The revival of interest in civil society, especially as opposed to the state, was triggered in central Eastern Europe by the emergence of opposition to the Communist regime in Poland in 1976. A discourse on civil society surfaced in France soon afterward as a prime referent for democratic projects on the part of significant groups of intellectuals and a variety of collective actors who sympathized with the East European struggle against totalitarianism.[15] Since then, the idea that civil society is the antecedent (or antithesis) of the state has entered into everyday practice. It now takes an effort, as Bobbio explains, to convince oneself that for centuries the same expression was used to designate that collection of institutions which, as a rule, today constitute the state and which nobody would call civil society without running the risk of a complete misunderstanding.[16] As in other parts of the world, the concept of civil society soon gained currency and attracted the attention of a number of modern Arab political thinkers. More recently, it has entered the vigorous debate among intellectual elites over the aspired model of state, and has become one of the most popular concepts within the circles concerned with political science and sociology. It has also been referred to by the advocates of democracy in the Arab world, both Islamists and secularists, as an analytical tool to diagnose the political predicament of the modern Arab state, and to call for the replacement of its totalitarian model with a more liberal one. Ghannouchi notes that it has also become one of the most important political concepts used by Arab "secularists" as a weapon in the war against the Islamic movement, especially in Egypt and Tunisia.[17]

Ghannouchi seems aware of the deep and distant roots of the Western concept of "civil society" but tends to emphasize its eighteenth-century association with the social contract as proposed by Locke and Rousseau. "Civil society was proposed as a counter to the natural state that preceded it. Humans in the natural state were said to have been dominated by anarchy, power, oppression, and hegemony, whereas the newly conceived civil society is founded on a contract among free individuals."[18]

Arab secularists identify the concept of civil society with secularism, and therefore, traditional Islamic society is discounted as a version of civil society. Put simply, a civil society, which is assumed to be a prerequisite of democracy and pluralism, is only attainable if religion is restricted to the private sphere. Some Egyptian secularists have been using the term *madani* (civil) to counter the term Islamic. A symposium was actually organized in Cairo with the title "The Civil State Versus the Islamic State."[19] This is perhaps why a debate has been going on regarding the term *madani*. Islamic circles within Egypt prefer the term *ahli* (which means both civil and civic) because it is believed to be more indigenous. It is argued that long before the word *madani* was introduced by Arab modernists, *ahli* described the huge sphere of activity that was independent of the state, including schools, *awqaf*, mosques, charitable organizations, and so on. And therefore, if *madani* is assumed by secularists to be associated with a Western-style modernity and consequently with secularism, *ahli* is supposed to be a more Islamic term. Civil society is thus rendered in Arabic *al-mujtama' al-ahli* instead of *al-mujtama' al-madani*.[20] However, Ghannouchi is not in favor of this distinction and is of the opinion that the debate, which has been taking place mostly in Egypt, over the preference of terminology is not worth spending time on. What matters, as far as he is concerned, is the meaning of the term, and so long as *madani* and *ahli* mean the same thing, the argument about the difference or the preference is futile.[21] Ghannouchi will find that many Islamic, as well as secularist, thinkers disagree with his assertion that the two terms are synonyms. It may not be farfetched to presume that his insistence on using the term *madani* instead of *ahli* stems from his unwillingness to concede to the secularist claim that *madani* entails the marginalization of religion.

Ernest Gellner provides a much more sophisticated argument than that suggested by Arab secularists for excluding Islamic society from the category of civil society. For although he acknowledges that Islamic *Ummah* (or community) is successful and enduring, he insists that Islamic society, which he adds to a class of what he calls segmentary communities, is very different from the Western notion of civil society, even though it may satisfy its plausible initial definition. A segmentary community is said to be one that avoids central tyranny by firmly turning the individual into an integral part of the social sub-unit. He argues that it may indeed be pluralistic and centralization-resistant, but it does not confer on its members the kind of freedom required and expected from civil society. He demands that civil society should not therefore be identified with any and every plural society within which well-established institutions counterbalance the state. He warns that unless segmentary societies are clearly excluded, the definition of civil society he invokes will include them and will mistakenly identify them with what he believes the Western notion of civil society to be.[22]

Gellner provides a definition of civil society that according to him is simplest, immediate, and intuitively obvious, a definition he considers to be deficient because it would include under the notion of civil society many forms of social order that would not satisfy the Western conception. The definition goes as follows: "Civil society is that set of diverse non-governmental institutions which is strong enough to counterbalance the state and, while not preventing the state from fulfilling its role of keeper of the peace and arbitrator between major interests, can nevertheless prevent it from dominating and atomizing the rest of society."

Whether an Islamic society is segmentary or not, Gellner seems to have no illusion that if segmentary societies are to be contrasted with civil society, because the sub-communities on which they depend are too stifling for modern individuals, Islam provides a further contrast. In his opinion, it exemplifies a social order which seems to lack much capacity to provide political countervailing institutions or associations, which is atomized without much individualism, and which operates effectively without intellectual pluralism. But Gellner has other objections that are more specifically applied to Islamic society. The first is that the Muslim world displays a strong tendency toward the establishment of an *Ummah*, an overall community based on the shared faith and the implementation of its law. The second is that Muslim polities are pervaded by clientalism; there is government by network. Thus, the formal institutional arrangements matter far less than do the informal connections of mutual trust based on past personal services, on exchange of protection from above for support from below. The third is that law governs the details of daily life, but not the institutions of power. For Gellner, a defining characteristic of modern civil societies as experienced in the West is that they enable subjects, who are interacting, to question power and authority, and to constantly undermine the very certainties of their existence. This he expresses in the term "reflexivity," which is, according to him, incompatible with the state in the Muslim society where the ruled judge their rulers by applying the religious norms of sacred law rather than the secular principles of a "civil society":

> Severe and fastidious about the implementation of the sacred prescriptions, they are not otherwise over-sensitive about the internal organization of political authority, nor greatly perturbed by its clientalist structure and its unfastidious methods and partiality. Nothing else is expected of politics. Authority is accountable to God for implementation of religious-legal rules, but not to man for the practice of some civil idea.

Gellner would not be entirely wrong if his analysis were applied to the current state of Muslim societies. There is no doubt that contemporary Muslims, including many scholars and Islamic activists, have been over-preoccupied with partial, even trivial, legal matters while neglecting the central issues regarding the constitution of the very authority that is supposed to oversee the implementation of these rules. Modern Islamic writers, chief among whom Mawdudi and Qutb, have, through the introduction of the notion of *hakimiyah* (God's sovereignty), created the illusion that the conflicts taking place in Muslim polities are those between God and some people, and not, as has always been the case, between different groups of people, none of whom dispute God's authority, but all dispute that of each other.[23] But it would be erroneous to apply this description to the entire history of Islam. In fact, the great schism in the Muslim community and the emergence of various schools of political thought were all over the organization of political authority. Gellner has also gone wrong in attributing the absence of a viable society in Muslim polities to religion or to ideology. El-Affendi, a critic of Gellner, sees a double misunderstanding in his analysis:

> Civil society refers, of course, to the institutions of society that are engaged in fulfilling functions other than the politico-military one. Since the main business of modern societies had tended to be economic, there has been a tendency, since Marx, to emphasize the economic component of civil society. This tends to obscure the complexity of the socio-economic dimension of civil society, as well as the actual diversity of societies and their structure, and peddles the implicit ethnocentric notion that all societies have to conform to a certain historical ideal. Secondly, on the basis of this mistaken conception, the past and actual vibrancy of Muslim civil society is thus overlooked.[24]

What Gellner has overlooked is the fact that Muslim societies, throughout history, were characterized with the ability to safeguard the basic orientation of society against state encroachment, be it foreign or local. In other words, Muslim societies had a characteristic capacity to develop and sustain structures to defend freedoms against oppressive state mechanisms. El-Affendi goes as far as accusing Gellner of exhibiting essentialism and orientalistic oversimplifications as he denies the *Ummah* the status of civil society for being uniquely based on a shared faith. Such claim, he stresses, is manifestly false. The very definition of a community involves some shared values or "faith" on which it is based.[25] Clearly, the term "community" here is assumed, as it is frequently in the Islamic literature, to be synonymous with civil society.

Another critic of Gellner, John Keane, finds in Gellner's treatment an unfortunate tendency to conflate different forms of civil society and to speak of civil society in economic and masculinist terms. He also perceives his thesis that Islam is incapable of achieving civil society as bordering on orientalist prejudice.[26]

In his account of civil society, Gellner presumes that a reflexive civil society is one in which there is little space for religion. He does not consider an Islamic civil society to be possible because, according to him, Islam contains within it the presumption of an absolute God that cannot be challenged or reflected upon. But can one really "question" or "reflect" without addressing oneself to the frame of reference within which such questioning and reflecting takes place? Emanating from its own frame of reference, a Muslim society deals with the question of reflexivity through *ijtihad*. It also does so through the concept of *al-bayniyah* (from *bayna*, between), which means that the human condition is such that it is compelled, or condemned as Jean-Paul Sartre would say, to engage in *ijtihad*. *Al-bayniyah* is a concept developed as part of the endeavor by contemporary Islamic thought to discover new "middle" analytical categories that distinguish Islamic discourse from the discourse of Western modernity.[27] It is the distance that separates the creator from the created; it is a human space where man can exercise his freedom and use his reason, becoming thereby a responsible trust-bearing creature.[28] This distance, according to Ghannouchi, comprises the huge *faragh* (space) within Islam where the process of *ijtihad* is exercised.[29]

As for the question of the compatibility of the sacred with civil society, any ethical system implies a level of transcendence, which implies in turn a concept of the sacred and the absolute. If ethics is relative, absolutely relative that is, it ceases to be ethics and becomes temporary procedures.[30] Hence is the idea of the return of the sacred, in the sense that man should not play god; that there is a limit, a finite quality of the human condition that could be said paradoxically to be a key ingredient of reflexivity. It would follow that living in an actually existing civil society is to recognize that man ought not, and cannot, play the role of god. This is a point that is surfacing again within the European tradition, and it comes principally after Martin Heidegger (1889-1976).[31] A notable example of this is that of Vaclav Havel, who has been speaking on radio to the nation every Sunday afternoon about the importance of cultivating civil society in the Czech Republic, while maintaining a strong belief in the sacred.[32] Many Christian organizations show willingness to be absolutely tolerant of different conceptions of God, for they realize that toleration is a key aspect of civil society. So, they believe in God, and they show respect for the sacred while seeing, at the same time, the role of the church as an activist role in generating compassion, solidarity, justice, and greater freedom within civil society.[33] Hence, contrary to what Gellner claimed, a concept of the sacred is an indispensable feature of civil society, or at least is not incompatible with it.

Ghannouchi, who listened attentively to Ernest Gellner as he spoke in June 1995 at the London School of Economics about his *Conditions of Liberty*, disagrees with his characterization of Islamic society.[34] He insists that the concept of civil society applies to the model of society the Muslims had known through much of their history. Ghannouchi concedes that few Islamists have thus far looked into the concept of civil society. However, those who do, he maintains, find it compatible with the concept of an Islamic society. As far as they are concerned, Islamic society rejects dictatorship, asserts the freedom of choice, respects human rights, and considers the community to be superior to the state whose powers are restricted by *Shari'ah*, by the authority of the scholars and by consensus.[34] It was this kind of a relationship between the state and society in the Islamic experience that afforded society a wide scope for initiative, organization, and self-sufficiency. Ghannouchi sees no harm in adopting the concept "civil society" provided it is cleansed of what he refers to as "some historic ambiguities" such as the attitude toward the relationship between the political and the religious and the supposition that civil society and secularism are inseparable. These ambiguities, he maintains, are alien to the essential import of civil society, namely that man and his interests have precedence over any form of hegemony. Such ambiguities, he explains, shroud the concept of "civil society" because its emergence and development in the course of European civilization had been associated with the liberal philosophy "which believes in the absolute supremacy of the worldly, individualist, and rational over the religious or the spiritual."[36] Ghannouchi sees no reason why the concept of civil society, just like the concept of democracy, should be monopolized by liberal thought. After all, liberal thought is said to be based on a distrust of values and the forms of authority that warrant respect for them. It separates the realm of impersonal reason, which should be that of public life and utility, from the realm of beliefs, which should be confined to private life. Furthermore, it does not credit the existence of social actors defined both by values and by social relations but rather validates private interests and preferences, seeking as much leeway for their exercise as is possible without infringing on the interests and preferences of others.[37]

Defining Civil Society

At the Civil Society symposium that was organized by the Beirut-based Centre of Arab Unity Studies in January 1992, the following definition was proposed:

> Civil society as we understand it is the sum of political, economic, social, and cultural institutions that act each within its own field independently of the state to achieve a variety of purposes. These include political purposes such as participating in decision making at the national level, an example of which is the activity political parties engage in. They include vocational purposes such as those served by the trade unions to uplift the standard of professions and defend the interests of union members. They include cultural purposes such as those served by the unions of writers and cultural societies with the aim of spreading awareness in accordance with the inclinations and convictions of the members of each union or society. And they include social purposes the accomplishment of which contributes to the attainment of development.[38]

Ghannouchi endorses this definition, describes it as reasonable and considers it more acceptable than Gellner's restrictive definition. Today, the concept of civil society, Ghannouchi explains, is associated with non-governmental organizations which seek—as mediators between the state and the individual members of society—to improve and bolster the intellectual, spiritual, and moral standards of these members and of the community as a whole. The purpose of these organizations would be to achieve as much self-sufficiency and independence from the state as possible, curbing its intervention power, and when necessary, maturing into a pressure force that influences the state and supervises its performance. This conception, he adds, concurs with the role of the *Ummah* as conceived by him as well as by an increasing number of contemporary Islamic thinkers, some of whom have chosen to use the term *Ummah* in lieu of civil society.[39]

The term *Ummah*, which is often translated into English as community, has many imports, whether as mentioned in the Qur'an and *hadith* or as developed through history. Of pertinence here is its meaning as a political community, which it derives from the historic Madina Document, known as the Constitution, that defines treaty relations between the different groups inhabiting Madina and its environs, including the Muslim tribes of Madina, Muslims who emigrated from Mecca, and Jews. The Constitution starts with the pronouncement that all these groups constitute "one distinct *Ummah* apart from other people."[40] The meaning of the term *Ummah* in the Constitution is clearly not synonymous with religion, and this is another proof that Gellner was wrong to assume that *Ummah* only implied a religious community. Rather than supplanting or abolishing tribal bonds, the Constitution regulates relations among tribes, and between them and the outside world, on the basis of the higher order of the *Ummah*. *Ummah* here is a concept of daily life that also stands for a certain kind of identity and defines a social unit. Hence, Ghannouchi sees that inasmuch as it denotes a society that is founded to a large extent on freedom and voluntary cooperation politically, where authority is not repressive, as well as socially and culturally, that is with regard to relations among its individual members, then the society Muslims established more than fourteen centuries ago was a civil society. It was a model of civil society that was not based politically on the legitimation of power, but on a contractual formula by which society is the employer of the state, and the state's mission is to serve society.[41] This is the ideal, Ghannouchi maintains, which only a true Islamic society is capable of realizing.

But, this is not exactly what the prevalent notion of civil society is about; it is more about the contrast between society and the state. Civil society is said to be the place where economic, social, ideological, and religious conflicts originate and occur and that state institutions have the task of solving them either by mediating or preventing or repressing them.[42] Or at best, and as a result of the dual colonization by the state of society and by the latter of the former, partly due to the transformation in the role of the state and partly due to the development of various forms of societal participation in political choice, it may be said that society and state act as two necessary moments, separate but contiguous, distinct but interdependent, internal articulations of the social system as a whole.[43]

However, Ghannouchi insists, perhaps with the intention of Islamizing the concept, that if civil society is one in which power is not monopolized by the state, but rather shared between the government—the political authority—and society, where the balance is in favor of the latter, and if it is one in which the state has no monopoly over the people's sustenance, so that private ownership is guaranteed; initiatives, whether individual or collective, are free; and the state monopolizes neither education, nor the rendering of social or cultural services, then this according to him is one of the characteristic features of an Islamic society. For similarly, the Islamic society, as he envisages it, organizes itself through institutions that are free, voluntary, and independent of the state. It is by virtue of their independence that these institutions fulfil many of the people's needs; and by doing so they secure society against paralysis and protect it from total dependence on the state. Not only would the interests of individual members of society be in jeopardy were the state to monopolize power, culture, and services, but the political process as a whole would suffer and crises would hit hard. That is why, he observes, the totalitarian state which swallows society, and in which the people are more likely to suffer deprivation, has proven to be a complete failure.[44] In saying so, Ghannouchi is taken to allude to the current situation in the Arab region, and in North Africa in particular. In spite of the abundance of resources, Arab post-independence despotic regimes, whose main priority since they came to power has been to destroy and disempower traditional society, have generated stifling economic crises that would have destabilized them had it not been for "the protection and support they receive from their Western allies."[45]

One of the ingredients of reflexivity, which Gellner stipulates as a condition for the inclusion of a given community in the category of civil society, is suspicion of the state or sensitivity to power, that is to "who gets what, when, and how." Ghannouchi maintains that suspicion of the power to be is more profound and well established in Islamic society than in Western society. He explains that since the coup against *al-Khilafah ar-Rashidah* (the Rightly Guided Caliphate), Muslims have harbored the conviction that the ideal Islamic state model was betrayed. The crystallization of civil society in Islamic history occurred to compensate for the loss incurred and confront the dangers emanating from the implosion of the first *Ummah* following the coup. Society no longer trusted the power to be and the people felt they could no longer rely on it. Gradually, the state relinquished many of the tasks that used to be undertaken by *al-Khilafah ar-Rashidah* prior to the coup such as the dispensation of *awqaf* funds, education, adjudication, and even legislation. By virtue of such empowerment, the source of which is clearly the people's veneration of the "Text" and scholars, not only did the emerging civil society compensate for the loss of some of the state's functions, but it undertook to protect the members of community from the state.[46] This is an important criterion overlooked by Gellner as he, in contradiction of some of his own conclusions about the difference between Islam and Marxism,[47] labeled each of the two societies as an *Ummah*. Equating both is, according to Gellner's own criteria, inaccurate. Whereas the Muslim *Ummah* is precisely a civil society before becoming a political community, the communist order had been imposed on pre-existing civil societies from outside by a "faithful" minority. This is why the communist order did not survive the state from which it derived its existence, while the Muslim *Ummah* survived the Mongol genocide, colonialist domination, and all sorts of assorted disasters and calamities.[48]

Civil Society and Religion

In liberal thought, as conceived by Ghannouchi, civil society is supposed to be founded on "a civil sentiment," on an upbringing that encourages law abiding. It is a society in which moral obligation and the need to coexist with others is an overwhelming sentiment. Hence, civil society contrasts the natural society. Therefore "civility" is the transition from the natural condition to the political condition, where an individual would concede in a political society some of his or her freedom for the sake of coexisting with others and attaining certain social benefits that would bring peace, security, and development. It is assumed that in the natural condition an individual enjoys unlimited freedom but individually lacks the ability to develop his or her intellectual, literary, and artistic talents because such a development essentially requires coexisting under an umbrella of law and authority. Hence, the founders of the theory of social contract assumed that in the transition from the natural condition to the civil condition—that is to the political condition—man conceded, or lost, some of his freedom in exchange for the benefits gained by socializing.[49]

However, Ghannouchi notes that as a result of extreme secularization in some countries, the concept of civil society has been used to counter religious practice. This has been more so in Francophonic cultures, those that are influenced by the French experience, which had known a violent conflict between the church and the revolution. The radical secularist culture generated by such conflict has pushed in the direction of excluding religion, barring it from having any influence on social process. Some of the foes of religion in the Arab world, who are strongly opposed to the Islamic project, including the bolshevists—those whom Ghannouchi calls the "enemies of liberalism and contractual society," have adopted the French tradition and have disguised themselves in the robes of civil society so as to undermine their Islamic foes.[50] Indeed, stressing that the concept of civil society has been used in Tunisia as a weapon against the Islamists, sociologist Abdelqadir Zghal points out that Tunisian Communists, both Marxists and Leninists, have made use of the concept to counter the Islamists, though after some hesitation.[51]

The influence of the French Revolution's thought upon North African secularists, which had in the past driven many of them to an extreme form of Marxism, is seen by Ghannouchi as a major obstacle that hinders dialogue between them and the Islamists. These secularists, he observes, have been less influenced by the Anglo-Saxon thought, which is much more tolerant in its view of the relationship between the religious and the political. Hence, he explains, those who have been influenced in the Arab world by the Latin modernist culture have sought in recent years to use the concept of civil society not as a tool of struggle against dictatorship but as a weapon in the war against the phenomenon of Islamic resurgence.

> In so doing, they have endeavored to impart on civil society an anti-religion, anti-Islam, dimension. By portraying the civil to be a function of the secularist, and secularism to be a condition for democracy, Islam has been portrayed as an associate of obscurantism and despotism. Arab societies are then told to choose between a combination of religion, dictatorship, and totalitarianism on the one hand, and civility, democracy, freedom, and secularism on the other.[52]

Ghannouchi describes this attitude as an "arbitrary dogmatization" of a procedural concept (that is of civil society), a dogmatization of a Marxist or French heritage imported and removed from its original habitat and stripped of its sociological and historical significance. He finds it necessary to stress that the European tradition is not, and should not be thought of as, based exclusively on the French experience of conflict between religion and modernity. In Anglo-Saxon societies, no such sharp conflict between the religious and the civil, or the religious and the political, has been experienced. The church, and this he insists is a well-established fact, was a central station along the path to modernity. In other words, religious reform was a principal contributor to the Enlightenment, and this meant that religion gradually ceased to be an obstacle. From the Reformation onward, religion acted, with varying degrees, as a catalyst in the process that reinstated the value of mundane action whereas prior to that mundane activity was portrayed as antithetical to religion.

Ghannouchi observes that today the religious establishment in the West is not only one of the main institutions but is the largest institution ever of civil society. Represented in the church (though increasingly pluralistic—mosques, synagogues, Hindu temples, and so on), the religious establishment is well organized and enjoys an independent status which qualifies it to contribute substantially to checking and balancing the power of the state in favor of society. The church has a significant moral and spiritual influence on the public. It possesses a large network of educational, social, and relief organizations and is financially independent of the state thanks to the collections it makes and to the revenues obtained from its huge investments, which make it one of the richest institutions of civil society. The church provides the members of the community with spiritual warmth and moral protection against the "atheistic" culture that is propagated by the "institutions of the secular state in the West." While contributing to the initiation and maintenance of dialogue, the church provides, through the various charities that belong to it, financial aid to the destitute and the needy. The church in the West is not, therefore, considered antithetical to civil society.

Wondering why some circles insist on perceiving civility as a rebellion against religion, Ghannouchi calls for a distinction between the modern, civil, and benevolent roles played by the church today and the historical inhumane and anti-social role played by the religious establishment in the Middle Ages. Then, extermination wars, colonial ambitions, and horrible repression were carried out in the name of religion. Then too, intellectual and scientific progress was suppressed and innovation prohibited in the name of Heaven. That was the era when legitimacy was bestowed upon despotic governments that exploited the weak and prospered on the spread of myths and illusions.

Islam and Civility

To Ghannouchi, civility is the transition from the legitimacy of power and necessity in the natural state to the legitimacy of law, or to what he calls the people's legitimacy, the legitimacy of choice. This process represents a transition from the condition of natural association with the clan, where man is born to find himself an affiliate of a tribe to whom he pays homage. Such an association is likened to the one that exists in the communities of bees. It is argued that it would not be possible to call the community of bees or the community of ants a "civil society." Although they do exist as a community, theirs is a natural community, belonging to which is involuntary and the administration of which is instinctive. In contrast, a civil society is a community whose members associate together voluntarily; it is one in which relations are governed by law, which itself is an expression of the members' free will. Whereas the community, which has the potential and the power to develop it further, chooses law in civil society, this is not the case in the communities of the bees and the ants. In the latter case, the system of operation is instinctive; law is not only unchangeable but is adhered to by the members involuntarily.

Hence, a tribal society cannot, according to Ghannouchi, be called a civil society because belonging to it and administering its affairs has very little to do with reason, free will, or free choice. Individuals belong to a particular tribe because they happen to be born into it. They cannot choose to belong to another tribe, and they are compelled to carry the legacy of their forefathers irrespective of its burden. An Arab poet from the tribe of Ghuzayyah had described this condition of barbarity saying: "I am only a Ghuzayyan; if Ghuzayyah strays, I follow suit, and if it heeds guidance, this is my route." What Islam had done, Ghannouchi explains, was to transfer, or elevate, the people from the stage of instinctive, or natural, belonging—as seen in the tribal condition—to the level of belonging to the community of faith. The free choice transfer had been from inherited modes of involuntary belonging to the tribe to a voluntary belonging to an Islamic society. The first Islamic society was therefore a civil society to which individuals progressed from the primitive society of the tribe. This resembles what is known today as the modern state or modern political association. However, the latter, in Ghannouchi's view, still carries some residues from the tribal society because its association is founded on race, color, language, or history, whereas an Islamic association is founded solely on faith which individuals embrace freely. Hence, true civility, he argues, is found in the Islamic society because belonging to it is not founded on instinct or fear. Furthermore, an Islamic society is administered by a state whose relationship with its citizens is based on *bay'ah*, a contract from which the ruler derives the authority to order or forbid, which in turn is an authority that is bound by law or *Shari'ah*.

Society and Law

A ruler in an Islamic state, Ghannouchi explains, has no right to disregard *Shari'ah*, the law derived from religious texts. While the texts are capable of being interpreted in so many flexible ways, the ruler has no right to monopolize the right to interpretation and has no authority to impose on the public any particular interpretation. Such an authority lies in the hands of the *'ulama'* (scholars). However, the authority of the *'ulama'* is not to be compared to that of the church in Christianity. "No such religion-monopolizing paradise-selling establishment exists in Islam whereby religion is turned into a natural authority before which the people lose all power and afford to do nothing but submit to its monopoly of understanding and interpreting religious text, and to its imposed code of prohibitions."

While respecting its *'ulama'*, an Islamic society does not lose its freedom of choice. The *'ulama'* interpret religion in their capacity as *mujtahidin* (plural of *mujtahid*, a jurist formulating independent decisions in legal or theological matters based on the interpretation and application of the four *usul*, that is the four foundations of Islamic jurisprudence: Qur'an, Sunnah, *qiyas* [analogy], and *ijma'* [consensus]). The *'ulama'* are not representatives of some kind of an official establishment that monopolizes speaking in the name of the Lord or interpreting His revelation. What the *'ulama'* suggest is no more than their understanding, or their *ijtihad*, a proposal submitted to the community, which has the final word, accepting or rejecting. This, Ghannouchi points out, is an excellent example of the compatibility of democracy, which he sums up as the right of the public to free choice, with Islam. An *ijtihad* that is accepted by the majority is usually adopted, though on most matters there could be more than one *ijtihad*. In this case people subscribe to the *ijtihad* they feel more comfortable with. In this, Ghannouchi finds clear evidence that an Islamic society is a pluralistic society in which religion neither suppresses the mind nor confiscates the right of individuals and communities to free choice. "Islam as a religion has neither been turned into an establishment nor is it monopolized by any particular institution, whether private or public. It remains a source of inspiration and guidance, and is available to all members of the community."

Ghannouchi does not suggest a mechanism through which the community in a modern Muslim society may choose from among various *ijtihadat* (plural of *ijtihad*), or how a chosen *ijtihad* may become law. Nevertheless, it may be assumed on the basis of his discussion of the concept of *shura* that such a task would be undertaken by an elected parliament in coordination with a council of legal experts appointed to the council on the basis of their qualifications.[53] In a modern Muslim civil society, one would expect scholars to organize themselves and their activities in associations or syndicates that would cooperate in one way or another with the council of experts as well as with parliament. This would naturally apply to a majority Muslim society. However, where Muslims are a minority, and today it is estimated that about one-third of the Muslims in the world are minorities in the countries in which they live, the best option for such minorities, according to Ghannouchi, would be to enter into alliances with secular democratic groups. They can then work toward the establishment of a secular democratic government that will respect human rights, ensuring security and freedom of expression and belief.[54] In other words, they serve their interests by being party to consolidating the civil society in which they live because this would be the best guarantee for their freedom of worship and freedom of choice.

In traditional Muslim societies, scholars proposed their *ijtihad* to the people who made the final choice. This explains why, throughout the history of Islam, certain Muslim communities chose one instead of any of the other several schools of jurisprudence that emerged from time to time. Some opted for the Hanafi school of *ijtihad* while others chose one of the other three later schools: the Maliki, the Shafi'i, or the Hanbali. While these four schools had been the most popular, other schools remained restricted to the shelved writings of their founders. This, Ghannouchi emphasizes, was not due to an action by a particular political authority nor due to a policy adopted by this state or that, but the outcome of free choice. In other words, schools of *ijtihad* materialize out of the interaction of Islam with specific social and cultural conditions. Once these conditions change, changes would have to be made by the school to accommodate the new circumstances. A failure to do so would inevitably cost an intractable school of jurisprudence its hold on the public who might opt for another, and are free to do so.[55]

Civility and Faith

What distinguishes an Islamic civil society from any other society, according to Ghannouchi, is Islamic faith, which, he suggests, has a profound civilizing influence on believers. As a result civil society is consolidated.[56] Ghannouchi bases his argument on a number of observations. To begin, Islamic faith declares all humans to be equal, having all been the descendants of Adam and having been the creation of the one and only Lord. Secondly, before their Creator, humans, irrespective of their color, race, or gender, are judged according to their deeds. Thirdly, divine honor is bestowed upon all, and no human is held responsible unless in possession of intellect and the freedom to choose. Fourthly, the entire universe with all its resources and laws has been tailored to serve humans who are encouraged to use their intellect and physical power to search for the best means of making use of this universe, which Ghannouchi describes as God's full-of-goodies table from which no human is to be excluded.[57]

Accordingly, those who choose to embrace Islam are told that working hard to earn their living is the only honorable way to fulfil their material needs and preserve their dignity. This, Ghannouchi clarifies, is not only encouraged but is considered a religious duty, an act of worship. A person who exerts his physical energy and spends his time seeking to provide for himself and his dependants is more honorable in the eyes of God than he who dedicates himself exclusively to worship expecting others to provide for his needs. Prophet Muhammad is reported to have said "An upper hand (which is giving) is better and more beloved to God than the lower one (which is receiving)." Furthermore, by attributing richness to God, Islam encourages people to seek richness through hard work. At the same time, poverty is condemned for being a burden and a companion to infidelity. While the right to private ownership is sanctified, Islam strictly forbids exploitation, monopoly, and the acquisition of wealth other than through lawful and legitimate means. Wealth is assigned a social mission that is fulfilled through the concepts of *zakat* and *sadaqa*, which constitute the foundation of the Islamic social security system. *Zakat* is one of the five pillars of Islam, the others being *shahadah* (declaration of faith), *salat* (prayer), *siyam* (fasting), and *hajj* (pilgrimage). Muslims with the financial means *(nisab)* to do so are obliged to give a certain percentage of their wealth (2.5 percent of net worth, deducted annually) as *zakat*. Other forms of wealth such as cattle, crops, and so on, are "*zakat*-able" in their own way. Although it has commonly been defined as a form of charity, almsgiving, donation, or contribution, *zakat* differs from these activities primarily in that they are arbitrary actions. *Zakat*, by contrast, is a formal duty not subject to choice. It compels believers to disburse a specific amount of their wealth; it conditions their identity as Muslims on their willingness to adhere to this fundamental precept of Islam. *Sadaqah* comprises *zakat* as well as all other voluntary charitable contributions.[58] Whereas *zakat* is a compulsory small percentage paid annually by the rich, many other forms of *sadaqah* (charitable contributions) are encouraged. These are optional and neither a minimum nor a maximum is specified. Ghannouchi subscribes to the opinion that if poverty strikes and the wealth collected from *zakat* and other forms of *sadaqah* is insufficient to alleviate the suffering and meet the requirements of the population, the state has the right to levy additional taxes until the crisis is surmounted. This opinion is derived from the principle that preserving life, and saving the community as a whole, has priority over preserving the wealth of individuals.[59]

Islamic faith's civilizing influence also derives from the fact that the authority of religion in Islamic society is founded on the freedom of *ijtihad*, which provides a large space for innovation and creativity. Ghannouchi's views on *ijtihad* have already been addressed in the section entitled Society and Law. But what may be of interest here is that in as much as it encourages *ijtihad*, Islamic faith motivates *jihad* by generating within the believer a passion for freedom. Referring to Malik Bennabi's work on democracy, Ghannouchi quotes him as saying that Islamic faith accomplishes two objectives: first, it liberates man from servitude rendering him un-*slaveable*, and secondly, it prohibits him from enslaving others. This, he argues, is where the concept of *jihad* lies. He defines *jihad* as the constant endeavor to struggle against all forms of political or economic tyranny; life has no value in the shade of despotism. Islam wages war against despotism using the weapon of *al-amr bil-ma'ruf wan-nahy 'anil-munkar* (enjoining good and forbidding evil) through a series of actions the minimum of which is by the heart, that is by boycotting evil and disliking it. This may then progress, depending on ability and resources, to condemning evil through the use of various means of non-violent expression, such as speaking up, writing, or demonstrating, or to the use of force. What matters here is that oppression should never be given a chance to establish itself in Islamic society. The Muslim is supposed to be a conscientious individual responding with appropriate action to whatever injustice that may be perpetrated in society. He is thus a force of positive change, a citizen whose faith reinforces within him the sense of responsibility. This, Ghannouchi stresses, is one of the fundamental concepts of a civil society that is based on voluntary belonging. Not only does Islamic faith permit a Muslim to resist despotism and rebel against it, but it makes it incumbent upon him to do so with whatever means available to him. It is understandable that a Muslim may lose his life struggling against oppression. But this is not the end of the story. A Muslim is promised a great reward for his or her sacrifice in the life after death. In other words the effort made is not wasted and the sacrifice is not in vain. "A magnificent reward awaits a Muslim who loses his life in the cause of fighting oppression. *Iman* (believing) plays an essential role in sustaining the determination of individuals and communities to rise against injustice. *Iman* disarms the pragmatists who like to use the pretext of an unfavorable balance of power to justify inaction."[60]

Quoting the Prophet as saying, "The noblest of *jihad* is speaking out in the presence of an unjust ruler;" and "Hamza is the master of martyrs, and so is a man who stands up to an unjust ruler enjoining him and forbidding him, and gets killed for it," Ghannouchi explains: "On the surface it would seem that the struggler who loses his life loses the cause, but in reality it is the tyrant who suffers a crushing defeat both in this life and in the Hereafter. After all, idols can only be brought down once the masses acquire the courage to stand up to them and defy their authority prior to bringing them down."[61]

Hence, martyrdom in the Islamic standard is not failure, and a martyr is not a loser but a hopeful who offers his life for what is much more valuable and, at the same time, eternal.

Tawahush

In spite of the attribution of civility and civil society to the Western liberal tradition, Ghannouchi finds signs of *tawahush* in modern Western societies.[62] *Tawahush*, from the Arabic word *wahasha* (to be unable to warm or reconcile, or to be alienated or become estranged), means the return to a wild or savage state, to barbarity. *Tawahush* can be said to mean a return to the "state of nature" as described by Hobbes: a state in which individuals are selfish, greedy, and power-seeking, in which an unending civil war of each against all rages, and in which human life becomes solitary, poor, nasty, brutish, and short.[63]

The examples Ghannouchi cites as signs of this *tawahush* include the throwing to his death of a young Moroccan man into the waters of the river Seine in the heart of the

French capital, Paris, by supporters of a right wing political party. He cites the example of the recurrent arson attacks by extreme right wing German youth on homes belonging to members of the Turkish community in several German towns, with the savage burning alive of many blameless women and children. He considers this to be a serious reversal of civility, a detour in the direction of a more "jungle" way of life. This savagery, in his opinion, is a return to a barbaric condition that had seemingly only been abated by economic growth, the source of much of which had not been local resources, but the colonial pillage of other nations' resources.[64] What Ghannouchi seems to imply is that the xenophobia exhibited in such cases is economically motivated. Evidently, the high rate of unemployment within indigenous populations in Europe has frequently been blamed on competition from cheaper and less demanding foreign laborers.

Ghannouchi suggests that humans, by nature, have the readiness to become brutes. Such readiness is inherent in the human personality, which is in constant struggle with what he refers to as the factors of ascent and the factors of descent. He sees that the Western solution to this problem, apart from inventing the concept of the monopolization of physical violence by the state, has been colonialism. Not only were the natural resources of other nations pillaged and brought home to improve the living conditions of citizens, but also criminals and rebels of all sorts were banished to remote colonies.[65] In other words, in addition to reaping economic benefits, European powers found in colonialism a means of resolving some of their social problems.

Colonialism in his view is responsible for more than just that. He goes as far as blaming the West for the present signs of *tawahush* in various parts of the Muslim world. This *tawahush*, he maintains, is atypical of Muslim societies. The phenomenon of violence is a reaction to Westernization, the colonial process undertaken by the Western invaders to divide the Muslims, nurture hostilities among them, and perpetuate their weakness and backwardness through the installation of puppet Western-supported governments in territorial states they themselves created.[66]

He cites as an example the violence in Algeria, which, he insists, could not have erupted, or at least lasted this long, had the French not clung to the ruling military junta supporting it in spite of its coup against the democratic process.[67] He notes that in Algeria, as in other Muslim countries where violence is prevalent, *tawahush* has been instigated by state security agencies to undermine the efforts by moderate Islamic movements to promote civility and peaceful reform. Prior to the coup against democracy in Algeria, the Islamic Salvation Front (FIS) had succeeded in defusing potentially explosive human bombs made of the clusters of thousands of deprived and trivialized young men who were driven by the system into desperation. Within the ranks of the Front, these mostly unemployed and frustrated individuals not only found something useful to do in the present and were made to see hope in a better future, but were refined into accepting, and engaging in, a peaceful process of change through the ballot box. When FIS leaders were sent to prison, their party outlawed, the ballot boxes crushed by tanks, and thousands of their colleagues banished to desert concentration camps, the survivors of this extermination campaign had no choice but to take to the mountains, wherefrom they undertook to fight those who, cheered by local secularists and condoned by the West, turned the dream of the Algerian people into nightmare.[68]

The other example Ghannouchi cites to prove his point that colonialism is responsible for the signs of *tawahush* in the Muslim world is that of the State of Israel, which, he reminds, was created, and continues to be sustained, by the West.[69] He considers the violence in Palestine to be a struggle for national liberation. This for him is a legitimate battle to undo the colonial project initiated by Britain and assisted by other Western countries that lend support to the Zionist entity out of the desire to expiate the sin of oppressing the Jews in Europe.[70]

Thus, violence in the Arab world is politically motivated. It is either in response to the presence of Israel in the body of the Muslim *Ummah*, or in response to the policies of oppression and persecution pursued by Arab authoritarian regimes. Both Israel and Arab undemocratic regimes could not have survived without the financial, military, and intelligence support offered to them by the West in exchange for their services.[71]

Not many people outside the Islamic camp may endorse Ghannouchi's explanation. Several questions may be raised about the violence in Afghanistan. Here is a conflict that is raging among Islamic factions, which all advocate *Shari'ah* and claim to want to implement it but cannot agree on ruling the country; as a result, they have caused much more destruction than that incurred during the war of liberation against the Soviet occupation. Critics might even question his analysis of what is going on in Algeria of indiscriminate killing, the murdering of women and children, and the destruction of the country's infrastructure. Questions may also be raised about the murdering of innocent tourists in Egypt by gunmen who claim to struggle for the establishment of an Islamic system of government. Ghannouchi might in return have answers to all these questions, perhaps still concentrating more on the root of violence. But there is no evidence so far that in any of his writings he has addressed the dynamics of violence, including the likelihood of its degeneration into violence for the sake of violence, as one may suspect has been the case now in Algeria and Afghanistan. It remains to be seen whether in the future, and especially in the revised edition of his book *Al-Hurriyat*, Ghannouchi will address with more depth an issue that cannot be analyzed solely on the ground of being a reaction to foreign or domestic oppression. This has been the way in which he analyzed the attack on tourists in November 1997 in Egypt. In his condemnation of the attack, he opens his statement with a reminder that this crime was perpetrated at a time when Egypt had adopted a "steadfast Islamic and nationalist policy in defiance of the Zionist and American plans of hegemony against our *Ummah*." He goes on to say:

> The crime is a stab in the back of Egypt by a group that claims to belong to Islam. This group, having been scorched by the heat of oppression and by the unprecedented high rate of death sentences, as frequent as the falling autumn leaves, raged in madness, slaughtering and destroying unarmed guests with the alleged pretext of inflicting harm upon the state. So blind they were as not to observe the Qur'anic rule of individual responsibility: nor shall a bearer of burdens bear another's burden.[72]

Ghannouchi's main thesis with regard to the phenomenon of *tawahush* has been to suggest that faith is the main source of pacification in the case of Islamic civil society. In contrast, in Western civil society the prevention of *tawahush*, or the maintenance of civilized standards,[73] requires the dedication of enormous material resources in order to compensate for the erosion of the influence of religious deterrents. As religious values become increasingly insignificant, and consequently less influential, the pacification of people is achieved principally using the method of *tarhib* (from the root *rahaba*, that is, to frighten or terrorize) and *targhib* (from the root *raghaba*, to want or desire), in other words the stick and the carrot. Ghannouchi stresses that in the West, this has been made possible, on the one hand, by the state's monopoly of violence, and, on the other, by welfarism, the reward of the colonial pillage of other nations' resources, but not due to the influence of civil sentiment.[74]

Civil here denotes "good manners," which enable people to accept one another as members of a common social order, and so treat one another with due regard for social well-being and quotidian moral rights. In an ideal Muslim society, as envisaged by Ghannouchi, individual members acquire civil sentiment from Islamic faith and values, and therefore the pacifying role of the state is kept to a minimum. Ghannouchi's argument is that whereas religious values generate and cherish civil sentiment, liberalism, upon the values of which modern Western societies have been constructed, depresses it.[75]

When Ghannouchi speaks of liberalism, he gives the impression that the term, in the way he uses it, refers to the total sum of philosophies underpinning the Western civilization. His attitude may be vindicated by the fact that liberal ideas and values are so deeply entrenched in Western political and economic life that it is sometimes difficult to distinguish between liberalism and Western civilization.[76] Ghannouchi speaks of liberalism in terms of "having two faces, one bright and one dark."[77] The first, which he refers to as political liberalism, is exemplified by the democratic system and by the recognition and defense of rights and freedoms. The dark side, of which Ghannouchi is critical, is what he calls "the philosophical dimension of liberalism." The dark face is deemed to be most detrimental to humanity. This is so because "it is based on the belief in the absolute ability of the mind to independently organize life. It gives precedence to the individual over the community and excludes religious guidance and values from the organization of economics, politics, and social as well as international relations. It ignores the metaphysical component of man in favor of solely fulfilling his material needs."[78] Ghannouchi is particularly critical of individualism, defined as the belief in the primacy of the individual and understood to involve seeing the individual as more fundamental than human society and its institutions and structures. He is equally critical about materialism, which he defines as the belief that the economic process is capable of being regulated by market laws such as the principle of supply and demand.[79] By materialism, Ghannouchi here means capitalism, which in his view is inevitably linked to liberalism, a view that was expressed earlier by C. B. Macpherson, who wrote: "Liberal can mean freedom of the stronger to do down the weaker by following market rules; or it can mean equal effective freedom of all to use and develop their capacities."[80]

In a way, Ghannouchi seems to echo a Marxist critique of liberalism, namely that its ideas reflect the economic interests of a "ruling class" of property owners within capitalist society.[81]

On the basis of the above, critics of Ghannouchi may consider his view of liberalism too simplistic or reductionist. Liberalism, it is said, should be seen, not in fixed and abstract terms as a collection of unchanging moral and political values, but as a specific historical movement of ideas in the modern era that begins with the Renaissance and the Reformation. As such it has undergone many changes and requires a historical rather than a purely conceptual and inherently static type of analysis.[82] As an ideology, liberalism is said to be polysemic, incoherent, and embracing contradictory beliefs, notably about the role of the state.[83]

Liberal contradictory doctrines are said to belong to two traditions, classical liberalism and modern liberalism. Classical liberals, who may now be referred to as neo-liberals, believe that the only rights the citizen is entitled to are negative rights, those that depend upon the restraint of government power. Hence, they want government to interfere as little as possible in the lives of its citizens. They advocate negative rights, which are said to constitute a "private sphere" that includes strongly-defended civil liberties such as the freedom of speech, religious worship, and assembly. Modern liberals, who advocate a positive concept of liberty, on the other hand, believe that government should be responsible for delivering welfare services, such as health, housing, pensions, and education, as well as managing the economy.[84] Ghannouchi contends that he is well aware—though some of his critics may still argue that he does not seem to exhibit such an awareness in his analysis—that the term "liberalism" is a loose one, and that several components—political, economic, social, and philosophical—not necessarily linked may combine together to convey one or the other of its imports.[85]

The emergence of each set of liberal ideas was influenced by developments that led to major transformations in Western societies. As feudalism started breaking down in the seventeenth century and was being replaced by market or capitalist society, a new intellectual climate, called the Enlightenment or the Age of Reason, emerged in the eighteenth century. Rational and scientific explanations, notable among them John Locke's (1632–1704) natural rights theory, gradually displaced traditional religious theories, and society was increasingly understood from the viewpoint of the human individual. The late eighteenth and early nineteenth centuries witnessed the development of classical economic theory. In his *The Wealth of Nations*, drawing heavily upon liberal and rationalist theories, Adam Smith (1723–1790) advocated the idea that the market should be free from government interference because it is self-regulating. The further development of industrialization in the nineteenth century brought about the realization that the minimal state of classical theory was incapable of rectifying the injustices and inequalities of civil society. The bridge between classical and modern liberal theories was provided by John Stuart Mill (1806–1873) who in his *On Liberty* elaborated the idea that liberty was a positive and constructive force that gave individuals the ability to take control of their own lives, to gain autonomy or achieve self-realization.[86]

The unrestrained pursuit of profit advocated by classical liberalism, and particularly by social Darwinism, as advocated by Herbert Spencer (1820–1903) in his *The Man Versus the State*, prompted late nineteenth-century thinkers, notable among them T. H. Green (1836–1882), to warn that the economic liberty of the few had blighted the life chances of the many. Following J. S. Mill in rejecting the early liberal conception of human beings as essentially self-seeking utility maximizers, Green suggested that individuals had sympathy for one another and were capable of being altruistic. Influenced by Hegel (1770–1831), Green believed that the state was invested with social responsibilities for its citizens, and hence strongly advocated that the state should be viewed positively as an enabling state, exercising an increasingly wide range of social and economic responsibilities. As governments in the West sought in the early twentieth century to achieve national efficiency, more healthy work forces, and stronger armies they were also coming under electoral pressure for social reform from newly enfranchised industrial workers and in some cases the rural peasantry. As a result, the twenieth century witnessed the growth in state intervention in the form of social welfare. This coincided with the rejection, prompted by the increasing complexity of industrial capitalist economics and their apparent inability to guarantee general prosperity if left to their own devices, of the belief in a self-regulating free market and the doctrine of *laissez-faire*. Government interventionist policies, guided by the ideas of John Maynard Keynes (1883–1946) in his *The General Theory of Employment, Interest, and Money*, was adopted by most Western countries after the World War II. But the economic difficulties of the 1970s generated renewed sympathy for the theories of classical political economy. Thatcherism in Britain and Reaganomics in the United States, both motivated by faltering economic growth in the last quarter of the twentieth century, had been major reversals in modern liberalism in favor of a renewed faith in the free market and the values of individual responsibility.[87]

The above digression has not only been intended to prove the intricacy of liberal thought, a fact Ghannouchi is not unaware of, but also to establish the relevance of Ghannouchi's theory that *tawahush* increases as welfarism declines. In modern Western societies, he suggests, the pacifying function of the state has not been restricted to the monopoly of violence. Pacification has until recently been successful because of the rewards the state is able to distribute to individual members of the society out of the booties of colonialism.

> The needs of workers in Britain or France or the United States have so far been successfully assuaged, and their grudge against the owners of capital mitigated. This will continue to be the case so long as workers are guaranteed a share of capitalist gains in terms of employment, social security, or other benefits, even if this is only a crumb of what is being robbed from other nations. And this explains why workers in the Western countries did not heed the call of Marxism for a global workers' unity against capitalism. Western workers needed not respond to such a call so long as they reaped the fruits of capitalism.[88]

As economic growth falters and states are compelled to shrink their welfare programs, Ghannouchi predicts that the absence of rewards will trigger more *tawahush*. "Today, we witness a decline in revenue. Cracks have started appearing in the matrix of Western society and racist groups have become so insolent and daring." Borrowing an idea he heard from Gellner in a 1995 speech at the London School of Economics, he takes this analysis further to suggest that when "wolves" (states) are no longer able to leave "dogs" (citizens) any more crumbs to feed on, the "dogs" will turn into wolves. By then, there will be nothing left to devour but society itself. Samples of this transformation, he reminds, were seen in the riots of Los Angeles in America, the disturbances of Brixton and Liverpool in Britain, and the workers' strikes in France and Germany.

Citing the incident when a number of Los Angeles policemen beat a black driver just because of the color of his skin, Ghannouchi points out that such an occurrence cannot be regarded a feature of a long-lasting civil society. The incident and the riots associated with the trial of the policemen implicated in the attack were an expression of what American civil society hoards of injustices and frustrations. The events, he predicts, are likely to be repeated. "More riots could ensue in San Francisco, or in Chicago, or in New York. The Palestinian uprising would seem very mild compared to the catastrophic consequences of future "explosions" in the heartland of America or for that matter in the centers of big European cities such as London, Liverpool, Paris, and Berlin." This is due to the emancipation of what Ghannouchi calls '*awamil at-tawahush* (barbarity factors) that are inherent in Western societies, or what he describes as the "remnants of natural society" that is founded on power and greed in lieu of truth and justice.

However, pointing to the existence of these "barbarity factors" does not prevent Ghannouchi from recognizing that Western societies have within them civility factors too. He cites as the most notable manifestation of these factors the numerous voluntary organizations that defend human rights, combat racism, and undertake a variety of benevolent activities. He acknowledges that Western societies are pluralistic and complex, and that significant sectors of people cherish good values, which are not much different from those enjoined by Islam. But he warns that the conflict between the factors of civility and those of *tawahush* may eventually lead to unfavorable results if religious values are not reinstated and individualistic tendencies curbed. "When the civil sentiment is deepened it provides a stronger and much sounder foundation for the respect and observance of law. Good is recognized as good and evil as evil, and people would think of others as they would think of themselves, or as Kant put it act as if your action would be made universal."

He observes, however, that when such lofty values are wrapped in materialistic philosophy and in atheism, as in the case of Western liberal societies, they become too idealistic. This is because humans are instinctively inclined to think in terms of gain and loss.

> Most humans do good not because they love to do good, but because doing so may reap them some benefit or bring them a feeling of enjoyment or delight. Similarly, they avoid evil not because they dislike evil but because they are keen to escape what it may cause of harm, pain, or misery. It is true that there are those in the West who respect the law for the sake of the law. There are those who would stop at the red traffic light even at midnight when no one is watching. And there are those who would declare their real income to the Inland Revenue even though they might be able to conceal some of it without being caught.

Acknowledging that this is undoubtedly a fine civil sentiment, he wonders what percentage of the people respect the law without fear of punishment or hope for reward. He thinks it is a very small percentage. "Only a small minority of people, though a highly distinguished minority, do so. The majority respect the law either for the benefit it brings them or to avoid punishment." In addition, he points to a predicament. While those who violate the law may be penalized if caught, those who abide by it may receive no reward.

In his analysis, Ghannouchi does not compare Western liberal societies with the present societies in the Muslim world, but with some envisaged Muslim society that may exist sometime in the future or may have existed sometime in the past. This is what weakens his case and makes his argument sound too idealistic. For it can be argued that existing Muslim societies exhibit serious signs of *tawahush*. It may be argued too that the least that can be said about civil sentiment is that it is not in abundance there either. Individual members of Muslim societies are not any more law abiding than any other contemporary human society. But Ghannouchi defends his position by insisting that while modern Muslim societies are not entirely devoid of Islamic values, they have been to a great deal corrupted under the influence of secularization. "In most

Muslim countries, where very little personal freedom is allowed; brutal force is used with varying intensities to de-Islamize customs and conduct." What Ghannouchi means to say is that by de-Islamizing society, it is the modern Arab state that promotes *tawahush*. Islam in his firm belief is the most potent source of civilizing.

Ghannouchi conceives of an Islamic civil society as one in which faith has an authority over the conscience of individual members. In other words it has the power of a deterrent, discouraging individuals from violating the law. For the faithful, respecting the law brings immediate and deferred benefits. While on the one hand, a law-abiding citizen enjoys security, protection, and a variety of social services, on the other, a great reward awaits this righteous citizen on the Day of Resurrection. According to Islamic teachings, the reward in the Hereafter for a good deed is multiplied at least ten times. Unless forgiven after repentance, an evil deed may be punishable, not only in this life, but in the Hereafter too. Even if an offender were to escape punishment by temporal authorities, he or she would not be saved from the wrath of God. Here lies the significance of the Islamic concept of *taqwa*, understood as the constant presence of God in the life of the faithful. When the faithful pays the tax, or the *zakat*, or when he or she stops—even in the absence of the police or their cameras—at the red traffic light, he or she does so not only out of obligation toward the state or out of fear of its punishment, but because he or she believes it to be his or her religious duty to do so. *Taqwa* entails the belief that if no one is watching, God is. So, to a Muslim observing the law is not only conscience-satisfying but is, above all, an act of worship to gain the pleasure of the Almighty. It would follow that in the Islamic state, worldly deterrents are not the sole crime prevention measures. Abiding by the law, doing good, and avoiding evil, or what Ghannouchi sums up as civil sentiment, is reinforced by *taqwa*.[89]

In a further step toward identifying civility with Islam, Ghannouchi proposes another defining criterion. Civil society is one that is founded on the Prophetic maxim: "None of you truly believes until he wishes for his brother what he wishes for himself."[90] It is a civil society in which good is done and evil is avoided not out of fear of the state but in response to the call of religious conscience, exemplified in another Prophetic tradition: "God is compassionate to those who show compassion to his creatures on earth." Civility here means liberating oneself from selfishness. A person's civility is a function of his ability to transcend his egoism and control his desires. In contrast to these Islamic values, Ghannouchi does not see in liberal philosophy a good answer to the question of why one should do good. It is possible that Ghannouchi has utilitarianism in mind as he raises this question. Although it is by no means representative of liberal thought or attitude, this theory has had considerable impact on liberalism.[91] Jeremy Bentham (1748–1832), assisted by James Stuart Mill (1773–1836), rejected the natural rights theory and proposed the idea that individuals were motivated by self-interest and that these interests could be defined as the desire for pleasure, or happiness, and the wish to avoid pain.[92]

Doing good because it brings you pleasure or protects you from harm is fair but not enough, Ghannouchi stresses.

> One may ask, what good does it do me to sacrifice my pleasures, or to go through the trouble of serving my kin or my neighbor or be good to the poor, or donate part of my wealth to a school, or hospital, or any other charitable cause? For many people, good is

what brings pleasure, and evil is what causes pain. An incentive of some kind is needed for someone to call off, for instance, a vacation to the Caribbean, and instead donate the cost of such pleasure and joy to those who are deprived of all joy in many war- or starvation-stricken parts of the world.[93]

The ideas of J. S. Mill, Green, and others, who criticized utilitarianism in favor of a more optimistic view of human nature, may be thought of as better explanations within the liberal tradition of what motivates an individual to do good. But, what motivates an individual to seek personal self-development en route what J. S. Mill calls self-realization?[94] Ghannouchi insists that although it is true that in every community there are those who do good surely for the sake of doing it, they are the exception and not the norm. Most people, he maintains, fulfil obligations because in the end an interest is served, either in the form of gaining certain benefits or averting harm. In other words, humans are by nature more willing to satisfy their desires than gratify their conscience. As Ghannouchi explains, Islam recognizes this weakness and responds by imparting a dimension to interest or benefit that transcends the worldly and the material. Benefit is not restricted to this life. Whereas some reward may be collected before death, a more important, most valuable, and eternal reward is collected in the life after death. Hence, is the centrality of the life-after-death concept to the Islamic way of life. Individuals are trained to sacrifice their own personal interests to serve the public interest. When they make sacrifices, they do so because they are promised a great reward if they forfeit what is immediate and temporary in exchange for that which is delayed but everlasting.[95]

Secularism: The Bear and the Fly

Ghannouchi considers secularism to be an impediment to the preservation and development of civil society. In the Western experience, he agrees, secularism had to a great extent emancipated Western mind from the hegemony of the church; it had reinstated value to temporal activity, restored dignity to man, and invested authority in the people. Nevertheless, he finds it to be detrimental to any human society. As a result of the marginalization of religion, secularism in Western liberal societies has compounded the effect of individualism in reinforcing selfishness and encouraging a feverish drive for making profit and fulfilling materialistic needs with little or no consideration for spiritual needs.[96]

In spite of the initial role played by secularism in consolidating civil society, it has, in Ghannouchi's view, ended doing the exact opposite. Allied with liberalism, which he considers to be "a synonym for selfishness, greed, and individualism," secularism will eventually do away not only with the notion of civility but with society itself, turning it into terrifying isolated islets, conditions within which resemble those prevailing in today's big cities of the West. He sees in Western cities manifest signs of erosion and a great potential for the eruption of *tawahush*.

> What civility remains in Western cities, what warmth, what compassion? They have become isolated islets crowded with millions of people. Inhabitants neighbor each other in body but not in soul. They fear each other, and some of them make a living out of terrorizing their fellow citizens. A person may live twenty, thirty, or even fifty years without

knowing much about his closest neighbors, let alone communicating or cooperating with them. Secularism is to blame for this serious deterioration in humanity. It is true it had liberated man from the oppressive church, but it went too far and liberated man from the values of altruism and humanity.[97]

Ghannouchi likens the effect of secularism on society to the example of the bear and the fly. Instead of killing the fly, the bear ended killing his fellow bear whom he intended to rid of the annoying insect.[98] It is true that secularism has emancipated the European human mind and unleashed man's potentials, but it is turning him into a selfish beast that has no consideration for others. A clear example of this, according to him, is what has befallen social relations. "The family has become meaningless, and both maternity and paternity lost the essence of being based on sacrifice." Arguing that setting up a family requires commitment and sacrifice, Ghannouchi finds no justification in the secularist logic for giving up pleasure and for losing physical beauty as a price for begetting children and caring for a family.[99]

Borrowing an expression used by Tunisian writer Muhsin al-Mili,[100] Ghannouchi argues that secularism in its eventuality is an antithesis to the concept of civil society; "it is the death of man." Secularism brings about the death of man because it views him as a body with a set of material needs, thus eliminating the most important feature that distinguishes him from other creatures, his metaphysical dimension. Unlike animals, man is not content with appeasement, but searches for the aesthetic and metaphysical symbols in the very things that fulfil his desires. Man is motivated by curiosity and is thus constantly searching for answers to questions about the ontology, causality, and teleology of the world. What secularism does is to "reify" man, turn humans into material objects, and this is the death of man.[101] Once this happens, and in spite of all laws and checks, man will be tempted, whenever it is possible, to escape the checks because man's motivation is to gain more and lose less, solely in material terms. The death of man means that society is no longer organized on the basis of civility but on the basis of Mafia-like competing interests that rob citizens and ravage society while covering each others' tails, sharing the spoils, and bribing those in power. Hence, the secularist state, even in its democratic form, cannot survive without the exercise of a great deal of violence; much more than would be needed in an Islamic state.

> In the past, secularist Western states exported many of their problems to their colonies. It was there that much of the violence was exercised against communities in the colonies and in fighting other colonial states over hegemony and spoils, some of which was needed to appease the public at home. The war effort meant more industrialization, more employment, higher standards of living, and greater ability to provide social benefits to the population as a whole.[102]

What Ghannouchi means to say is that the less a Western state is able to exercise violence abroad, the more violent it is likely to become at home. With less carrots to placate individual members of society, and in the absence of religious deterrence, more sticks are needed to restrain the public. In contrast, the Islamic model envisaged by Ghannouchi solves this problem through the concept of taqwa. The need for violence is significantly reduced when both the rulers and the ruled fear God, or to put it in another way, the level of violence is inversely proportional to the level of piety.[103]

Ghannouchi observes that the erosion of the piety factor in Western democracies has, at the political level, manifested itself in the sharp deterioration in the reputation of politicians. "A politician is no longer an exemplar of morality to whom citizens or future generations can look up. Today's shrewd politician is he who has a better ability to cheat and master the arts of fraud and hypocrisy. The shining mask of liberalism veils faces of wolves, whose main concern is to avoid a scandal."[104]

He cites Italy as an example, where reportedly few politicians have no links to the Mafia. The predicament of Western liberal society, as seen by Ghannouchi, is that no solution is found within the secularist framework for the problem of reconciling altruism, a prerequisite of civil society, with the inborn human trait of selfishness. Such a problem, he insists, has a solution only within a religious framework. Faith alone is capable of extending the span of life beyond this world, and of setting up a system of justice that transcends earthly justice to a divine one that gives hope to those to whom earthly justice is never served.[105]

However, despite his opposition to secularization of Muslim societies, Ghannouchi can see that secularism in the West is not one distinct well-defined concept. On average, and in spite of some excesses, "it is a compromise that separated church and state. Such a separation has meant that religion retains its role and its institutions." This is where as a politician Ghannouchi may at times state that he does not mind a similar separation in his own country to resolve the crisis of the modern state. He may say so while still insisting that Islam has no church and that it does not recognize this sort of separation between religion and politics, for Islam caters to both *addini* and *as-siyasi*. But in reality, he insists, this is not the problem facing the Muslims today. Whereas in the European experience secularism liberated the state from the church, in the case of modern Arab states what is needed is to liberate religion from the state. This is what Ghannouchi means when he reiterates that in Tunisia, for instance, the choice is not between secularism and Islam but between despotism and democracy, and when he asserts that what is claimed to be secularism in North Africa is nothing but false or pseudo-secularism. In other words, a true democratic state, even if secularist, is better than a despotic state, even one claiming to be Islamic. Of course for him it is still not the best. What is best, in his conviction, would be an Islamic democratic state, one in which the sources of legitimacy are *Shari'ah* and the *Ummah*.

The tension perceived in Ghannouchi's treatment of secularism emanates from the fact that at one point he hails it for having in the West been associated with progress and democracy while at another he considers it the source of all evils and the promoter of barbarity. Whereas, it would seem as a political thinker, he condemns secularism, as a political leader he is willing to accept what he calls a Western-style secularist regime, one that respects human rights and recognizes the right of the people to choose freely their government in a fair election. But Ghannouchi sees no contradiction between the two positions. When asked about his response to this apparent tension in his discourse, he insists that there is no tension and no contradiction. He maintains that if we were to handle the matter with some degree of relativity, we would find no contradiction between considering secularism a philosophy of self-deception, barbarity, tyranny, and alienation and considering it a progressive democratic movement.

It is a philosophy of self-deception, of barbarity, of tyranny, and of alienation because in one of its most popular definitions it means desacralizing the world and viewing objects, ideas and values as utilizable things. Consequently, those who are more capable and more resourceful are in a better position to make use of these things. Power becomes the source of value and is used to legitimize every action undertaken by the powerful to achieve his objectives and desires. It is the intoxication of self-deceiving power where desire for control is unchecked by moral or religious values; it is barbarity fulfilled—as in nazism, fascism, communism, and capitalism—in the annihilation of nations and civilizations, in the destruction of nature, and in using man as a mere tool for the purpose of making profit. It is a philosophy of alienation because it strips man of his most important characteristic. While sharing some characteristics with other natural creatures, man is unique in his ability to transcend nature. The more he transcends the more he fulfils his humanness. Hence is the importance of religion as an indispensable source not only for transcending nature but also for achieving a balance between the physical and the metaphysical in the life of man, a balance between the Heaven and the earth, between the clay and the Divine Breath, between economics and ethics, between conscience and law. This is what renders secularism an oddity, an alienation from the profound longing within man for transcending nature and for communicating with God. In this sense, secularism is a philosophy of solitude and bereavement. It leads to the severance of all social ties that can only be founded on man's transcendence of nature and of his selfishness. Only through such transcendence will man experience altruism and compassion that are indispensable if family ties are to be maintained. Secularism, in as much as it means this worldly, restricts man and condemns him to that which contravenes his nature. Man is created to live in two realms. He is bigger than this world, and condemning him to imprisonment in this world—which is the secularist disposition—is condemning him to estrangement and is a destruction of his greatest resource, his ability to transcend this world while existing within it.[106]

For him, secularism is self-contradictory. For as it marginalizes religion and desacralizes the world it offers itself as an alternative absolute, a sacrosanct, that employs all methods of deception and violence to track and uproot the other. He sees evidence of this in the intolerant attitude of secularist societies toward religious minorities. An example of this is the banning of the headscarf and denying a girl who wears it her right to education in France. This, he stresses, is a model of secularist self-contradiction. Within the same framework he sees recent calls for the proclamation of "the end of history" and the pillage perpetrated by the Western world during the colonial era. "In the name of this new sanctity, peoples and civilizations were plundered and nature destroyed. Selfishness has replaced justice and compassion. The globe's resources are controlled by an overfed minority that throws millions of tons of food into the sea while millions of humans starve to death."

Ghannouchi's view that secularism is a progressive democratic movement is not, in his opinion, contradicted by the above. For compared to theocracy and feudalism in the history of Europe, secularism in the West has succeeded, notwithstanding its aforementioned evils, in awakening the Western mind from its theocratic slumber enabling it to take hold of the reins of power.

As a consequence, many illusions were dispelled and secrets of the universe were discovered and utilized for the benefit of humanity. Man's inalienable rights to life, to freedom of expression, and to participating in administering public affairs were recognized. The sovereignty of the people was recognized and, for the first time since the eclipse of the short-lived Rightly Guided Caliphate, peaceful alternation of power was accomplished. For the first time too, a constitutional framework to inhibit despotism, even if at least in theory, was formulated and thus state powers were restricted by the rule of law. A ruler has become an ordinary human being whose task is to serve his people. Equality was established and opportunities were created for empowering society through the formation of independent institutions that accomplish for society a great deal of independence from the state and that enable it to pressure, rectify, and replace governments.

Ghannouchi goes on to explain that no matter how critical one may be of secularism, it should not be denied its achievements as a progressive movement. One of the great accomplishments of secularism, as he sees it, is the space it provides for pluralism and for a reasonable degree of tolerance and coexistence. He calls on Muslims to recognize that the presence of millions of them in the West today, for the first time in such big numbers, is the fruit of several factors including the secularist revolution that liberated the state from the hegemony of the church. He explains that this is what has prompted him at times, in the absence of an Islamic *shura* (democratic) system of government, to call for a secular democratic system that fulfils the category of the rule of reason.

As a leader struggling for political reform in a state that recognizes no political party other than its own ruling party, Ghannouchi's compromise in exchange for recognition is to accept a liberal secularist model that permits freedom of association and freedom of speech. It is a question of choosing between evils, and the lesser of the two if one has no third choice is Western secularism. This is the situation in which most Islamic movements nowadays find themselves.[107] Under normal circumstances, that is when the Muslim community can establish "the system of its intellectual, political, economic, international, and other relations on the basis of Islam and in conformity with its faith and cultural heritage, an Islamic system of government is the only choice." However, in the exceptional situation when "the community of believers is unable to accomplish its goal of establishing an Islamic government directly" (even when it is in a majority situation), power-sharing becomes a necessity. This would be the best option in order to guarantee respect for civil liberties, human rights, political pluralism, independence of the judiciary, freedom of the press, and freedom for mosques and Islamic institutions.[108] In such a liberal environment, which Western-style secularism may create, Ghannouchi's task would be to compete with everyone else to convince the public of his model of Islamic democracy.[109]

The next chapter will discuss Ghannouchi's theory that the modern Arab state, the territorial state, is itself an obstacle to democratization. Foreign intervention, without which such territorial state could not have come into being or continued to exist, is another major obstacle that will be dealt with in the next chapter.

6

The Territorial State and
the New World Order

If a modern democracy has been defined as a system of governance in which rulers are held accountable for their actions in the public realm by citizens, and if popularly elected governments are supposed be able to exercise their powers without obstruction or control by unelected officials (for example, the military),[1] the territorial state in the Arab world is far from being democratic. The policies of modern Arab states have generally been aimed at stifling the public will and concentrating power in the hands of military or quasi-military bodies that consolidate their power through the unchecked use of violence. A genuine democratic transition would inevitably mean changing the very character and mandate of this state, a development the prevalent "world order" is most anxious to prevent. Evidently, the position of the world order, both old and new, is calculated purely on the basis of economic interests, and thus principles are excluded from the equation. In this way, a double standard policy is justified and consequently the most democratic nations of the world stand vehemently opposed to the transition to democracy in regions where their interests are best served by autocratic or oligarchic systems of governance. This chapter will discuss Ghannouchi's theory that both the territorial state and foreign influence, or the "world order," are two major "symbiotically" interrelated obstacles that hinder the progress of democracy in the Arab world, and particularly in North Africa.

The Territorial State

Ad-dawlah al-qutriyah (territorial state) is the term widely used in Arabic literature to describe the political entity that came to being following the disintegration of the Ottoman Empire. Although founded following the example of the nation-state in the European tradition, the territorial state is not a natural growth of its own socio-economic history or its own cultural and intellectual tradition.[2] It has in the main come to the region as an "imported commodity," partly under colonial pressure and partly under the influence of imitation and mimicry.[3] Some researchers go as far as considering the state exclusively European and insist that until the nineteenth century no mention of the state was ever made in the Islamic political discourse. Nazih Ayubi subscribes to this opinion and stresses that with a few partial exceptions, notably Egypt, Morocco, Tunisia, Oman, Yemen, and Turkey, the state—as a concept and as an institution—has been a recent introduction in the Middle East.

> Until the beginning of the nineteenth century, Muslims had thought of politics in terms of the *Ummah* (a term originally connoting any ethnic or religious community but even-tually becoming nearly synonymous with the universal Islamic community) and *khilafah* or *sultan* (i.e., government or rule of respectively a more religious or a more political character). A concept of the "state" that may link these two previous categories of analysis (i.e., the community and the government) was not to develop until later on.[4]

The rise of the nation-state has customarily been located in late eighteenth-century Europe. Its emergence has been linked to the ideas that gave rise to the American Revo-lution in 1776 and the French Revolution in 1789.[5] On the basis of Max Weber's definition of the state as "a human community that claims the monopoly of the legiti-mate use of physical force within a given territory," the nation-state is said to be a mod-ern phenomenon. It is characterized by the formation of a kind of state that has the monopoly of what it claims to be the legitimate use of force within a demarcated terri-tory. It seeks to unite the people subjected to its rule by means of homogenization, cre-ating a common culture, symbols, reviving traditions and myths of origin, and some-times inventing them.[6] The rise of this phenomenon is said to be the product of a multidimensional process changing the relations of power in society. The main elements of this process included the consolidation of territorial units by bureaucratic absolutist states that for the first time were able to hold the monopoly of the means of violence inside their territory; the transformation of frontiers delimiting different states in clearly fixed borders; the emergence of the bourgeoisie as a new class especially receptive to the ideas of the Enlightenment (emphasizing the cult of liberty, equality, and particularly the idea of state power rooted in popular consent); and a new role of monarchs and rulers that was characterized by a fundamental change in the relation between rulers and ruled.[7]

In contrast, the rise of the modern Arab territorial state is located in the European colonial campaigns. The impact of industrial techniques upon warfare and communica-tions favored the relatively quick processes by means of which leading European pow-ers conquered the lands of the so-called Third World in the nineteenth and early twen-tieth centuries. The kingdoms and empires existing in most parts of these areas were defeated and, in many cases, destroyed. New states—called colonies or protectorates—were formed in their place. The colonial authorities named the new states, drew their borders, built up their capital cities, and established a central administration and politi-cal institutions to suit their economic needs and prestige.[8] Indeed, most modern Arab territorial states owe their existence to the colonial era, which was most instrumental in drawing up boundaries in their present form, in redirecting economic relations away from the Middle East and toward Europe, and additionally in defining—often very arti-ficially—the units that were to be singled out as distinct states. The end result of colo-nialism was the institutionalization and consolidation of territorial states in the image of the European pattern.[9] During the colonial era, which is referred to in some Arabic literature as the mandatory period, the institutions of traditional Arab society were seriously undermined and new realities of partition were created. Borders had been drawn, colonial interests preserved, national liberation figures banished or imprisoned, regional parliaments or local councils set up and constitutions formulated, flags designed and national anthems written. In other words, features resembling those of the European nation-state were created and draped on the emerging territorial states that lacked in sovereignty.[10]

Ghannouchi traces the origin of the modern state in the Arab region in much the same way. Encouraged by the eruption of the Iranian revolution in 1979 and the subsequent establishment of the Islamic Republic of Iran, he wrote an article in 1980 to emphasize the association of post-independence state in the Muslim world with Western imperialism.[11] To Ghannouchi, the Western invasion of the Arab world is one in a long series of calamities that have afflicted the Muslim *Ummah* since the Ommiad coup in 661 A.D. against the Rightly Guided Caliphate. It was this coup that "had inclined the state toward an increasingly imperial model and had begun the gradual alienation of Islam from political life, restricting its influence to cultural, educational, and spiritual activities." In his opinion, the very concept of the state was deformed, and "dictatorial" regimes reigned successively with the effect of alienating the masses from exercising their political role. Such regimes "encouraged a lifestyle engrossed either in play and distraction in the company of poets such as Abu Nuwas and Bashshar, or in asceticism and mysticism in pursuit of spiritual bliss in the company of Sufis such as Abu al-'Atahiyah, Ibn al-Farid, al-Hallaj, and Ibn 'Arabi."[12] Consequently, "Islamic life was afflicted with stagnation and an appropriate climate was prepared for foreign invasion by the Mongols" (c. 1258), by the "old crusaders" (c. 1096) and by the "new crusaders: Napoleon Bonaparte and his brothers." The latter refers to nineteenth- and twentieth-century European colonialists, who—in Ghannouchi's opinion—had realized Islam's revolutionary and liberating potentials, and had thus planned meticulously and with extreme caution in order to thwart them.

> They took over the reins of government in the Muslim world and earnestly sought to empty Islam of its revolutionary contents by means of controlling educational institutions. They managed to raise a generation of Muslims who could not envisage of revolution except if attributed to France, Italy, Britain, Russia or, of late, China, a generation in whose minds Islam has been associated with all that is reactionary and backward.[13]

But the colonialists, Ghannouchi explains, could not maintain a presence in the Muslim countries for long. "Just as the old invaders were driven out, the new invaders had come under the hammer of independence movements." Quoting General Charles De Gaulle as saying "we have realized that colonialism is no longer profitable," Ghannouchi concludes that Western invading powers were compelled to withdraw their armies, allowing for the proclamation of the establishment of a chain of independent states. These states were entrusted to what he calls cultured elites that grew in the lap of colonialism.

> Lacking in merit and aptitude, the Western-infatuated elites have pursued with utmost enthusiasm the objective of destroying what has remained of the features of Islamic life in order to construct on their relics a model that is certainly not Islamic, but that is not Western either. The appearance of the model is indeed Western: costumes, architecture, language, and bureaucracy. But it is an emulation of the West emanating not from pride and self-confidence but from an inferiority complex.[14]

The post-independence territorial state model depicted by Ghannouchi may be said to belong to what Max Weber called sultanism. This is a model of state whose administration and military force are purely personal instruments of the master, where domination operates primarily on the basis of discretion.[15] According to Linz and Stepan, the term sultanism connotes a generic style of domination and regime rulership that is, to quote Weber, an extreme form of patrimonialism. In sultanism, the private and the public are fused, there is a strong tendency toward familial power and dynastic succession, there is no distinction between a state career and personal service to the ruler, there is a lack of rationalized impersonal ideology, economic success depends on a personal relationship to the ruler, and, most of all, the ruler acts only according to his own unchecked discretion, with no larger, impersonal goals.[16] Furthermore, under sultanism, there is no rule of law, no space for a semi-opposition, no space for regime moderates who might negotiate with democratic moderates, and no sphere of the economy or civil society that is not subject to the despotic exercise of the sultan's will.[17]

Although Ghannouchi agrees that the Weberian characterization of this model of state applies fully to the modern Arab state, he is vehemently opposed to the name given to it. Weber's use of sultanism[18] to describe this model emanates from the notion of oriental despotism, which Ghannouchi not only discounts as unscientific but also regards to be part of the Western colonial enterprise. "Sultanism is a product of the 'culture' created by the Westerners to demonize the Orient, to justify the colonial onslaught against it, and to give credence to the notion that it is incompatible, in every respect, with their own 'enlightenment,' which they sought to impose on the rest of the world."[19]

He insists that the characteristics of the sultanistic regimes, which Weber and those who subscribe to his theory take to be anti-modernist and anti-democratic, do not apply to the systems of government known by the Muslims in the past. It is true, he acknowledges, that sultanates were not similar to modern democratic nation states.

> Nevertheless, they were not as ugly as Weber sought to portray them. While it is also true that these sultanates were not an embodiment of the Islamic ideal represented in the Rightly Guided model of the Caliphate in Madina—where the ruler was the people's servant instead of the people being the subjects and servants of the sultan, the manner in which government operated was far more superior and advanced than anything Europe had known until modern times.[20]

According to Ghannouchi, the Weberian sultanistic characteristics apply to the "modernization state" created and supported by the West in various parts of the Muslim world. In contrast to the despotic nature, for instance, of the Arab modern state, sultanates in Muslim history were not absolutist. For example, he explains, the power of legislation was never the prerogative of the sultan.

> Law making was an independent process and so was the judiciary. Society enjoyed numerous defense mechanisms starting from the belief that man is a dignified creature whose honor, rights, and freedom are God-given. These also included the role of extended families and tribes in providing individuals with protection, and the institution of *awqaf* (endowment), which established and administered, independently of the sultanate, mosques, schools, and social welfare services.[21]

To prove his point, Ghannouchi draws attention to the differences between two models of current Arab states: Yemen, which retains some aspects of traditional Arab society, and Tunisia, which, as it stands today, is a product of enforced modernization. In the former model, the state deals with a society empowered by its traditional institutions such as tribes, *sufi* orders, and the *awqaf*, that act together to the effect of serving society and curtailing the state's tendency to violate the rights of individuals. In the latter model, "pseudo-modernity" has destroyed the traditional institutions of society, thus pulverizing the community into vulnerable individuals who cannot be saved from encroachment on their basic rights by state institutions.[22]

As far as Ghannouchi is concerned, the Arab post-independence territorial state generated nothing but total failure.[23] At the economic level, he argues, the Muslim world is still tied down to "super financial centers" that rob it of its resources in exchange for a trifle price. The Muslim world, he explains, is burdened with the "crises of the West," which determines the rates of exchange for currencies in Muslim countries and which mediates in almost every single commercial transaction involving a Muslim country even if it were with another Muslim country. He laments that in spite of the enormous resources the Muslim world possesses, Islamic countries continue to be menial subordinates to international banks and big Western companies. At the political level, Ghannouchi sees that more than half a century after independence "the Muslim world is still shredded into 'chips' divided in allegiance between the superpowers." Describing the condition that prevailed during the Cold War, he notes that a Muslim country dares not express support for another Muslim country, even if only verbally, without first consulting the masters in the East or the West. With reference to the war in Afghanistan and the revolution in Iran, both of which had then still been fresh developments, he describes how some states in the Muslim world could not express support for the first because of their ties with Russia while some others not only failed to express support for the second because of their ties with America, but went as far as voting in favor of a U.S.-sponsored U.N. Security Council resolution that imposed sanctions against Iran. Political independence, he concludes, finds expression only in slogans and flags or in the regional conflicts "among the children of the one *Ummah*."[24]

At the cultural and educational levels, Ghannouchi finds that "the Western-devised cultural and educational model" is still predominant in the Muslim world. "Arts, literature, fashion, architecture, furniture, wedding parties, receptions, theater, cinema, education curricula, and the media continue to stem from the assumption that the West is the model to be emulated if one is to be civilized and avoid being branded as reactionary or backward." He cites in this regard the example of the ongoing debate on the question of Arabizing education and on whether the Arabic language is capable of expressing the modern sciences. At the legal and legislative level, Ghannouchi points out that although most Islamic countries have constitutions that pay homage to Islam, such declaration is given no regard when legislating laws or making rules according to which state institutions are operated and administered. "Brothels, taverns, gambling houses, usurious transactions, and displays of dance and nudity are all licensed by the authorities and protected by law."[25]

What Ghannouchi aims at is to question the validity of the claim of independence by modern territorial states in the Muslim world. The struggle for liberation and independence in much of the Muslim region has ended, at best, with transferring its countries from the epoch of direct colonialism to the epoch of indirect colonialism. The latter, in his assessment, is worse than the former "because our spirit of resistance is weakened and we end up in a state of apathy and triviality, lost in the realm of delusion."[26]

But it is not only because of its failure and lack of independence that Ghannouchi considers the modern Arab territorial state to be an obstacle to Arab renaissance and development. "Because of the territorial states imposed on them, Muslims are painfully torn between their common faith, culture, and history on the one hand and the reality of partition on the other."[27] He goes further to consider the territorial state in its present form antagonistic to the basic tenet of Islam, *tawhid*. Meaning both monotheism and unity, *tawhid* for Ghannouchi is the foundation upon which Islam, in all its intellectual, political, social, and cultural aspects, is based.

> There are numerous manifestations of *tawhid*. The manner in which the universe is run through a set of harmonious rules and laws designed so magnificently so as never to contradict one another is one. A second manifestation is the oneness of the origin of humans, being all the descendants of Adam. A third manifestation is the oneness of the source of all divine messages to humans, God the Creator. Hence, the Muslims are *ummat-u-tawhid* (the community of unity and monotheism).[28]

Ideally, Ghannouchi argues, *ummat-u-tawhid* is supposed to be governed by a single political regime that derives its legitimacy first from the supreme *nass* (text), which provides the outlines for state administration as well as for conduct, morality, and legislation, and secondly from the principle of *shura*.[29]

Conflicting Theories

But Ghannouchi is aware that the modern territorial state, especially in the Arab region, has its advocates. He acknowledges that at least two theories in contemporary Arab thought exist regarding the territorial state.[30] The first theory considers the territorial state an old recurrent phenomenon and not the product of "a foreign conspiracy hatched jointly by the English and the French," who are accused of having plotted to bring about the downfall of the Islamic caliphate. The territorial state is said to have long preceded the downfall of the caliphate that in turn is said to have collapsed because of factors inherent in the divisive and tribal nature of the Arabs.[31]

Ghannouchi recognizes that this first theory finds supporters within both Islamic and nationalist camps in the Arab region.[32] Unlike most Islamic movements elsewhere in the Muslim world, the Sudanese Islamic movement under the leadership of Dr. Hassan Turabi has, by way of accepting nationalism as a legitimate expression of the individual characteristics of each community, recognized the legitimacy of the territorial state. While consenting that Muslims should not recognize the legitimacy of the artificial borders inherited from the colonial order nor succumb to the divisive sentiments designed to separate Muslims into different nations, Turabi stresses that Muslims should nevertheless recognize the reality of the distinct existence of separate communities within the Muslim world.[33] This eventually led to acceptance, in the Islamic Charter of 1965, of the principle of the national state, which excluded extra-territorial Muslims from its citizenship.[34] Moroccan scholar and political leader Muhammad 'Allal al-Fasi (1906–1973) has similarly claimed that Morocco was always a territorial state and that although its people embraced Islam, they never relinquished their sovereignty. He believed that the territorial state of Morocco included the Western Sahara, Mauritania, and territories that had been annexed to western and southern Algeria by the French.[35] Muhammad Jabir al-Ansari, a Bahraini nationalist thinker, maintains that, contrary to what he considers to be a general misconception, the territorial state has always been the norm rather than the exception. Some people, he charges, confuse the concept of Islamic cultural unity with the concept of the unity of the Arab Islamic state. The former, he argues, had evidently been existent in the history and conscience of Arabs and Muslims whereas the latter had only been a dream that materialized for a very short period of time during the first century of Islam and then disappeared forever. The territorial state, he explains, has been the product of divisive factors inherent in the Arab psyche and culture and not due to a colonial design.[36]

The second theory considers the territorial state a colonial product that has incurred upon the Arabs nothing but misfortune. Ghannouchi is a strong proponent of this theory. While agreeing that some territorial states preceded the colonial era, he insists that such states did not view themselves, nor were they viewed by their subjects, as independent nations. "Old territorial states existed as political entities inter-linked through the concept of Islamic unity and by means of the caliphate."[37] To elucidate the difference between the modern territorial state and the old one, Ghannouchi traces back the origin of the old territorial state.

> For some time, the early Islamic *fuqaha'* (jurists) insisted that the idealistic situation, where a single state represented the entire *Ummah*, should alone be recognized as legitimate. However, eventually they succumbed to the status quo and recognized the legitimacy of the existence of more than one political entity within the same *Ummah*. The *fuqaha'* were faced with real problems that required practical solutions. Within a very short period of time, the territory under Islamic rule expanded manifolds and the size of the population grew massively. Thus, the emergence of semi-autonomous political entities, or "territorial states," was inevitable. The history of Islam witnessed the emergence and coexistence of several such states, including those that existed in al-Andalus (Muslim Spain), in the Maghreb, and in India. Notwithstanding the existence of these states, *khilafah* (caliphate), the symbol that represented the overall political unity of the *Ummah*, persisted. *Shari'ah* was still the frame of reference for all Muslims, the *fuqaha'* held on to the prerogative of legislation, and borders between states remained open. A Muslim could travel freely from one state to the other without restrictions. Thus, the conditions of "citizenship" remained simple; whoever belonged to the *Ummah* was a citizen irrespective of the state or the power to be, and thus a Muslim could settle wherever he or she wished because wherever he or she went he or she was a full-fledged citizen. In other words, in spite of the existence of more than one state, the social matrix of the *Ummah* remained intact. Tribes, *sufi* orders, and schools of jurisprudence permeated and transcended borders, which anyway were so flexible, expanding or shrinking depending on the power of the relevant state. The expansion of a state, or its seizure of additional territory, did not represent an alien invasion by a colonial power. To the subjects, it did not matter who ruled them so long as it was a Muslim.[38]

Ghannouchi cites as an example the adventures of the Islamic historian and sociologist Ibn Khaldoun (1332–1406). He was born in Tunis where at the age of sixteen he worked for a while as a government clerk. He then moved to Algiers where he worked as an administrator in its own government. Later on, he traveled to Morocco where he was appointed as a *hajib*, the equivalent of a state minister. Some time later, he moved to al-Andalus and ascended the scale of public office all the way up to the position of prime minister. He returned to Algiers where he retired for a while and spent some time writing his memoirs and documenting his political career. Then he moved to Egypt where he worked as *qadi-al-qudat* (chief judge). During the Mongol invasion, he went to Ash-Sham[39] where he acted as *safir* (ambassador) mediating between Ash-Sham government and Holaku, the commander of the invading Mongol army.[40] It is evident for Ghannouchi that the *Ummah* in effect transcended the state. The situation that prevailed through much of Islamic history resembled a modern federal system. In other words, the state in the Islamic tradition was an executive set-up under the overall control of a strong community. Hence, the central theme was not power but *'aqidah* (faith).[41]

This quasi-federal arrangement, Ghannouchi explains, resembled more the United States of America than the European Union, that is in terms of the level of cohesiveness or bondage and in terms of the existence of a supreme common constitutional framework. The loss of absolute political unity was substituted for by ideological unity. Although the *Ummah* was no longer governed by a single administration, it was spiritually and organically intact and united. Ghannouchi cites the example of the independent states that existed in North Africa since the sixteenth century. They had all paid allegiance to the Ottoman sultan. The ties with the sultan might have been feeble at times, but citizens of these different states felt the sultan spoke in their name, they responded to his declaration of *jihad* whenever he made one. Subjects regarded the territorial state, the product of a status quo, the lesser of the two evils when compared with the outcome of sedition and civil war, but they did not view it as the legitimate state.[42] To the *fuqaha'*, the state that replaced *al-Khilafah ar-Rashidah* (the Rightly Guided Caliphate)[43] was known as *dawlat-ut-taghallub* (the state of overpowering), because unlike the *Khilafah* it did not express the public will. It was a revolutionary state that came to being by force to represent certain tribal or sectarian interests. Still, in spite of all of this, Ghannouchi maintains, such a state did not undermine the unity of the *Ummah*, and should therefore be distinguished from the modern territorial state. "In spite of the resemblance between the two models in some aspects of appearance, in essence they are completely different."[44]

Faking National Identity

Unlike territorial states that existed in the pre-colonial era, the seeds of modern territorial states were sown in a different soil, under completely different conditions. For Ghannouchi, the modern territorial state is an alien commodity "that was brought and imposed upon us" in order to divide the one *Ummah* into many different nations.[45] For example, the creation of a Tunisian *Ummah*, which Ghannouchi stresses was promoted by the secularist elite of Tunisia, as well as of other *Ummahs* elsewhere in the Arab homeland, is a colonial design.

> The territorial state was never intended to serve the interests of the *Ummah*, nor did it
> come to being because this was what the *Ummah* wished or willed; it was founded so as
> to serve foreign interests in accordance with foreign wishes and willpower. Its whole purpose
> was to Westernize life and, therefore, its project is in essence at odds with the Islamic

project. In a bid to bestow some kind of legitimacy upon these new *Ummahs* new national identities were forged in emulation of the European experience, and the fragmentation of the one *Ummah* was accomplished in the name of national self-determination.[46]

The secular concept of national identity was, in Ghannouchi's assessment, the germ that crept into the body of the *Ummah* and afflicted it with the diseases of division and disloyalty.[47]

Nationalism in the European experience is said to have been a natural corollary of some specific aspects of modernization, a phenomenon connected with the emergence of industrial society.[48] Its emergence is said to be located in the late eighteenth century and after.[49] More precisely, the doctrine of nationalism was born during the French Revolution. The revolutionaries in France who rose up against Louis XVI in 1789 did so in the name of the people, and understood the people to be the French nation. Their ideas were influenced by the writings of Jean Jacques Rousseau, often thought of as the founder of modern nationalism, who had advocated that government should be based upon popular sovereignty or, in Rousseau's words, general will.[50] The French Revolution destroyed forever faith in the divine and unassailable right of monarchs to govern and sparked a struggle against the privileged classes in the name of a sovereign nation of free and equal individuals.[51] Nationalism in the Western tradition was therefore a revolutionary and democratic creed, reflecting the idea that subjects of the crown should become citizens of France.[52] During the Revolutionary and Napoleonic Wars, 1792–1815, much of continental Europe was invaded by France, giving rise to both resentment against France and a desire for independence.[53]

In contrast, Ghannouchi suggests that in the Arab region nationalism was imported and imposed by colonial powers with the objective of dividing the *Ummah*.

> It was the notion of Arab nationalism that turned the Muslim Arab against the Muslim Turk under the illusion that, by virtue of a British promise, this was going to herald a new era of independence and national sovereignty. Not only was the promise never fulfilled, but also the entire region was divided into colonies that later on were promoted to the status of "states" in the midst of which a foreign entity, Israel, was created.[54]

Ghannouchi refuses to accept that divisive factors inherent in the Arab psyche and culture, summed up in the nomadic factor,[55] have all the while been responsible for the existence of territorial states. While recognizing that the Arab territory is more or less an ocean of desert with small islets of cities and towns scattered here and there, he stresses that Islam has had a powerful civilizing influence; its main mission is to transform and promote Arab Bedouins into a civilized community of believers, the *Ummah*.[56] Following Ibn Khaldoun, Ghannouchi associates nomadic life with *tawahush* (barbarity) and *Ummahtic* association with *tamaddun* (civility).

He does not deny, however, that in spite of associating within the *Ummah*, which transcends and defies the desert environment, the Arabs have retained, with varying degrees, some nomadic traditions and traits, and thus some aspects of barbarity that may be revived and reinforced by geographic and ecological factors. He argues that the Arabs, like many other nomadic communities that embraced Islam over the years, such as the Turks and the Mongols, managed, in spite of converting to Islam, to preserve some aspects of their own culture. This, he explains, was possible because Islam does not preclude specific cultural legacies so long as they do not contravene its basic tenets, and this is why, he points out, so much diversity exists within the one Islamic *Ummah*. It would therefore be erroneous, according to Ghannouchi, to assume that the nomadic nature of the Arabs has been responsible for the creation of the territorial state. To the contrary, he argues, Islam started in Mecca and then moved to Madina, both of which are recognized as two very important urban centers where the task of transforming the Arabs from the state of *jahiliyah* (ignorance and barbarity) into the state of civility was undertaken. To prove his point, Ghannouchi refers to the Qur'anic text, where he finds evidence of contempt for nomadic conduct: "The desert Arabs say 'we have believed.' Tell them 'you have no faith.' They should instead say: 'we have submitted.' For not yet has faith entered their hearts."[57]

Ghannouchi's interpretation of this verse is that the desert Arabs were initially scorned for having had a rather superficial conception of Islam, a conception that would not have attained them the *iman* (faith) with which they could truly be transformed from barbarity to civility. The Qur'an associates barbarity with disbelief and hypocrisy: "The Bedouin Arabs are the worst in unbelief and hypocrisy, and most fitted to be in ignorance of the command which Allah has sent down to His Messenger."[58]

On the basis of the Qur'anic text, Ghannouchi also suggests that the difference between the Bedouins who are civilized by Islam and those who are not is to be seen in the way they conceive of their role and responsibility within and toward the *Ummah*: "Some of the Bedouin Arabs look upon their payments (that is, of *zakat*) as a fine, and watch for disasters for you. But some of the Bedouin Arabs believe in Allah and the Last Day, and look on their payments as pious gifts bringing them nearer to Allah."[59]

Ghannouchi takes his argument further to suggest that Prophet Muhammad had strictly forbidden the Bedouins who embraced Islam, and had already moved from the desert to the city, from ever returning to nomadic life. His objective of these arguments is to show that the values of Islam have the influence of repressing and even purging the remnants of barbarity, including the tendency to be divisive and rebellious. Hence is his assertion that reversion from civility to barbarity is considered a grave sin. It is in these terms, according to Ghannouchi, that the phenomenon of *hawadir* (plural of *hadirah*, center of civilization or metropolis), which were established wherever Islam reached, is explicable. "*Hawadir* were possible because Islam is a civilizing project; it could not have flourished and bloomed except within a progressive civilizational context." In saying so, Ghannouchi seems to want, without indulging in details, to strike a comparison between the Islamic conquest and other conquering powers in the known history of humanity. Whereas the former brought with it civilization, the latter were mainly concerned with pillaging and destroying vanquished communities. At the same time, Ghannouchi also seeks to emphasize that a tribal nomadic lifestyle is an unfit medium for development and progress.[60] Quoting Ibn Khaldoun's famous observation "where Bedouins prevail, ruin is the fate," Ghannouchi concludes that since Bedouin life is based on pasturing and plundering, it is a wandering lifestyle that can support neither agriculture nor industry.[61]

However, Ghannouchi's arguments may be quite vulnerable. For even though Islam has a civilizing potential, and thus the ability to curb the nomadic tendency toward dissent, its influence is far from uniform or universal. It has an impact on individuals only in as much as they believe in it and adhere to its values. He may even seem to contradict his own conviction, as discussed in chapter one, that by being a Muslim a person is not necessarily civilized. Furthermore, it may be argued that the creation of Arab territorial states at the turn of the century on the relics of the Ottoman Empire could not have been possible, even if the European colonial powers willed or wanted it to be, without the involvement of Arab agents. One may cite the example of the Arab nationalist campaign led by Sherif Hussein of Mecca (1856–1931) and composed primarily of Arab chieftains and their tribes. It would not be farfetched to suggest that Lawrence of Arabia (1888–1935) might have managed to instigate the Arabs against their Turkish brothers because he cleverly identified within the Arabs what Ghannouchi would like us to believe has been successfully cleansed by Islamic faith, namely *jahiliyah*, or barbarity. Ghannouchi might have sounded less idealistic had he argued instead that colonial designs might have benefited greatly from the re-generation of Arab nomadic tendencies. Capitalizing on the decline of the Muslims and the alienation of Islam's teachings and values, the colonialists succeeded in dividing the Arab world and creating modern territorial states in the Arab region.

State-Society Conflict

Ghannouchi's other criticism of the modern Arab territorial state is that since its creation it has relied primarily on violence in order to consolidate its existence. In the absence of any proper representation of the interests of the public, repression has driven thousands of intellectuals into exile or into prison. In other words, the territorial state has been at war with its own citizens. Repressive practices, perpetrated by security and intelligence services acting extra-judicially, occur across the Arab region: in Saudi Arabia, Bahrain, and Oman in the Peninsula; in Egypt, Syria, Iraq, and Palestine in the Arab *Mashriq*; and in Libya, Tunisia, Algeria, and Morocco in the Arab Maghreb. Indeed, it has been observed that the tendency within sultanism, whose criteria are fulfilled by Arab territorial states, is to use para-state groups linked to the "sultan" to wield violence and terror against anyone who opposes the ruler's will. As Linz and Stepan explain, these para-state groups are not modern bureaucracies with generalized norms and procedures; rather, they are direct extensions of the sultan's will. "They have no significant institutional autonomy. As Weber stressed, they are purely personal instruments of the master."[62]

Ghannouchi's verdict is that the territorial state is an "evil" that should be confronted. This may seem to contradict his declared commitment to democratization unless the struggle for democratization is the kind of confrontation he has in mind. Alternatively, one may assume that he does not think any more, presumably since the failure of democratization projects in North Africa in the late 1980s and early 1990s, that the territorial state in its present form is "democratizable" and as such it stands as an obstacle to democratization. Ghannouchi's pessimism regarding the prospect of democratizing Arab territorial states, or "sultanates"—a term that may safely be applied to all Arab states irrespective of the type of regime—is shared by Linz and Stepan. They observe that given a lack of rule of law and civil liberties on the one hand and personalistic penetration of the entire polity by the sultan on the other, the two prerequisites for (democratic) reform, an organized non-violent democratic opposition and regime moderates with sufficient authority to negotiate a pact, do not exist.[63]

But if the territorial state is incapable of shouldering the Islamic project, and is also incapable of supporting a genuine transition toward democracy, since it neither represents the public will nor is keen on serving the public interest, is not its removal a prerequisite for restoring the glory of the *Ummah*? Can this illegitimate Western-dominated territorial state be transformed into its own people's truly independent state? As an obstacle hindering the process of political reform and transition to democracy, how should the territorial state be dealt with? Having become the leading political opposition in almost all present day territorial states, are the Islamists required to combat this state, which has been so oppressive and repressive? Should bringing about its downfall become one of their main objectives? What are the options available to the victims of the territorial state?

While it is incumbent upon the Islamic movement to show no hesitation in resisting the projects of Westernization and the attempts to partition the *Ummah*, Ghannouchi warns that it is imperative that the appropriate method of resistance be chosen. This would require a thorough study of the existing reality, of what the *Ummah*, as well as the movements of reform, can afford. The rule he seeks to emphasize in this regard is that resisting an evil should never lead to a bigger evil. This is a fundamental rule in the Islamic jurisprudence, and in this context it is specifically applied to the use of force against the authority in power. Most Islamic jurists, for many centuries, have opposed resorting to the use of force as a means for achieving political reform. To them it was a matter of choosing the lesser of the two evils. When the choice is between freedom and despotism, freedom is definitely the choice. But when the choice is between despotism and sedition or anarchy, the traditional position of Islamic *fuqaha'* has been to avert sedition, which here means the total collapse of law and order and the spread of killing. This position gave rise to the dictum "oppressive government is better than persistent sedition."[64]

Although other theories of change have existed, some of which continue to be popular with some quarters within the spectrum of Islamic revivalist trends, Ghannouchi cautions that the quasi-unanimous position of the *fuqaha'* on this matter should be respected. While endeavoring to change evil is the duty of a Muslim, it is incumbent upon Muslims to observe the rule of *muwazanah* (from the root *wazana*, that is to weigh or balance). In other words, the least evil of options should be favored. An unwise choice, he warns, is like choosing to fight a battle inside a run-down house, and thus run the risk of being crushed not by the enemy but by the collapsing walls and roof of the house.[65] He cites both Lebanon and Somalia as examples of what may happen when a struggle against *qutriyah* (territorialism) leads to a situation worse than the territorial state, where entities more primitive than the territorial state itself, due to tribalism, sectarianism, or factionalism, are created.[66] Ghannouchi's reservation regarding the use of violence to reform the territorial state is vindicated once again by the observation made by Linz and Stepan. Given the absence of the rule of law and widespread para-state violence in a sultanistic state, the democratic path is virtually not available without external monitoring and guarantees.[67] Indeed, had it not been for the influence of Syria and the United States of America on various political and religious factions in Lebanon, civil war, which lasted from 1978 to 1988, would not have come to an end. Lebanese elections—though it could be argued are not really fully democratic—would not have been held. Not finding any external parties interested enough, or powerful enough, to put an end to factional fighting and restore law and order, Somalia continued to be stateless and torn by a devastating tribal warfare until October 2000.

Ghannouchi is confident that the "Westernizing" territorial state, or *dawlat-u-taghrib*, is destined to fail. The factors leading to its failure, he notes, are inherent within it. Even if one were to assume that the long term objective of its proponents is to establish a Western-style state in which religion is excluded or marginalized, and in which public opinion is mobilized in order to achieve happiness through scientific and technological development, the West will never permit such a project to blossom. In recent times, he reminds, the West has intervened repeatedly in order to thwart development projects, even when undertaken by states that were not so friendly toward Islam.

> The modernization projects led in the last century by Muhammad Ali in Egypt and Khairuddin at-Tunisi in Tunisia were vehemently fought. This century, the projects of Jamal Abd-un-Nasir and Saddam Hussein and all the projects undertaken by secularists within the framework of the modern territorial states for the purpose of attaining advanced scientific and military technology were aborted in one way or another.[68]

In other words, the territorial state is self-destructing because the West upon whom it relies for protection and sustenance will not let it achieve any noble objectives. Therefore, reformers are advised not to be hasty; they should not think that their decisive battle is with the territorial state. The battle in Ghannouchi's opinion is a long-term one, and is one that is waged at all levels in order to restore the political and civilizational edifice of the *Ummah*. Notwithstanding his emphasis on the importance of the state, to the extent of considering it a prerequisite for the proper and full implementation of *Shari'ah*, Ghannouchi cautions against overstating the state. "Aspirations should not all be attached to it."[69]

What Muslims should do instead is dedicate their resources to reviving and reinvigorating the *Ummah*. The territorial state has, since its inception, targeted civil society, which had already been weakened by the colonizer, in order to remove all potential obstacles that may hinder or resist its authoritarian regime. The shift in the balance of power was rapid, and it has, since the dawn of colonization, always been in favor of the state against society. A strong society is the solution, and creating one should be given priority. Ghannouchi argues that what kept the *Ummah* going for more than fifteen centuries is that classical Islamic scholars played a crucial role, as they saw the state deviate from the ideal model, in consolidating society so as to resist state encroachment. Therefore, in modern times, he suggests, tribal affiliations and sufi orders should be encouraged rather than discouraged; private institutions, such as schools and welfare associations, should be established and promoted whenever and wherever possible.

Furthermore, the territorial state does not exist in a void or in isolation from the rest of the world. It is part of a global project, or more precisely a world order, which is under the hegemony of the West. To illustrate this point, Ghannouchi cites the example of Kuwait: "Saddam Hussein so naively thought he could get away with occupying Kuwait, which he perceived as no more than a small entity that could be annexed through a pleasure ride. Soon he discovered that the matter was not as simple as he imagined, for there was a sophisticated world order that recognized such small entities and protected them."[70]

The territorial state—no matter how small—should, according to Ghannouchi, be seen as a component of a greater global entity that determines the balance of power.[71]

The World Order

Ghannouchi's line of argument leads to the assumption that since the Arab territorial state was created by foreign powers, and is maintained by a "world order" that is the overall balance of these powers, this "order" constitutes a major obstacle hindering democratization in the Arab world.

Contrary to the claims of its leaders, the new world order, according to Ghannouchi, is not interested in promoting the values of democracy, modernity, human rights, and international law. At the international arena, the new world order is not motivated in its activities by the desire to extend such noble values to regions of the world where they are still lacking. It has rather been motivated by the urge to serve its own interests through the domination of the globe and controlling its resources. The Arab region is of crucial strategic importance to the West. Since genuine democracy, through which the people's interests are represented and defended by a freely elected government, eventually loosens the grip of the Western world order on the Arab region, its spread to the Arab countries has been not only discouraged but also thwarted.[72]

In Ghannouchi's analysis, the attitude of the world order, whether old or new, toward Islam has not changed since the first European invasion of the Arab region. Nevertheless, he conceives of this world order as only one component of a sophisticated phenomenon referred to generally as the West. Most Islamic writers, and occasionally Ghannouchi himself, tend in their writings to use the terms as synonyms. This is not surprising because at the political level Western Europe and the United States of America have normally pursued policies deemed by most Muslims to be hostile and detrimental to Islamic interests. However, Ghannouchi recognizes that a great deal of oversimplification is made by Islamic analysts when dealing with the West, a phenomenon whose roots, in his opinion, should be traced to ancient Greece.

> Enriched by the Romans, and then fed on the teachings and values of Christianity, the Western civilization went through different stages and had its ups and downs. When the Islamic civilization was at its climax, the Western civilization had reached a decadent middle age best known for its religious wars, feudalism, injustices, oppression, and backwardness. Then the two civilizations exchanged positions thanks to the movement of religious reform. Scientific discoveries, liberalization, and finally industrialization swept through the Western world, which eventually accomplished virtual dominion of the entire world.[73]

Ghannouchi suggests that Western campaigns to dominate the world were in the old times, that is prior to the Enlightenment, justified in the name of converting heathens in America, Africa, and Asia to Christianity. The advent of *intégrisme scientiste* more than two centuries ago provided a new justification for colonial expansion. This has been the transfer of scientific and secular values to the primitive nations that endured under the hegemony of *age theologique*, an idea attributed to the French Auguste Comte (1798-1857) and to his English counterpart John Stuart Mill (1806-1873). To prove his theory, Ghannouchi cites the example of Jules Ferry, the French prime minister between 1881 and 1885, who stood before the French parliament to answer the question "what kind of civilization is that which is imposed by force." The answer was: "Upper races have a practical right over lower races."[74] The justification was to change again with the advent of the so-called new world order, which is said to have materialized upon the collapse of the Communist bloc, thus marking the end of the Cold War. The Gulf War in 1991 signaled the launch of the new world order, which claims to uphold international law and defend the interests of the international community. The real objectives of this world order, as seen by Ghannouchi, have been to maintain control of the oil resources, protect Israel, and achieve American hegemony on the entire globe.[75]

Greed and Fear

Ghannouchi cites the experience of his own country, Tunisia, as an example of western hegemony. The French, in the last century, colonized much of North Africa and ruled Tunisia from 1883 to 1956. In fact, French intervention in Tunisian affairs preceded the 1883 military occupation with the effect of aborting what Ghannouchi describes as a genuine reformation and modernization project launched in 1867 by Khairuddin at-Tunisi.

> French diplomats in Tunis incited the Bey entourage to resist the reforms while enticing the Bey to indulge in extravagant spending, especially the construction of palaces, using funds borrowed from Western banks. While gradually exhausting the state's budget, this attitude increased the influence of the Western lenders in the country. Eventually, Tunisia was taken over by France for having failed to honor its foreign debts. The Bey was then told to suspend the constitution and to expel Khairuddin, the founder and leader of the reform movement.[76]

Foreign intervention brought an end to the first modernization project in Tunisia, described by Ghannouchi as "an enlightened Islamic project that sought to learn and borrow from the Western civilization without conceding the country's Arab and Islamic identity." Under foreign influence, the doors to the country's markets were rendered wide open to foreign commodities and the economy was made increasingly dependent upon the West. Had the reform process been allowed to continue, Ghannouchi maintains, it would have transformed the country and enabled it to join the world of modernity upon Islamic foundations. "The colonizers thwarted the reform process and placed the country under French mandate subjecting it to Westernization, to pseudo-modernization. The colonizers' program was aimed at destroying Tunisia's specific cultural identity, undermining its economic independence, absorbing it into the French culture, and transforming it into a subordinate rather than a partner of the West."[77]

The French, according to Ghannouchi, exercised their influence at several levels. On the one hand, they marginalized Arab-Islamic education by establishing French educational institutions. On the other, they destroyed Tunisian traditional industries and linked the local economy to their own, rendering the country completely dependent on France. The French also targeted the *awqaf* (endowment) establishment. In other words, the French were the first to strip Tunisian civil society of its strength and independence. Ghannouchi maintains that pre-colonization Tunisian society was teeming with movement and modernization ideas.

> Prior to the seizure of the country by the French, the state had limited control over society whose educational, religious, and legal institutions were independent. When the people rose up to defend their beleaguered society, preserve their cultural identity, and struggle

for the independence of their country, the French proclaimed the country independent, handing it over to their own disciples, Tunisian pseudo-secularists, who continued the work, and who turned out to be much more efficient in Westernizing the country than their masters.[78]

The same story, Ghannouchi suggests, was repeated in various parts of the Muslim world where Western-supported pseudo-modernist elites reigned, deriving legitimacy not from the people, but from Western-aided violence. The result, he asserts, was disastrous. On the one hand, development projects failed and resources were squandered due to corruption and mismanagement, and as a result the future of many generations to come has been pledged to foreign creditors.[79] On the other hand, the policy of undermining traditional institutions of civil society, and forcing the people to renounce their own culture and heritage in favor of an imported one, led to the creation of a huge gap of mistrust between the ruling elite and the public. Ataturk of Turkey, the Shah of Iran, and Bourguiba of Tunisia are, according to Ghannouchi, examples of such pseudo-modernists, who turned out to be corrupt dictators.[80]

While in the past European colonial powers invaded Muslim land mainly for economic reasons, today Western powers not only have interests to defend, but they also fear the revival of Islamic power, a "nightmare" they seek to prevent from coming true. This issue has preoccupied Ghannouchi for quite some time, but more so since he settled in Britain in 1991. Having been exposed to the media coverage on Islam in the aftermath of the Gulf War and the abortion of the democratic process in Algeria, he has sought to refute the claims that Islam poses a threat to the West. The anxieties expressed by certain circles in the West were unjustified, and in his opinion, the leaders of the new world order are misled and ill-advised on Islam. This is especially so with regard to the question of fundamentalism. The applicability of the term fundamentalism to Islam or to Muslims is rejected by Ghannouchi. He considers this term to be the product of Christian culture "that lacked a concept for *ijtihad*."[81]

The term fundamentalism, perceived as vacuous, derogatory, and explaining a phenomenon that is alien to Islam,[82] has been rejected by most Muslim thinkers and also by some Western academics who have studied and written on the phenomenon of Islamic resurgence.[83] The general attitude in the West today is to describe all those who call for a return to the fundamentals of Islam fundamentalist or *intégrist*. In a strict sense this could include all practicing Muslims who accept the Qur'an as the literal word of God and the Sunnah (example) of Prophet Muhammad as a normative model for living. Both fundamentalism and *intégrisme* are often equated with political activism, extremism, fanaticism, terrorism, and anti-Westernism. According to John Esposito, the two words are too laden with Christian presuppositions and Western stereotypes.[84] In the Arab region, *usuliyah*[85] is used by secularist writers and journalists as an equivalent to the term fundamentalism to describe Islamic activism. In this case it is generally taken to mean the advocating of *Shari'ah*.[86]

Ghannouchi believes that a state of panic prevails in the Western world while very little effort, in his opinion, is made to understand the transformations that are taking place in Muslim countries. He detects an utter failure in the West to recognize that in response to decades of corruption, injustice, and oppression, a new Muslim generation of highly educated intellectuals has shouldered the responsibility of reforming society and applying true modernity, which he defines as the attainment of freedom, dignity, and effective power sharing and benefiting from the positive aspects of Western civilization. Pseudo-modernity, in contrast, is the mere copying of the negative aspects of the Western civilization at the expense of Muslim faith and culture.[87]

> One of the main objectives of modern reformists is to pursue an open-minded forward-looking policy in dealing with national and international issues. Their aim is to rid themselves of narrow-minded territorialism under the pretext of which, and as a result of whose false claim to modernity, the entire Muslim community was squeezed to one corner until it almost suffocated after failing to resolve any of its problems.

By the reformist trend Ghannouchi means the current Islamic revival movement, commonly referred to in Western media and Western political circles as Islamic fundamentalism, or political Islam. The Islamic revival movement, which Ghannouchi suggests may in some aspects be compared to the Protestant reform movement in Europe's Renaissance, is a process of vivid intellectual revival that encompasses social, economic, and political aspects. "It emanates from a profound belief in liberty and political participation." This, he explains, is the fruit of a genuine development in the thinking of contemporary mainstream Islamists, who have as a result earned many enemies within the ruling elites that resist reform and reject the principle of power sharing. "They have also gained enemies within the West to whom threatened Arab ruling elites turn for help and support in their campaign against the alleged common enemy, the fundamentalist threat." Ghannouchi appreciates that the choice for Western powers has not been easy. Western powers are torn between the principles they believe in, such as democracy, liberty, and human rights, and what they perceive to be their interests in the region. The latter is in line with the Western colonial inclination toward cultural hegemony and profound inability to deal with the "other" unless the other is in subservient position. This has led to the failure to realize, or recognize, that today Islam, as a culture and a way of life, has become the choice of the Muslims throughout the Muslim world as evident from the successes achieved by the Islamists in elections held in Algeria, Tunisia, Yemen, Turkey, and other countries. "If democracy is permitted to take its course in the Muslim world, Islam will undoubtedly rule because nothing today has the aptitude to compete with its equality-promoting, justice-serving, and prosperity-generating values."

Myth of a New Threat

Ghannouchi regrets that there are what he calls "programmed minds" in the West who find it difficult to envisage a free and prosperous "Islamic" Middle East in which wealth is well distributed, and which can become a partner to, rather than an enemy of, progress and international peace. He points to the negative coverage Islam receives in the Western media. Intentionally, or out of sheer ignorance, the media, especially in the United States of America, exploit the Western public's confused state of mind vis-à-vis Islam. They have succeeded to a large extent in isolating the Muslims and in portraying Islam as an antagonist of the West and its civilization. He cites as an example the media coverage of the New York World Trade Center bombing. The media focused on the religious identity of the defendants with the consequence of incriminating Islam itself.[88] He is outraged by what he considers to be a damning evidence of hypocrisy and double standard. For although the Jewish Defense League has reportedly been implicated in the perpetration of no less than seventy bombings in the United States, no one accused the Jews or Judaism of terrorism, let alone the suspicion that there was a deliberate attempt of a cover-up. What he finds most deplorable is the persistent campaign against Islam by the Western media. Since the eruption of the Iranian revolution, the Western media have been feeding the public with distorted images that cause resentment and fear and that portray Islam as a threat. Islam is alleged to be fundamentally opposed to democratic values and to the aspirations of humanity in accomplishing peace, freedom, progress, and equality.

In addition to the role played by the media in mobilizing public opinion against Islam, politicians, missionary establishments, and strategic and academic research centers are accused of constantly reinforcing the terrifying images relayed from the legacy of ancient conflicts between Islam and Europe to today's Western public opinion. Ghannouchi cites as an example a statement made by former German Chancellor Helmut Kohl at a convention of German defense affairs experts in February 1994. In his statement, which Ghannouchi says represented a declaration of war against Islam and Islamic activists, Kohl reportedly said: "The Islamic movements of North Africa have become a source of increasing concern for Bonn and Paris and are being carefully monitored. Security plans for Europe and the Mediterranean basin need careful attention in light of what is happening in Algeria, Morocco, Tunisia, and Egypt." Kohl is also said to have warned against the possibility that "radicals" may obtain medium range missiles, which could be used to hit targets one thousand kilometers away.

Suspicion and apprehension is further heightened by the existence of large Muslim communities in major cities in the West. Ghannouchi notes that Western countries have only recently experienced the presence of such large Muslim communities in their midst. This phenomenon, he suggests, sustains the feelings of apprehension toward Islam, which some Westerners perceive as a threat to their own lifestyle. He associates it with the rise in xenophobia and the boost in the popularity of the extreme right, which blames the rise in unemployment and crime on Muslim immigrants. In France, he observes, the Islamic threat has become a domestic issue; it is exploited in political campaigning in a country "whose wound of defeat in Algeria has not healed, and who is known for its extreme secular heritage that is rather hostile to Islam." Ghannouchi explains that the roots of this hostility are to be found in the Enlightenment. Some of its pioneers such as Voltaire, "had no hesitation, by way of flattering the religious and political establishments of their time, to express hatred for Islam and instigate war against it." Voltaire, who had written a book of slander against Prophet Muhammad, excluded the Muslims from the right to tolerance in his famous essay of 1762. He considered the Turks to be a curse and called for their extermination. He confessed to Catherine the Great that the sacking of the Ottoman Empire would enable him to die content, adding his one regret that he would die without having taken part in killing the Turks.[89] This mode of thinking is by no means restricted to a remote period of history. In his book *Le nouveau monde*, Pierre Lelouche, key adviser to Jacques Chirac, French majority leader and presidential candidate, warned against the growing dangers of fundamentalism and dictatorship in the Muslim world. Former Belgian interior minister and European Parliament member Joseph Michele played the same tune, saying: "We run the risk of becoming like the Roman people, invaded by barbarian peoples such as Arabs, Moroccans, Yugoslavs, and Turks."[90]

Such statements, which heighten the tension between Islam and the West, express an intense degree of anxiety, commonly referred to now as Islamophobia. This phenomenon is the product of a situation where, according to Ghannouchi, the powers of selfishness and lust have defeated the powers of goodness within the human individual in dealing with fellow humans, within elites in dealing with the masses, and within strong nations in dealing with weaker nations. At the global level, the strong north oppresses the weak south, and within the north as within the south there are oppressors and oppressed.[91]

Indeed, Islamophobia has become a feature of the new world order that was proclaimed by former American President George Bush during the Gulf War, and in the aftermath of the collapse of the Soviet Union in 1991. It gained currency as a new link was being forged between the political decision-making process of the power centers of the international system and political theories reflected in Fukuyama's *The End of History* and Huntington's *The Clash of Civilizations*.[92] Encouraged by the collapse of the Communist bloc, Fukuyama declared the ultimate victory of liberal democracy and argued that it may constitute the end point of mankind's ideological evolution and the final form of human government and as such constitute the end of history.[93] As he wrote, the prevalent spirit in the West was probably more of jubilation than of fear. Fukuyama's thesis was received with enthusiasm by American foreign policy makers because it provided them, during the Gulf War, with the political rhetoric needed to mobilize the whole world for the achievement of their own strategic planning in the Gulf War.[94] However, it did not take long for his theory to crumble under the impact of serious developments, in the heart of Europe, that led to the war over Bosnia.

In contrast to Fukuyama's idealistic belief in the unavoidable and irresistible universalization of Western values, Huntington came up with a realistic and cautious attempt, without reference to a universal set of values or an international order, to explain the alternative civilizational processes that mobilize the masses into political action and confrontation. Huntington predicted that the clash of civilizations would dominate global politics and that the fault lines between civilizations would be the battle lines of the future.[95] There are six reasons why, according to Huntington, this clash is inevitable: differences among civilizations are basic; cultural characteristics are less easily compromised; interactions among peoples of different civilizations are increasing in a negative way; modernization is exacerbating religious fundamentalism; non-Western elites are becoming more indigenized; and economic regionalism is getting stronger through culture and religion.[96] Huntington's theory would appear to complete the picture drawn in Fukuyama's by providing the hegemonic powers with a theoretical justification for the overall political and military strategies required to control and reshape the international system. Fukuyama proclaims Western values and political structures to have an intrinsic and irresistible universality, while Huntington proclaims that it is the other civilizations that are responsible for the political crisis and clashes, and thus the West is justified in taking pre-emptive measures against other civilizations. Islam figures prominently as a threat in Huntington's "clash of civilizations," especially as he warns against what he calls "the Confucian-Islam connection that has emerged to challenge Western interests, values, and power."[97]

Ghannouchi observes that one of the factors that has contributed to the misrepresentation of Islam in the Western media has been the influence of "the clash of civilizations" on many writers and journalists, especially in the United States of America. The proponents of "the clash of civilizations" theory are more interested in emphasizing the points of difference than of agreement between the Western and Islamic civilizations. "This theory has provided the powers of selfishness with added ammunition."[98]

Israel and the Zionist Lobby

The most hostile element of the powers of selfishness, according to Ghannouchi, is Israel, which he accuses of "insisting on playing the tune of the East-West, or Islam-West, conflict."[99] Ghannouchi observes that soon after the end of the Cold War, Israel, which reaped most of its fruits playing the role of defender of Western interests against the spread of communism—fearing that it might lose the gains made thus far—nominated Islam as the new threat. In what amounts to blackmail, and in order to guarantee the continued flow of Western aid and support, "the Israeli instigators of hatred and hostility worked hard to instill fear in the hearts of Westerners." Ghannouchi supposes that the Israelis must have been horrified to see the West accomplish its objectives in the Gulf without requiring their assistance. Thus, in order to restore their entity's traditional status and role and to guarantee the continuation of generous American aid, it was necessary to portray their own enemy, Islam, as the new threat to Western interests in the region and the world over. Consequently, Israel is confirmed as the West's strategic ally that ought to be supported and funded in order to confront the new threat. "Zionist media and diplomacy have been banging the drums of war against Islam, and have been mobilizing powers and offering expertise to fight against it." Ghannouchi refers to the endeavor of former Israeli President Chaim Herzog, who addressed the European Parliament (EUP) soon after the Gulf War in 1991, instigating it against the fundamentalist threat. Reportedly belittling EUP members and accusing them of ignorance with regard to the Middle East, Herzog insisted that fundamentalism posed the greatest threat to the world.

Ghannouchi also cites as an example the visit former Israeli Prime Minister Yitzhak Rabin made to Washington in the early 1990s. During that visit, Rabin demanded that the United States support Israel in its war against the Islamists, "the enemies of peace, who threaten the regimes of Algeria, Egypt, Tunisia, and other countries in the region." Addressing the Federation of Jewish Organizations in Washington, Rabin reportedly said:

> We are not sure that President Clinton and his team fully realize the threat of Islamic fundamentalism and the decisive rol Israel plays in combating it. The Arab world and the entire world will pay dearly if this Islamic cancer is not stopped. . . . By fighting Muslim terrorists we aim to awaken the world that is sleeping unaware of an important fact, namely that this danger is serious, real, and threatens world peace. Today, we the Israelis truly stand in the firing line against fundamentalist Islam. We demand all states and nations to focus their attention on this huge threat inherent in Islamic fundamentalism.

Former Israeli Foreign Minister Shimon Peres is similarly cited as addressing in February 1993 a group of American officials inside the White House, saying: "The U.S.

should increase its aid to Israel instead of reducing it because Israel is waging a ferocious war against Islamic extremism."

Israel, Ghannouchi adds, has a powerful lobby in the West, and especially in the United States of America. He cites as an example AIPAC, an American Zionist organization, which called in its 1993 annual conference for the necessity of confronting the threat of Islamic fundamentalism, and urged the United States to rely on its Israeli ally to accomplish this objective. American Zionist writers too undertake to promote Israel and its services to the American public. Paul Model is quoted as saying:

> The Americans must comprehend that Israel has served them for many years when it stood as a barrier preventing the spread of the communist threat in the Middle East. Now, following the disappearance of this threat, a new bigger threat has emerged, namely Islamic fundamentalism, against which Israel stands because it threatens the Middle East and the entire Christian world. Hence, it is incumbent upon the Americans to fully support Israel so as to confront this new threat.

Within this framework, Ghannouchi points to an abundance of writings by prominent journalists and academics such as Judith Miller, Bernard Luis, Martin Kramer, and Yusef Budenski. He accuses them of adopting the method of exaggeration and generalization in their campaign against Islamic fundamentalism.

> No effort is made to provide clear definitions for concepts such as the vague and obscure term fundamentalism. This term has been indiscriminately applied to every Muslim activist, and in some cases to every Muslim. No distinction is made between the mainstream moderate trend within the Islamic movement, which struggles for reform peacefully from within the system, and a minority trend that opted to respond to state violence with counter-violence.

Patronizing the West

A clear example of what Ghannouchi complains about is the writings of Judith Miller. She has written profusely to warn the American administration, and the West in general, against reconciling themselves with Islamists. She warns that "radical political Islam" placed atop the societies of the Middle East has created a combustible mixture.[100] Therefore, "those who believe in universal human rights (and women's rights in particular), democratic government, political tolerance, and pluralism, and in peace between the Arabs and Israelis cannot be complacent about the growing strength of militant Islamic movements in most Middle Eastern countries, or about the numerous and increasing ties among such movements and between Iran and Sudan." She demands that Western governments be concerned about these movements and, more important, oppose them. "For despite their rhetorical commitment to democracy and pluralism, virtually all militant Islamists oppose both. They are, and are likely to remain, anti-Western, anti-American, and anti-Israeli."[101]

The militant Islamists Miller refers to include among others, as she explicitly mentions, Rachid Ghannouchi's Ennahda movement, the Muslim Brotherhood, FIS, and the governments of Iran and Sudan. She asks: "Why should one suspect the sincerity of the Islamists' commitment to truth, justice, and the democratic way?" The answer very simply is: "In short, because of Arab and Islamic history and the nature and evolution of these groups."[102] Extremely critical of some U.S. State department officials' attempts to open dialogue with the Islamists, with special reference to former U.S. Assistant Secretary of State Edward Djerejian's bid to make a distinction between Islamists who resort to violence and those who do not, Miller demands:

> American officials formulating new policies toward Islam and the Arabs should be skeptical of those who seek to liberate Arabs through Islam. First, they should understand that no matter how often and fervently Islamic groups assert their commitment to democracy and pluralism, their basic ideological covenants and tracts, published declarations and interviews (especially in Arabic) appear to make these pledges incompatible with their stated goals of establishing societies under Islamic laws and according to Islamic values. Far too many Middle Easterners, and Islamists in particular, have learned how to mollify the West (and deceive their own potential adherents, many of whom genuinely crave democracy, greater political expression, and an end to political expression) by manipulating the words of democracy. Moreover, to most Islamists, and to many Arabs today, democracy translates as majority rule. There is an almost total disregard for minority rights, an essential component of liberal democracy. If the majority want an Islamic state, Islamists maintain, then the minority or minorities—be they religious, ethnic, or female—who do not will have to put up or shut up, or accept a far worse fate.[103]

Ghannouchi has one explanation for what he considers a "feverish campaign" against not only Islamists but also Islam. "The writings of Miller can only be explained in terms of her Zionist inclinations and what she might consider a "noble" cause in support of Israel. This is not much different from the "noble" cause claimed by the Serbs as they annihilated the Muslims allegedly on behalf of the civilized world."[104]

Another example is that of Daniel Pipes, editor of *Middle East Quarterly*, which is published in Philadelphia. Pipes' mission is to alert the U.S. administration to the alleged threat of Islamic groups. He demands that the United States should not encourage or cooperate or communicate with such groups but should instead confront them. He suggests that just as the United States supported the right against the left in the past, it should now cooperate with the left, following the disappearance of its threat, against the new right, Islamic fundamentalists. He calls for supporting secular groups in their fight against fundamentalists, and for standing by France in its support for the military regime in Algeria. He recommends supporting existing governments even though "we know they are corrupt simply because they do not threaten our interests in North Africa and Egypt, whereas the success of the fundamentalists will harm these interests."[105]

In his correspondence with Western politicians and academics, Ghannouchi expresses concern over the role he believes the Zionists play in damaging the prospects of peaceful coexistence between Islam and the West. In a long letter to Lord Avebury, chairman of the Human Rights Committee at the British Parliament, Ghannouchi complains:

> The Zionist issue stands as an obstacle hindering the progress of dialogue and cooperation between the Muslims and Western nations. Whenever we invite our European neighbors to a discussion of our bilateral relations and of the means to develop them further

toward more understanding and more cooperation, and whenever we make an effort to highlight the common ıssues of ınterest (relıgıon, culture, and economic cooperatıon), they always ınsist that the file of the Jewish question must have precedence and be given priority. By so doing, they keep the files of our relations wıth them closed, as if saying that they can be opened only once the Zionist issue is settled. Nevertheless, we continue to stress and explain to our Western neighbors that these files should remain separate and be dealt with independently.[106]

Ghannouchi's anxiety is shared by politicians and academics around the Muslim world. It is a concern that emanates from the ever growing power of the Zionist lobby that in many instances seems to dictate the terms of diplomacy in the West, particularly in the United States of America. These terms now include the necessity of supporting dictatorship against democracy if the latter is deemed of no service to the West and to its alleged strategic ally in the Middle East, Israel.

Warmongers

Another source of agitation against Islam in the West, or another "element of selfish-ness" according to Ghannouchi, is the arms merchants "who have been saddened by the decline in their business opportunities as a result of the termination of the Cold War." To maintain their revenues, Ghannouchi suggests, warmongers have joined the search for a new enemy, and have invested heavily in the campaign against the alleged Islamic threat, fighting which has become a profitable business. "Maintaining the sta-tus quo in the Arab world, where undemocratic corrupt governments squander resources on heaps of useless armament or on security tools and equipment used to control the population and muzzle critics, is of interest to arms manufacturers."[107]

Many parties for a variety of different ends have exploited the anxieties Western countries have vis-à-vis Islamic extremism. The arms industry and those who stand to earn huge commissions for playing the double role of purchaser and broker are anxious to preserve their privileges. In doing so, they adopt a hostile position toward any at-tempt to democratize the Arab region lest freely elected and accountable decision-makers interrupt the squandering of national resources on arms. But Ghannouchi points out that local dictators have learned the rules of the game well. "One of them need only cry 'fundamentalist threat' to obtain from the West what he needs, or to get away with any evil-doing without being rebuked or condemned."[108]

Ghannouchi's concern over the squandering of Arab resources over arms deals, which are said to benefit only those who sell them and those who earn high commissions for facilitating them, has been voiced by other Islamic leaders.[109] It is estimated, according to figures taken from London's International Institute for Strategic Studies and from the U.S. Agency for Monitoring Arms and Disarmament, that between 1976 and 1985 Saudi Arabia, Kuwait, the United Arab Emirates, and Oman alone spent $210 billion on defense.[110] Substantial amounts of these funds are believed to find their own way back to the accounts of senior officials, mostly ruling family members, in the purchas-ing countries. The press in Britain frequently publishes reports about such dealings. Commissions amounting to £600 million were reportedly paid to two Saudi royal fam-ily members for their role in facilitating an £8.6 billion Tornado deal.[111]

Implications for Islam-West Relations

Greed might have been the main motivation in the past for Western colonial policy. Today, according to Ghannouchi, it is greed plus a fear-hostility composite that dictate the attitude of the new world order toward the world of Islam, an attitude that does not favor democratization in Muslim countries.[112] Ghannouchi observes that whereas democratic movements in Latin America and Eastern Europe receive full Western support, no enthusiasm is shown for the democratic process in the Islamic region. In both Latin America and Eastern Europe, liberalization, including democratization, is conducive to Western interests. In the Muslim world, Ghannouchi suggests, democratization is not preferable lest it leads to the rise of Islamic powers and the decline of authoritarian territorial states that serve Western interests at the expense of national interests.

> No threat was posed to Western interests by the falsification of election results in Tunisia. Nor were such interests threatened by the crushing of ballot boxes by armored vehicles in Algeria and the banishment of the winners in the Algerian elections to detention camps deep in the Sahara. The West had no reason for complaint. Was Saddam Hussein a democrat when the West provided him with military and economic aid? Or was the Kuwaiti government so democratic as to deserve the intervention of more than thirty countries in an unprecedented alliance and show of force? Didn't Saddam persecute his own people for several decades with the knowledge of the West? Or was it only on the 2 August 1990 that the West discovered that Saddam was a dictator?

Ghannouchi insists that these are not only his own concerns and that such questions are being asked by millions of Muslims around the world. He regrets that because of the double-standard policies of Western governments, the West is increasingly perceived by practicing and non-practicing Muslims alike as a conspirator against the interests of Arabs and Muslims.

> The political stances of the West are blamed for blurring the vision of many Muslims who see a monolithic black and white image that never changes. Today's Westerners are believed to be the same as those whose horses marched up to their knees in the blood of Muslims when Jerusalem was invaded. They are the same as those who destroyed the Islamic caliphate, colonized our countries, and imposed secularism and partition on us. They are the ones who, through Westernization and intelligence intrigues, captured the hearts and minds of a generation of our children. They instituted them as despotic rulers and supplied them with material and moral support in order to embezzle our resources, sustain backwardness in our countries, and deny us the right to democracy. They are the ones who implanted in the heart of our *Ummah* an alien and hostile entity, Israel, so as to sustain division and fragmentation. They are the ones who provide unconditional support to this entity and watch in acquiescence the daily crimes committed by its troops. Bosnia is another Palestine in central Europe. Before the eyes of the European states and the United Nations, an entire people have been raped and annihilated by bloodthirsty Serb bandits. The Serbs enjoy overt and covert support in their bid to destroy a state that could have become a model of coexistence among religions and ethnicities and that could have been a meeting point between Islam and Christianity.

Ghannouchi reiterates what he believes to be questions asked by millions of Muslims around the world:

Why were the Western fleets deployed to protect Kuwait from Saddam while very little was done to rescue the people of Bosnia? Why does President Clinton warn and threaten the strugglers of Hamas as they defend their homeland? Why is he moved by the killing of Zionist occupation soldiers who for years had no mission other than repressing the uprising of Palestinian men, women, and children, breaking their limbs in front of cameras, while on the other hand he remains silent toward the crimes perpetrated against the peoples of Bosnia, Kashmir, Tajikistan, Azerbaijan, and Southern Lebanon? Why is democracy in Haiti supported and fleets are rushed to its aid while despotic regimes in Algeria and everywhere else in the Muslim countries are protected? Muslims find no convincing logic for these scandalous Western double standards except one simple explanation: because they are Muslims they have no right to live decently, that is if at all their right to life is recognized.

But Ghannouchi is keen to stress that this picture of the West is not wholly true. He warns Muslims against making the same mistake they blame the West for making, namely the mistake of generalizing. For in spite of "the organized campaign to which strategic minds and apostles of politics in the West have been subjected in the direction of incriminating the Islamic movement as a whole and even Islam itself, there are courageous voices inside some Western research centers and within political circles as well as the media that resist the enormous pressures and blackmail." These persons, Ghannouchi explains, distinguish between Islam and fundamentalism; they perceive Islam as a civilization-enriching religion. They resist the temptation to presume Islam the new enemy that replaces communism and they recognize that fundamentalists are not one thing or a simple reality but a broad spectrum of trends. They believe that the West, including the United States, should not be an enemy of Islam or the Islamic movement, but an enemy of radicalism, whether Islamic or secular.

Ghannouchi points to a phenomenon that attracted his attention in the early 1990s. It is the attempt by some senior American officials to bridge the gap between Islam and the West. The trend, which was strongly criticized by Zionist writers such as Miller and Pipes, was crowned with the 1992 Meridian speech by Edward Djerejian, Assistant U.S. State Secretary. It was expressed also by his successors Robert H. Pelletreau and Anthony Lake in 1994. The same trend, Ghannouchi observes, appeared in the October 1993 speech by Prince Charles at the Oxford Centre for Islamic Studies. Within the sector of academia, Ghannouchi hails the contributions of a number of prominent scholars and researchers, including John Esposito, John Voll, Yvonne Haddad, John Entelis, Graham Fuller, Jennifer Noyon, Francois Burgat, Roger Garaudy, and John Keane.

Together with such esteemed persons, Ghannouchi hopes that thinkers from both sides will continue the search for a common ground on which Muslims and non-Muslims will stand and by way of which a better future can be created. This, he believes, is especially important at a time when some of what he describes as the instigators of hatred insist on talking about the eventual or inevitable conflict between Islam and the West, a prediction that, in his view, stands on no solid grounds. "For the advance in technology, sciences, and communications leaves no option before the nations of the world, if they are indeed in pursuit of a viable future, but to endeavor to know each other, to communicate and to cooperate."

But even if such agreement is reached, Ghannouchi deems it necessary to recognize that "legitimate" conflict will continue. This is not a conflict between Christianity and

Islam, or between Islam and Judaism, for "we are not against a people because of their religion or because of their color. We alone have recognized everybody else, and have been waiting for others to reciprocate." The legitimate conflict according to Ghannouchi, which he maintains derives legitimacy from Islamic faith, is a conflict between truth and falsehood. "It is a struggle against oppression and aggression, and against despotism and hegemony irrespective of their justification, whether in the name of Islam or in the name of democracy. For the worst form of despotism is that practiced in the name of noble slogans."

While seeking this common ground, Ghannouchi warns that it is time for the "masters" of the world order to come to terms with Islam. "Islam has come back to restore dignity to its followers, to liberate them from despotism, to regain the *Ummah*'s usurped legitimacy, to restrict the powers of the state, and to establish and reinforce the power of the people, the power of civil society." In other words, Islam is not a threat to the West if it is not taken by the West to be one.

Ghannouchi is also keen to remind the Western world that history has shown that Islam has a successful record of resisting those who encroach on its community or on its territory. So, none should be fooled by the present weakness of the Muslims, and none should take for granted the treaties and deals that are being concluded falsely and unjustly in the name of Islam or in the name of its people. "These are deals of capitulation and humiliation and not the choice of the peoples." This is clearly a reference to the peace treaties between the Arabs and Israel, which Ghannouchi, like other Islamists, believes are not designed to serve justice but to prolong colonial hegemony in the Muslim world.

Ghannouchi is unequivocal about his reasons for opposing peace with Israel. Palestine, he stresses, has been usurped from its rightful owners and inhabited instead by aliens brought to it from various parts of the world. It has a special religious status in the heart of every Muslim as well as a very important strategic and historic position in the heart of the Muslim world. Therefore, any arrangement aimed at waiving it, irrespective of the justification, is null and void.[113] When Ghannouchi talks about Israel, he is keen to explain that "we are not here talking about the Jews as a community, nor about Judaism as a religion." He stresses that "our *Ummah* coexisted with Judaism, and is still willing to do so," and that it never happened in "our history that we ever declared war against a religion or its followers."[114] As far as he is concerned, what the Muslims are facing in Palestine is a foreign occupation. They are facing a process of appropriation of an entire homeland, of the properties and homes of a people that have been forced to live in exile and banishment. "Palestinian refugees watch with their own eyes their homes being occupied by immigrants who are brought here from distant continents. They see their civilizational heritage, which also belongs to the *Ummah*, being destroyed day and night."[115] In the name of what justice, he asks, are we to condone this savagery? "Who is prepared to sign the document of conceding these rights, this heritage, and these shrines? And what value will such signing have in the eyes of truth, justice, and history?"[116] As for the solution, Ghannouchi recognizes there is a predicament. For him, as for most Islamists, the state of Israel is illegitimate and just peace can only be established following its dismantlement. But clearly, such a mission seems impossible, at least on the short, and even medium, range in light of the present balance of powers in favor of Israel and its allies. "That is why if our generation is too weak to restore rights, this is understandable, for 'On no soul does God place a burden greater than it can bear.'"[117] But he warns that it would not be right, nor would it be honorable, "to pledge posterity to weakness or confiscate the right of our children to endeavor to accomplish what we have been unable to accomplish ourselves."[118]

> Our *Ummah* will tear every document signed in a state of capitulation and incapacity and will disregard every treaty that in a moment of weakness is forged to strip it of its right to struggle for the restoration of what has been usurped. The crusaders' occupation of Jerusalem lasted for about a century, but still no person or party declared willingness to waiver the right of the *Ummah* to it because of their inability at the time to regain it.[119]

On a number of occasions, Ghannouchi has tried to communicate his ideas to policy makers in the West, and especially in the United States of America, whose government has, apparently in response to pressure from the Tunisian government, repeatedly denied him an entry visa. The first of such communication was a letter he sent to Mr. Edward Djerejian, former Assistant Secretary of State for Near East and South Asian Affairs, commending him for what he considered an important and unprecedented statement made by a senior American official on Islam. On 2 June 1992, Djerejian affirmed that Islam's rich civilizational heritage contributed to enriching Western civilization, pointing to the fact that millions of Americans now believed in Islam and that the Islamic movement was not a monolithic structure. Later on, in his address to the National Association of Arab Americans in Washington on 11 September 1992, Mr. Djerejian declared: "We do not view Islam as the next 'ism' confronting the West or threatening world peace. That is an overly simplistic reaction to a complex reality. It is evident the Crusades have been over for a long time."[120]

In his letter to Djerejian dated 14 June 1992, Ghannouchi expressed delight at what he considered to be a new trend in the American policy toward Islam and Muslims. Hoping that this trend would be strengthened and translated into policy, Ghannouchi assured Djerjian that the Muslims believe in building bridges between civilizations, peoples, and religions, and believe in dialogue as the best way to resolving disputes and disagreements. This belief, he explained, is integral to Islam, which has since its inception recognized believers in other faiths by accepting and respecting all preceding religions and prophets.[121] In the letter, Ghannouchi made a point of having had difficulty writing to someone like Djerejian, the reason being that it is not customary for an Islamist leader to write to a senior American official owing to America's policies toward Islam and the Islamic movements, which Ghannouchi criticizes for alternating between denial, neglect, simplistic generalizations, and hurried labeling with extremism and fundamentalism.[122]

Having hailed Djerejian for his position on Islam, and after explaining to him the plight of the Tunisian people and their struggle against autocracy, Ghannouchi put a question to him: How can the U.S., which claims to lead the struggle for human rights and democracy in the world, continue to provide political, financial, and moral cover to such corrupt and bankrupt regimes such as the one in Tunisia?[123]

Regrettably, Djerejian and several other officials, known in Washington as Arabists for their moderate positions on Islamic issues, have almost entirely been replaced by officials known to be prominent figures within the Zionist lobby. This has made the Clinton administration the most pro-Israel administration in the history of the United States of America and the most unsympathetic to Islamic causes.

Nevertheless, Ghannouchi insists that there is a lot of goodness in the West, and that the door should remain open. His message to Westerners, and to the Americans in particular as expressed in his letter to Djerejian, is:

> We want you to know that we the Muslims harbor no ill feelings for you or for your superpower status, but we want our freedom in our own countries; we want our right to choose the system we feel comfortable with. We want the relationship between you and us to be based on friendship, and not subordination. We see a potential for an exchange of ideas, for a flow of information and for cultural exchange in an era governed by the rules of competition and cooperation rather than the rules of hegemony and subordination. We call on you to halt your aggression against our people and against our religion. We invite you to a historic reconciliation, to rapprochement and to cooperation. After all, you are the closest of all other humans to us, in terms of geography, religion, civilization, and interests.[124]

According to Ghannouchi, the myth of the "Islamic threat" has over the years been fed not only by greedy, selfish, or sinister elements in the West, but as well by the ignorance and backwardness of the Muslims. Some of those who claim to defend Islam pronounce views that undermine or belittle some of the best accomplishments of humanity in the field of freedom and human rights. The Islamic arena is not void of people who claim to speak in the name of Islam while inflicting a lot of harm on it. Under the pretext that democracy is imported from the West, they ignorantly denounce it and completely reject it.[125] This is the other front along which Ghannouchi has been defending the cause of democracy, and this will be the topic of the next chapter.

7

Islamist Obstacles to Democracy

The obstacles to the progress of democracy are not confined to the factors outlined in the preceding chapters, namely the project of secularization and modernization, the nation-state and the new world order. An impediment, though in Ghannouchi's assessment less serious than those dealt with hitherto, exists within the realm of Islamic political thinking and activism. It is the opposition, or hostility, to democracy by some Islamic quarters, within factions as well as within academia. The grounds for hostility range from considering democracy antithetical to Islam to considering it a Western design against it. The dispute within Islamic circles over democracy has had serious ramifications. Inter-Islamic factional conflict has been attributed, in many cases, to the disagreement on the stance toward democracy, or more generally toward the question of governance. Ghannouchi considers the rejectionist attitude toward democracy an obstacle that undermines the endeavor of mainstream Islamic movements, such as Ennahda and the Muslim Brotherhood, to bring about peaceful political reform in the Arab region. This chapter will review the opinions of some of the opponents of democracy and then discuss Ghannouchi's response to them.

Rejectionist Theses

Ayman Dhawahiri, an ideologue of the Egyptian Jihad faction, believes democracy to be *shirk-u-billah* (assigning partners with God).[1] He understands *tawhid* (monotheism) to entail the belief that legislation is the sole prerogative of God whereas democracy, as he understands it, is the rule of the people for the people. Whereas in democracy the legislator is the people, in *tawhid* God is the legislator. Hence, democracy is *shirk* (idolatry) because it usurps the right to legislation from the Almighty and puts it in the hands of the people.[2] Alleging to base his conclusions on the writings of Mawdudi and Qutb, Dhawahiri denounces democracy as a new "religion" that deifies humans by awarding them the right to legislate without being bound by a superior divine authority. His entire discourse is based on the argument that since democracy is the recognition of the sovereignty of the people, it would have to mean the denial of God's sovereignty. Consequently, those who believe in democracy, like the post-Qutb Muslim Brotherhood, by accepting the rule of the people instead of the rule of God, compare with those who assign partners with God. It follows that the members of the people's assembly (parliament) are the idols, and those who elect them commit, by doing so, the arch-sin of *shirk*. Thus, participating in the democratic process at whatever level is *haram* (forbidden) and those who perpetrate it are apostates and infidels.[3]

In addition to what has become known as *al-jama'at al-jihadiyah* (jihadi groups), those who believe that existing governments should be fought and removed by force, Hizb-ut-Tahrir (Liberation Party) believes that democracy is *nizam-u-kufr* (a system of blasphemy) that was marketed in the Muslim countries by the blasphemous West.[4] Not only is democracy said to have nothing whatsoever to do with Islam, but it completely contradicts its code in all issues, both major and minor; it is said to contradict its source, the ideology it emanates from, the foundations it is based on, and the ideas and systems it has come up with. Therefore, it is strictly *haram* for Muslims to adopt it, implement it, or call for it.[5] In addition to stressing that democracy emanates from the unacceptable ideology of excluding religion from public life and of awarding sovereignty to the people, unlike the *jihadi* trend, Hizb-ut-Tahrir (HT) goes further to argue that democracy eventually does not achieve what its advocates claim it will. In this regard, the ills of democracy and its negative impact on societies that adopt it are highlighted. In the West, as is the case in America and Britain, it is argued, elected members of parliament do not represent the majority of the people but represent business interests. It would therefore be misleading, and even an act of falsification, to claim that parliaments in democratic countries represent the majority of the public. This is notwithstanding the assertion that majority rule is considered un-Islamic because it could lead, as has happened in the West, to legalizing forbidden matters such as *riba* (usury) and *liwat* (sodomy). The concept of public liberties, it is claimed, is the worst thing the democratic system has come up with; it transforms the human community into herds of animals. Examples from public life in the West, cited to prove that democracy eventually leads to a decline in morality and to exploitation of the majority by the minority, include individualism, disintegration of the family, promiscuity, homosexuality, capitalism, and exploitation.[6]

In spite of this dogmatic stance, HT members in Jordan participated in democratic elections several times in the past. By doing so, they fully accepted the terms of the political game as set by what is to their standards a non-Islamic regime. In 1951, HT founder Taqiyy-ud-Din an-Nabhani nominated himself but lost to his opponent Abdullah Na'was from the Ba'th party. In the 1954 elections, HT nominated five candidates in the West Bank, which was then under Jordanian jurisdiction. Dawud Hamdan was nominated in the city of al-Quds; Abdul-Qadim Zallum, As'ad Tamimi, and Abdulqadir al-Khatib in the city of al-Khalil (Hebron); and Ahmad ad-Da'ur, in the city of Tolkarm. Only ad-Da'ur won because he entered into an arrangement with the Muslim Brotherhood. Like every other candidate ad-Da'ur gave the constitutional oath of allegiance to the king and the homeland but added the phrase "and to God." In 1956, HT once more participated in the elections and contested for seats in al-Quds, al-Khalil, Jenin, and Tolkarm, and this time too only ad-Da'ur won.[7]

It is not clear whether HT in the 1950s was not yet opposed to democracy or whether its participation in the Jordanian elections was a violation of its own doctrine. What is undoubted, however, is that the party is now among the Islamic factions most hostile to democracy. Little wonder that a scathing attack was launched against Ghannouchi's *Al-Hurriyat al-'Ammah Fid-Dawlah al-Islamiyyah* (Public liberties in the Islamic state) by HT ideologue Mahmud Abdulkarim Hasan.[8] Ghannouchi is accused of having been vanquished by the Western civilization to the extent that, like millions of other misguided Muslims, he is no longer able to think except on the basis of the utilitarian principle of this civilization. Ghannouchi is diagnosed by Hasan as suffering from a feeble understanding of Islam, an "illness complicated by considerable civilizational backwardness and immense infatuation in the Western civilizational progress, an imbalance that induces some people to reconcile many of the ideas of Islam with the ideas of the Western civilization." Ghannouchi's method of analysis is described as *inbitahi* (from the root *bataha*, meaning to prostrate or lay low), a method known for its tendency to come up with new titles and new treatises to justify one's deviation and to misguide the Muslims.[9] The focus of HT critique of Ghannouchi's *Al-Hurriyat* is the concept of *maslaha* (exigency). Ghannouchi is accused of fabricating and twisting classical *ijtihad*, such as that of Imam Ash-Shatibi—in defense of whom Hasan took the initiative of reproaching Ghannouchi—in order to "turn Islam upside down."[10] The HT ideologue concludes that Ghannouchi's book, to which he refers as "this piece of work," comes up with a new method of thinking or legislating based on *maslaha*, a method that is falsely attributed to Ash-Shatibi for the purpose of bestowing some sort of legitimacy on an illegitimate discourse. Ghannouchi is said to "clearly harbor Western concepts that are alien to Islam, such as democracy and public liberties, for whose benefit he seeks to alter Islam's concepts claiming they are flexible and capable of modification whenever we want depending on our interests or according to our own reasoning."[11]

Ghannouchi is condemned by both *jihadis* and *tahriris* for being a *mubtadi'* (innovator) and an *i'tidhari* (apologist). Similar accusations are leveled at him within other Islamic circles by individuals or groups who disagree with his approach to dealing with both the Islamic heritage and the Western civilization. Members of some of the *salafi* groups in the United Kingdom, for instance, have repeatedly attempted to veto decisions by university Islamic societies to invite him to talk to students and other members of the Muslim community.[12] More extreme elements even consider him to be worse than infidels.[13]

More than that, Ghannouchi has been accused of serving Western designs. Abdul Rashid Moten, a lecturer at the department of Political Science at the International Islamic University in Malaysia, whose political affiliation is unclear, argues in a recent paper that democracy is a Western conspiracy.[14] According to Moten, the West is eager to impose this value, which is said to be incompatible with Islam, on the Muslim countries as part of cultural imperialism. It would follow, thus, that Islamic thinkers who stand for the cause of democracy in the Muslim world serve Western interests. Moten's paper revolves around the notion that Islam already has a system of governance that is superior to democracy. The exertions of Westernized Muslim thinkers, and he includes in his list together with al-Afghani and Abduh two contemporaries, Abdul Karim Soroush and Rashid Ghannouchi, to devise a theory of Islamic democracy or to demonstrate the compatibility of Islam and democracy are said to lend further credence to the false belief in the eminence of the democratic system. Such Westernized Muslim thinkers, he charges, have trivialized the fundamental principles of an Islamic political system:

The practice of *shura*, meaning people's participation in governing themselves, was turned into parliamentary democracy; *ijma'*, denoting the consensus of the *Ummah* or of the leading *'ulama'* on a regulation was held to be synonymous with public opinion; and *maslaha*, referring to the adoption of a course which is considered to be in the best interest of the community, was developed into the liberal notion of utility.[15]

Moten goes on to claim that, despite their full backing by the establishment, such Westernized thinkers never enjoyed the status of an *'alim* (a person well-versed in religious sciences) and their ideas were never considered by the Muslim masses as genuine Islamic responses to the Western onslaught. "Islamic liberalism was an urban elite phenomenon and remained confined to a handful of Western-educated elite."[16]

Hakimiyah versus Democracy?

Such Islamists in Ghannouchi's view are not only an obstacle to democratization but to progress and development as a whole. Their problem is two-fold; on the one hand they have no specialized or adequate knowledge in the humanities, and on the other they are indoctrinated with some shallow literature on Islam. Consequently, they tend to define things with extreme simplicity. For instance, he explains, they understand Islamic government to mean *hukm-u-llah* (God's rule) and democracy to mean *hukm-ush-sha'ab* (people's rule). Not only are issues of politics too complex to be simplified in this manner, but the concept of *hukm-u-llah* is totally misunderstood. *Hukm-u-llah*, Ghannouchi stresses, is supposed to be a liberation movement, a revolution against despots who monopolize wealth, power, and law-making, and against clerics who monopolize the right to interpret God's will and who claim to speak in His name. *Hukm-u-llah* is a revolution in the sense that it limits a governor's powers, rendering them more executive in nature than legislative. *Hukm-u-llah* does not mean that God comes down and governs humans, but means the sovereignty of law, which, Ghannouchi notes, is a fundamental feature of the modern state, the state of law and order. If, according to this conception, a government in Islam is not to be monopolized by a despot or an oligarchy, it follows that *hukm-u-llah* refers to, and implies, *hukm-ush-sha'ab*, that is the rule of the people or their representatives who in the Islamic tradition used to be referred to as *ahl-ul-hal wal-'aqd*, whose power is limited by, and derived from, *Shari'ah*.[17]

Ghannouchi suggests that the position of hostility toward democracy within the Islamic camp emanates from a number of factors. The first is a profound misconception of democracy, which he traces to the ideas of Sayyid Qutb on the concept of *hakimiyah*.[18]

Sayyid Qutb (1906–1966), who was imprisoned for ten years in 1954 and then executed in 1966, became the leading ideologue of the Ikhwan (Muslim Brotherhood) in Egypt from the mid-1950s. His book *Ma'alim Fit-Tariq* (Milestones), which was written in response to Nassir's persecution of the Ikhwan, acquired a wide acceptance throughout the Arab world especially after his execution and more so following the defeat of the Arabs in the 1967 war with Israel. In it, he put forward the thesis of *jahiliyah* (ignorance or barbarity or idolatry) from which Islam came to deliver the world.[19] Qutb divided social systems into two categories: the order of Islam and the order of *jahiliyah*. The latter was decadent and ignorant, and was typical of the situation that prevailed in Arabia before Prophet Muhammad had received the Word of God, when men revered not God but other men disguised as deities.[20] Drawing on this, he divided Muslim society itself into two realms, that of Islam and that of *jahiliyah*. Judging the world as he saw it then, Qutb declared that looking at the sources and foundations of modern ways of living, it becomes clear that the whole world is steeped in *jahiliyah*, and asserted that all the marvelous material comforts and high-level inventions do not diminish this ignorance.[21] This *jahiliyah*, Qutb explains, is based on rebellion against God's sovereignty on earth. It transfers to man one of the greatest attributes of God, namely *hakimiyah*, and makes some men lords over others. The modern *jahiliyah* is not in that simple and primitive form of the ancient *jahiliyah*, but takes the form of claiming that the right to create values, to legislate rules of collective behavior, and to choose any way of life rests with men, without regard to what God has prescribed. The result of this rebellion against the authority of God is the oppression of His creatures. Thus the humiliation of the common man under the communist systems and the exploitation of individuals and nations due to greed for wealth and imperialism under the capitalist systems are but a corollary of rebellion against God's authority and the denial of the dignity of man given to him by God.[22] In this respect, Qutb asserts, Islam's way of life is unique, for in systems other than Islam, some people worship others in some form or another. Only in the Islamic way of life do all men become free from the servitude of some men to others and devote themselves to the worship of God alone, deriving guidance from Him alone, and bowing before Him alone.[23] What really concerns Qutb is that *jahiliya* "is now present not only in the capitalist West and the Communist East," but has also infected the world of Islam. "All that is around us is *jahiliyah*. Peoples' imaginings, their beliefs, customs, and traditions, the sources of their culture, their art and literature, their laws and statutes, much even of what we take to be Islamic culture, Islamic authorities, Islamic philosophy, Islamic thought: all this too is of the making of this *jahiliyah*."[24]

The term *hakimiyah* (sovereignty), which Qutb constantly refers to while arguing against man-made political systems, was originally coined by Mawdudi, who distinguishes between Islamic and *jahili* (barbaric) societies. Mawdudi argues that in a *jahili* situation, the edifice of politics rises on the foundations of *al-hakimiyah al-bashariyah* (human sovereignty) whether such sovereignty rested in the hands of an individual, a family, or a class, or was the sovereignty of the public:

> Legislating in this kind of reign is entirely in the hands of man. All laws are made and replaced according to desires and to provisional interests. So is the case with political plans, which are only drawn or altered as dictated by the passion for utility and the provision of interests. In such a reign, no word is given precedence and no affair is awarded prevalence except if such were the functions of those who are most cunning, most resourceful, and most capable of fabricating lies; those who have reached the pinnacle of deceit, cruelty, and guilefulness; and those who have seized full control and are recognized as leaders in their community where, in their "laws," falsehood becomes truth just because its proponents have power and have the ability to terrorize, and where, in their courts of law, truth becomes falsehood just because it has no supporter or defender.[25]

Ghannouchi's position on this matter is that *hakimiyah* is a controversial concept. "It is what one takes it to mean."[26] If understood correctly, Ghannouchi explains, *hakimiyah* is a sound idea. He understands it to mean that God is the absolute sovereign, but in the sense that the authority of anything or anybody else is relative and is derived from God:

Just as we move, develop, innovate, and behave in nature within the framework of what we call natural law, which is not our own making, similarly we should accept that our laws and our human relations are best placed within the framework of Divine Law, which we call *hakimiyah*. Whereas natural law is imposed on us, that is we have no choice but to accept it and deal with it, *hakimiyah* is optional, that is we are free to accept it or reject it.[27]

Choosing to accept *hakimiyah*, Ghannouchi stresses, is in itself an exercise of the right to freedom of choice. "By accepting it one never loses his or her freedom." But for Ghannouchi *hakimiyah* does not mean that God intervenes constantly in running the affairs of humans on earth. He merely provides them with broad guidelines to help them make the right choices. The exercise of *hakimiyah* is therefore a human endeavor that involves interpreting divine guidelines and coming up with new *ijtihad* whenever necessary. Hence, differences and disagreements are to be expected and should be tolerated. As Ghannouchi understands it, *hakimiyah* is not a code or a legal instrument or a computer program that when a button is pressed a divine judgment is revealed. Nor does *hakimiyah* mean for him that every question has an answer. To the contrary, he insists, a single question may have several different legitimate and acceptable answers.[28]

Faraghat for Ijtihad

The second factor, which Ghannouchi suggests contributes to some Islamists' hostility toward democracy, is the lack of understanding of the nature of Islam as well as of the historical development of the Muslims' approach to the question of governance. He proposes the idea that Islam includes *faraghat* (plural of *faragh*, that is space), or areas left for humans to fill in accordance with the respective needs and exigencies of times and places.[29]

Ghannouchi finds irrefutable evidence to the existence of these *faraghat* in the documented conduct of the Prophet and the attitude of his *Sahaba* (Companions). He distinguishes in the activities of the *Sahaba* between what he calls *ad-dini* (the religious, sacred, or absolute) and *as-siyasi* (the political, profane, or relative). He also observes that no disputes ever erupted among the early Muslims in matters pertaining to the first category, *ad-dini*, that is in matters of *'aqidah* (faith), *'ibadah* (worship), or *akhlaq* (morality). Nor were there disagreements among them, for instance, on the fundamentals of family law or those of the code of penalties known as the *hudud*. He asserts however that they disagreed over matters pertaining to the second category, *as-siyasi*; that is on how to administer political affairs, on how to manage disputes and resolve problems pertaining to public office, and on the qualifications and powers of rulers. Ghannouchi quotes a renowned Muslim historian Ash-Shahrastani[30] as saying that it was on the question of *khilafah* (caliphate), or power, that Muslims drew their swords, fought each other, and shed the blood of one another.[31]

The dispute which Ghannouchi refers to erupted soon after the death of the Prophet in 632 A.D.[32] The companions rushed to what is known as *Saqifat Bani Sa'idah* to discuss filling the political position of "head of state" vacated by the Prophet's departure. Some suggested that two heads be appointed, one from the *muhajirun* (the immigrants from Mecca) and one from the *ansar* (the Madinites who sheltered and supported them). This was in accordance with an Arab old custom, that when a tragic event befell the community, its elders, who were not necessarily duly appointed or elected, met and deliberated what to do. In this particular instance, the conferees were the cream of the Companions' generation, the most senior figures in both the *muhajirun* and the *ansar*. Nevertheless, it was not easy for them to reach a unanimous decision, and when they did 'Umar bin al-Khattab, who then was to become the second *khalifah* (caliph), is reported to have said "that was a lucky escape," that is from what seemed an imminent disaster.[33]

Ghannouchi's *faraghat* theory begins with the assumption that the *Sahaba* were not left, that is by the Prophet, with a set of rules as to how to choose his successor. They were compelled to perform *ijtihad* in order to find their own ways and means. Ghannouchi considers this to be one of the miracles of Islam, and not, as some may be misled to think, a weakness.[34] If Islam is the final divine revelation to humanity, he argues, it is only appropriate that no fixed prescriptions are given for matters that are of changing nature. By virtue of such *murunah* (flexibility), and thanks to the existence of *faraghat*, whereby Muslims can exercise their *ijtihad* to devise suitable solutions for emerging problems, Islam is said to be fit for all times and places. Ghannouchi strongly rebukes those "zealots" who have not acquired sufficient knowledge about Islam, and who do it a great deal of harm by claiming, while seeking to defend it, that it has ready answers for all questions and solutions for all problems. "It would be rather naive to think that all is required for the *khilafah* to be reinstated would be for Muslims to execute a set of *ahkam* (rules). What role remains for the *Ummah*, for *ijtihad*, or for *'aql* (reason) if Islam is conceived of as encompassing, or catering for, all requirements?"[35]

Ghannouchi suggests that certain verses of the Holy Qur'an are misinterpreted to mean that every single problem, whether major or minor, has a ready-made solution in Islam. Verses, which are construed as implying that Muslims need not look for answers anywhere else, include "This day have I perfected your religion for you, completed my favor upon you, and have chosen for you Islam as your religion,"[36] and "Nothing We have omitted from the Book."[37] What is really meant, Ghannouchi explains, is that while some answers are provided to specific questions, only guidelines exist in the case of most other questions so that Muslims may search for the detailed answers in accordance with the requirements of their respective times and places.[38] To exemplify this, he draws attention to the Qur'anic declaration that "There is no moving creature on earth but its sustenance depends on Allah."[39] For in spite of such a declaration many creatures, including entire human communities, die of thirst or hunger. "Where is their sustenance?" he asks. "Their sustenance has indeed been stored in the earth and in the heavens, but to become readily available it would require exploring, an exertion of efforts, on the part of those to whom it has been destined."[40]

He cites as an example the prolonged periods of famine that hit Iraq and the Arabian peninsula prior to the discovery of petroleum. "Millions may have perished out of hunger while walking on land that stored beneath it valuable resources that waited until the Westerners came and discovered them." The example of the Arabs who perished in famine, he adds, is similar to that of the camel that dies out of thirst in spite of carrying water in its hump. As much as it is necessary to explore and search for sustenance through hard work, it is essential for the Muslims to explore the universe and look into other people's accomplishments in order to derive within the guidelines of their faith answers and solutions.[41] So, just as no sustenance becomes available without exploration, no questions get answered, or problems get resolved, without *ijtihad*.

An important source of misconception regarding the relationship between that which is *dını* and that which is *siyası* has been the interpretation of the Sunnah (the Prophet's tradition). Sunnah, the sayings, actions, and lifestyle of the Prophet, is the second most important source of guidance after the Qur'an. Ghannouchi finds it necessary to remind people that not every thing the Prophet did or said or condoned was *dını*. After all, the prophet was a human being, and like humans he liked certain foods and disliked others, and this had nothing to do with *halal* (that which is permissible) or *haram* (that which is forbidden). Furthermore, on matters where no divine revelation was made, the Prophet sometimes opted for choices that turned out not to be best. The *Sahaba* lived those moments, not only when the Prophet conceded his own *ıjtıhad* or changed an earlier position after having listened to advice from one or more of his companions, but also when he was blamed by the Qur'an for pursuing a policy out of personal *ijtihad* that was not, in the given circumstances, most appropriate. Consequently, they recognized, and could tell, much more easily than any successive generation of Muslims, the difference between the Prophet's divinely guided choices and those that were his own personal preferences. Whereas their attitude toward the former category was full obedience, they had no hesitation to regard the second an area of *faragh*, where they too could exercise *ıjtıhad* if and when necessary, whether during the life of the Prophet or after his death.[42]

As part of the process of learning the new way of life brought to them by Islam, the *Sahaba* showed no reluctance to ask, whenever unsure, whether a particular decision was made upon a divine revelation or out of *ıjtıhad*. They had to do so because they once learned a lesson that cost them their crops. The Prophet was born and raised in Mecca, a barren land that sustained no agricultural life. When he migrated and settled down in Madina, famous for its palm trees, he noticed that farmers pollinated trees manually. He suggested to them that perhaps there was no need to do so. Upon his advice, they did not pollinate the trees, and for that particular season they had a very low harvest. When they complained to him he said to them that was *shu'un dunyakum*, that is a matter of your livelihood, something they knew better about, and should tackle as they deemed appropriate.[43]

Another famous incident that proves Ghannouchi's point that the Prophet was not always guided by divine revelation has to do with military tactics. As the Muslim army deployed for the first battle in the history of Islam, at the Oasis of Badr, the Prophet ordered his troops to take a position that would have left the water wells between them and their opponents. One of the *Sahaba* by the name of al-Habbab ibnul-Mundhir asked whether that was a position God guided the Prophet to or a matter of *ar-ra'y wal-harb wal-makidah* (opinion and war strategy-making), in other words a choice based on personal *ijtihad*. The Prophet said it was *ar-ra'y wal-harb wal-makıdah*. The companion, who had been an experienced war commander, suggested that strategically the position was not the best, and that it would be better to deploy beyond the wells so that the enemy could not have access to the water. The Prophet agreed and the companion's plan was implemented.[44]

The fact Ghannouchi seeks to highlight is that the edifice of Islam, which Prophet Muhammad left behind, was complete with regard to the foundations and the structural components pertaining to *ad-dını*. Apart from that, the structural components pertaining to *as-siyası* were left for the coming generations to devise and add. In the political field for instance, the Sahaba had to build on the foundation of shura in order to devise a mechanism for choosing the successor of the Prophet. The mechanism was neither fixed nor sacred; it kept changing, progressing each time, from one successor to another. What was common to the four caliphs, whose era is known as al-Khilafah ar-Rashidah (the Rightly Guided Caliphate), is that none of them inherited power from his father and that they were all nominated and elected by the Ummah, or its representatives. This, Ghannouchi points out, was revolutionary in the sense that no similar system of government existed at the time whereby the community had a say in electing its ruler.[45] It was also revolutionary in the sense that it was not rigid. Successive caliphs effected modifications to the system of election that perhaps could, had it not been interrupted, led to the institutionalization of shura. Whereas the second caliph was nominated by his predecessor, the third was nominated by a council of six senior members of the community. The methodology in the latter case may in certain respects be compared to modern democratic procedure. The council of six was appointed by Caliph 'Umar who had been suffering from fatal wounds sustained in an assassination attempt on his life. He ordered the six senior Sahaba to nominate to the community one of them excluding his own son whom he insisted should only play the role of an observer and a moderator.[46] When the short listing came down to two, 'Uthman and 'Ali, the opinions of the members of the community, both men and women, were polled to determine who of the two the community favored more. They were so close, that eventually each of them was asked separately whether he would pledge to follow the teachings of the Qur'an, the Sunnah (way) of the Prophet, and that of the first two caliphs. 'Uthman said he would, while 'Ali said he would pledge to follow the Qur'an and the Sunnah of the Prophet, but not that of the first two caliphs.[47] Ghannouchi suggests that perhaps 'Ali felt confident that he was no less capable of making ijtihad himself, and that what the first two caliphs, who would have been his predecessors, had come up with of ijtihad was not binding for him. This, Ghannouchi assumes, might have been the first indication of the developing tension between the desire to maintain the tradition and the need for ever more ijtihad to cope with changes.[48] Clearly, the inclination toward the first was stronger, and that is why, presumably, 'Ali lost the nomination to 'Uthman.

In addition to accusing them of misinterpreting the Qur'an and the Sunnah and of incomprehension of the way the Sahaba conducted their affairs following the death of the Prophet, anti-democracy Islamists, whether jihadis, tahriris, or salafis are diagnosed by Ghannouchi as lacking in knowledge and understanding of Islamic history as a whole. This in his opinion is particularly true with regard to how the Muslims approached the question of governance.[49] Evidently, the Prophet died at a time when the Islamic territory was expanding very rapidly and when entire communities had been embracing the new religion. On the one hand, the city-state had become an empire-state. The territory governed by the Muslims was no longer just the city of Madina and its outskirts but the whole of Arabia. Muslim armies were preparing to conquer the Ash-Sham and Iraq, and before too long the whole of North Africa had become Islamic. On the other hand, new converts with diverse cultures and ethnicities had become the bulk of the Ummah. In other words, the Ummah lost its relative homogeneity. Many of the Sahaba who had previously been the bulk of the state's population had died or spread across the vast Muslim empire; a very small minority of them remained in the capital.[50]

The changes constituted serious challenges in dealing with the different methods pursued by the Prophet's successors. The first challenge was that of *ar-riddah* (the turning away or back, or apostasy, from Islam), which Ghannouchi views as a military insurrection rather than an act of apostasy.[51] Some Arabs claimed that the death of the Prophet necessitated the removal of certain obligations, such as *zakat*. This suggests that *ar-riddah* was an attempt to deny Islam's political aspect. The renegade Arabs wanted to remain Muslim but felt they did not have to pay allegiance to the Prophet's successors, that is, to the Islamic government of the day, and therefore wanted to absolve themselves of what such an allegiance entailed. The first caliph, Abu Bakr, consulted his fellow *Sahaba* some of whom, led by 'Umar, suggested that it was not appropriate to fight the *murtaddun* (apostates) because they had not categorically, but only partly, rejected Islam. Abu Bakr was resolute and insisted on fighting them until they submitted fully to Islam, both its spiritual and temporal authorities.[52] Ghannouchi sees that disagreement among leading *Sahaba* over this issue is clear proof that it was a matter of *ijtihad*.[53]

What Ghannouchi refers to as "the challenge of territorial expansion and increase in population," had ushered an epoch of post-Prophetic *ijtihad*.[54] Following the death of the first caliph, Abu Bakr, his successor, 'Umar bin al-Khattab, responded to the challenge in a number of ways. Firstly, he modified the manner in which booties were distributed. According to a Qur'anic injunction, booties are supposed to be divided into five equal shares, one goes to *bayt-ul-mal* (the state treasury) while the remaining four shares are distributed among conquering troops. 'Umar decided that this no longer served the interests of the *Ummah*. He decreed that immovable assets were to be excluded from distribution.[55] He feared that if all gains were automatically distributed, not only would wealth accumulate in the hands of the few, but none would be left for the coming generations. Ghannouchi describes 'Umar's era as one characterized by a high dynamism of *ijtihad*.[56] He observes that 'Umar effected more changes and encouraged more innovations than any of the other four caliphs. He was the first to borrow from other cultures. He obtained administrative methods and procedures from the Persians so as to cope with his expanding state. This, Ghannouchi regrets, is what some contemporary Islamists fail to appreciate.[57] The spaces, or *faraghat*, Ghannouchi refers to need not, therefore, necessarily be filled with local *ijtihad*. "Muslims can, and should, borrow if necessary from others."[58] He observes too that what 'Umar did was to follow the example of the Prophet who emulated the Persians in ordering his followers to excavate a ditch around Madina to protect it from invading tribes. When his Meccan opponents saw the ditch they were horrified. "Muhammad has innovated something the Arabs never knew before," they exclaimed.[59]

Just as the Arabs knew not of ditching as a means of defense, they had no administrative system. By the time 'Umar became caliph, the traditional system of distributing funds to members of the public had become rather laborious and extremely inefficient. He learned about the Persian *devan* system, which he borrowed and implemented, Arabizing it into *diwan*.[60] By doing so, 'Umar laid the foundation for a huge process of learning from other civilizations, as part of which the Muslims translated Greek and Persian writings in philosophy, mathematics, astronomy, and medicine to establish a great civilization upon whose foundations modern Western civilization now stands.[61]

Al-Khilafah ar-Rashidah (The Rightly Guided Caliphate) was in many respects an extension of the era of Prophethood. Together, they constituted what Ghannouchi describes as short-lived golden period. Several factors may have contributed to the decline of this ideal model of governance, but the principal one according to Ghannouchi is the fact that this experiment was too revolutionary, too advanced, and out of keeping with the political climates of the time, whether in Arabia or elsewhere. In other words, it was a big leap forward, which the slow, gradual, and steady progress of history could not embrace. Ghannouchi's explanation is that "perhaps God wanted the years of *an-Nubuwah* (Prophethood) and *al-Khilafah ar-Rashidah* to stand as a model, a minaret, and a source of guidance and inspiration for successive Muslim generations."[62] In other words, even if this short-lived experiment is impossible to re-accomplish, it will always be looked up to as the ideal against which all other accomplishments are measured and assessed. This is something some Muslims fail to comprehend, Ghannouchi asserts. "They fail to see that *al-Khilafah ar-Rashidah* was an exceptional rare occurrence in the history of Islam. Or else, why hasn't this model ever been repeated in the past fourteen centuries?"[63]

Ghannouchi's own answer to this question is that it simply cannot be repeated. Of course, many Muslims would prefer to believe that it can, and should, be repeated. Some even insist that only 100 per cent of the original model is acceptable, and no less. But the fact is, and this is what Ghannouchi tries to show, that 100 per cent may never be attainable until the exact conditions that prevailed during that golden era are repeated, and this is impossible in the present and inconceivable in the foreseeable future. Perhaps the main reason why such a model cannot be repeated is the fact that it was a model of a city-state. Hence is the predicament the Muslims found themselves in when their city-state rapidly grew into a vast empire.

However, the downfall of the *al-Khilafah ar-Rashidah* model, and the emergence of *al-mulk al-'adud* (snapping dynasty) model, cannot be explained merely by the hypothesis that the ideal model was perhaps too advanced or that it was only intended to be a minaret, or a lighthouse, or that it was meant to act as a source of guidance and inspiration for Muslim generations to come. The rapid changes in the nature of the Islamic state, which the Muslims could not at the time cope with at an equal rate, is the principal cause of decline. The disproportionate transformation of the caliphate from a city-state to an empire-state disabled the government of the day, preventing it from coping with developments. In the meantime, the *Sahaba* were keen to preserve, as much as they could, the model they inherited from the Prophet. One may cite as an example the events of what is known in the history of Islam as *al-fitnat-ul-kubra* (the great sedition), which led to the assassination of 'Uthman (the third caliph), and henceforth to a series of *hurub* (inter-Muslim wars; pl. of *harb*) that were indeed the midwife that brought into being *al-mulk al-'adud*.[64] Toward the end of 'Uthman's reign disgruntled groups, of what is known as *ath-thuwwar* (the rebels), arrived in Madina from Yemen, Egypt, and Iraq during the pilgrimage season to protest against what they considered injustices perpetrated by *al-wulat* (pl. of *wali*: a caliph's deputy or provincial governor). The rebels demanded the dismissal of *al-wulat*, but 'Uthman refused to meet their demands. They then insisted that he should abdicate. He told them that this was not a matter for them to decide but for the community of *Sahaba*, and this cost him his life.[65]

The failure here was manifold. On the one hand, the capital of an enormous empire could easily be occupied and taken hostage by a small group of rebels. There was no security whatsoever, and with many people off to *hajj* (pilgrimage) the caliph, who is the head of state, had no protection. Some Muslims offered to stand up to the rebels and defend 'Uthman, but he refused to allow them fearing that the blood of too many people would be shed because the rebels could not be outmatched.[66] On the other hand the caliph clearly had no mechanism by which he could institutionally observe, control, or bring to account his deputies some of whom were several weeks' ride away. Ghannouchi is of the opinion that although the rebels may have had committed a criminal act by murdering 'Uthman, their grievances were genuine. Thousands of people had embraced Islam upon the promise of justice and equality, but the corrupt relatives of the caliph, who administered some of the very distant provinces, delivered neither.[67] 'Uthman governed for a total of twelve years before he was murdered. In the first six years, he is said to have done well in terms of controlling his deputies and of responding to complaints against them from the public. In the second half of his reign, however, and bearing in mind the fact that he had already become more than eighty years of age, his grip on his deputies loosened.[68]

What Ghannouchi finds interesting is that some of the junior members of the community of *Sahaba* had already begun to realize that dramatic changes in the nature of both state and society were occurring, and increasingly felt the need to respond to them. One of them was al-Hasan, the elder son of the fourth caliph, 'Ali, and grandson of the Prophet, who tried to alert his father to the new reality. The assassins of 'Uthman came to 'Ali and offered to give *bay'ah* (pay homage) to him as the new head of state. 'Ali declined and told them that this was not a matter for them to decide but for the people of Madina, specifically for *al-muhajirun* and *al-ansar*, or the community of *Sahaba*. Al-Hasan advised his father not to be content with the *bay'ah* of the *Sahaba* and to insist on *bay'ah* from all the other provinces such as Yemen, Iraq, and Egypt, because the *Ummah* was no longer just the *Sahaba*. 'Ali did not think much of his son's advice, who in turn warned his father that he too would one day be murdered, and indeed he was.[69]

Ghannouchi observes too that the decline of the ideal model of *al-Khilafah ar-Rashidah* was accelerated by the fact that the development of the system of government, in spite of the strides achieved during 'Umar's time, fell short of the full transformation of the state into an institution. For instance, while *shura* was truly implemented, no proper *shura* council was set up, or mechanism developed, to closely monitor and audit the performance of the caliph and his deputies. "The inability of 'Uthman, toward the end of his reign, to control his deputies was the first manifestation of this deficiency."[70]

With the Ommiad takeover tribalism was reinstituted and *al-mulk al-'adud* established. Ghannouchi suggests that *al-mulk al-'adud* was a blend of three main components: Islam, tribalism, and a variety of administrative systems borrowed from other cultures.[71] It was a form of governance positioned half way between the ideal form, represented in the *al-Khilafah ar-Rashidah* and the tribal or imperial forms that prevailed elsewhere at the time. Tribalism, Ghannouchi stresses, was the evil component; its role was to create a schism, thus dividing the *Ummah* and separating the state from society. This, he explains, was initially resisted by the *'ulama'* (scholars), who sought to maintain the unity and integrity of the *Ummah* and who wanted the tradition of *al-Khilafah ar-Rashidah* to continue. It was the *'ulama'*, who by the way consisted of the *Sahaba*, that were then in power. When *al-Khilafah ar-Rashidah* was replaced by *al-mulk al-'adud*, many of the *'ulama'* joined, or supported, rebellious movements to reverse the status quo, which they termed kusrawiyah (an adjective derived from Khosrau, the designate of the Persian king). Ghannouchi cites as an example the historic fact that each of the four Imams, the founders of the four main schools of jurisprudence, supported the revolutionaries in one or another of such rebellious movements.[72] Abu Hanifah and Malik for instance supported the Ibn al-Ash'ath revolution while Ash-Shafi'i almost lost his head for supporting the revolutionaries of his time.[73] But all these revolutions were futile and proved incapable of reinstating the ideal model of government. Little wonder that several hundred years later Ibn Khaldoun (1332–1406)—and on this Ghannouchi agrees with him—ridiculed in his Al-Muqaddimah the preachers who incite the public to rise against the state. For states are founded on 'asabiyah (clan solidarity)[74] and can only be replaced by a stronger 'asabiyah and not by rhetoric.

The bloodshed and destruction caused during the first century of Islamic history by the repeated attempts to reinstate al-Khilafah ar-Rashidah gave rise to a new discourse. The 'ulama' started warning against a greater evil than al-mulk al-'adud, namely fitnah (sedition), a reference to inter-Muslim fighting. The 'ulama' had agreed by then that although armed struggle to change a regime may not in principle be haram (prohibited), it becomes so if the outcome is bloodshed and destruction. But there were, as there usually are in every age, extreme positions. Ghannouchi cites the example of Abu al-Hasan al-Ash'ari, founder of the ash'ariyah school of thought, who declared it to be strictly haram to rise against the ruler. But such a position, Ghannouchi explains, might have been prompted by the fact that in spite of the huge sacrifices made, the rebels who rose against al-mulk al-'adud only reasserted the status quo and reproduced the autocratic models that prevailed at the time. Ghannouchi is, himself, critical of the opposition parties that rose against the state in the first century of Islam:

> The opposition groups which condemned the Ommiad coup and struggled to reinstate al-Khilafah ar-Rashidah were driven by persecution and the legacy of autocracy to crystallize models or alternatives that were far away from the shura-guided model they sanctified and much more autocratic than the regime they rose against. Even the Khawarij, who were most vehemently opposed to hereditary rule, did not differ from their opponents when they had the opportunity to set up their own state except in that they handed power over to another dynasty. As for the Shiia, they dropped the principle of shura altogether in favor of the concept of wasiyah (designation).[75]

Nevertheless, the 'ulama' eventually embarked on a comprehensive strategy, described by Ghannouchi as peaceful but not conciliatory, to reduce the powers of al-mulk al-'adud.[76] State powers had to be restricted in order to curtail its hegemony and prevent it from overwhelming society. The search for viable means to achieve this end led to the development of 'ilm-ul-usul, the science of the four foundations of Islamic jurisprudence: Qur'an, Sunnah, qiyas (analogy), and ijma' (consensus). The objective was to refute the rulers' claim of a divine right to unconditional obedience. In this way, rulers, it is argued, were stripped of the religious cloak they tended, with the assistance of what is known as 'ulama'-us-sultan (ruler's scholars), to drape their government in. 'Ulama'-us-sultan is the term applied to scholars who provide rulers with desperately needed legitimation by means of interpreting the text in a manner that suits their desires or meets their requirements. Ash-Shafi'i (d. 820) is believed to have been the first to set the rules of 'ilm-ut-tafsir (the science of expounding explanatory commentary on the Holy Qur'an).

In the era of *al-Khilafah ar-Rashidah*, a caliph knew his limits and sincerely believed that public obedience was conditional upon his own obedience to the Qur'an and Sunnah and his observance of *shura*. After his election, Abu Bakr, the first caliph, told his fellow Muslims: "I have been appointed as your leader whilst I am not the best man among you. I am following (the norms established by the Prophet) and not establishing new practices. So if I get it right help me, and if I go astray redirect me."[77] Until the end of this era, caliphs acquired legitimacy from the Qur'an and the Sunnah on the one hand and from the *Ummah* on the other. However, the advent of the Ommiad dynasty introduced a new source of legitimacy, namely *'asabiyah*. Gradually the balance shifted from the traditional sources of legitimacy to this new element, which nevertheless still needed a religious cover that was often provided by *'ulama'-us-sultan*. Such expedience was manifested in the interpretation of relevant Qur'anic verses such as the one in chapter 4: "O you who believe, obey Allah, and obey the Messenger, and those charged with authority among you. If you differ in anything among yourselves, refer it to Allah and His Messenger, if you do believe in Allah and the Last Day. That is best and most suitable for final determination."[78] The first task of the *mufassirun* (interpreters of the Qur'an), was to establish stringent conditions for earning the obedience and respect of the public.[79]

Their second task, according to Ghannouchi, was to deny the rulers the power of legislation and to assign its responsibility to the jurists. This consequently liberated the judiciary from the authority of the state, and hence both legislators and judges, who in fact were the *'ulama'* themselves, functioned freely and independently.[80]

The third task was to develop a non-governmental financial institution to guarantee the independence not only of the legislature and the judiciary but also the society as a whole. Known as the *awqaf* (endowment fund), this institution derived legitimacy from the Prophetic tradition: "When a child of Adam dies his (or her) good deeds cease except for three: a current charity, a knowledge that others benefit from, and a righteous child who would invoke God's Mercy upon his (or her) parent."[81] Accordingly, the scholars emanated from a strong religious position when they encouraged the Muslim public to donate generously for the establishment of public institutions such as schools, orphanages, traveler guest houses, and other charitable projects. So, once they managed to define the rules for the proper understanding and correct interpretation of Islam, the *'ulama'* turned to society, via the rendering of services in various educational and social fields, to further weaken the state and limit its powers. In doing so, they sought in every conceivable way to refute initial claims by the Ommiad caliphs that the collection and dispensation of funds was, by way of a divine will, their responsibility. Ghannouchi credits early Muslim *'ulama'* for successfully preventing the transformation of the Islamic state at the hands of the Ommiads into a theocracy.[82]

At the time, the *'ulama'* enjoyed formidable power. A caliph or his deputy, instead of summoning a scholar to his palace, would usually apply for permission to meet the scholar in his own house or *majlis* (court) and would feel honored to have been awarded such an opportunity.[83]

Ghannouchi finds strong evidence in history to support the theory that Muslims had a viable civil society that derived its strength from the *'ulama'*, who controlled the legislature, the judiciary, the schools, and the mosques by virtue of their financial independence. Their power emanated from the people's respect and reverence for, and therefore obedience to, them, a reality felt and dreaded by the rulers. "The power of the *'ulama'* considerably mitigated the negative impact of the transformation of the Islamic state from *al-Khilafah ar-Rashidah* to *al-mulk al-'adud*."[84]

Another notable achievement of the *'ulama'* was the development of a new science known as *'ilm maqasid ash-shari'ah* (the science of the purposes of *Shari'ah*), whose objective was to prevent the rulers from exploiting what Ghannouchi calls *zawahir an-nusus* (the literal meaning of Qur'anic text).

> A ruler might have been tempted to claim that so long as he did not order his subjects to violate the commandments of God, he would have to be obeyed in every other matter. Such an argument would have been intended to expand and consolidate the ruler's powers, especially as pertains to the dispensation of wealth. The scholars established through this branch of Islamic science that *Shari'ah* is not a mere text, but a set of rules intended for serving and preserving the interests of humans.[85]

Ghannouchi attributes the founding of this science to Imam al-Haramayn al-Juwayni (1028–1085).[86] It was then further developed and refined by a number of scholars such as Al'izz ibn 'Abdessalam, Ibn Taymiyah, and Ibn al-Qayim. The apex of this development was reached by Abu Ishaq Ash-Shatibi whose studies and thoughts were complementary to those of his predecessor Imam Ash-Shafi'i. The contribution of Ash-Shatibi is of significance to Ghannouchi's theory of *faraghat*. Drawing on the Qur'anic verses, "We sent you not but as a mercy for all creatures,"[87] "Allah does not wish to place you in difficulty, but to purify you, and to complete His favor to you,"[88] and "In the Law of Equality there is (saving of) life to you,"[89] Ash-Shatibi concludes: "Upon exploration of *Shari'ah* we have concluded that it was only set up to serve the interests of man. This is a conclusion that no one can dispute. Canon laws were made for only one purpose and that is to serve the interests of humans in this life and in the hereafter."[90]

In his *Al-Muwafaqat*, which is one the foremost treatise in this field, Ash-Shatibi categorizes into three classes the exigencies which divine messengers were sent to fulfil in the lives of humans. These are *masalih daruriyah* (essential requirements) without which life would be ruined, *masalih hajiyah* (requirements pertaining to general needs) without which man can survive but may be in distress and hardship, and *masalih tahsiniyah* (ameliorative requirements) whose absence would not seriously undermine the quality of life.[91]

However, the strategy of the *'ulama'*, though mostly successful, did not proceed unhindered. On the one hand, the gradual sophistication of the caliphate institution and its transformation from a simple traditional Arab-style clan rule to a powerful bureaucracy posed a real challenge to the *'ulama'*. The climax of the tension between the two institutions was reached during the era of the Abbaside caliph al-Mansur, who built a powerful state apparatus based on an army whose recruits were mostly of Khurasani descent and a bureaucracy led by the Barmakid family, which continued the Sassanian traditions of financial administration.[92] The bureaucrats, who had become so influential, entered into conflict with the *'ulama'* and sought to undermine their authority through the establishment of an alternative political theory. Whereas the *'ulama'* considered the ruler a servant whose powers are determined and restricted by *Shari'ah*, bureaucrats, who derived influence from the ruler's power, wanted him to become an absolute ruler and wanted the *'ulama'* to be under his jurisdiction and not independent of him.

To counter the influence of the independent *'ulama'*, rulers resorted to establishing their own religious entourage, which consisted of scholars that were prepared to issue *fatawa* (pl. of *fatwa*) appealing to the public for unconditional obedience. Ghannouchi traces this development to the early years of the Ommiads, when attempts were made to corrupt the *'aqidah* (Islamic faith) by introducing *'aqidat-ul-jabr* (the ideology of fatalism). He considers *al-jabriyah*, the school of thought that teaches the inescapability of fate, to be a movement aimed at justifying absolutism on religious grounds.[93] Its founders argued that if every thing is fated, then the ruler, whether "good" or "bad," is God's will. It would follow then that whoever stands up to the ruler commits a sin for opposing the will of God.[94] To refute *'aqidat-ul-jabr*, the independent *'ulama'* responded by reinforcing *'aqidat-ul-ikhtiyar* (the ideology of free choice), the belief that man has a choice and is therefore responsible. The debate over this issue continued until Abu al-Hasan al-Ash'ari (873–941) came up, in the fifth century of Hegira, with what seemed at the time a middle course solution. His theory, known as *al-kasb* (from the root *kasaba*, that is, to earn), tackled the question of *sababiyah* (causality). Under the pretext of defending God's will, he denied the link between cause and effect and ended up endorsing *'aqidat-ul-jabr*. He argued that burning is not necessarily caused by fire, nor does fire necessarily burn. Similarly, thirst may be extinguished without water, and water does not necessarily extinguish thirst.[95] Ghannouchi blames this ideology, which he supposes must have been a source of comfort for despotic rulers, for the decline of the Muslim civilization.[96] He also blames Sufism, which he suspects rulers also encouraged, for effectively denying that man had a will or a freedom of choice. He maintains that by subjugating the *murid* (novice of a Sufi order) to his *shaykh* (order leader), Sufism stripped its followers of their will power. "Both *'aqidat-ul-jabr* and Sufism had the influence of narcotics; at times the entire *Ummah* seemed intoxicated."

The relevance of the above to today's debate on democracy within Islamic circles is that most of those who hoist the banner of an ideological warfare against democracy in contemporary times do so on the basis of similar intoxicating beliefs. *Al-Khilafah ar-Rashidah*, it is claimed, is the only acceptable system of governance, and until it is reinstated, by way of some unspecified—and perhaps unknown—magical formula, every other activity that is assumed to be the responsibility of the caliph is *haram* because it obstructs the coming of the caliph. In this sense, Hizb-ut-Tahrir, which openly denounces democracy and condemns Muslims who call for an Islamic democracy, is a modern manifestation of *'aqidat-ul-jabr* as much as the so-called *jihadiyun* are a modern manifestation of the *Khawarij*. Ghannouchi observes that these groups share in common the inability to distinguish between *ad-dini* and *as-siyasi* in the Sunnah of the Prophet and in the history of the Muslims. But he warns that this *ad-dini/as-siyasi* dichotomy is not to be understood to mean a separation as in the Western experience between religion and the state, for Islam is "a comprehensive way of life and God is the Lord both in the mosque and in the market, in the school and in the factory." What it means, he stresses, is a distinction between the areas that have been filled by divine commandments and the areas that were intentionally left vacant so as to be filled with what is needed to cope with changes through *ijtihad* but within the framework of *'aqidah*.

Still, the problem is not as simple as it may seem. The current tension between states and various Islamic movements, whether identified as mainstream or extreme, is the product of a radical change in the traditional relationship, which remained the norm for several centuries, between the state and the *'ulama'*. Throughout these centuries, Ghannouchi explains, the *Ummah* was ruled in accordance with a historic settlement between scholars and rulers, a division of labor and a power-sharing arrangement whereby rulers took charge of government affairs while scholars pacified society in exchange for keeping traditional institutions free from state intervention. Such an arrangement did not completely prevent armed mutinies from erupting every now and then, here and there. For this reason, the scholars maintained a pragmatic attitude, whenever the rebels failed, and this was usually the case, the endeavor would be labeled as *fitnah* (sedition), but if at all successful in seizing power and forming the new government, the rebels were "deservedly" given allegiance and granted legitimacy. What is noteworthy, Ghannouchi stresses, is that the coup in every case was directed against the ruling elite, with little, if any, impact on society itself. The situation remained as such until, as Ghannouchi puts it, the civilizational cycle was completed. The cycle, as he sees it, started with the mission of *tawhid* (monotheism) that emerged out of Arabia more than fourteen centuries ago and ended when division and backwardness overwhelmed the *Ummah* under the leadership of the Ottoman dynasty in Istanbul less than a century ago.

Since its creation in the aftermath of World War I, the modern territorial state has had a different approach to dealing with scholars. They are given one of two choices, either become part and parcel of the state institution, or suffer persecution, banishment, and even death. Some scholars have chosen to support the rulers, drawing on the attitude of traditional *'ulama'*. While recognizing that some of these scholars may have opted for this position not necessarily out of a personal ambition but out of what they deem to be the public good, Ghannouchi criticizes them for failing to realize the profound change in the nature of the state. Scholars who have joined the ranks of the opposition have been the source of much of the contemporary literature that inspires various Islamic groups. Sometimes, the same literature inspires both mainstream groups that adhere to peaceful means of change and radical groups that believe in the use of force. The writings of Sayyid Qutb, Mawdudi, and al-Banna, for instance, are studied by mainstream Islamic groups and also provide the right material for justifying the use of force as a means to get rid of what is seen as the evils of the secularist state and to establish pure Islamic governance. Ghannouchi points out that the reason for this seemingly confusing situation is that from the point of view of many scholars declaring a regime to be blasphemous does not necessarily justify the use of force against it. Possessing the means of change is the most important criterion for deciding the type of methodology to be pursued for effecting change. It is true, he adds, that Islam makes it incumbent upon a Muslim to remove injustice and eliminate evil. But Islam calls on its followers to contemplate and choose the methods that are least costly and most rewarding. This is the essence of the message inherent in the tradition: "He who sees an evil should change it by hand, but if he cannot then by tongue and if he still cannot then by heart. This is the minimum one is expected to do."[97]

Ghannouchi is keen to emphasize that while struggling against external obstacles to democracy in the Muslim world, it is of equal importance to struggle against endogenous obstacles through education, re-reading of Islamic history, and activation of *ijtihad*. His writings and lectures, especially since he was exiled, are considered an important contribution to this effort. This is particularly so because in the United Kingdom and the other European countries he has been to, he has been confronted with arguments put forward by *jihadi*, *tahriri*, and *salafi* trends that not only oppose democracy but take it to be their main occupation, in spite of enjoying the fruits of democracy in the West, to attack and discredit those who defend its cause, including Rachid Ghannouchi.

The political environment prevalent in much of the Muslim world today does not make Ghannouchi's task easy. In fact, it is this political environment that encourages the spread of radical ideas and the growth of extremist groups. Ghannouchi himself is a victim of a regime that does not tolerate the most moderate of ideas if deemed threatening to its monopoly of power. His movement, Ennahda (the Renaissance Party), is outlawed and its members are persecuted or banished for no crime other than calling for democratization. The absence of mainstream Islamic groups creates an ambient environment for what Francois Burgat calls bilateral radicalization.[98] Not only in Tunisia, but in Algeria, Egypt, Libya, Iraq, and Syria, just to mention a few examples, despotism has led to the creation of repressive environments with an almost total lack of basic freedom and a complete disregard for human rights. Force is used to secure the status quo and to silence critics. This tends to marginalize majority mainstream Islamic movements and increase the membership of small radical groups. The radicals respond to repression with acts of violence and regimes mobilize the security forces or the army to quell the rebels or frustrate their plans. In time, a vicious cycle of violence and counterviolence becomes a way of life.

8

Ghannouchi's Detractors

Ghannouchi's ideas and his political stances have earned him many critics within and outside Islamic circles. The central theme in Ghannouchi's thought is that democracy is compatible with Islam, and that Muslims need to incorporate it into their political thought in order to institutionalize the concept of *shura*. His theme is based on the belief that civilizational products and achievements are universal. What may be called Greek, Islamic, or Western civilizations are only phases in a single human civilizational cycle, and thus the material and intellectual products of any particular phase are inheritable by subsequent phases. The belief itself is not new. It is prominent in Ibn Khaldoun's works and is said by its proponents to have its origin in the Islamic creed itself. Prophet Muhammad's mission, Muslims believe, was not aimed at repealing what had existed before him or abrogating the divine messages that preceded him, but at endorsing and complementing the goodness in all of them. It was in this spirit that ancient Muslim scholars translated and revived Greek philosophies and explored with enthusiasm the contributions of other cultures in all fields of knowledge.

The unwholesome relationship between Europe and the Muslim world since the beginning of the colonial era has been an impediment to what might otherwise have been a smooth exchange or peaceful interaction. Since the middle of the nineteenth century, intellectuals in the Muslim world have belonged to one of two strongly opposed groups, one infatuated with the European accomplishments, seeing nothing negative about them and believing Europe's route to progress to be the only option, and the other completely opposed to Europe, despising it, seeing nothing positive in it, and insisting that the route to progress is to be found nowhere other than in the Muslims' own heritage. Ghannouchi adopts a middle course, and as a result he is criticized by both radical secularists and radical Islamists. The critique of the radical Islamists, already dealt with in the preceding chapter, emanates primarily from groups such as Hizb-ut-Tahrir and the so-called *jihadi* and *salafi* trends. The Islamic critique of Rachid Ghannouchi was dealt with in the preceding chapter.

Ghannouchi's non-Islamist critics denounce him more for his political standing than for his thoughts, that is more as leader of Ennahda than as an Islamic thinker. His writings on democracy, public liberties, and human rights are cause for admiration rather than contempt. For this reason, much of the critique directed against him by non-Islamist critics is based on presuming him insincere in his defense of democracy and human rights. He is accused of using these values to camouflage his struggle for power. Several attempts have been made by press reporters to prove his embroilment in inciting or plotting violence. Ghannouchi accuses the Tunisian government of indirect involvement in a number of press campaigns aimed at discrediting him. Recent court cases in the United Kingdom have substantiated his claims. Apparently embarrassed by repeated criticism of its human rights record by international humans rights organizations, the Tunisian government may have indeed sought vindication in proving Ghannouchi's guilt. At least thirty-six reports on human rights violations in Tunisia were published by Amnesty International alone between the beginning of 1991 and the end of 1992. More than twice as many reports were published between 1992 and 1996 by Amnesty International and other organizations such as Human Rights Watch and the New York-based Lawyers Committee for Humans Rights. The U.S. State Department and the European Community too have been critical of the Tunisian government's human rights record.[1]

Government-Sponsored Critique

Ghannouchi and his colleagues in Ennahda implicate the Tunisian government in at least two attempts aimed at discrediting Ghannouchi by associating him with violence and extremism.[2] The first attempt, it is alleged, was draped in academic research, the second in investigative journalism.

In 1992, Michael Collins Dunn, a senior analyst at International Estimate Inc., a Washington consulting firm, authored a book entitled *Renaissance or Radicalism: Political Islam, the Case of Tunisia's al-Nahda*, which he then summarized in a paper entitled "The al-Nahda Movement in Tunisia: From Renaissance to Revolution" in *Islamism and Secularism in North Africa.*[3] Dunn sets out to prove what he claims to be evidence that Ennahda, under the leadership of Rachid Ghannouchi, evolved or was driven toward a far more radical revolutionary position than it originally appeared to hold. Relying on information which Ennahda insists were taken from Tunisian government reports as well as from writers who had been known to harbor hostility toward the Islamic movement in Tunisia, Dunn arrives at the conclusion that although there have been many observers who doubt some or all of the details of the plot the Tunisian government accused Ennahda of, and although one may certainly raise questions about the interrogations that resulted in some of the testimony and confession, "there was enough external evidence of a new commitment to confrontation on the part of Ennahda in 1989–1991 to lead to the conclusion that at least the general outlines of the 'plot' are credible."[4] The external evidence Dunn refers to is Ghannouchi's persistent criticism of the Tunisian regime under both Bourguiba and Ben Ali. Ghannouchi's attitude is alleged to have emanated from his inclination toward Iran. He is said to have led a radical pro-Iran faction within the movement to contrast a more moderate pro-Saudi faction led by his deputy Moro. Dunn deduces from Ghannouchi's speeches and messages, as well as from the MTI 1986 Basic Program, that Ghannouchi must have given the impression to his followers that it would be possible for them to declare their enemies, in accordance with the doctrine of *takfir*, as *kuffar* (unbelievers), thus opening the way for resorting to violence because *kuffar* are to be dealt with through *jihad*.[5]

Ghannouchi has responded to the allegations made by Dunn in a letter to Lord Avebury, chairman of the British Parliament Human Rights Committee, upon the latter's request. Ghannouchi maintains that Dunn's book is full of errors and distortions, having been based mostly on information obtained from Tunisian government press statements, including the text of a press conference held by the interior minister, police files, and articles published in local government-owned press.[6] Ghannouchi's explanation for this "plot" is the government's desperation to justify "the terror campaign it has been waging" against Ennahda.[7]

Dunn's approach relies on the proposition that Ennahda is torn between two strong personalities, that of Ghannouchi, who is radical, and that of Moro, who is moderate. Mourou is described as a democrat who dissented from the movement because he was opposed to violence, the course Dunn alleges Ennahda eventually pursued. There is no evidence in Dunn's work that he has studied the writings of Ghannouchi. Instead, it would seem, he judges him on the basis of a few out-of-context excerpts probably rendered to him by Tunisian sources. Dunn's conclusions are in stark contradiction to those arrived at by many other Western scholars and researchers—such as Francois Burgat, John Esposito, John Voll, Linda Jones, and Robin Wright, to name a few—who have studied, and written about, Ghannouchi and his movement.[8]

Ghannouchi is naturally keen on disputing the allegations made by Dunn. His allegation that Mourou had left the movement to protest its involvement in violence is discounted as baseless. Ghannouchi insists that the circumstances surrounding Moro's decision to resign from Ennahda would have to be taken into account in order to understand his motives. A group of young men, reportedly associated with Ennahda, had been accused by the government in Tunisia of storming a barracks belonging to a ruling party militia and causing the death of a guard. The authorities seized the opportunity to crack down on the movement. A campaign was launched throughout the country, and thousands of arrests were made among the members and supporters of Ennahda. This is said to have been beyond the forbearance of Mourou, "whose physical, psychological, and social conditions did not help him endure the hardships of the terror campaign."[9] He, together with some of his colleagues, chose to renounce the movement and resign from it in the hope of evading the repressive measures that were bound to be taken against them by the authorities. However, their hopes were soon shattered. When they applied for permission to set up a political party, that is after having fulfilled all the conditions and criteria set up by the authorities, their application was rejected. Instead, the security authorities orchestrated, through the local government-owned press, a defamation campaign against them to destroy them. Using special photography and video dubbing techniques, the regime produced and circulated photographs and a video film to convince the public that Mourou was caught in the act of adultery. Although few people believed it, the allegation has destroyed him. The assertion within Ennahda ranks is that this defamation campaign was launched in response to a press statement made by Moro, who denied that Ennahda had anything to do with the incident known as Bab Souika as a result of which the entire movement was outlawed.[10] In his press statement, the first since his resignation from the movement, Mourou blamed the government for creating an environment conducive to violence. None of these details seem to have been of available to Dunn, whose book shows no evidence of contacts with any of Ennahda leaders. One would normally expect in a work like his that at least Rachid Ghannouchi would be interviewed.

Lord Avebury responded to Ghannouchi's letter with a letter in which he stated that he had seen nothing in the views expressed by Rachid Ghannouchi, or those attributed to him by others, to justify the charge that he was involved in a conspiracy to overthrow the government by force. Lord Avebury said that the fact that Ghannouchi had been granted asylum in Britain showed that the British government did not think there was any basis for the charge either.[11]

As Ghannouchi's asylum application in Britain was still being processed, the *Sunday Telegraph* published two articles alleging that he was responsible for the 1987 bombing of four Tunisian hotels in which five British tourists were injured, and that he was additionally involved in other terrorist outrages in Tunisia, including a 1991 plot to assassinate its president. The paper further alleged that Ghannouchi refused to participate in the democratic process in his country, insisting on overthrowing the established government and founding an Iranian-style republic.[12] Confident that the reports were based exclusively on Tunisian government propaganda and that their objective was to undermine his asylum application, Ghannouchi took the *Sunday Telegraph* to court. In July 1996, the *Sunday Telegraph* offered to settle out of court. Ghannouchi agreed, and the publishers, a former editor of the *Sunday Telegraph*, and a journalist employed by the newspaper apologized to him for the allegations published by them and accepted that "his convictions by Tunisian State Security and Military Courts in 1987 and 1992 were unsafe."[13]

The London Saudi-owned Arabic daily *Ash-Sharq al-Awsat* published the same allegations, quoting from the *Sunday Telegraph*.[14] Ghannouchi took the paper to court. More than four years later, he agreed to settle out of court and the paper published the following statement of apology:

> *Ash-Sharq al-Awsat* wishes to clarify that the claims [it] published [quoting] the *Sunday Telegraph* are unfounded. Mr. Ghannouchi is not a terrorist and he has not committed any terrorist action. On the contrary, he has constantly condemned such [terrorist] actions. Furthermore, Mr. Ghannouchi was under arrest in Tunisia at the time of the bombings in August 1987, a fact that refutes the allegation of his involvement in these incidents. In addition, Mr. Ghannouchi has been living in exile since 1989, a fact that belies the allegation of his involvement in the conspiracy which the Tunisian authorities claim was plotted against President Ben Ali in 1991. *Ash-Sharq al-Awsat* apologizes for having published the allegations originally published by the *Sunday Telegraph* regarding Mr. Rachid Ghannouchi, who has won a court case against the paper. Having agreed to an out of court settlement, *Ash-Sharq al-Awsat* publishes this clarification in adherence to the truth and as an obligation toward the readers and toward Mr. Ghannouchi.[15]

Similar allegations against Ghannouchi were repeated by the *Sunday Express*.[16] The paper alleged that Ghannouchi had masterminded the terrorist bombing of defenseless British tourists at a Tunisian hotel in August 1987, in which five holiday makers had received serious injuries, and that he had entered into a deal with the British authorities whereby he was granted political asylum in the United Kingdom in return for agreeing to reveal the secrets of Muslim terrorist groups to the intelligence services. Ghannouchi believed that this time the purpose of the article was not only to discredit him in the eyes of the British public, but also to damage his reputation within Islamic circles by claiming that he collaborated with the intelligence services against fellow Islamists. He took the newspaper to court. The editors of the *Sunday Express* admitted that their allegations were published in reliance in part upon information provided by the Tunisian Embassy in London. In the settlement of the lawsuit, they agreed to the following:

> Having undertaken further enquiries subsequent to the commencement of these proceedings, the Defendants (The Editor of *The Sunday Express* in 1995 and its publisher) now recognize that the Plaintiff (Rachid Ghannouchi), who was held incommunicado by the Tunisian authorities during the six months prior to the August 1987 bombing, was not responsible, and could not have been responsible, for the outrage. Further, the Defendants acknowledge that the Plaintiff is not linked with Muslim terrorist groups and that he could not have entered into the kind of agreement with the British authorities that was described in their article. The Defendants are here publicly to acknowledge these facts, to retract the allegations that appeared in the article of 6 August 1995 and to apologize. They have, in addition, agreed to pay a substantial sum in damages to the Plaintiff and to pay his legal costs.[17]

Arab Secularist Critique

Ghannouchi has often been the target of secularist vengeance for his critique of secularism. Seemingly finding little ammunition to undermine his ideas, the focus is turned to his intentions. Bahey Eddin Hassan, director of the Cairo Institute for Human Rights Studies and a known opponent of what he calls political Islam, names Ghannouchi as an example of the "Machiavellianism rampant in the political Islamic trend."[18] He regards as a major obstacle hindering dialogue with political Islam the great "flexibility" that characterizes the leaders of political Islam, manifest in their willingness to adopt a certain position and its opposite. This, he claims, is explained historically by the resort to *taqiyyah*, "which allows Islamists, in the phases of weakness, to declare positions contradicting their beliefs and to conceal those opinions which contradict those of others." He cites as an example what he calls "one of the most prominent symbols of moderation in political Islam." It is Rachid Ghannouchi, who is accused of hypocrisy: "For while he is noted for his condemnation of violence, he considers terrorist and assassination acts in Algeria a part of what he calls a popular revolution."[19] Hassan refers to Ghannouchi as an example of the dualism in standards said to be "most evident in the political Islamists' hard criticism of the records of human rights in their countries while they keep silent on the violations in Iran and Sudan, or even consider them the model of the Islamic project and a victory for Islam, or otherwise justify them on the grounds of political specificity."[20]

The practice of *taqiyyah*, which Islamic leaders, such as Ghannouchi, are alleged to resort to, in this context implies hypocrisy. The term is derived from the Arabic root *waqa*, which means to shield or protect or avoid. As a concept, *taqiyyah* is the precautionary dissimulation of religious belief and practice in the face of persecution. It is more a Shiite concept than a Sunni one, for since the death of the Prophet, Shiite Muslims have considered themselves subject to persistent religious persecution by the Sunni majority, the holders of political power. So what started as a passive or silent resistance developed later on into active dissimulation of true beliefs when required to protect life, property, and religion itself.[21]

Rachid Ghannouchi, who had the opportunity to respond to Hassan's remarks at the same function where the latter made them,[22] rebutted the allegations and accused Hassan of making "outrageous errors that severely undermined his credibility." Ghannouchi finds no explanation for such an attack on his intentions except as "an act of vengeance for settling a score with a political foe using the cover of the global human rights movement."[23] What Ghannouchi alludes to is that Hassan is a veteran Nassirist "who, together with many of his comrades, converted to liberalism and espoused the cause of human rights to survive the loss of their glory. When Nassirism was in power, there was no concern for human rights. In fact they were violated in the name of the struggle against imperialism." Hence is the charge made by Ghannouchi that Hassan was "employing non-political tools to attack a political foe, and in so doing his action resembles what had happened in Tunisia when secularists used the concept of civil society as a sword to fight Islamic foes."[24] On the question of supporting violence in Algeria, Ghannouchi accused Hassan of having taken out of context a remark made by him in an article where he describes the general situation in Algeria as revolutionary.[25] Nowhere in Ghannouchi's writings or speeches is the violence in Algeria condoned or justified. However, like most other observers of the Algerian affair, he does indeed call attention to the root of the crisis and condemns the military coup, which in his opinion has led to "anarchy, carnage, and mayhem."

On the sympathetic position adopted by Islamists toward Iran and Sudan, Ghannouchi contends that here too the expression of sympathy is taken out of context. He warns that his discourse on this matter is not to be construed as one of unconditional support for the government in either country. He calls attention to his distinction between what would be his assessment of the human rights record of either government and his condemnation of what is seen as an unjust Western campaign, involving economic sanctions against not only Sudan and Iran but also Libya and Iraq, the consequences of which are deprivation and suffering by millions of ordinary people who may have little say in the policies of their governments. In other words, the context of Ghannouchi's statement of sympathy is not one of condoning policies of undemocratic regimes but of denunciation of a selective American policy of imposing sanctions against "unfriendly" regimes.

Although one would not expect Ghannouchi to pay the same level of attention to the domestic policies of Sudanese and Iranian governments as he does to the government in his own country, as an Islamic leader he would be expected to criticize violations of human rights or lack of democratization just as he would in the case of any other Arab or Islamic country. But has Ghannouchi been commenting on the human rights situations in Arab and Islamic countries other than Tunisia? Has he really been selective in this regard? There is no evidence that he has. Or is it the case that he should not comment on the violations perpetrated against his colleagues in his own country unless he equally comments on the violations perpetrated by every other Arab or Islamic government against its opponents? Violations of human rights are perpetrated, as reported by regional and international human rights groups, by many Muslim governments from as far in the east as Indonesia to as far in the west as Morocco. Had Ghannouchi been a leader of a human rights monitoring organization he would definitely have been blamed for failing to report, or comment on, all such violations. But he is a leader of a Tunisian political organization that has its local objectives and pressing priorities. Furthermore, even though as a thinker he may be expected to raise and respond to issues of more general interest than just Tunisian affairs, he is continually pressed by his colleagues in the movement, being their leader and official spokesman, to take every care in dealing with issues of concern to third parties so as not to earn additional enemies or incur further restrictions on the movement and its members. This is an area that requires delicate calculation. The outcome of any such political calculation is always bound to be a source of discomfort for some supporters as well as for some opponents. For instance, some of Ghannouchi's ex-colleagues now tell us, as shall be discussed below, that they were not pleased with his strong denunciation of the American-led international alliance against Iraq in the Gulf War in 1991. Such a position, they argue, earned him and his movement the dislike of Kuwaiti Islamists upon whose financial support many less fortunate Islamists relied until Iraq invaded Kuwait in the summer of 1990.

Ghannouchi maintains that in both Iran and Sudan there are Islamic projects that are far from complete. Both experiments fall well short of an aspired modern Islamic democratic state. Nevertheless, he credits both regimes for having shown signs of flexibility and tendency toward slow and gradual democratization. In the second edition of his *Al-Hurriyat al-'Ammah Fid-Dawlah al-Islamiyyah* (Public liberties in the Islamic state) he is particularly critical of the ruling Islamic elite in the Sudan for having relied, in just the same way as ruling secularist elites did before, on the state apparatus in order to change the structure of society.[26]

> The ongoing [political] project in Sudan seems to be based on the idea of deconstructing the traditional sectarian structure of society in prelude to re-constructing it on a modern national Islamic foundation. In doing so, the ruling elite in Sudan joins Arab modernist elites which consider that the state has a mission that justifies the use of violence and the curtailment of freedom in order to guarantee the success of this project. In this case, the state's primary mission is not to express public will but to find it, even to create it. If such a mission is legitimate, and it is as far as I am concerned illegitimate, then the prospects of its success in pulling people with chains to paradise is, in my understanding, rather weak simply because God has created the children of Adam with a natural disposition for the love of freedom. Any project of salvation that comes through this route, irrespective of the amount of good it alleges to carry to the people, is invariably met with rejection. This has been the experiment of modernization in Egypt, Tunisia, Turkey, and the Soviet Union.[27]

However, Ghannouchi finds hope in what he calls the Islamic pragmatic culture of the Sudanese Islamic Movement, a culture that is bound to "make it in the near future, once more, accept political pluralism as a true expression of diversification within Sudanese society." He is encouraged by the fact that the government in Khartoum has recognized the political parties of the south and believes it would be impossible for the parties of the north to remain banned.

> The Sudanese Islamic project's chances of success in lasting, growing, and changing the current balance of power are realistic but remain very limited if its [leaders] do not reduce the ceiling of their ambitions and if they fail to interact well with the components of their society, with their surroundings, and with their age. They should not count on the state

as a source of their existence and a guarantor of their future. They should accept the notion of power sharing, pluralism, and open contestation. It should not be their objective to possess power irrespective of the cost.[28]

Irreconcilability

Ghannouchi's thoughts have been criticized by Arab secularist writers who claim that it is inconceivable that Islam can be reconciled with what is deemed to be strictly secularist values such as democracy and modernity.

A typical work in this regard is the recent book by Haydar Ibrahim Ali entitled *At-Tayyarat al-Islamiyah Wa-Qadiyat ad-Dimuqratiyah* (Islamic currents and the question of democracy). Ghannouchi suspects that the book was published by Markaz Dirasat al-Wahdah al-'Arabiyah (Arab Unity Studies Centre) in Beirut "under pressure from certain quarters to atone for its earlier publication" of Ghannouchi's book *Al-Hurriyat al-'Ammah Fid-Dawlah al-Islamiyyah* (Public liberties in the Islamic state). When *Al-Hurriyat* was first published the Tunisian government and some radical Arab secularists expressed dismay and outrage at the publishers.

In his book, Ali, an ex-Marxist and prominent figure within the self-exiled Sudanese opposition, seeks to discredit Islamist democratic discourse in two ways: first by proving the impossibility of reconciling Islamic values with democracy, and second by proving that Islamists are pragmatists who do not really believe in what they profess. In dealing with Ghannouchi, Ali starts with praising his intellectual aptitude and unique contribution to Islamic political thought. He quotes him at length only to conclude that his thought is based on an attempt to reconcile two distinct ideas irreconcilable by virtue of the difference in their historical development and their vision of the world. Such duality between the Islamic heritage and modernity, he argues, is the source of weakness, and hence contradiction in Ghannouchi's discourse.[29] Ghannouchi is criticized for searching for an Islamic humanism, one that stems from a religious frame of reference, which to the conviction of the author is a paradox, for it is an attempt to reconcile between the *ilahi* (divine) and the *insani* (human).[30] Referring to what he calls the predicament of Islamic humanism, Ali points to a contradiction between humanism and the concept of *al-istikhlaf* (vicegerency).[31]

Ali attributes Ghannouchi's Islamism to a feeling of deprivation and trivialization because he comes from the rural provinces, which did not enjoy the privileges of the urbanized provinces.[32] The idea that Ghannouchi was driven toward Islamism by economic factors was first put forward by Tunisian writer Abdelqader Zghal, who suggests that social conditions of production and socio-professional factors were at play in the development of Ghannouchi's political thought.[33] Associating the phenomenon of Islamism in Tunisia with the process of decolonization and the construction of the nation-state, Zghal argues that two important developments took place following independence: the first was the urbanization of the Tunisian countryside and the ruralization of the cities; and the second was the expansion of the education network throughout the whole country, including the most remote rural regions from the urban centers. These changes, he goes on, produced a new social periphery coming essentially from the many graduates and school-leavers who have been blocked in their social promotion and from a large sector of what he calls the new petite bourgeoisie coming mainly from the rural or semi-urban parts of the country and destabilized by the rapid changes and the new requirements of modernity and, as a result, downgraded in comparison to the new bourgeoisie. The conspicuous consumption of the latter and its slavish imitation not of Western values but of external manifestations of Western behavior are two of the factors that created the feeling of frustration of a large part of the new petite bourgeoisie and of the mass of educated people prone to unemployment or professional disqualification. He further argues that the feeling of frustration of the new social periphery could not express itself in terms of class struggle because of the broad diversity in the socio-professional status of its members. They could express their frustration politically only through moral judgment that would delegitimize the existing political system.[34]

This analysis is contradicted by the details of Ghannouchi's upbringing and development. As shown in chapter one, Ghannouchi grew up as a Nassirist and did not convert to Islamism until he became disenchanted with nationalism during his years of study in Syria. It would have been more accurate to suggest, on the basis of the facts of his life history, that his rural background—especially as he moved to the city to join az-Zaytouna for his studies—drove him in the direction of skepticism and lack of religious commitment.

Like Ali, Zghal finds ambivalence in Ghannouchi's endeavor to build a contemporary Islamic society that would dip into the Western culture without losing itself. He also describes him, though not without expressing an understanding on the ground that Ghannouchi is a politician, as one who speaks two languages. He even likens him to Bourguiba, who is said to have spoken two languages during the struggle for national liberation. For this reason Zghal declares Ghannouchi the illegitimate son of Bourguiba.[35] But the most serious accusation Zghal levels at Ghannouchi is that democracy and political pluralism for him, as well as for all Sudanese and Tunisian Islamists, are not values in themselves:

> The goal is still *al-islam din-wa-dawla*, that is, the fusion of policy and religion and the strict application by the state of the religious law, or *Shari'ah*. Political democracy and multi-partism are for them just a less costly means than armed struggle of putting pressure on the political decision makers and the first step in conquering the state machinery. The final goal is not a state under the laws of a constitution voted by the representatives of the citizens but an Islamic state following the precepts of the motto *al-islam dustourouna* (Islam is our constitution).[36]

Arab secularists and radical Islamists, in spite of the hostility they exhibit toward each other, share the conviction that democracy and Islam are irreconcilable, and that if you accept one you would have to renounce the other. Ghannouchi's secularist critics, however, accuse him of ambiguity and evasiveness on the question of democracy. He is accused of failing to come up with a procedural definition of democracy that would help contrast it with *shura*. Instead, he is said to deliberately "float" the concept of democracy in order to deny its attractiveness or ability. He is also criticized for speaking of different models of democracy, so as to indulge in criticizing the liberal model "as if it necessarily leads to corruption, moral decay, deviation, and exploitation."[37] It is suggested that liberal democracy, as it is, should either be accepted as a whole or rejected as a whole. Ghannouchi's arbitrary distinction between the concept of democracy and its liberal model is said to be a reflection of the confused treatment of the notion of democracy in the minds of Islamists.[38]

Indeed, Ghannouchi does not believe liberal democracy to be the ultimate model of democracy and is very keen to highlight, as has been shown in chapter three, what he regards to be liberal democracy's points of weakness. He is also unequivocal about his conviction that an Islamic model of democracy, which would be born out of a marriage between procedural democracy and Islamic values, is possible. He does not consider it to be a contradiction with this conviction to accept liberal democracy as a working model until an Islamic model is developed and proven workable. This theory may not be convincing for some secularists and Islamists alike, but it is becoming increasingly popular within the ranks of mainstream Islamism and among some secular academics. As for the claim of irreconcilability, the assumption that ideas are rigid systems that cannot interact, nor allow for any exchange, is indefensible. In fact the originality of Ghannouchi's thought stems from the fact that he searches, in both Western and Islamic cultures, for points of agreement that allow Muslims, while adhering to the principles of their creed and value system, to benefit from, and integrate into their own culture, valuable inventions that might help establish an Islamic democratic system of governance.

Silent Witness

An ex-member of Ennahda, and a former defender and close associate of Ghannouchi, Mohamed Elhachmi Hamdi, has recently joined the club of Ghannouchi's detractors. His critique appears primarily in his Ph.D. dissertation at the School of Oriental and African Studies at the University of London. Ghannouchi and other Ennahda members were hoping that Hamdi's research, which started in 1990, two years before he decided to leave the movement, would be the first academic work in English to vindicate Ennahda and provide an objective analysis of its history and convictions. However, from Ennahda's point of view, it turned out to be worse than anything they feared the most hostile of their critics would say about them. In spite of his dismay at the result, Ghannouchi has an explanation for what he considers to be a rather disappointing testimony. Hamdi, who had until the early 1990s been well-positioned and especially favored by Ghannouchi, was growing restless as he saw his role as spokesperson for the movement diminish. He had previously been asked to represent Ennahda abroad and to establish links, which he successfully achieved, with the media and political circles in Europe and in the Arab world. In the early 1990s, Ghannouchi left Tunisia and settled in London. Scores of senior Ennahda members joined him in his London exile or settled elsewhere in Europe. The movement started reorganizing itself and restructuring its offices, apparently minimizing the role previously assigned to Hamdi.[39] The straw that broke the camel's back and convinced Hamdi that he had no reason to remain in the movement was his loss of a bid to be appointed as chief editor of a newspaper the movement was contemplating publishing in London.[40] In May 1992, Hamdi announced his withdrawal from the movement. In a statement published in the London Arabic press he declared that he resigned because of disagreement over the priorities of Islamic and national work in the current period and over the methodology pursued by the movement. He further explained: "I have tried to keep the debate over these issues within the internal legitimate circles, and have called for the necessity of equal opportunities for all different views without discrimination. However, these attempts have failed and I felt that my affiliation to the movement was a mere formality that has no spirit and no meaning."[41]

Hamdi expressed confidence that the Islamic work in Tunisia was in need of serious and fundamental revisions regarding the vital issues that constitute its general strategy. In a remark interpreted by Ennahda as an attempt to distance himself from acts of violence the regime in Tunisia accused Ennahda of, Hamdi denounced violence, stressing that "no party will benefit from embroilment in violent conflict because no one, except the enemy, wins a battle waged against one's own brother and fellow citizens."[42]

Hamdi's former colleagues believe that this development necessitated a change in the purposes of his Ph.D. thesis. The purpose was now to retaliate from the movement that failed to appreciate his talents and that seemed ungrateful for his services. He set out to prove to his adversaries within the movement that he was capable not only of succeeding on his own, but also of damaging the movement by discrediting its leader, the very same person who always lent him a helping hand and promoted him in the face of strong opposition from other leading members who felt uncomfortable working with him. To some of them, he was an opportunist who was more interested in self-serving maneuvers than in safeguarding the interests of the movement.[43]

Entitled "An Analysis of the History and Discourse of the Tunisian Islamic Movement al-Nahda: A Case Study of the Politicization of Islam," Hamdi's Ph.D. arrives at a conclusion that reinforces the claims already made by Tunisian government agencies and Arab secularist critics of Ghannouchi. He accuses Ghannouchi of "double-talk and double-agenda" and of embroilment in violence. Despite having been active within the ranks of the Tunisian Islamic movement since 1978, Hamdi suddenly changed his convictions not only about Ghannouchi and Ennahda but also about the entire concept of Islamic activism. Hamdi now assumes that Islam as a religion is non-political. He regards Islamic movements, including Ennahda, to be opportunist political groups that use Islam to serve their ends and to conceal the hidden agenda of planning to seize power through violence.[44]

Throughout his dissertation, Hamdi remains a silent witness. He divulges very little of his own experience, of his own findings, or of his own assessment of what others, on whose writings he relies, say about Ennahda or Ghannouchi. The issues he raises in his dissertation and uses as indicators of how disastrous Ghannouchi's leadership of Ennahda has been, are the very same ones he strongly defended and skillfully explained just before he started having disagreements with Ghannouchi over the post of chief editor. In his introduction to the first volume of a collection of Ghannouchi's writings, published just before he withdrew from the movement in 1992 under the title *Minal-Fikr al-Islami Fi-Tunis*, Hamdi highlights the features of excellence in Ghannouchi's thought and in the Islamic Tunisian experiment.[45] Contrary to the way he depicts him in his Ph.D. thesis, Ghannouchi here is one of the greatest Islamic thinkers of our time. He is hailed as a great leader whose struggle along several fronts never ceased, a defender of human rights, women rights and workers' rights, a strict adherent to *shura*, a leader respectful of his colleagues and insistent on assessment and self-critique.[46]

I find myself fully convinced that the new epoch of Islamic work, present and future, requires new symbols and new trends in terms of thinking and methodology. We must contribute, everyone in his own way, to effecting this change. For each battle has its men. I can feel the currents of aspired revival blowing here in the Maghreb and there in the Sudan. They are accompanied by rightly-guided voices in the Occupied Territories, in Egypt, in Lebanon, and within expatriate communities. This is not to mention the lessons we have not yet derived from the revolution of Islam in Iran. All prospects are there for a real and necessary renaissance within the Islamic movement. So let these winds blow in every direction. It is within this framework that these writings of teacher Rachid Ghannouchi are presented. For he is one of the symbols of the new epoch in whose struggle and contribution we have great hope.[47]

No less devout is Hamdi's emphasis of the distinctiveness of Ghannouchi in his own documentation of the history of Ennahda in a book published in 1989. Nowhere in this book or in any of the literature Hamdi produced before his desertion is he seen to criticize Ghannouchi or the movement, or even demand revision or reform. All seemed well, and it was the Tunisian government to blame for everything.[48] In contrast, Hamdi now has no hesitation to claim the exact opposite. In his dissertation, Hamdi is found to err in no less than seventy-five positions. In a bid to discredit Ghannouchi, both as thinker and leader, he excludes historical facts, disregards texts, distorts some of Ghannouchi's remarks, relies on police reports based on confessions extracted under duress, and relies on forged political statements attributed to Ghannouchi, who strongly denies ever making them.

In the first category one may cite Hamdi's total silence with regard to the influence of Bennabi on Ghannouchi and on the movement as a whole. The trips made by the founders of the movement for three years to Algeria to meet and listen to Bennabi, and Bennabi's treatise on democracy translated by Ghannouchi in prison, are non-existent in the dissertation. What Hamdi sets out to prove is that Ennahda has been influenced by three main factors: the *tabligh*, to give an impression of radicalism in appearance; the Ikhwan (and Qutb in particular), to give an impression of radicalism in thinking; and Iran, to give an impression of radicalism in methodology. The clash with the Marxists on campus is analyzed in such away that it adds to the perception of the movement as a violent organization.[49]

Although his Ph.D. thesis is on the politicization of religion, Hamdi provides no definition of politicization and leaves it to the reader to conclude that it means using religion as a motivation and as a justification of the desire to seize power. Nor does he say what he understands Islam to mean, although it is apparent that his conception of Islam has now become a secularist conception of religion. This probably explains why he sees as a major defect in the Tunisian Islamic movement that its leader is not a professional religious scholar.[50]

Hamdi reduces the imprisonment period of Ghannouchi and several of his colleagues in the early 1980s to a period marred by disputation, especially between Salah Karkar and Ghannouchi, over who should run the movement and how. At the time when Ennahda members discount the reported dispute as insignificant, they accuse Hamdi of deliberately maintaining silence in his dissertation regarding the significant activities that took place within prison. The most important of these was the writing up of a draft of a comprehensive assessment of Tunisian society, which the movement felt was necessary prior to proposing its own Islamic alternative. The importance of this assessment document, entitled "Al-Mujtama' at-Tunisi: Tahlil Hadari" (Tunisian society: A civilizational analysis), is that it belies some of Hamdi's allegations including the claim that Ghannouchi had no interest in the Arab reformist school of the nineteenth century or in Khairuddin at-Tunisi, and his claim that there were no attempts to formulate a political or social theory because the leaders of the movement only reacted to events around them.[51]

Hamdi relies exclusively on sources known to have been staunchly opposed to the Islamic movement, and at the same time closely tied to the regime, to indict the leadership of the movement of setting up a secret military wing about which most members had no knowledge.[52] He himself, as a member, apparently was unaware of the existence of this wing. Had there been a military wing, why didn't the movement ever resort to using it in order to respond to persecution, and why had all forms of protestation been peaceful as admitted by Hamdi himself?[53]

In another category of errors one may cite the distortion of statements made by Ghannouchi so as to discredit him and to portray him in the image of an exclusionist who looks down upon others. Ghannouchi is accused of attempting to rewrite history and misrepresent the present.[54] Ghannouchi is quoted as saying: "We are the leading elite of the one million Muslims yearning for progress, civilization, and world peace under Islam. If we are to be mocked and insulted, our enemies should be clear and frank enough to mock and insult Islam itself. Only Islamists provide the real vision."[55]

We are told that this quote is taken from Ghannouchi's *Maqalat*. The quote is actually taken from part of a dialogue that Ghannouchi envisages taking place between him and another person who asks about the *ikhwanjiyah*, a derogatory term used by the government-sponsored media to describe the Islamists. The reason this dialogue is taking place is the rumored preparation by the government to crack down on Islamic activists. Ghannouchi asks: What is the danger? He is told it is the *ikhwanjiyah*. But who are the *ikhwanjiyah*? he asks. He gets this answer:

> They are those reactionary rigid persons, who do not drink wine, nor do they fornicate, nor do they gamble or steal or lie or swear. They perform prayer at its assigned times, they attend in the mosques praising the Lord, reciting the Qur'an and learning the *din* (religion). For them, *din* is neither mere utterances by the tongue nor mere geographic affiliation; it is faith, worship, conduct, and a way of life. Worship for them perfects one's conduct in the mosque, in the road, in the market, in school, and in the house. They call to prayer, to righteousness, and to renouncing superstition and bigotry wherever they may be. Imagine, they do not even smoke.[56]

The dialogue continues with the following:

> If such are the *ikhwanjiyah*, then they are not a misguided gang in the *Ummah* as you say. To the contrary, they are an enlightened group of Muslims, they are the vanguard of the one billion Muslims who aspire for progress and civilization in the shade of Islam, which is peace for the entire world. It would have been better, instead of condemning them and calling them names they have not called themselves, that you be clear and frank. It is Islam you should be prosecuting, condemning, describing as reactionary, and accusing of collaboration. For they are only its dynamic image (or they are trying at least to be so).[57]

There are several other examples of such distortion in Hamdi's Ph.D. thesis. One particular flagrant distortion is seen in the way he plays with the text of an interview conducted with Ghannouchi by Qusay ad-Darwish on the concept of Muslim and Islamist.[58] The twisting, omitting, and out-of-context quoting is aimed at proving that

Ghannouchi believes that his movement is the sole representative of faith.[59] In fact, nowhere in Ghannouchi's writings or statements is he found to claim, implicitly or explicitly, what Hamdi attributes to him.

To prove his point that Ghannouchi is not sincere about his claim to democracy, Hamdi relies heavily on two pieces of evidence, both of which were obtained from the files of the Tunisian government and both of which are vehemently denied by Ennahda and Ghannouchi. The first is the claim that Ennahda had a military wing that was preparing to seize power. The second is a document entitled "This Is the Day on Which the Truthful Will Profit from Their Truthfulness, This Is the Day Which You Were Promised." The document, which Hamdi attaches as an appendix to his thesis, is said to have been issued by the Ennahda leader and distributed within Islamic circles but never published in a magazine or a book.[60] In the alleged document Ghannouchi praises Saddam Hussein's wise and courageous leadership and declares that the man who dared attack Israel and resisted in the face of united international aggression deserves to be obeyed by Muslims in whatever he orders, and has the right to their money and lives.[61] This is the same document that was used by the *Sunday Telegraph*'s lawyers in the London case lodged against the paper by Ghannouchi to prove its allegation that he was a terrorist. Denying any connection with the document, which strangely appears nowhere in any published Islamic book or periodical, but not denying his opposition to the American-led alliance against Iraq, Ghannouchi insists that this document was fabricated by the regime in Tunisia in an attempt to discredit him.[62]

Reservations and Apprehensions

Ghannouchi's enthusiasm for democracy and his anxiousness to prove that liberal democracy can be a good starting point en route to achieving an Islamic model of democracy has been a source of concern to some Islamic observers. The anxiety stems from the apprehension that the borrowing of what may be considered a mere set of tools and measures, from a specific cultural environment to another that is culturally and historically different, and perhaps contradictory, may involve serious risks. Some of Ghannouchi's own friends have argued that previous attempts, within the context of reform, to borrow European administrative systems have had disastrous consequences. On the one hand, they constituted a bridge across which secularism crossed from Europe over to the Muslim world. On the other, such borrowing has led to the establishment of deformed systems of governance that are neither based on tradition nor on democracy. The deformation, they argue, has been the result of a combination of the worst elements in both the traditional system and the Western model to the effect of producing oppressive dictatorships throughout the Muslim world.[63]

The above line of critique emanates from Islamist thinkers who express reservation about what they see as Ghannouchi's overconfidence in democracy. Their position does not stem from the belief that democracy is incompatible with Islam, but out of their conviction that a sound system of governance would have to evolve out of the local, and within the specific historical, context. Their main concern is that Ghannouchi's ideas may be construed as implying that democratic procedures and tools can be borrowed without bringing with them what may be deemed as unwanted components of philosophy or ideology. Although Ghannouchi does make an effort to distinguish between philosophy and procedures, this seems insufficient to some Islamic thinkers who expect more concentration on cultural specificity. One of the most radical opinions in this regard is expressed by Abdelwahab Elmessiri, who considers it impossible to disengage procedures from their philosophical origins. He is particularly critical of what he calls Ghannouchi's "oscillation" between procedures and concepts, an oscillation that emanates from Ghannouchi's double role as a thinker and as a political leader.[64]

Furthermore, Ghannouchi is criticized for not addressing the changes that would be necessary for a truly pluralistic environment to prevail in the Arab world. In the Western case major economic, social, and political transformations took place over a long period of time prior to the restructuring of political life in a manner that permitted democratization and pluralization. The question is what sort of transformations, if any, are still to be seen in the Arab world. Since the beginning of the colonial era, through the struggle for independence, and finally the era of territorial statehood, no comparable transformations have taken place. For instance, the Sudanese experience has shown, and in this regard it may be considered representative of most Arab societies—perhaps excluding Tunisia—that tribal and sectarian factionalism impedes Western-style democratization and political pluralization. The point here is that democratic governments in Sudan have continually been controlled by one of the two major Sufi orders (functioning as political party) in the country, the Mahdi or the Mirighni, with the inevitable consequence of monopoly of power, rampant corruption, and disenchantment with democracy. Would pluralist democracy work in such an environment? Ghannouchi himself has expressed an opinion in support of the current attempts by the Sudanese government to introduce a new system of "popular democracy" based on representation in regional, ultimately progressing to national, congresses. Having trivialized the tribal factor as an obstacle to democratization, the failure of the democratic process in Sudan is attributed, in Ghannouchi's analysis, less to local factors than to foreign intervention, the most notable manifestations of which are the repeated coup attempts instigated by international and regional powers, and the war of attrition in the south, which, it is argued, could not have continued this long had it not been for the role played by intervening foreign powers. Still, Ghannouchi may be blamed for not addressing the "topography" and "geology" of the terrain to which democratic tools and procedures are to be transferred. Had his theory been applied exclusively to Tunisia, whose traditional social structure had seriously been mutilated, his ideas would have been less questionable.[65]

Conclusion

Rachid Ghannouchi's importance emanates from the high standard of his political discourse, which is distinguished by daring attempts to innovate and to introduce new dimensions in contemporary Islamic thought. The impact of his ideological and intellectual standing has extended well beyond the frontiers of Tunisia. His contribution to modern Islamic thought lies in his comprehension of both traditional Islamic literature and modern Western concepts and in his strong belief in the theory of the compatibility between Islam and Western thought in matters concerning the system of government, human rights, and civil liberties.

The significance of Ghannouchi also emanates from the fact that, unlike other Islamic thinkers who espouse the democratic cause, he is both a thinker and a leader of an Islamic movement. He is a credible authority within Islamic circles at the global level. His thoughts are in no way restricted to an intellectual debate at a time when the Islamic movement has emerged as a major political power in the Muslim world, and when power-sharing or power-taking experiments are in process. Ghannouchi is unprecedented within Islamic intellectual circles in his theory that civil society is an Islamic concept and that religion consolidates civil society whereas secularism, especially the model imported to the Muslim world under the guise of modernization, weakens it. He is the first Islamic thinker to address the problems facing the transition to democracy in the Arab world in the manner this book has analyzed. He started developing this thesis following the coup against democracy in Algeria in 1992, less than two years after the failure of the democratic experiment in his own country, Tunisia.

Having read Ghannouchi's written works since the early 1980s, the author finds that on fundamental issues, such as democracy, human rights, and civil liberties, his position has not changed. However, his position as leader of the main opposition party in his country requires that he take certain political factors into consideration, and this in turn is bound to give an impression of an inconsistency in his discourse. As a political leader he has been, on more than an occasion, compelled to make compromises, the most notable of which was his decision to remove the reference to Islam from the name of his movement in order to qualify for registering as a legal political party.

Ghannouchi's weakness may therefore be said to emanate from his dual role as a political activist and a political thinker. The limitation this imposes on his work is evident, for instance, in the fact that he chose, for pure tactical reasons, in the late 1980s, to change his strategy of criticizing the Personal Status Code, which prohibited polygamy. Instead, he declared that the code was in its broad guidelines acceptable to his movement. His justification was, and still is, that polygamy is not compulsory, and therefore it is not a priority. If polygamy is not a principal value in Islam, and if making an issue out of it is likely to harm the movement and reduce its chances of political success, then it can be forgotten about, at least for a while. The duality of his role may also explain his preference of highlighting the positive aspects of Western civilization to that of providing a deep and comprehensive critique of its negative side, something which most Islamic thinkers have been eager to do since the beginning of the twentieth century. This explains, also, why he has not felt, at least thus far, the need to write more deeply on issues of relevance to his theories. His treatment of liberalism, secularism, modernity, and modernization, for instance, shows clearly that his priority lies not in providing his readers with an exposition of the origin of these concepts or of the philosophies underpinning them. His priority lies in informing his readers of the positive and negative aspects of these concepts and in encouraging them to search for a common ground, a compromise of some sort, between Islam and the West.

Inevitably, Ghannouchi sometimes speaks more as a politician and at other times more as a thinker. The language he uses corresponds to the level and nature of his audience. Sometimes it is too sophisticated for an average Muslim to relate to. Sometimes it is more political analysis than philosophical argumentation. There is no evidence, however, that he contradicts himself or speaks different languages for pure tactical reasons. What is evident is that his emphasis may vary depending on the audience he addresses or the occasion at which he is invited to speak. Although in his most important book, *Al-Hurriyat*, the concept of democracy is discussed at length, much of his thought is conveyed through public talks or in papers submitted to seminars or conferences.

Although being a political leader can be a liability and is definitely a heavy burden, what distinguishes Ghannouchi from other Islamic political thinkers is his direct involvement in politics. It is true that the events that led to his exile and the banning of his movement have cost him some popularity among his own followers (in the 1995 leadership contest he won only 52 percent of the votes). It is also true that he took the blame for his decision to trust President Ben Ali, who upon coming to power promised to start a new era of democracy and freedom that turned to be an era of crackdown and persecution. It is even true that some disgruntled and former members of the movement allege that Ghannouchi is not qualified as political leader. Nevertheless, Ghannouchi is a democratically elected leader. In fact, no crucial decision was ever taken singularly by him; such decisions were always made through the practice of *shura*. In other words, to more than 50 per cent of his colleagues, Ghannouchi is a credible and capable leader. What is interesting to note in this regard is that his involvement in policy and decision making, and what this entails of risk taking, opens his eyes to issues not easily seen by those dedicated to theoretical research and pure academic thinking. Usually, having to make compromises or enter into alliances with other political powers, and having to take into consideration the supreme interest of the movement as a whole, is obstructive to free political thinking. In Ghannouchi's case, however, it has been a source of inspiration and motivation with all the light it sheds on the way Islamic movements operate and seek to improve the way they operate.

As a thinker and political leader, Ghannouchi's main preoccupation has been to resolve the problem his country, Tunisia, and other Arab countries as well, have been suffering from, namely the problem of despotism. He believes democracy to be the best available means of curtailing despotism. While he is conscious that democracy has ethical and philosophical underpinnings that procedures may unavoidably carry with them, this for him is a price worth paying in order to get rid of despotism. He believes that the difficulty to extrude, completely, procedures and mechanisms from their philosophical and ethical contents is not a good reason why Muslims should deprive themselves of the opportunity to rid themselves of authoritarianism. It is an opportunity, as he is keen to stress, for the Muslims to fill a gap created and maintained for centuries by the absence of despotism-checking mechanisms. What he is interested in, and what really motivates him, is not merely importing, copying, or emulating the charming goodies of the West. He is anxious about the existence of a serious domestic problem the solution for which, he is convinced, lies in a set of procedures the West has surpassed the Muslims not only in devising but also in testing, implementing, and improving.

Ghannouchi's discourse is likely to exhibit signs of tension for one other reason. In certain ways, he is a follower of the reformist school, which combines to its Islamic terminology a list of Western terms. This is evident in Ghannouchi's tendency to shift from one terminology to the other without prior warning. Democracy could become *shura* or vice versa, although it is clear from his writings that he does make a distinction between the two. He may similarly equate a modern day parliament with the vague classical concept of *ahl-ul-hall wal-'aqd*. This problem does not face Arab secularists, who do not have to deal with an Islamic epistemology and who, unlike Ghannouchi, see the solution in adopting an imported Western outlook. Nor does it face Islamic rejectionists of modernity, who are content with the Islamic heritage as it is and who see nothing worth taking from the West. The difficulty of Ghannouchi's task is that he sets out from a domestic reality in pursuit of a solution for his country's problem but at the same time one that does not undermine its cultural identity. Like the pioneers of the reformist school (Tahtawi, al-Afghani, Abduh, at-Tunisi, Rida, al-Kawakibi, and so on), Ghannouchi seeks to find an alternative to the old method of domestic conflict resolution. The old methods were crippled, rendered useless, by the advent of colonialism and the emergence of the modern state, which altered, and even destroyed, traditional society. In the past, tribes, extended families, 'ulama', Sufi orders, and the awqaf managed society and maintained peace, stability, and a balance of power that checked despotism.

The tension perceived in Ghannouchi's discourse may be caused not as much by his inability to construct a coherent thought on the issues he seeks to address as by the difficulty of the mission on which he has embarked. His mission is aimed at assimilating specific Western civilizational products and incorporating them into the Islamic culture and its epistemological system. For contrary to what Ghannouchi himself says, civilizations do not simply inherit one another. Each civilization has its own underpinnings and its own historical course. Civilizations may meet or cross at certain points, an exchange of some sort may occur between them, but a fundamental characteristic of each single one of them prevents one from becoming the other or from taking over its historical course. For instance, the Western civilization took from the Islamic civilization important scientific and philosophical theories, but it did not change its main direction or its underpinnings. The same applies to the Muslims today as they seek to benefit from the Western civilization. Whatever comes in is fed into the civilization's specific mill, which grinds the intake, digests it, and re-produces it prior to incorporating it into its own integrated system. Once this process is over, the intake ends up having characteristics that can hardly be related to its origin. In other words, this is not a process of mere accumulation. In order for the project of establishing an Islamic democratic system to succeed, Western democratic procedures and concepts would have to be melted and re-cast in order to become a natural component of the Islamic cultural system.

It is in this light that one may also explain the tension observed in Ghannouchi's discussion of the concepts of secularism, liberalism, and modernity. Ghannouchi belongs to a cultural system that recognizes the divine and considers revelation to be the ultimate frame of reference. At the same time he sees in Western modernity, including secularism and liberalism, positive aspects that can be of benefit to the Muslims. He embarks on yet another tough mission and travels through a rough terrain. He attempts to deconstruct Western concepts, assimilate what he believes to be positive, and eventually come up with a formula for an Islamic renaissance. The latter would have to be founded on Islamic values and capable of benefiting, at the same time, from the positive aspects of modernity.

Ghannouchi's work is still ongoing; he may not even have reached the zenith of his contribution yet. His exile in Britain has, despite the pain it causes him, been a blessing in disguise. His ideas on secularism, civil society, and the territorial state have matured during the first six years of his exile and will develop further in the coming years.

It is only understandable that a number of gaps remain to be filled within Ghannouchi's thought. For instance, despite the criticism directed at the modern state, very little work has been done to suggest what the modern Islamic state would look like. Much of what has been written by Islamic thinkers, including Ghannouchi in his Al-Hurriyat, is no more than a review of various classical Islamic opinions on state and government as they existed in the Muslim world centuries ago. Writings in this field fall short of tackling the question of power in a modern setting. In spite of his enthusiasm for an Islamic democracy, and while describing at length the obstacles precluding its materialization, Ghannouchi says very little about the process of transition itself. Many questions remain unanswered. In a period of transition toward a stable consolidated Islamic democracy what compromises would have to be made and what mechanisms would have to be installed; or what safeguards are needed in order to prevent a society undergoing pluralization and democratization from slipping into chaos? In the past, Islamic societies relied on traditional institutions such as the tribe, the extended family, the Sufi order, and the 'ulama' to settle disputes and resolve conflicts. Most of these institutions have been disempowered by colonialism and the modern state but they have not disappeared completely. There is strong evidence that in some Arab societies they are regaining influence and reasserting themselves. In what way will political parties competing for power in a modern Islamic democracy relate to such traditional institutions, and how can impediments to open, free, and fair contestation by such institutions be averted?

Ghannouchi is suspicious of the modern Arab territorial state. Not only is it an obstacle facing democratization but it is also antithetical to the democratic state. He has more recently been stressing the need to concentrate more on consolidating civil society instead of concentrating on reforming the territorial state. He is ever more convinced that the territorial state is part of a global power system and that tampering with it in the absence of a strong civil society can have disastrous consequences. However, very little has thus far been said by Ghannouchi on how the problem of the territorial sate can be resolved.

Whatever may be said about the weaknesses of Ghannouchi's discourse or the need for him to fill in some gaps here and there, he remains a very important and influential Islamic thinker at the threshold of the twenty-first century. His contribution to Islamic political thought, which is still continuing, will undoubtedly be remembered by future generations and reflected upon just as we today reflect upon the contributions of great men such as at-Tunisi, al-Afghani, and Bennabi.

Ghannouchi deserves recognition for a number of important contributions, including:

1. His contribution to the revival and redefinition of the language of civil society within Islamic political thought
2. His thesis that the project of secularization has its limits and that it is incompatible with civil society, and that indeed a post-secular civil society is thinkable and possible
3. His rethinking of the relationship between democracy and Islam, and the importance therefore of democratic procedures and ways of life for the survival and renewal of Islam
4. His elucidation of the Islamic concept of freedom and human rights
5. His analysis of the role played by the modern Arab state and the new world order in precluding the advancement of democracy in the Arab region.

These are not only valuable additions to Islamic political thought but also launching pads from which ambitious Islamic thinkers and researchers may take off.

Notes

Chapter One

1. el-Kray el-Qusantini, "At-Thawbit wat-Tajdid fil-Fikr al-Islahı Ghadat Khuruj al-Mihwar Min Tunıs," in *Actes du Ivè Séminaire sur l'Histoire du Mouvement National La Tunisie de 1939 à 1945* (Tunis: Ministère de l'Education, 1989), 104-14.

2. This and the following eight paragraphs contain information received from R. Ghannouchi, interview by the author, London, February 1998.

3. R. Ghannouchı, interview by the author, London, March 1995.

4. R. Ghannouchı, interview by the author, London, February 1998.

5. R. Ghannouchı, interview by the author, London, March 1995.

6. R. Ghannouchi, interview by the author, London, February 1998.

7. Ibid.

8. Ibid.

9. Ibıd.

10. M. El-Hadi az-Zamzami, *Tunıs al-Islam al-Janh* [Tunısia, the wounded Islam] (Bonn: n.p., 1994), 35.

11. *Al-Mawsu'ah al-'Arabıyah al-Muyassarah* [The concise Arab encyclopedia], vol. 1 (Cairo: Dar Al Sha'b, 1965).

12. M. az-Zamzami, *Tunis*.

13. R. Ghannouchi, interview by the author, London, March 1995.

14. M. az-Zamzamı, *Tunis*.

15. Linda Jones, "Portrait of Rachıd al-Ghannouchı," *Middle East Report* (July-August 1988): 20.

16. A. el-Affendi, "The Long March Forward," *The Inquiry*, London (October 1987).

17. R. Ghannouchi, interview by the author, London, March 1995.

18. Ibid.

19. az-Zamzami, *Tunis*.

20. Ibid.

21. Ibid.

22. R. Ghannouchi, interview by the author, London, March 1995.

23. Ibid.

24. R. Ghannouchi, interview by the author, London, June 1997.

25. R. Ghannouchi, "The Conflict Between the West and Islam, The Tunısian Case: Real-

ity and Prospects" (paper presented at the Royal Institute of International Affairs [Chatham House] on 9 May 1995).

26. R. Ghannouchi, interview by the author, London, February 1998.

27. This and the following seven paragraphs contain information received from R. Ghannouchi, interview by the author, London, March 1995.

28. Burgat and Dowell, The Islamic Movement in North Africa, Texas 1993, p. 57.

29. R. Ghannouchi, interview by the author, London, March 1995.

30. R. Ghannouchi, interview by the author, London, June 1997.

31. R. Ghannouchi, interview by the author, London, March 1995.

32. Ibid.

33. E. Kedourie, Politics in the Middle East (Oxford: Oxford University Press, 1992), 309.

34. Ibid. p. 298.

35. K. Jaber, The Arab Ba'ath Socialist Party (Syracuse, N.Y.: Syracuse University Press, 1966).

36. R. Ghannouchi, interview by the author, London, March 1995

37. R. Ghannouchi, interview by the author, London, June 1997.

38. R. Ghannouchi, interview by the author, London, March 1995

39. Ibid.

40. Ibid.

41. Ibid.

42. R. Ghannouchi, interview by the author, London, June 1997.

43. Kedourie, Politics in the Middle East 295–96.

44. R. Ghannouchi, interview by the author, London, March 1995.

45. Burgat and Dowell, The Islamic Movement, 60.

46. Kedourie, Politics in the Middle East, 297.

47. A. el-Affendi, "The Long March Forward."

48. Ibid.

49. S. Amin, Ad-Da'wah al-Islamiyah: Faridah Shar'iyah Wa Darurah Bashariyah [Calling to Islam: Mandated by Shari'ah and necessitated by humanity] (Amman: n.p., 1982). See also J. Esposito, The Oxford Encyclopedia of the Modern Islamic World, vol. 2.

50. R. Ghannouchi, interview by the author, London, June 1997.

51. R. Ghannouchi, interview by the author, London, March 1995.

52. Ibid.

53. J. Esposito, Islam: The Straight Path (New York: Oxford University Press, 1991).

54. R. Ghannouchi, interview by the author, London, March 1995.

55. R. Ghannouchi, interview by the author, London, June 1997.

56. Ibid.

57. M. Ahmad, "Islamic Fundamentalism in South India: The Jamaat-i-Islami and the Tablighi Jamaat," in Fundamentalism Observed, ed. Marain E. Marty and R. Scott Appleby (Chicago: University of Chicago Press, 1991), 437–530.

58. This and the following four paragraphs contain information received from R. Ghannouchi, interview by the author, London, March 1995.

59. R. Ghannouchi, interview by the author, London, June 1997.

60. R. Ghannouchi, interview by the author, London, March 1995.

61. H. E. Chehabi, Iranian Politics and Religious Modernism: The Liberation Movement of Iran Under the Shah and Khomeyni (Ithaca, N.Y.: Cotnell University press, 1990).

62. H. Ayoub, Tabsit al-'Aqa'id al-Islamiyah (Kuwait: Ar-Risalah, 1974).

63. R. Ghannouchi, interview by the author, London, March 1995.

64. Ibid.

65. M. Bennabi, Al-Qadaya al-Kubra [The grand issues], (Beirut: Dar-al-Fikr, 1991).

66. Ibid.

Chapter Two

1. R. Ghannouchi, interview by the author, London, June 1995.

2. Ibid.

3. R. Ghannouchi, interview with MSA-NEWS (*http://msanews mynet.net*), 10 February 1998.

4. Ibid.

5. Ibid.

6. Bennabi, *Al-Qadaya al-Kubra.*

7. R. Ghannouchi, interview by the author, London, June 1995.

8. R. Ghannouchi, *Tariquna Ilal al-Hadarah* [Our way to civilization] (Tunis: al-Ma'rifah Publications, 1975), 13.

9. R. Ghannouchi, interview by the author, London, June 1995.

10. Ibid.

11. This and the following eight paragraphs contain information received from R. Ghannouchi, "Barnamij al-Falsafa Wa Jil ad-Daya,'" in *Minalfikr al-Islami Fi Tunis*, vol. 2 (Kuwait: Dar al-Qalam, 1992), 33, 35.

12. R. Ghannouchi, interview by the author, London, June 1995.

13. Ibid.

14. Ibid.

15. Ibid.

16. Verse 8, Chapter 5. The Holy Qur'an, English *Translation of Mushaf al-Madinah an-Nabawiyah* (Medina: King Fahd Holy Quran Printing Complex, 1990).

17. R. Ghannouchi, interview by the author, London, June 1995

18. Ibid.

19. Ibid.

20. J. Esposito, *Islam and Politics*, 3rd ed. (Syracuse, N.Y.: Syracuse University press, 1991).

21. H. al-Banna, "Baynal-'Ams Wal-Yawm" [Between yesterday and today], in *Rasa'il al-Imam* [The messages of the imam] (Beirut: Mu'assat ar-Risalah, 1975), 249. No precise date is given for al-Banna's message, which is one of several, apart from the fact that it was just before the eruption of the Second World War.

22. Ibid., pp. 250–51

23. Ibid.

24. Ibid.

25. R. Ghannouchi, interview by the author, London, June 1995

26. R. Ghannouchi, "The Conflict Between the West and Islam, The Tunisian Case: Reality and Prospects" (paper presented at the Royal Institute of International Affairs, Chatham House, 9 May 1995).

27. Charles A. Micaub, Leon Carl Brown, and Clement Henry More, *Tunis: The Politics of Modernization* (London: Pall Mall Press, 1964), 10.

28. R. Ghannouchi, interview by the author, London, June 1995

29. R. Ghannouchi, "Tahlil Lil-'Anasir al-Mukawwinah Lidh-Dhahira al-Islamiyah Bi-Tunis" [Analysis of the constituent components of the Islamic phenomenon in Tunisia], in *Al-Harakat al-Islamiyah al-Mu'asirah Fil-Watan al-'Arabi* [Contemporary Islamic movements in the Arab homeland] (Beirut: Markaz Dirasat al-Wahda al-'Arabiyah [Arab Unity Studies Centre], 1987), 300–8.

30. Ibid.

31. For further details on these and other Islamic theological doctrines see J. Esposito, *The Oxford Encyclopedia of the Modern Islamic World*, vol. 4.

32. R. Ghannouchi, interview by the author, London, June 1997

33. Ibid.

34. Ibid.

35. R. Ghannouchi, "Tahlil Lil-'Anasir al-Mukawwinah."

36. Ibid., p. 301.

37. R. Ghannouchi, interview by the author, London, June 1997.

38. R. Ghannouchi, interview by Zainab Farran, Ash-Shira' (Beirut) (October 1994): 28–32. (English translation by MSANEWS at http://msanews.mynet.net)

39. R. Ghannouchi, "Tahlil Lil-'Anasir al-Mukawwinah."

40. R. Ghannouchi, interview by the author, London, June 1995.

41. S. Qutb, Milestones, English translation by Naushaba Publications, New Delhi 1991, p. 21.

42. S. Qutb, Islam: The Religion of the Future, English translation published by the International Islamic Federation of Student Organizations (IIFSO), Kuwait 1992, p. 126.

43. Ibid.

44. R. Ghannouchi, "Tahlil Lil-'Anasir al-Mukawwinah," 302.

45. D. Magnuson, "Islamic Reform in Contemporary Tunisia: Unity and Diversity," in Tunisia: The Political Economy of Reform, ed. I. William Zartman (London: Lynne Rienner, 1991), 181–82.

46. R. Ghannouchi, interview by the author, London, June 1995

47. See his interview with Francois Burgat, "How Can a Muslim Live in This Era?" in Political Islam: Essays from Middle East Reports, ed. Joel Beinin and Joe Stork (London: Tauris, 1997), 370–75.

48. Ibid.

49. R. Ghannouchi, interview by the author, London, June 1995

50. Ibid.

51. Ibid.

52. Sayyid Firjani, senior member of Ennahda, interview by the author, London May 1996.

53. R. Ghannouchi, interview by the author, London, June 1995.

54. This and the following two paragraphs contain information received from R. Ghannouchi, interview by the author, London, June 1997.

55. Ahmad Sudqi ad-Dajani, "Tatawur Mafahim ad-Dimuqratiyah Fil-Fikr al-'Arabi al-Hadith" [The development of the concepts of democracy in the modern Arab thought], in Azmat ad-Dimuqratiyah Fil-Watan al-'Arabi [The crisis of democracy in the Arab homeland] (Beirut: Markaz Dirasat al-Wahda al-'Arabiyah [Arab Unity Studies Centre], 1984), 115.

56. Albert Hourani, Arabic Thought in the Liberal Age 1798–1939 (Cambridge: Cambridge University Press, 1991), 69. See also R. S. Ahmad, Ad-Din Wad-Dawlah Wath-Thawrah [Religion, state, and revolution] (Cairo: al-Dar al-Sharkiyah, 1989), 34.

57. ad-Dajani, "Tatawur Mafahim," 121 (quoting Lewis Awad's The History of Modern Egyptian Thought).

58. Hourani, Arabic Thought in the Liberal Age, 70–71.

59. ad-Dajani, "Tatawur Mafahim," 121.

60. Faruq Abdessalam, Al-Ahzab as-Siyasiyah Fil-Islam [Political parties in Islam] (Cairo: Qalyoob Publishing House, 1978), 27.

61. ad-Dajani, "Tatawur Mafahim," 123.

62. Khairuddin at-Tunisi, Aqwam al-Masalik Fi Ma'rifati Ahwal al-Mamalik (Tunis: Ad-Dar At-Tunisiyah, 1972), 185.

63. ad-Dajani, "Tatawur Mafahim," 123.

64. R. S. Ahmad, Ad-Din Wad-Dawlah Wath-Thawrah, 44–47.

65. Jamal ad-Din al-Afghani, "Al-Hukumah al-Istibdadiyah" [The despotic government], in Abdulbasit Hasan, Jamal ad-Din al-Afghani (Cairo: Maktabat Wahba, 1982), 267–68.

66. Ibid.

67. R. S. Ahmad, *Ad-Dın Wad-Dawlah Wath-Thawrah*, 44–47.

68. F. Abdessalam, *Al-Ahzab as-Sıyasıyah Fıl-Islam*, 28.

69. A. al-Kawakibi, *Taba'ı' al-Istıbdad* [Traıts of despotism] (Algıers: Mofam, 1988), 187.

70. Ibid., 169.

71. A. al-Kawakibi, *Umm-Ul-Qura* [Mother of villages] (Beırut: Dar Ash-Shuruq al-'Arabı, 1991). Also ad-Dajani, "Tatawur Mafahim," 124.

72. Hourani, *Arabic Thought ın the Liberal Age*, 228.

73. ad-Dajanı, "Tatawur Mafahım," 124–25.

74. M. Rashid Rida, *Al-Khalıfah* [The caliphate] (Caıro: az-Zahra Publications, 1988), 9.

75. R. Ghannouchi, interview by the author, London, June 1995.

76. R. Ghannouchi, "Al-Mılkıyah az-Zira'iyah Fıl-Islam" [Agrarıan property ownership in Islam], in *Minal-Fikr al-Islamı Fı-Tunıs* [From the Islamıc thought in Tunisia], vol. 2 (Kuwait: Dar al-Qalam, 1992), 130–44.

77. Ibıd.

78. R. Ghannouchi, ınterview by the author, London, June 1995.

79. Ibıd.

80. Enneıfer's interview wıth Francois Burgat ın J. Beınin and J. Stork, eds., *Islam: Essays from Mıddle East Reports*, 370–75.

81. R. Ghannouchi, interview by the author, London, June 1995.

82. The *khums* is a tax owed by the Shiite community for the support of *sayyıds*, who are believed to be the descendants of the Prophet.

83. R. Ghannouchi, "Ath-Thawrah al-Iraniyah Thawrah Islamiyah" [The Iranian revolution is an Islamic revolutıon], in *Maqalat* [Articles] (Paris: Dar al-Karawan, 1984), 77–84.

84. Ibid.

85. Ibid.

86. Ibıd.

87. Abu Dawud narrated through Abu Hurayra that Prophet Muhammad said: "God sends to this Ummah at the head of each century a person that renews for ıt its religion."

88. R. Ghannouchı, "Qadat al-Harakah al-Islamıyah al-Mu'Asırah: al-Banna, al-Mawdudı, al-Khomeyni" [Leaders of the Contemporary Islamic Movement: al-Banna, Mawdudı, and Khomeynı], in *Maqalat*, 87–105.

89. Ibid.

90. R. Ghannouchı, ınterview by the author, London, June 1995

91. Ibıd.

92. Ibid.

93. Ibid.

94. R. Ghannouchi, *Al-Mar'ah al-Muslımah Fı Tunis Bayna Tawjıhat al-Qur'an Wa Waqı' al-Mumıtama' at-Tunısı* [Muslim woman ın Tunisia between Qur'anıc dırectives and realıties of Tunısian socıety], 2nd ed. (Kuwaıt: Dar al-Qalam, 1993), 87–108.

95. R. Ghannouchi, interview by the author, London, June 1995.

96. Ibid.

97. A. Zghal, "The New Strategy of the Movement of the Islamic Way" Manipulatıon or Expression of Political Culture?" in *Tunısıa: The Political Economy of Reform*, ed. I. William Zartman, London: Zynne Rıenner, 216.

98. R. Ghannouchi, interview by the author, London, June 1997.

99. Ibid.

100. Ibid.

101. I. Wılliam Zartman, "The Challenge of Democratic Alternatives in the Maghrib," in J. Ruedy, *Islamısm and Secularısm ın North Africa* (London: Macmillan, 1994), 206–08.

102. L. Zeytoun, Ennahda senıor member, ınterview by the author, London June 1997.

103. Ghannouchi, Al-Hurriyat, 335-38.

104. R. Ghannouchi, interview by the author, London, June 1995.

105. Ibid.

106. Ibid.

107. Ibid.

108. R. Ghannouchi, interview by the author, London, June 1995

109. R. Ghannouchi, "Al-Mujtama' at-Tunisi: Tahlil Hadari" [Tunisian Society: A Civiliazational Analysis], unpublished MTI document, 1983.

110. Ibid.

111. Ibid.

112. R. Ghannouchi, interview by the author, London, February 1998.

113. Some of these articles are published in the collections of Ghannouchi's works entitled Maqalat; and Minal-Fikr al-Islami Fi-Tunis [From the Islamic thought in Tunis], 2 vols. (Kuwait: Dar al-Qalam, 1992).

Chapter Three

1. Ghannouchi, Al-Hurriyat, 17.

2. The book was translated by Jalal al-Matrahi and published in Tunis. No date is given. The original, which is assumed to be in French, is untraceable and no details of it are given in the Arabic edition.

3. This was published in 1983 by Dar ar-Rayah in Tunis under the title Al-Islam Wad-Dimuqratiyah. Ghannouchi was assisted in the translation of this work by an-Nuri, an imprisoned colleague.

4. Adh-Dhikra ath-Thalitha Liharakat al-Ittijah al-Islami (The third anniversary of the MTI), Carthage, 6 June 1984.

5. Ibid.

6. This is in reference to a long hadith (Prophetic tradition) related by Muslim on the authority of Umar bin al-Khattab who said: "One day while we were sitting with the Messenger of Allah, may the blessings and peace of Allah be upon him, there appeared before us a man whose clothes were exceedingly white and whose hair was exceedingly black. . . . " For full text of the hadith and its English translation see Ezzeddin Ibrahim and Denys Johnson-Davies, trans., An-Nawawi's Forty Hadiths (Beirut: Dar al-Koran al-Kareem, 1976), 28-33.

7. This and the following eleven paragraphs contain information received from Malik Bennabi, "Ad-Dimuqratiyah Fil-Islam" [Democracy in Islam], in Al-Qadaya al-Kubra 134-64. The name of the translator in this edition is not given. But according to Ghannouchi, this is a re-publication of his own translation with a slight modification in the title from "Islam and Democracy" to "Democracy in Islam."

The English translation of Pericles' statement is taken from David Held, "Democracy: Past, Present, and Possible Future," Alternatives 18, no. 3 (summer 1993): 259-71.

8. This and the following four paragraphs contain information received from R. Ghannouchi, Al-Hurriyat, 17.

9. President's Declaration on 7 November 1987, Tunisian External Communications Agency.

10. J. Esposito and J. Piscatori, "Democratization and Islam," The Middle East Journal 45, no. 3 (Summer 1991): 427-440.

11. R. Ghannouchi, interview by the Jordanian weekly newspaper Assabeel (Amman), 4 July 1995.

12. Ibid.

13. Ibid.

14. Ghannouchi, Al-Hurriyat.

15. N. Hicks, *Promise Unfulfilled: Human Rights in Tunisia Since 1987* (New York: The Lawyers Committee for Human Rights, October 1993), 6–14.

16. This and the following six paragraphs contain information received from R. Ghannouchi, interview by the author, London, February 1998. See also Ghannouchi's interview with MSA-NEWS (*http://msanews.mynet net*), 10 February 1998, 31, 32, 34.

17. L. Siedentop, *Tocqueville* (Oxford: Oxford University Press, 1994), 32.

18. Ibid., 33.

19. Ghannouchi, *Al-Hurriyat.*

20. This and the following paragraph contain information from I. Berlin, "Two Concepts of Liberty," in *Four Essays on Liberty* (Oxford: Oxford University Press, 1969), 122–23, 126, 131, 132, 134.

21. C. Taylor, "What's Wrong with Negative Liberty?" in *Philosophical Papers*, vol. 2 (Cambridge: Cambridge University Press, 1985), 211–13.

22. Ghannouchi, *Al-Hurriyat.*

23. Berlin, "Two Concepts of Liberty," 148.

24. Ghannouchi, *Al-Hurriyat.*

25. R. Ghannouchi, "Al-Islam Yuwli 'Inayatan Kubra Lil-Mujtama' al-Madani" [Islam attaches great importance to civil society], *Al-'Alam* (London), no. 612 (14 March 1998), and no. 613 (21 March 1998).

26. Ibid.

27. R. Ghannouchi, *Al-Hurriyat*, quoting 'Allal al-Fasi, *Maqasid Ash-Shari'ah al-Islamiyah Wa-Makarimuha* (Rabat: ar-Rislah Publications, 1979), 247.

28. Ghannouchi, *Al-Hurriyat*, 43.

29. Ibid.

30. Ibid., 44.

31. R. Ghannouchi, *The Right to Nationality Status of Non-Muslim Citizens in a Muslim Nation*, trans. M. El Erian (The Islamic Foundation of America, 1990), 60.

32. Ibid., 60–61.

33. Ghannouchi, *Al-Hurriyat*, 290.

34. Ibid.

35. Ibid.

36. Ghannouchi, *The Right to Nationality*, 85.

37. Said Hawwa, *Al-Islam*, vol. 2 (Syria: Dar as-Salam Publications, n.d.), 17.

38. R. Ghannouchi, *The Right to Nationality*, 85. For arguments along these lines, see for instance Abdulkarim Zaidan, *Ahkam Ahl Adh-Dhimmah Wal-Musta'manin* (Beirut: Ar-Risaleh, 1976).

39. R. Ghannouchi, *Al-Hurriyat*, 291. For more details of the contemporary debate on the political rights of non-Muslims see for instance Tariq el-Bishri, "Ahkam al-Wilayah al-'Ammah Li-Ghayr al-Muslimin," in *Ash-Shar'iyah as-Siyasiyah Fil-Islam* [Political legitimacy in Islam], ed. Azzam Tamimi (London: Liberty for Muslim World Publications, 1997).

40. Ibid.

41. Ibid., 48.

42. Ibid., 50.

43. Ibid., 55. Ghannouchi's views on property ownership were discussed in more detail in the previous chapter.

44. Ibid.

45. Ibid., 57.

46. Ibid., 71. The first definition is quoted from Ali Abdulwahid Wafi, *Huquq al-Insan Fil-Islam* [Human rights in Islam] (Cairo: Dar Nahdat Misr, 1967); the second definition is quoted from Abdelhadi Abu Talib, *al-Marji' Fil-Qanun ad-Dusturi Wal-Mu'assasat as-Siyasiyah* [Reference of constitutional law and political institutions] (Casablanca: Dar Al-Kitab, 1980).

47. R. Ghannouchi, interview by the author, London, June 1995.

48. R. Wright, "Islam and Liberal Democracy: Two Visions of Reformation," *Journal of Democracy* 7, no. 2 (April 1996).

49. Ghannouchi, *Al-Hurriyat*, 75.

50. Tawfiq Ash-Shawi, *Fiqh Ash-Shura Wal-Istisharah* [Jurisprudence of Shura and consultation] (Cairo: al-Wafa' Publications, 1992), 11.

51. Hasan at-Turabi, *Ash-Shura Wad-Dimuqratiyah* [Shura and democracy] (Casablanca: al-Furqan Publications, 1993), 6.

52. Ghannouchi, *Al-Hurriyat*, 76.

53. Ibid., 76.

54. Ibid., 77.

55. A. Heywood, *Political Ideologies: An Introduction* (London: Macmillan, 1992), 275.

56. This and the following two paragraphs contain information from Ghannouchi, *Al-Hurriyat*, 228-47. Note where Ghannouchi uses the term state to denote government.

57. C. Macpherson, *The Life and Times of Liberal Democracy* (Oxford: Oxford University Press, 1977), 7.

58. J. Keane, "Introduction: Democracy and the Decline of the Left," in N. Bobbio, *Democracy and Dictatorship* (Oxford: Polity Press, 1997), ix-x.

59. P. Schmitter and T. Karl, "What Is Democracy and Is Not," in *The Global Resurgence of Democracy*, eds. L. Diamond and M. Plattner (Baltimore and London: John Hopkins University Press, 1996), 49-62.

60. Ghannouchi, *Al-Hurriyat*, 77.

61. Ibid.

62. J. Cohen and A. Arato, *Civil Society and Political Theory*, 3rd ed. (Cambridge, Mass.: MIT Press, 1994), 4.

63. Ibid., quoting J. Schumpeter, *Capitalism, Socialism, and Democracy* (New York: Harper & Row, 1942), 232-302.

64. Ibid., 5-6.

65. Ibid., 6-7.

66. Macpherson, *The Life and Times*, 5

67. Ghannouchi, *Al-Hurriyat*, 83.

68. Ibid., 84.

69. A. Heywood, *Political Ideologies*, 271.

70. Ghannouchi, *Al-Hurriyat*, 84.

71. Ibid.

72. A. Elmessiri, "Ma'alim al-Khitab al-Islami al-Jadid" [Features of the new Islamic discourse], in *Ash-Shar'iyah as-Siyasiyah Fil-Islam*, ed. A. Tamimi 165-88.

73. This and the following seven paragraphs contain information from Ghannouchi, *Al-Hurriyat*, 83, 84, 86, 87.

74. R. Ghannouchi, "Islam and Freedom Can Be Friends," *The Observer* (London), 19 January 1992, 18.

75. Ibid.

76. Ibid.

77. R. Ghannouchi, "The Basic Principles of an Islamic State" (paper presented to a symposium on Christian-Islamic Dialogue, Germany, June 1994).

78. In his book *Al-Muwafaqat*. A reference is made to his theory earlier in this chapter.

79. R. Ghannouchi, "Human Rights in Islam" (paper presented to a Symposium of the Association of Muslim Lawyers, Birmingham, 18 June 1995).

80. This and the following five paragraphs contain information from Ghannouchi, *Al-Hurriyat*, 78, 79, 82-83.

81. W. Jordan, *The State: Authority and Autonomy* (Oxford: Blackwell, 1985).

82. W. P. Shively, *Power and Choice*, 3rd ed. (New York: McGraw-Hill, 1993), 113.

83. Ghannouchi, *Al-Hurriyat*, 92.

84. R. Ghannouchi, "The Islamic Conception of the State" (paper presented to the Conference of Young Muslims in London, April 1992).

85. Ibid.

86. In his book *Al-Islam Wa Usul al-Hukm* (Islam and the fundamentals of government), first published in Cairo, Egypt, in 1925.

87. R. Ghannouchi, *Al-Hurriyat*, 89.

88. R. Ghannouchi, "The Islamic Conception of the State."

89. Ibid.

90. R. Ghannouchi, *Al-Hurriyat*, 94.

91. R. Ghannouchi, "The Islamic Conception of the State."

92. Ibid.

93. Ibid.

94. Ghannouchi, *Al-Hurriyat*, 94.

95. R. Ghannouchi, "The Islamic Conception of the State."

96. R. Ghannouchi, "Human Rights in Islam."

97. Ibid.

98. Ibid.

99. R. Ghannouchi, "The Islamic Conception of the State."

100. R. Ghannouchi, "Public Liberties from an Islamic Perspective," (paper presented to the Annual Conference of the Muslim Students Union, Italy, 24 December 1994). The concept of freedom has already been discussed earlier in this chapter.

101. Ibid. Ghannouchi often cites examples to support this theory from Zagrid Honk, *God's Sun Shines on the West*, Beirut: Dar El-Jil, 1993; and Murad Hofman *Islam the Alternative*, Reading: Gamet, 1993.

102. R. Ghannouchi, "Human Rights in Islam."

103. Ibid.

104. Ibid.

105. R. Ghannouchi, "The Basic Principles of an Islamic State."

106. F. Huwaidi, *Al-Islam Wad-Dimuqratiyah* [Islam and democracy] (Cairo: al-Ahram translation and Publishing, 1993), 111.

107. R. Ghannouchi, "The Basic Principles of an Islamic State."

108. A. Ali Belhaj, *Ghayat al-Murad Fi Qadaya al-Jihad*, an Islamic Salvation Front (FIS) publication, January 1994, no place of publication given.

109. R. Ghannouchi, "The Basic Principles of an Islamic State."

110. Ghannouchi, *Al-Hurriyat*, 98

111. Ibid.

112. R. Ghannouchi, "The Basic Principles of an Islamic State."

113. Ibid.

114. Ibid.

115. R. Ghannouchi, interview by the author, London, 28 February 1997.

116. Hourani, *Arabic Thought in the Liberal Age* (, and H. Enayat, *Modern Islamic Political Thought* (London: Macmillan, 1982).

117. R. Ghannouchi, "The Basic Principles of an Islamic State."

118. M. Asad, *The Principles of State and Government in Islam* (Gibraltar: Dar al-Andalus, 1985).

119. Ibid., 43.

120. Ghannouchi, "The Basic Principles of an Islamic State."

121. Ibid.

122. Ibid.

123. A. Tamimi, Ash-Shar'iyah as-Siyasiyah Fil-Islam, 240.

124. N. Bobbio, The Future of Democracy (Oxford: Polity Press, 1987), 18.

125. Ibid.

126. This and the following three paragraphs contain information received from R. Ghannouchi, interview by the author, London, February 1998.

127. Ghannouchi, Al-Hurriyat, 87–88.

128. Ibid.

239. Ibid., 88.

Chapter Four

1. Ghannouchi, "The Conflict Between the West and Islam."

2. Ghannouchi, Al-Hurriyat, 264.

3. Ibid.

4. Ibid., 265–68.

5. Ibid., 270–79.

6. R. Ghannouchi, "On the Eve of the Elections: Tunisia Mourns Its Loved Ones" (lecture at the London School of Economics, London, 24 February 1994).

7. R. Ghannouchi, "Islam and the West: Prospects and Realities" (paper presented to the weekly seminar of the Centre for the Study of Democracy at the University of Westminster, London, 6 October 1992).

8. P. C. Schmitter, "Is It Safe for Transitologists and Consolidologists to Travel to the Middle East and North Africa?" (paper presented at the Conference on Legitimacy and Governance: Transformation of Societies and Political Systems in the Middle East and North Africa, Paris, 11–13 July 1995).

9. J. Linz and A. Stepan, Problems of Democratic Transition and Consolidation (Baltimore: Johns Hopkins University Press, 1996), 3.

10. Ibid.

11. Ibid., 7.

12. R. Ghannouchi, interview by the author, London, June 1995. Ghannouchi's conception of democracy is discussed in more detail in chapter three.

13. Ibid.

14. Ibid.

15. R. Ghannouchi, "Our View of Modernity and Democracy" (paper presented at the Symposium of Islam and Democracy in North Africa, London School of Economics, 29 February 1992).

16. Ibid.

17. R. Ghannouchi, interview by the author, London, June 1995.

18. On the basis of the interviews conducted with Ghannouchi by the author, during which his conception of secularism, secularization, and civil society was explored, his forthcoming third edition of Al-Hurriyat is being edited so as to incorporate a discussion of these issues, with emphasis on the importance of reinvigorating civil society as a means of facilitating the process of democratization

19. R. Ghannouchi, "At-Taghrib Wa-Hatmiyat Ad-Diktaturiyah" (Westernization and the inevitability of dictatorship), in Maqalat , 167–70. The article was published first in London's Al-Ghuraba' 6, no. 6 (September 1980).

20. R. Ghannouchi, interview by the author, London, February 1997.

21. Ibid.

22. Ibid.

23. Ibid.

24. J. Hastings, ed., *Encyclopedia of Religion and Ethics*, vol. 2 (Edinburgh: T & T Clark, 1971), 347. See also W. Outhwaite and T. Bottmore, eds., *Blackwell Dictionary of 20ᵗʰ Century Social Thought* (Oxford: Blackwell, 1995).

25. Mircea Eliade, ed., *The Encyclopedia of Religion*, vol. 13 (New York: Macmillan, 1987), 159.

26. Renee Fregosi, "From the Secular to the Politico-Religious," *Contemporary European Affairs* 2, no. 4 (1989), 21.

27. Eliade, *The Encyclopedia of Religion*, vol. 13, 162.

28. Hastings and Clark, *Encyclopedia of Religion and Ethics*, vol. 2, 347.

29. Ibid., 348.

30. Ibid.

31. Ibid.

32. Fregosi, "From the Secular," 21.

33. Ibid., 22.

34. Roger Scruton, ed., *The Dictionary of Political Thought* (London: Pan Books, 1983), 253.

35. Outhwaite and Bottmore, *The Blackwell Dictionary of 20ᵗʰ Century Social Thought*, 573.

36. Scruton, *The Dictionary of Political Thought*, 250.

37. Ibid., 253–54. Kemalism is the advocacy of the doctrines and policies of Kemal Ataturk (1880–1938), who abolished the Ottoman Caliphate and founded the modern secular Turkish republic in a spirit of Turkish nationalism.

38. R. Ghannouchi, "The Conflict Between the West and Islam."

39. Ibid.

40. R. S. Ahmad, *Ad-Din Wad-Dawlah Wath-Thawrah*, 31.

41. R. Ghannouchi, "The Conflict."

42. R. Ghannouchi, interview by the author, London, June 1995

43. A. Elmessiri, *Tafkik al-Khitab al-'Ilmani* [Deconstructing the secular discourse], a four-volume Arabic language encyclopedia, forthcoming, summer 2002.

44. Ibid.

45. R. S. Ahmad, *Ad-Din wad-Dawlah Wath-Thawrah*, 33.

46. Ibid., 34.

47. Ghannouchi, *Al-Hurriyat*, 252.

48. Hourani, *Arabic Thought in the Liberal Age*, 246–47.

49. Ibid.

50. R. S. Ahmad, *Ad-Din wad-Dawlah Wath-Thawrah*, 51.

51. Hourani, *Arabic Thought in the Liberal Age*, 256–57.

52. Ibid.

53. R. Ghannouchi, interview by the author, London, June 1995.

54. R. Ghannouchi, "Al-Harakah al-Islamiyah Wal-Mujtama' al-Madani" [The Islamic movement and civil society] (paper presented at Pretoria University, South Africa, August 1994).

55. R. Ghannouchi, "The Conflict."

56. This and the following five paragraphs contain information from R. Ghannouchi, "Secularism in the Arab Maghreb . . . What Secularism?" (paper presented to the Collapse of Secularism seminar, Centre for the Study of Democracy, University of Westminster, London, 10 June 1994).

57. R. Ghannouchi, interview by the author, London, 28 February 1997.

58. Ibid.

59. A. Giddens, *The Consequences of Modernity* (Cambridge: Polity Press, 1990), 1.

60. J. Habermas, *The Philosophical Discourse of Modernity*, trans. F. Lawrence, (Oxford: Policy Press, 1987), 5.

61. A. Touraine, *Critique of Modernity* (Oxford: Blackwell, 1995), 9.

62. Ibid.

63. A. Giddens, *Modernity and Self-Identity: Self and Society in the Late Modern Age* (Cambridge: Polity Press, 1991), 3.

64. Touraine, *Critique of Modernity*, 9.

65. Ibid.

66. Habermas, *The Philosophical Discourse*, 1.

67. Giddens, *The Consequences of Modernity*, 139.

68. Ibid.

69. Ibid.

70. Ibid., 64.

71. Munir Shafiq, "Hal al-Hadatha Mutaha Aslan?" [Is modernity readily available?], *Al-Mujtama'*, no. 1290 (3 March 1998), 55.

72. Ghannouchi, "Secularism in the Arab Maghreb."

73. Ibid.

74. From a speech given by the former president of Tunisia on 2 April 1963.

75. Ghannouchi, "The Conflict Between the West and Islam."

76. Ibid.

77. Ibid.

78. Ghannouchi, "Secularism in the Arab Maghreb."

79. Ibid.

80. Ibid.

81. A. al-Ibrahimi, "Algeria Now: Crises and Mutations in Gestations" (public lecture, SOAS, London, 2 June 1994).

82. *Le monde diplomatique*, 1 January 1992.

83. Ghannouchi, "Secularism in the Arab Maghreb."

84. Ibid.

85. N. Hicks, *Promise Unfulfilled*, 62.

86. During the March 1994 elections Dr. Moncef Marzouki, former president of the Tunisian League of Human Rights, and Mr. Abderrahman Hani, a minor politician, were both arrested for nominating themselves for the post of president of the republic. Even though a constitutional obstacle prevented either from making it on to the ballot, the regime was furious. See Francis Ghiles's article in the *Financial Times* of 18 March 1994, and Ennahda's 22 March 1994 statement on the elections.

87. In a symposium on the German policy in Africa organized by the German Corporation for Africa on 27 April 1994, a German expert by the name of Dr. Koon noted that the dominant impression in some African states, such as Tunisia, is that if the state combats fundamentalism it is more likely to get what it wants from the West and that it will not be accused of violating democracy.

88. Ghannouchi, "Our View of Modernity and Democracy."

89. Ghannouchi, "Secularism in the Arab Maghreb."

90. Ghannouchi, "Our View of Modernity and Democracy."

91. Keane, "Secularism."

92. Ghannouchi, "Our View of Modernity and Democracy."

93. Ibid.

94. R. Ghannouchi, interview by the author, London, 28 February 1997.

95. Ibid.

96. Ibid.

97. Ghannouchi, "Our View of Modernity and Democracy."

98. Ghannouchi, "The Conflict Between the West and Islam."

Chapter Five

1. This and the following two paragraphs contain information from R. Ghannouchi, "Al-Harakah al-Islamiyah Wal-Mujtama' al-Madani."

2. R. Ghannouchi, "The Conflict Between the West and Islam."

3. Ibid.

4. R. Ghannouchi, "Tunisia: The Islamic Movement and Civil Society," paper presented at Pretoria University, South Africa, August 1994.

5. I. Ahmad, The Social Contract and the Islamic State (New Delhi: Kitab Bahavan, 1981), 102.

6. J. Keane, "Despotism and Democracy," in Civil Society and the State: New European Perspectives, ed. J. Keane (London and New York: Verso, 1988), 35–36.

7. W. Kawtharani, "Al-Mujtama' al-Madani Waddawlah Fit-Tarikh al-'Arabi" [Civil society and the state in Arab history], in Al-Mujtama' al-Madani Fil-Watan al-'Arabi (Beirut: Markaz Dirasat al-Wahda al-'Arabiyah [Arab Unity Studies Centre], 1992), 119.

8. E. Gellner, Conditions of Liberty, Civil Society, and its Rivals (London: Hamish Hamilton, 1994), 43.

9. Keane, "Despotism and Democracy."

10. Ibid., 37.

11. Ibid., 39–50.

12. Ibid., 1.

13. Gellner, Conditions of Liberty, 1.

14. J. Keane, Reflections on Violence (London: Verso, 1996), 10.

15. Cohen and Arato, Civil Society and Political Theory, 31–36.

16. Bobbio, Democracy and Dictatorship, 40.

17. Ghannouchi, "Al-Harakah al-Islamiyah Wal-Mujtama' al-Madani."

18. Ibid.

19. Huwaidi, Al-Islam Wad-Dimuqratiyah, 192.

20. The Arabic word ahl has many meanings including: relatives, folks, family, kin, kinsfolk, wife, people, and inhabitants. The adjective ahli (m) or ahliyah (f) has frequently been used to mean civil, such as in harb ahliyah (civil war). The word madan means to urbanize or to civilize or even to refine. Madina is the word for city and madani has several meanings including urban, city-dwelling, polished, and civilized.

21. R. Ghannouchi, interview by the author, London, 28 February 1997.

22. This and the following two paragraphs contain information from Gellner, Conditions of Liberty, 5, 8–10, 22–23, 26, 29.

23. A. el-Affendi, "Rationality, Civil Society, and Democracy in the Modern Muslim Context: Prolegomena to a Meta-archaeological Investigation" (paper presented to the Second International Conference on Islamic Thought, Istanbul, 25–27 April 1997).

24. Ibid.

25. Ibid.

26. Keane, Reflections on Violence, 11.

27. A. Elmessiri, "Ma'alim al-Khitab al-Islami al-Jadid," 165–88.

28. Ibid.

29. R. Ghannouchi, "Ad-Dini Was-Siyasi Fil-Islam" [The religious and the political in Islam] (lecture at Cardiff Islamic Society, January 1997).

30. A. Elmessiri, interview by the author, April 1997.

31. J. Keane, interview by the author, London, 4 March 1997.

32. Ibid.

33. Ibid.

34. E. Gellner, "The Enemies of Civil Society" (lecture at the London School of Economics, 19 June 1995).

35. Ghannouchi, "Tunisia: The Islamic Movement and Civil Society."

36. Ibid.

37. A. Touraine, *What is Democracy?* trans. David Macey (Boulder, Colo.: Westview Press, 1997), 45.

38. S. Ismail, "Al-Mujtama' al-Madani Wad-Dawlah," in *Al-Mujtama' al-Madani Fil-Watan al-'Arabi* (Beirut: Markaz Dirasat al-Wahda al-'Arabiyah [Arab Unity Studies Centre], 1992), 292.

39. Ghannouchi, "Tunisia: The Islamic Movement and Civil Society."

40. Imad-ud-Din Khalil, *Dirasa Fis-Sirah*, 3rd ed. (Beirut: ar-Risalah Publications, 1978).

41. R. Ghannouchi, interview by the author, London, June 1995.

42. Bobbio, *Democracy and Dictatorship*, 25.

43. Ibid., 43.

44. R. Ghannouchi, interview by the author, London, June 1995.

45. Ibid.

46. R. Ghannouchi, interview by the author, London, 28 February 1997.

47. See for instance his paper "Marxism and Islam: Failure and Success," in *Power-Sharing Islam?*, ed. Azzam Tamimi (London: Liberty for Muslim World Publications, 1993).

48. el-Affendi, "Rationality, Civil Society, and Democracy."

49. R. Ghannouchi, interview by the author, London, June 1995.

50. Ibid.

51. Abdelqadir Zghal, "Al-Mujtama' al-Madani Was-Sira' Min-Ajl al-Haymana al-Aydilujiyah Fil-Maghrib al-'Arabi," in *Al-Mujtama' al-Madani Fil-Watan al-'Arabi* (Beirut: Markaz Dirasat al-Wahda al-'Arabiyah [Arab Unity Studies Centre], 1992), 431.

52. This and the following seven paragraphs contain information from R. Ghannouchi, interview by the author, London, June 1995.

53. Ghannouchi, *Al-Hurriyat*, 138.

54. R. Ghannouchi, "The Participation of Islamists in a Non-Islamic Government," in *Power-Sharing Islam?*, ed. A. Tamimi, 51–63.

55. R. Ghannouchi, interview by the author, London, June 1995.

56. Ibid.

57. Ibid.

58. as-Sayid Sabiq, *Fiqh as-Sunnah*, vol. 1 (Beirut: Dar al-Fikr, 1977), 276.

59. R. Ghannouchi, interview by the author, London, June 1995.

60. Ibid.

61. Ibid.

62. Ibid.

63. T. Hobbes, *Leviathan* (London: Penguin Classics, 1985), 185–86.

64. R. Ghannouchi, interview by the author, London, June 1995.

65. Ibid.

66. R. Ghannouchi, interview by the author, London, 28 February 1997.

67. Ibid.

68. Ibid.

69. Ibid.

70. From a letter by R. Ghannouchi to Lord Avebury, dated 17 August 1993.

71. R. Ghannouchi, interview by the author, London, 28 February 1997.

72. A political statement signed by Rachid Ghannouchi, president of Ennahda Movement, dated 18 November 1997.

73. Norbert Elias, "Violence and Civilization: The State Monopoly of Physical Violence and its Infringement," in *Civil Society and the State*, ed. J. Keane, 177–98.

74. R. Ghannouchi, interview by the author, London, 28 February 1997.

75. Ibid.

76. Heywood, *Political Ideologies*, 17.

77. R. Ghannouchi, interview by the author, London, 28 February 1997.

78. Ibid.

79. Ibid.

80. Macpherson, *The Life and Times*, 1.

81. R. Ghannouchi, interview by the author, London, 28 February 1997.

82. A. Arblaster, *The Rise and Decline of Western Liberalism* (Oxford: Basil Blackwell, 1984), 11.

83. Heywood, *Political Ideologies*.

84. Ibid.

85. R. Ghannouchi, interview by the author, London, 28 February 1997.

86. J. S. Mill, *On Liberty and Other Essays* (Oxford: Oxford University Press, 1991).

87. Heywood, *Political Ideologies*.

88. This and the following six paragraphs contain information from R. Ghannouchi, interview by the author, London, June 1995.

89. R. Ghannouchi, "Taqwa Is the Best Remedy for Fear" (paper presented to the Fear and Politics Seminar, CSD, University of Westminster, London, 7 July 1995).

90. A *hadith* related by al-Bukhari and Muslim. Translation taken from *An-Nawawi's Forty Hadiths*, trans. Ezzeddin Ibrahim and Denys Johnson-Davies

91. Heywood, *Political Ideologies*.

92. Arblaster, *The Rise and Decline of Western Liberalism*.

93. R. Ghannouchi, interview by the author, London, June 1995.

94. Mill, *On Liberty and Other Essays*

95. Ghannouchi, "Taqwa Is the Best Remedy."

96. R. Ghannouchi, interview by the author, London, June 1995.

97. Ibid.

98. Ibid. The example is attributed to Sartre.

99. Ibid.

100. Muhsin al-Mili, *Al-'Ilmaniyah Aw Falsafat Mawt al-Insan* [Secularism or the philosophy of the death of man] (Carthage: The Tunisian Press, 1986).

101. R. Ghannouchi, interview by the author, London, 28 February 1997.

102. Ibid.

103. Ibid.

104. R. Ghannouchi, interview with the author, London, June 1995.

105. Ibid.

106. This and the following three paragraphs contain information from R. Ghannouchi, "Hal al-'Almaniyah Falsafat Ghurur Wa-Tawahush Am Falsafat Taqaddum Wa-Taharrur?" [Is secularism a philosophy of self-deception and barbarity or a philosophy of progress and liberation?] (paper written in response to a question put to Ghannouchi by the author, London, 30 March 1998).

107. R. Ghannouchi, "The Participation of Islamists in a Non-Islamic Government."

108. Ibid.

109. R. Ghannouchi, interview by the author, London, June 1995.

Chapter Six

1. Schmitter and Karl, "What Democracy Is . . . and Is Not," 49–62.

2. Nazih Ayubi, *Over-stating the Arab State: Politics and Society in the Middle East* (London: I. B. Tauris, 1995), 3.

3. Ibid., 21

4. Ibid.

5. M. Guibernau, *Nationalisms, the Nation-State, and Nationalism in the Twentieth Century* (Cambridge: Polity Press, 1996), 51.

6. Ibid., 47

7. Ibid., 51–52.

8. Ibid., 116.

9. Ayubi, *Over-stating the Arab State*, 86.

10. M. Dahir, "Al-Mujtama' al-Madani Waddawlah Filmashriq al-'Arabi," in *Al-Mujtama' al-Madani Fil-Watan al-'Arabi* (Beirut: Markaz Dirasat al-Wahda al-'Arabiyah [Arab Unity Studies Centre], 1992), 405–6.

11. R. Ghannouchi, "Al-'Alam al-Islami Wal-Isti'mar al-Hadith" [The Islamic world and modern colonialism], in *Maqalat*, 161–64.

12. Ibid.

13. Ibid.

14. Ibid.

15. Linz and Stepan, *Problems of Democratic Transition and Consolidation*, 51–54.

16. Ibid.

17. Ibid.

18. The Arabic word *sultan* has a number of related meanings including power, dominion, authority, mandate, and legitimation. It also denotes the possessor of power, a ruler. The term first appeared as the official title of a ruler under the Seljuks of Baghdad (1055–1157), under whom governmental power and coercive force were monopolized by the *sultan* and his *wazir* (minister) while authority remained vested in the Abbasid caliph as *imam* of the *Ummah*. Classical scholars dealt with this dualism, giving rise to several theories aimed at defining the roles of, and relations between, *sultan* and *imam*. Prominent among such scholars are al-Mawardi (d. 1058), al-Juwayni (d. 1085), and al-Ghazali (d. 1111). In subsequent centuries, various combinations of the theories devised by these three scholars concerning the functions and powers of the sultanate were used as ideological justifications for authoritarian regimes. For further details see Esposito, *The Oxford Encyclopedia of the Modern Islamic World*, vol. 4, 135.

19. R. Ghannouchi, interview by the author, London, February 1998.

20. Ibid.

21. Ibid.

22. Ibid.

23. Ghannouchi, "Al-'Alam al-Islami Wal-Isti'mar al-Hadith."

24. Ibid.

25. Ibid.

26. Ibid.

27. R. Ghannouchi, "Kayfa Nuwajih Tahaddi ad-Dawlah al-Qutriyah" [How to confront the challenge of the territorial state] (paper presented in Arabic to the Annual Winter Conference of the Muslim Students Society, Manchester, January 1995).

28. R. Ghannouchi, interview by the author, London, 28 February 1997.

29. Ibid.

30. Ghannouchi, "Kayfa Nuwajih."

31. See for instance M. J. al-Ansari, *Takwin al-'Arab as-Siyasi Wamaghza Addawlah al-Qutriyah* [The Arabs' political formation and the implication of the territorial state] (Beirut: Markaz Dirasat al-Wahda al-'Arabiyah [Arab Unity Studies Centre], 1994).

32. Ghannouchi, "Kayfa Nuwajih."

33. A. el-Affendi, *Turabi's Revolution* (London: Grey Seal, 1991), 166.

34. Ibid.

35. M. al-'Alami, *'Allal al-Fasi, Ra'id al-Haraka al-Wataniyah al-Maghribiyah* (Rabat: ar-Risalah Press, 1972).

36. al-Ansari, *Takwin al-'Arab as-Siyasi*, 89–91.

37. Ghannouchi, "Kayfa Nuwajih."

38. Ibid.

39. The province that now consists of Syria, Lebanon, Jordan, and Palestine.

40. Ibn Khaldoun, *Al-Muqaddimah* (Beirut: Dar al-Hilal, 1983).

41. R. Ghannouchi, interview by the author, London, 28 February 1997.

42. Ghannouchi, "Kayfa Nuwajih."

43. *Al-Khilafah ar-Rashidah* lasted from the death of the Prophet in approximately 634 to around 660 A.D.

44. R. Ghannouchi, interview by the author, London, 28 February 1997.

45. Ibid.

46. Ibid.

47. R. Ghannouchi, *Al-Qawmiyah Wal-Islam* [Nationalism and Islam] (draft of an article written in the early eighties for publication in the Persian language periodical *Twaheed*, date of publication not known).

48. E. Gellner, "Ethnicity, Culture, Class and Power," in *Ethnic Diversity and Conflict in Eastern Europe*, ed. P. F. Surgar (Santa Barbara and Oxford, ABC-Clio, 1980), 237–40.

49. A. Giddens, *The Nation-State and Violence* (Cambridge: Polity Press, 1985), 116–19.

50. Heywood, *Political Ideologies*, 137.

51. J. Keane, "Nations, Nationalism, and the European Citizen," *CSD Perspectives* (Autumn 1993): 9.

52. Heywood, *Political Ideologies*.

53. Ibid.

54. Ghannouchi, "Al-Qawmiyah Wal-Islam."

55. As argued for instance by M. J. al-Ansari in his *Takwin al-'Arab as-Siyasi*.

56. Ghannouchi, "Kayfa Nuwajih."

57. Ibid., quoting *The Holy Qur'an*, Chapter 49, Verse 14.

58. Ibid., quoting *The Holy Qur'an*, Chapter 9, verse 97.

59. Ibid., quoting *The Holy Qur'an*, Chapter 9, verses 98 and 99.

60. The term progress, which in Arabic is *taqaddum* from the root *qadama* (to move forward), is used by Ghannouchi to mean scientific and technological accomplishments, whereas development, which in Arabic is *tanmiyah* from the root *nama* (to grow), refers to economic success.

61. Ghannouchi, "Kayfa Nuwajih."

62. Linz and Stepan, *Problems of Democratic Transition*.

63. Ibid.

64. Ghannouchi, "Kayfa Nuwajih."

65. Ibid.

66. Ibid.

67. Linz and Stepan, *Problems of Democratic Transition*.

68. Ghannouchi, "Kayfa Nuwajih."

69. Ibid.

70. Ibid.

71. Ibid.

72. R. Ghannouchi, "Islam and the West: Prospects and Realities" (paper presented at the Centre for the Study of Democracy, University of Westminster, 6 October 1992).

73. Ibid.

74. Ibid.

75. Ibid.

76. R. Ghannouchi, "The Conflict Between the West and Islam."

77. Ibid.

78. R. Ghannouchi, interview by the author, London, 28 February 1997.

79. This has been blamed on the policy of *étatisme* adopted in many Arab countries, for example Egypt, Syria, Iraq, Tunisia, and Algeria, mostly since independence, sometimes after a coup, until the early 1970s when public policy changed in response to fiscal crises and the pressure/temptation from globalized capitalism and from its international institutions. This led, in the case of Tunisia for instance, to serious social upheavals in the early 1980s when the fragility of the country's economic system had already been exposed. The rate of growth of GNP declined from the previous levels of 5.2 per cent during the first half of the 1970s and 6.3 per cent during the second half of the 1970s, to only 2–3 per cent during the four years from 1982 to 1986. The balance of payments deteriorated, commercial deficit grew, and by 1986, with the collapse in petroleum prices and a drop in tourism and agriculture, foreign currency reserves were nil and foreign debt amounted to $5 billion (representing 60 percent of GDP), while an amount of $1.2 billion was due for debt servicing. It was at this juncture that the state had to resort to the International Monetary Fund and the World Bank (Ayubi, *Over-stating the Arab State*).

80. Ghannouchi, "Islam and the West: Prospects and Realities."

81. Ibid.

82. Larbi Sadiki, *Authoritarianism, Islamism, and the Search for Arab Democracy* (Ph.D. diss., Australian National University, Canberra, 1996), 18.

83. For example, John Esposito, who, recognizing the inadequacy of the term, speaks of "Islamic revivalism and Islamic activism." See Esposito, *The Islamic Threat*, 7–8. Francois Burgat suggests that fundamentalism and other such terms as Islamism, Khomeynism, and *intégrisme*, have been inflated by Western writers intrigued and disturbed by what they see of rapid changes in the Muslim world. See Burgat and Dowell, *The Islamic Movement in North Africa*, 2.

84. Esposito, *The Islamic Threat*, 7.

85. The Arabic *usuliyah* is a derivative of the word *asl* (sing.) and *usul* (plural), meaning root, origin, foundation, fundamental, or principle. *'Ilm-ul-usul* refers to the branch of knowledge that specializes in the study of the four foundations of Islamic jurisprudence, known also as *usul-ul-flqh*, that is Quran, Sunna, *qiyas* (analogy), and *ijma'* (consensus). A fundamentalist, *usuli*, is, therefore, one who specializes in this field of knowledge.

The English fundamentalism is a term said to refer to the belief that the Bible possesses complete infallibility because every word in it is the word of God; a belief that is usually accompanied by the condemnation of modern thought. The Western perception of fundamentalism is heavily influenced by American Protestantism, a movement in twentieth-century Protestantism emphasizing the literally interpreted Bible as fundamental to Christian life and teaching. The use of the term was then extended to describe the movement within any religion toward the fundamental doctrine out of which the religion has grown, and a refusal to depart from it in order to accommodate extraneous social or moral requirements. For many Christians, fundamentalism is pejorative or derogatory, being applied rather indiscriminately to all those who advocate a literalist biblical position and thus are regarded as static, retrogressive, and extremist. As a result, fundamentalism often has been regarded as referring to those who are literalists and wish to return to, and replicate, the past.

The French *intrégrisme* was coined by the French right-wing intellectual Charles Maurras, who was an anti-democrat and a supporter of the Vichy government during the Nazi occupation of France from 1940 to 1945. He introduced the term to denote the aim of bringing all distinct characteristics of a nation within purview of its political organization, so that, for example, the Roman Catholic Church in France would be regarded as an integral part of the political structure of the country, along with the language, customs, and traditions of the people. His opponents denounced the initiative as fascist because of its attempt to incorporate the functions of civil society into those of the state.

Intégrisme is the term most often used to refer to the Islamists in the French language media in France and in North Africa. See Marty and Appleby, Fundamentalism Observed; and Bruce Lawrence, Defenders of God: The Fundamentalist Revolt against the Modern Age (New York: Harper and Row, 1989).

86. See the documentation of the famous debate between Islamists and secularists at Cairo's International Book Exhibition, edited by Husni Abul-Yazid and published under the title Misr Bayna ad-Dawlah ad-Diniyah Wal-Madaniyah [Egypt between the civil and religious state] (Cairo: al-dar al-masriya Publishing House, 1992).

87. This and the following paragraph contain information from R. Ghannouchi, "Islam and the West" (paper presented to a symposium in Copenhagen, May 1994).

88. This and the following two paragraphs contain information from R. Ghannouchi, "Islam and the West: Concord or Inevitable Conflict?" in After the Cold War: Essays on the Emerging World Order, ed. Keith Philip Lepor (Austin: University of Texas Press, 1997).

89. Ibid., quoting J. Keane, "Power-Sharing Islam?" in Tamimi, Power-Sharing Islam?

90. Ibid.

91. R. Ghannouchi, "The Conflict Between the West and Islam."

92. A. Davutoglu, "The Clash of Interests: An Explanation of the World [Dis]order," Intellectual Discourses 2, no. 2 (1994).

93. Francis Fukuyama, The End of History and the Last Man (New York: The Free Press, 1992).

94. Davutoglu, "The Clash of Interests."

95. Samuel Huntington, "The Clash of Civilizations," Foreign Affairs (summer 1993). The theme of the paper was later expanded into Huntington's The Clash of Civilizations and the Remaking of World Order, 1996.

96. Ibid.

97. Ibid.

98. R. Ghannouchi, interview by the author, London, March 1995.

99. This and the following four paragraphs contain information from Ghannouchi, "Islam and the West: Concord or Inevitable Conflict?"

100. Judith Miller, "The Challenge of Radical Islam," Foreign Affairs (spring 1993): 45.

101. Ibid.

102. Ibid., 47

103. Ibid., 51.

104. Ghannouchi, "Islam and the West: Concord or Inevitable Conflict?"

105. Daniel Pipes, "An Islamic Internationale?" Forward (July 22, 1994). See also his article "Islam's Intramural Struggle," The National Interest, no. 35 (spring 1994).

106. R. Ghannouchi, "A Letter to Lord Avebury" in The Renaissance: A Civilizational Project, a collection of documents about the Ennahda Movement and the writings of its leader Rachid Ghannouchi, no date or place of publication. Ghannouchi's letter to Lord Avebury is dated 25 August 1993.

107. R. Ghannouchi, "Islam and the West: Concord or Inevitable Conflict?"

108. R. Ghannouchi, "Islam and the West."

109. Salim Azzam, Tabdid Amwal AnNnaft Al-'Arabi, Man-Il-Mas'ul [Who is responsible for squandering Arab petro-funds?] (London: The Islamic Council, 1986).

110. Ibid.

111. Ibid. See for example The Observer of 20 October 1985, and The Sunday Times of 2 December 1984.

112. This and the following nine paragraphs contain information from Ghannouchi, "Islam and the West: Concord or Inevitable Conflict?"

113. R. Ghannouchi, interview by Ad-Dustur (Jordan), Amman, 14 July 1993.

114. Ibid.

115. Ibid.

116. Ibid.

117. The Holy Qur'an, Verse 286, Chapter 2.

118. R. Ghannouchi, interview by Ad-Dustur.

119. Ibid.

120. Edward Djerjian, speech at the National Association of Arab Americans, Washington D.C., 11 September 1992.

121. R. Ghannouchi, unpublished letter to Edward Djerjian, dated 14 June 1992.

122. Ibid.

123. Ibid.

124. R. Ghannouchi, "Islam and the West: Concord or Inevitable Conflict?"

125. R. Ghannouchi, "Islam and the West."

Chapter Seven

1. A. Dhawahiri, Al-Hasad al-Murr: al-Ikhawn al-Muslimum Fi Sittin 'Aman, p. 8. No place or date is given, but it was evidently published between 1991 and 1992. The publication is identified on the front cover as a Jihad Group Publication. The document, whose title would read in English The Bitter Harvest: The Muslim Brotherhood in Sixty Years, is intended to substantiate the group's claim that the Muslim Brotherhood have strayed away from the Path of Guidance.

2. Ibid.

3. Ibid., 11–13.

4. Hizb-ut-Tahrir, Ad-Dimuqratiyah Nizam Kufr (Democracy is a system of blasphemy), 5. No date or place of publication is given.

5. Ibid.

6. Ibid., 11–23.

7. Musa Zayd al-Kilani, Al-Harakat al-Islamiyah fi al-Urdun wa Filastin [The Islamic movements in Jordan and Palestine] (Beirut: Mu'ssasat ar-Risalah, 1991).

8. Mahmud Abdulkarim Hasan, "Radd Iftira'at 'Ala al-Imam Ash-Shatibi" [Refuting false allegations attributed to Imam Ash-Shatibi], Al-Wa'y (August 1994): 21–30. Al-Wa'y is the official publication of HT in Lebanon.

9. Ibid.

10. Ibid.

11. Ibid.

12. One such attempt was made when Ghannouchi was invited in January 1997 to speak to the Muslim public in Swansea. The Salafis lost their bid.

13. A Muslim convert from the Caribbean by the name of Sheikh Faisal, who claims to be a leader of the so-called jihadi trend in the United Kingdom, is alleged to have told a crowd of Muslim students in Swansea in March 1997 that those who believe in democracy such as Rachid Ghannouchi are worse than Christians and Hindus.

14. Abdul Rashid Moten, "Democratic and Shura-Based Systems: A Comparative Analysis," Encounters 3, no. 1 (March 1997). Encounters is published by the Islamic Foundation, Leicester, U.K.

15. Ibid.

16. Ibid.

17. R. Ghannouchi, interview by the author, London, June 1995.

18. R. Ghannouchi, Interview by the author, London, June 1997.

19. Kedourie, Politics in the Middle East, 332.

20. Dilip Hiro, Islamic Fundamentalism (London: Paladin, 1989), 67.

21. S. Qutb, Ma'alim Fit-Tariq [Milestones], 8th ed. (Beirut: Dar Ash-Shuruq Publications, 1980); and Qutb, Milestones.

22. Ibid.

23. Ibid.

24. Ibid.

25. A. Mawdudi, Al-Islam Wal-Jahiliyah [Islam and barbarity], 2nd ed. (Dar-at-Turath al-Arabi, 1980), 14–15.

26. R. Ghannouchi, interview by the author, London, June 1997.

27. Ibid.

28. Ibid.

29. Ghannouchi, "Ad-Dini Was-Siyasi Fil-Islam."

30. Ash-Shahrastani (1086–1153) is a highly authoritative historian from Shahrastan in Persia. He is particularly known for his extensive studies into factionalism. His most famous book, to which Ghannouchi refers here, is Al-Milal Wan-Nihal in which Ash-Shahrastani provides a detailed study of the various political, religious, and philosophical factions that emerged in the history of Islam until his time.

31. Ghannouchi, "Ad-Dini Was-Siyasi Fil-Islam."

32. Ibn Kathir, Al-Bidayah Wan-Nihayah [The beginning and the end], 3rd ed. (Beirut: Maktabat-ul-Ma'arif, 1980).

33. Imam as-Suyuti, Tarikh al-Khulafa' [History of the caliphs] (Cairo: al-Fajjalah Press, 1969), 67.

34. Ghannouchi, "Ad-Dini Was-Siyasi Fil-Islam."

35. Ibid.

36. The Holy Qur'an, Verse 3, Chapter 5. This and all subsequent translations of Qur'anic verses are taken from The Holy Qur'an English Translation of the Meaning and Commentary (Medina: King Fahd Holy Qur'an Printing Complex, 1990).

37. The Holy Qur'an, Verse 38, Chapter 6.

38. Ghannouchi, "Ad-Dini Was-Siyasi Fil-Islam."

39. The Holy Qur'an, Verse 6, Chapter 11.

40. Ghannouchi, "Ad-Dini Was-Siyasi Fil-Islam."

41. Ibid.

42. Ibid.

43. This incident is reported in all well-known references on Sira (prophet's life-history) including Ibn Hisham. For a good political analysis of Sira see also Khalil, Dirasa Fis-Sirah; and Mustafa as-Siba'i, As-Sirah an-Nabawiyah, Durus Wa 'Ibar (Beirut: al-Maktab al-Islami, 1972).

44. Ibn Kathir, Al-Bidayah Wan-Nihayah, vol. 3, p. 267. Badr is about eighty miles to the west of Medina. It was then strategically positioned on the trade route from Mecca to Ash-Sham (Syria and Palestine).

45. Ghannouchi, "Ad-Dini Was-Siyasi Fil-Islam."

46. Imam as-Suyuti, Tarikh al-Khulafa'.

47. Ibid.

48. Ghannouchi, "Ad-Dini Was-Siyasi Fil-Islam."

49. R. Ghannouchi, interview by the author, London, 28 February 1997.

50. These developments are detailed in at-Tabari, Tarikh ar-Rusul Wal-Muluk [History of messengers and kings] (Cairo: Dar al-Ma'arif, 1961); and Ibn Kathir, Al-Bidayah Wan-Nihayah.

51. Ghannouchi, Al-Hurriyat, 48–51.

52. Imam as-Suyuti, Tarikh al-Khulafa'.

53. Ghannouchi, "Ad-Dini Was-Siyasi Fil-Islam."

54. Ibid.

55. Imam as-Suyuti, Tarikh al-Khulafa'.

56. Ghannouchi, "Ad-Dini Was-Siyasi Fil-Islam."

57. Ibid.

58. Ibid.

59. Imaduddin Khalil, Dirasa Fis-Sirah. This happened during the battle known as al-khandaq (the ditch) five years after Muhammad migrated to Medina. The Islamic city-state was besieged by the invading tribes of the Arab pagans, and the ditch was suggested by Salman al-Farisi, a Muslim Sahaba of Persian origin. See also S. Al Yahya, Al-Harakat al-'Askariyah Lir-Rasul al-A'zam Fi Kaffatayy al-Mizan [The military campaigns of the Great Prophet in the balance], vol. 2 (Beirut: ad-Dar al-'Arabiyah Lilmawsu'at, 1983), 302–14.

60. Imam as-Suyuti, Tarikh al-Khulafa'.

61. An account of the impact of the Arab Islamic civilization on the West is detailed in Sigrid Hunke, Shams-Ul-'Arab Tasta' 'Alal-Gharb [Allahs Sonne uber dem Abendland unser Arabisches Erbe] (Beirut: Dar al-Afaq al-Jadidah, 1993).

62. Ghannouchi, "Ad-Dini Was-Siyasi Fil-Islam."

63. Ibid.

64. One of the best, and most detailed, accounts of these events is given in Ibn al-'Arabi, Al-'Awasim Min-al-Qawasim (Cairo: al-Maktaba as-Salafiyah, 1968).

65. Ibn al-'Arabi, Al-'Awasim; see also Imam as-Suyuti, Tarikh al-Khulafa', and Ibn Kathir, Al-Bidayah Wan-Nihayah.

66. Ibid.

67. Ghannouchi, "Ad-Dini Was-Siyasi Fil-Islam."

68. Ibn al-'Arabi, al-'Awasim.

69. Ibid.

70. Ghannouchi, "Ad-Dini Was-Siyasi Fil-Islam."

71. Ibid.

72. Ibid.

73. Ibn Kathir, Al-Bidayah Wan-Nihayah.

74. 'Asabiyah is derived from the root 'asaab (to bind) and 'asab (union), and refers to a socio-cultural bond that can be used to measure the strength of social groupings. (Esposito, The Oxford Encyclopedia of the Modern Islamic World.)

75. R. Ghannouchi, "The Islamic Movement and the Dilemma of Choosing Between State and Society" (paper presented at the Islam and Modernity Symposium, SOAS, London, 6 July 1996).

76. Ghannouchi, "Ad-Dini Was-Siyasi Fil-Islam."

77. Ibn Kathir, Al-Bidayah Wan-Nihayah.

78. The Holy Qur'an, Verse 59, Chapter 4.

79. Ghannouchi, "Ad-Dini Was-Siyasi Fil-Islam."

80. Ibid.

81. A hadith reported by Muslim in "Kitab al-Wasiyah," and listed in an-Nawawi, Riyad as-Salihin (Beirut: Dar ibn Hazm, 1989).

82. Ghannouchi, "Ad-Dini Was-Siyasi Fil-Islam."

83. A. al-Badri, Al-Islam Baynal 'Ulama' Wal-Hukkam [Islam between the scholars and the rulers] (Medina: al-Maktaba al-'Ilmiyah, 1965), 36–38. Numerous examples are narrated by Muslim historians, including one involving two most prominent scholars, Imam Malik and Imam Ash-Shafi'i. When the latter was still a young man longing to join the majlis of the former as a pupil, he asked a family friend, the wali (deputy caliph or governor) of Mecca, to ask the wali of Medina to intercede on his behalf so as to convince Imam Malik to include him in his study

circle. The *wali* of Mecca wrote a letter to his colleague the *wali* of Medina, which Ash-Shafi'i took to him in person. Ash-Shafi'i reported that when he delivered the letter to the *wali* of Medina, the latter said to him: "Young boy! Walking from here to the bottom of the valley in Mecca barefooted is easier for me than walking to the house of Malik; for I never feel so humiliated except when I stand at the door of Malik." Ash-Shafi'i said astonishingly: "May Allah grant you righteousness, why don't you just send for him?" The *wali* said: "How preposterous! I do not guarantee that even if I rode to his house he would let me in." Eventually both left for Malik's house. They knocked on his door, and it took a while for a servant to respond. The *wali* said to her: "Tell your master the *wali* of Medina is at the door." She went back in. After a while she returned to them and said: "My master says *salam* to you (greets you), and tells you that if you have come to ask a question then write it down and you will get a written answer. Otherwise, if it is conversing with him that you are after, then you already know where his *majlis* is and it is there you should seek him. So go away." It is reported that Malik later on strongly rebuked Ash-Shafi'i for asking a ruler, somebody who is not so honorable, to intercede in a matter that is so honorable, namely the seeking of knowledge.

84. Ghannouchi, "Ad-Dini Was-Siyasi Fil-Islam."

85. Ibid.

86. Al-Juwayni is originally from Nisabur, a town in the northeast of Persia. He traveled to Baghdad where he did his studies and then settled in Hijaz, teaching at both Mecca and Medina. Hence is his title Imam al-Haramayn, that is Imam of the two Sacred Shrines.

87. *The Holy Qur'an*, Verse 107, Chapter 21.

88. *The Holy Qur'an*, Verse 6, Chapter 5.

89. *The Holy Qur'an*, Verse 179, Chapter 2.

90. Abu Ishaq Ash-Shatibi, *Al-Muwafaqat*, vol. 2 (Beirut: Dar al-Ma'rifah, n.d.), 6–8.

91. Ibid.

92. Imam as-Suyuti, *Tarikh al-Khulafa'*.

93. Ghannouchi, "Ad-Dini Was-Siyasi Fil-Islam."

94. Ibn Hazm, *Al-Fasl Fil-Milal Wal-Ahwa' Wan-Nihal* (Cairo: Al-Misriyah, 1964).

95. Al-Ash'ari's doctrine is outlined in his book *Maqalat al-Islamiyyin Wa-Ikhtilafat al-Musallin*, 2 vols., ed. Helmut Ritter (Istanbul: FranzSteiner, 1929–1933).

96. This and the following two paragraphs contain information from Ghannouchi, "Ad-Dini Was-Siyasi Fil-Islam."

97. This Prophetic *hadith* is reported by Muslim in the section on Iman, and is listed in an-Nawawi, *Riyad as-Salihin*.

98. F. Burgat, "Bilateral Radicalization," in *Power-Sharing Islam?*, ed. A. Tamimi.

Chapter Eight

1. See also the annual reports published by Amnesty International, Human Watch, the Lawyers Committee for Human Rights, and the U.S. State Department's Country Report. See for instance Amnesty International's report "Tunisia: Incommunicado Detention and Torture," March 1992; and The Lawyers Committee's document *Promise Unfulfilled. Human Rights in Tunisia Since 1987*, New York, October 1993.

2. Ghannouchi, "A Letter to Lord Avebury," in *The Renaissance: A Civilizational Project*. Ghannouchi's letter to Lord Avebury is dated 25 August 1993.

3. Edited by John Rudy and published in 1994 by Macmillan Press in association with the Centre for Contemporary Arab Studies, Georgetown University.

4. Dunn, "The al-Nahda Movement in Tunisia", 160.

5. Ibid. 154–58.

6. Ghannouchi, "A Letter to Lord Avebury."

7. Ibid.

8. See for instance Burgat and Dowell, *The Islamic Movement in North Africa*; Esposito, *The Islamic Threat, Myth or Reality?*; Esposito and Voll, *Islam and Democracy*; Jones, "Portrait of Rashid al-Ghannoushi,"; and R. Wright, "Islam and Liberal Democracy: Two Visions of Reformation," 72.

9. Ghannouchi, "A Letter to Lord Avebury."

10. This was made to a reporter of the London Arabic daily *Ash-Sharq al-Awsat*, published on 24 January 1992.

11. Lord Avebury's letter to Ghannouchi, London, 28 September 1993.

12. *The Sunday Telegraph* (London), 14 November 1993. The articles were titled "Victims Fury at Asylum for Bomber" and "Fanatic in Our Midst."

13. The apology was published in the 26 July issue of *The Sunday Telegraph* and repeated once more on 28 July 1996.

14. *Ash-Sharq al-Awsat* (London), 15 November 1993.

15. Ibid.

16. *The Sunday Express* (London), 6 August 1995. The article was titled "Shameful Deal Lets a Fugitive Terrorist Enjoy Life in Britain."

17. From a press release issued by Peter Carter-Ruck and Partners, Ghannouchi's solicitors, London, 2 October 1997.

18. B. Hassan, "Toward Human Rights Enforcement in the Arab World: A Comprehensive Strategy," in *Islam and Justice* (New York: Lawyers Committee for Human Rights, January 1997, 147–63.

19. Ibid.

20. Ibid.

21. Esposito, *The Oxford Encyclopedia of the Modern Islamic World*.

22. This was the Political Islam and Human Rights Symposium organized in London by the New York based Lawyers Committee for Human Rights in May 1996.

23. R. Ghannouchi, "The Islamists and Human Rights: A Comment on Bahey Eddin Hassan's Paper," in *Islam and Justice*, 165–70.

24. Ibid.

25. The article was published in *Ash-Sha'b* (Cairo) on 23 August 1994.

26. R. Ghannouchi, draft of amendments to be incorporated in the second edition of *Al-Hurriyat*.

27. Ibid.

28. Ibid.

29. H. Ali, *At-Tayyarat al-Islamiyah Wa-Qadiyat ad-Dimuqratiyah* [Islamic currents and the question of democracy] (Beirut: Markaz Dirasat al-Wahdah al-'Arabiyah [Arab Unity Studies Centre], 1996), 236.

30. Ibid., 238.

31. Ibid., 247.

32. Ibid.

33. A. Zghal, "The New Strategy of the Movement of the Islamic Way," 206.

34. Ibid., 212.

35. Ibid., 216.

36. Ibid., 205.

37. Ali, *At-Tayyarat al-Islamiyah*, 249.

38. Ibid., 250.

39. R. Ghannouchi, interview by the author, London, February 1998.

40. L. Zeytoun, interview by the author, London, June 1997.

41. Mohammed Elhachmi Hamdi, "Press Statement," *Al-Quds al-Arabi* (London), 13 May 1992.

42. Ibid.

43. L. Zeytoun (senior Ennahda member), interview by the author, London, June 1997.

44. Mohamed Elhachmi Hamdi, "An Analysis of the History and Discourse of the Tunisian Islamic Movement al-Nahda: A Case Study of the Politicization of Islam" (Ph.D. diss., School of Oriental and African Studies, University of London, July 1996), 245–58.

45. Mohamed Elhachmi Hamdi, "Malamih at-Tamayuz Fi-Tafkir al-Ghannouchi Wafi at-Tajruba al-Islamiyah at-Tunisiyah" [Distinctive features of Ghannouchi's thought and of the Tunisian Islamic experiment], in *Minal-Fikr al-Islami Fi-Tunis*, vol. 1 (Kuwait: Dar-ul-Qalam, 1992), 5.

46. Ibid., 22–27.

47. Ibid., 30.

48. Mohamed Elhachmi Hamdi, *Ashwaq al-Hurriyah: Qissat al-Haraka al-Islamiya Fi-Tunis* [Longings for freedom: The story of the Islamic movement in Tunisia] (Kuwait: Dar al-Qalam, 1989).

49. Hamdi, *An Analysis*, 47.

50. Ibid., 54.

51. Ibid., 54.

52. The allegation is made quoting Abdallah Imami, *Tanzimat al-Irhab Fil-'Alam al-Islami: Unmudhaj al-Nahda* [Terrorist organizations in the Islamic World: The model of Ennahda] Tunis: Al-Dar al-Tunisi li-l-nashr, 1992.

53. Hamdi, *An Analysis*, 86.

54. Ibid., 126.

55. Ibid., 128.

56. R. Ghannouchi, "Da'watun Ilar-Rushd," in *Maqalat*, 71. This was an article first published in *Al-Ma'rifah* (Tunis), 8 January 1979.

57. Ibid.

58. ad-Darwish, *Hiwarat* [Dialogue] (London: _Khalil Media Service, 1992), 14–19.

59. Hamdi, *An Analysis*, 129. Compare for instance the quotation given by Hamdi here and the original text of the interview in ad-Darwish, *Hiwarat*, 14–19.

60. Ibid., 286.

61. Ibid., 183.

62. R. Ghannouchi, interview by the author, London, February 1998.

63. See for instance the debate among a group of Islamic thinkers in Tamimi, *Ash-Shar'iyah as-Siyasiyah Fil-Islam*.

64. A. Elmessiri, interview by the author, London, 26 October 1996.

65. Nur-ud-Din al-'Waididi, "Taqdim Kitab al-Hurriyat al-'Ammah Fid-Dawlah al-Islamiyah," *Al-Insan* (Paris) 3, no. 13 (December 1994).

Bibliography

Primary Sources

'Akif, Mahmud. Letter to Rachid Ghannouchi, 29 July 1994.

Avebury, Lord. Letter to Rachid Ghannouchi, 28 September 1993.

Ennahda Movement. *Harakat an-Nahdah Fidh-Dhikra al-Khamisata 'Ashrata Li-Ta'sisiha, Durus al-Madi Wa-Ishkalat al-Hadir Wa-Tatallu'at al-Mustaqbal* (Ennahda on its fifteenth anniversary: Lessons from the past, present problems, and future ambitions), London, 6 June 1996.

——. *The Manifesto*, Tunis, 1988.

——. *The Renaissance: A Civilizational Project.* Ennahda document. Date and place of publication unknown.

——. Unpublished collection of political statements issued by Rachid Ghannouchi in his capacity as leader of Ennahda Movement between 1992 and 1997.

Ghannouchi, Rachid. "Al-'Alam al-Islami Wal-Isti'mar al-Hadith" (The Islamic world and modern colonialism). In *Maqalat.* Paris: Dar al-Karawan, 1984. The article was published first in *Al-Aman* (Beirut) 2, no. 62 (11 April 1980).

——. "Al-'Amal al-Islam Wa-Qutta' at-Turuq." *An-Nur* (Algiers), 8 July 1991.

——. "America's Strategy," article written in April 1992 for publication in *The Observer* but was not published.

——. "Barnamij al-Falsafa Wa Jil ad-Daya'." In *Minalfikr al-Islami Fi Tunis.* Vol. 2. Kuwait: Dar al-Qalam. Originally published in *Al-Ma'rifah* magazine, no. 10 (1973).

——. "The Basic Principles of an Islamic State." Paper presented to a symposium on Christian-Islamic Dialogue, Germany, June 1994.

——. "The Conflict Between the West and Islam, The Tunisian Case: Reality and Prospects." Paper presented at the Royal Institute of International Affairs, Chatham House, London, 9 May 1995.

——. "Dars-Ul-Jaza'ir" (Algeria's lesson). *Ar-Rayah* (Rabat), 24 February 1992.

——. "Ad-Dimuqratiyah Wal-Wad' at-Tunisi Aw al-Jabha ad-Dimuqratiyah Lil-Inqadh" (Democracy and the situation in Tunisia or the Democratic Front for Salvation). *Al-Insan* 2, no. 8 (August 1992).

——. "Ad-Dini Was-Siyasi Fil-Islam" (The religious and the political in Islam), lecture at Cardiff Islamic Society, January 1997.

——. "Falsafat al-Islam as-Siyasiyah" (Islam's political philosophy). Paper given at a seminar organized by the Iranian Students Society, London, January 1998.

———. "Fil-Bid' Kanal-Masjid" (The mosque was in the beginning). Date and place of publication unknown.

———. "Hal al-'Almaniyah Falsafat Ghurur Wa-Tawahush Am Falsafat Taqaddum Wa-Taharrur?" (Is secularism a philosophy of self-deception and barbarity or a philosophy of progress and liberation?). Paper written in response to a question put to him by the author, London, 30 March 1998.

———. "Hal Tasluh as-Sahwa al-Islamiyah Asasan Li-Nahdatin Hadhariyah" (Is the Islamic awakening fit to be a basis for a civilizational renaissance). Lecture in Arabic at the Annual Winter Conference of the Muslim Students Society, Manchester, England, January 1995.

———. "Al-Harakah al-Islamiyah Wal-Mujtama' al-Madani" (The Islamic movement and civil society). Paper presented at Pretoria University, South Africa, August 1994.

———. "Al-Harakah al-Islamiyah, al-Waqi' Wal-Aafaq" (The Islamic movement: Reality and prospects). Lecture at the Conference of Turkish Students Society, Markfield, England, 15 July 1995.

———. Al-Hrakah al-Islamiyah Wat-Tahdith. Beirut: Dar al-Jeel, 1980.

———. "Human Rights in Islam." Paper presented to a Symposium of the Association of Muslim Lawyers, Birmingham, 18 June 1995.

———. Huquq al-Muwatanah, Huquq Ghayr al-Muslim in Fil-Mujtama' al-Islami. (Citizenship rights, rights of non-Muslims in the Islamic society). Herndon, Va.: The International Institute of Islamic Thought, 1993.

———. Al-Hurriyat al-'Ammah Fid-Dawlah al-Islamiyyah (Public liberties in the Islamic state). Beirut: Markaz Dirasat al-Wihda al-'Arabiyah, 1993.

———. "Islam and Freedom Can Be Friends." The Observer (London), 19 January 1992.

———. "Islam and the West." Paper presented to a symposium in Copenhagen, May 1994.

———. "Islam and the West: Concord or Inevitable Conflict?" In After the Cold War: Essays on the Emerging World Order. Edited by Keith Philip Lepor. Austin: University of Texas Press, 1997.

———. "Islam and the West: Prospects and Realities." Paper presented to the weekly seminar of the Centre for the Study of Democracy at the University of Westminster, London, 6 October 1992.

———. "Al-Islam Wan-Nidham ad-Dawli" (Islam and the world order). Date and place of publication unknown.

———. "Al-Islam Yuwli 'Inayatan Kubra Lil-Mujtama' al-Madani" (Islam attaches great importance to civil society). Al-'Alam (London), no. 612 (14 March 1998) and no. 613 (21 March 1998).

———. "The Islamic Conception of the State." Paper presented at the annual spring conference of the Young Muslims Organization, London, April 1992.

———. "The Islamic Movement and the Dilemma of Choosing Between State and Society." Paper presented at the Islam and Modernity Symposium, SOAS, London, 6 July 1996.

———. "Islamic Movements in a Pluralist Society: Future Directions." Lecture at Markfield: The Islamic Foundation, U. K. 12 April 1997.

———. "The Islamists and Human Rights: A Comment on Bahey Eddin Hassan's Paper." In Islam and Justice. New York: Lawyers Committee for Human Rights, January 1997.

———. "Al-Islamiyun Wa-Khiyar ad-Dimuqratiyah" (The Islamists and the democratic option). Qira'at Siyasiyah, Tampa, Fla. summer 1993.

———. "Jadwa Istikhdam al-Quwwa" (The feasibility of using force). Unpublished paper, Summer 1996.

———. "Kalimat Wafa' Lis-Sadiq az-Za'im Layth Shbailat" (A word of loyalty to friend and leader Lath Shbailat). Date and place of publication unknown.

———. "Kayfa Nuwajih Tahaddi ad-Dawlah al-Qutriyah" (How to confront the challenge of the territorial state). Paper presented in Arabic to the Annual Winter Conference of the Muslim Students Society, Manchester, England, January 1995.

——. Letter to Abdullah Jaballah (president of Algeria's an-Nahda), on the occasion of his movement's conference in Algiers; date unknown.

——. Letter to Algerian Prime Minister Beleid Abessalam, 29 August 1992.

——. Letter to Edward Djerjian, the former assistant secretary of state for Near East and South Asian Affairs, 14 June 1992.

——. Letter to the Deportees (Palestinians expelled to South Lebanon by Israel), 25 December 1992.

——. Letter to the Deputy Prime Minister of Malaysia, no date.

——. Letter to Erbakan (leader of the Turkish Refah Party), May 1993.

——. Letter to Lord Avebury, dated 17 August 1993, published in *The Renaissance: A Civilizational Project*, a collection of documents about Ennahda Movement and the writings of its leader Rachid Ghannouchi, no date or place of publication given.

——. Letter to Mahmud 'Akif (editor of *'Alam al-Ahdath*, Centre of Civilizational Studies in Cairo) commenting on his centre's report about Tunisia; 8 July 1994.

——. Letter to Mu'adh (Ghannouchi's eldest son), 18 October 1992.

——. Letter to President Mu'ammar Qadhdhafi, 30 April 1992.

——. Letter to the prime minister of Malaysia, no date.

——. Letter to Sheikh Abdelaziz bin Bazz, June 1993.

——. Letter to Tasnim (Ghannouchi's eldest daughter), June 1993.

——. Letter to Tony Blair condemning the attitude of members of Hizbutahrir who shouted at Blair and his wife as they visited the Central Mosque in London to congratulate the Muslims on the occasion of Eid, April 1997.

——. *Al-Mabadi' al-Asasiyah Lid-Dimuqratiyah Wa-Usul al-Hukm al-Islami* (The basic principles of democracy and the fundamentals of Islamic governance). Casablanca: al-Furqan Publications, 1994.

——. "Manhaj at-Taghyir Fin-Nizam al-Ijtima'i al-Islami" (The method of change within the Islamic social system). Lecture at the FOSIS Training Camp, Markfield, England 18 July 1993.

——. *Maqalat* (Articles). Paris: Dar al-Karawan, 1984.

——. *Al-Mar'ah al-Muslimah Fi Tunis Bayna Tawjihat al-Qur'an Wa Waqi' al-Mujtama' at-Tunisi*. [Muslim woman in Tunisia between Qur'anic directives and realities of Tunisian society). Kuwait: Dar al-Qalam, 1993.

——. "Mawqi' as-Sultah Wash-Shura Fil-Islam" (The position of power and *Shura* in Islam). Paper presented at the Muslim Student Society's Annual Winter Conference, Manchester, England, February 1998.

——. "Al-Milkiyah az-Zira'iyah Fil-Islam" (Agrarian property ownership in Islam). In *Minal-Fikr al-Islami Fi-Tunis* (From the Islamic thought in Tunisia). Vol. 2. Kuwait: Dar al-Qalam, 1992. This was originally a talk delivered by Ghannouchi at Sahib Tayi Mosque in Tunis on May 1981.

——. *Minal-Fikr al-Islami Fi-Tunis* (From the Islamic thought). 2 vols. Kuwait: Dar-al-Qalam, 1992.

——. "Al-Mujtama' at-Tunisi: Tahlil Hadari: (Tunisian society: A civilizational analysis). Unpublished treatise authored by Ghannouchi while in prison in Tunisia in 1983.

——. "On the Eve of the Elections: Tunisia Mourns Its Loved Ones." Lecture at the London School of Economics, London, 24 February 1994.

——. "Our View of Modernity and Democracy." Paper presented at the Symposium of Islam and Democracy in North Africa, London School of Economics, 29 February 1992.

——. "Palestine as a Global Agenda." In *The Spirit of Palestine*. London: ZAD S.L., 1994.

——. "The Participation of Islamists in a Non-Islamic Government." In *Power-Sharing Islamic?* Edited by Azzam Tamimi. London: Liberty for Muslim World Publications, 1993.

——. "Public Liberties from an Islamic Perspective," a paper presented to the Annual Conference of the Muslim Students Union in Italy, 24 December 1994.

——. Al-Qadar 'Inda Ibn Taymiyah (Destiny in the thought of Ibn Taymiyah). Tunis: Halq al-Wadi, 1989.

——. "Qadat al-Harakah al-Islamiyah al-Mu'asirah: al-Banna, al-Mawdudi, al-Khomeyni" (Leaders of the contemporary Islamic movement: al-Banna, Mawdudi, and Khomeyni). In Maqalat. Paris: Dar al-Karawan, 1984. First published in Al-Ma'rifah, 5, no. 4 1 April 1979.

——. "Qadaya Wa-Mafahim Lil-Hiwar" (Issues and concepts for dialogue). In Al-Mutawassit, no date.

——. "Al-Qawmiyah Wal-Islam" (Nationalism and Islam). Draft of an article written in the early 1980s for publication in the Iranian Persian periodical Twaheed, no date.

——. "Ramadan 'Ala-L-Abwab Fasta'iddu" (Ramadan is at the doors, so get prepared). Letter from London to Ennahda members on the occasion of the fasting month of Ramadan, date unknown.

——. The Right to Nationality Status of Non-Muslim Citizens in a Muslim Nation. Translated by M. A. El Erian. Islamic Foundation of America, 1990.

——. "Risala Ilas-Sabirin" (A letter to those who are patient). Letter from London to Ennahda members, date unknown.

——. "As-Sakit 'An Ghazwi-S-Sudan Shaitanun Akhras" (An indifferent person to the invasion of Sudan is a mute Satan). Filastin al-Muslimah (London), March 1997.

——. "Secularism in the Arab Maghreb . . . What Secularism?" Paper presented to the Collapse of Secularism Conference, organized by Centre for the Study of Democracy, University of Westminster, London, 10 June 1994.

——. "Sha'bu-D-Dawlah Am Dawlat-Ush-Sha'b" (The state's people or the people's state). Al-Fajr (Tunis), 12 May 1990.

——. "Ash-Shaykh Muhammad Salih Annayfar (1903–1993)." Date and place of publication unknown.

——. "Ta'ammulat Fil-Wad' al-'Arabi as-Siyasi" (Reflections on the Arab political situation). London: London Islamic Dialogue Forum, June 1993.

——. "Tabi'at al-Mashru' as-Suhyuni" (Nature of the Zionist project). Lecture at the First Islamic Conference on Palestine, Tehran, 4 December 1990.

——. "At-Taghrib Wa-Hatmiyat ad-Diktaturiyah" (Westernization and the inevitability of dictatorship). In Maqalat. Paris: Dar al-Karawan, 1984. The article was published first in London's Al-Ghuraba' 6, no. 6 (September 1980).

——. "Tahlil Lil-'Anasir al-Mukawwinah Lidh-Dhahira al-Islamiya Bi-Tunis" (Analysis of the constituent components of the Islamic phenomenon in Tunisia). In Al-Harakat al-Islamiyah al-Mu'asira Fil-Watan al-'Arabi (Contemporary Islamic movements in the Arab homeland). Beirut: Markaz Dirasat al-Wahda al-'Arabiyah (Arab Unity Studies Centre), 1987.

——. "Taqwa Is the Best Remedy for Fear." Paper presented to the Fear and Politics Seminar, CSD, University of Westminster, London, 7 July 1995.

——. Tariquna Ila al-Hadarah (Our way to civilization). Tunis: al-Ma'rifah Publications, 1975.

——. "Ath-Thawrah al-Iraniyah Thawrah Islamiyah" (The Iranian revolution is an Islamic revolution). In Maqalat. Paris: Dar al-Karawan, 1984. First published in Al-Ma'rifah 5, no. 3, (12 February 1979).

——. "Tunisia: The Islamic Movement and Civil Society." Paper presented at Pretoria University, South Africa, August 1994.

——. "Al-Usuliyah al-Waraqa al-Wahida al-Lati La'iba Biha Arafat" (Fundamentalism, the only card Arafat played with). Date and place of publication unknown.

——. "Wakhajlatah Ya-Tunis" (How shameful, Tunisia). Al-Mutawassit (London) 27 May 1993.

——. "Zaman Ta'aqub an-Nukhab" (Age of the succession of elites). Date and place of publication unknown.

MTI (Islamic Tendency Movement). *Adh-Dhikra ath-Thalitha Liharakat al-Ittijah al-Islami* (The third anniversary of the MTI). Carthage, 6 June 1984.
———.*The Founding Manifesto*. Tunis: MTI, 1981.

Secondary Sources

Abdessalam, F. *Al-Ahzab as-Siyasiyah Fil-Islam* (Political parties in Islam). Cairo: Qalyoob Publishing House, 1978.
el-Affendi, A. "The Long March Forward." *The Inquiry*, London October 1987.
———. "Rationality, Civil Society, and Democracy in the Modern Muslim Context: Prolegomena to a Meta-archaeological Investigation." Paper presented to the Second International Conference on Islamic Thought, Istanbul, 25–27 April 1997.
———. *Turabi's Revolution*. London: Grey Seal, 1991.
———. *Who Needs an Islamic State?* London: Grey Seal, 1991.
Al-Afghani, J. "Al-Hukumah Al-Istibdadiyah" (The Despotic Government) in Abdulbasit Hasan's *Jamal Ad-Din Al-Afghani*, Cairo, Maktabat Wahba, 1982.
Ahmad, I. *The Social Contract and the Islamic State*. New Delhi: Kitab Bahavan, 1981.
Ahmad, M. 'Islamic Fundamentalism in South India: The Jamaat-I-Islami and the Tablighi Jamaat' in *Fundamentalism Observed*, edited by Marain E. Marty and R. Scott Appleby, Chicago, University of Chicago Press, 1991.
Ahmad, R. *Ad-Din Wad-Dawlah Wath-Thawrah* (Religion, state, and revolution). Cairo: al-Dar al-Sharkiyah, 1989.
Al-'Alami, M. *'Allal Al-Fasi, Ra'id Al-Haraka Al-Wataniyah Al-Maghribiyah*, Rabat: Ar-Risalah Press, 1972.
Algar, H. *Islam and Revolution I: Writings and Declarations of Imam Khomeyni (1941–1980)*. Berkeley: Mizan Press, 1981.
Ali, H. *At-Tayyarat al-Islamiyah Wa-Qadiyat ad-Dimuqratiyah* (Islamic currents and the question of democracy). Beirut: Markaz Dirasat al-Wahdah al-'Arabiyah (Arab Unity Studies Centre), 1996.
Amin, Sadiq. *Ad-Da'wah al-Islamiyah: Faridah Shar'iyah Wa Darurah Bashariyah* (Calling to Islam: Mandated by Shari'ah and necessitated by humanity). Amman: n.p., 1982.
Amin, Samir. "Qadiyat ad-Dimuqratiyah Fil-'Alam ath-Thalith" (The issue of democracy in the third world). *Al-Fikr ad-Dimuqrati*, Nicosia, Cyprus November 1990.
al-Ansari, M. *Takwin al-'Arab as-Siyasi Wamaghza Addawlah al-Qutriyah* (The Arabs' political formation and the implication of the territorial state). Beirut: Markaz Dirasat al-Wahda al-'Arabiyah (Arab Unity Studies Centre), May 1994.
Arblaster, A. *The Rise and Decline of Western Liberalism*. Oxford: Basil Blackwell, 1984.
Asad, M. *The Principles of State and Government in Islam*. Gibraltar: Dar al-Andalus, 1985.
A. Al Ash'ari, *Maqalat Al Islamiyyin Wa Ikhtilafat Al-Musallin*, 2 vol., edited by Helmut Ritter. Istanbul: FranzSteiner, 1929, 1933.
el-Awa, M. *On the Political System of the Islamic State*. Indianapolis, Ind.: American Trust Publications, 1978.
Ayoub, H. *Tabsit al-'Aqa'id al-Islamiyah*. Kuwait: Ar-Risalah, 1974.
Ayubi, N. *Over-stating the Arab State: Politics and Society in the Middle East*. London: I. B. Tauris, 1995.
Azzam, S. *The Concept of the Islamic State*. London: The Islamic Council of Europe, 1979.
———. *Tabdid Amwal an-Naft al-'Arabi, Man-Il-Mas'ul* (Who is responsible for squandering Arab petro-funds?). London: The Islamic Council, 1986.
al-Badri, A. *Al-Islam Baynal 'Ulama' Wal-Hukkam* (Islam between the scholars and the rulers). Madina: al-Maktaba al-'Ilmiyah, 1965.

el-Bahiyy, M. *Al-Fikr al-Islami al-Hadith Wa-Silatuhu Bil-Isti'mar al-Gharbi* (Modern Islamic political thought and its connection with western colonialism). 12th ed. Cairo: Maktabat Wahbah, 1991.

al-Banna, H. *Rasa'il al-Imam* (The messages of the Imam). Beirut: Mu'assat ar-Risalah, 1975.

——. "Limadha Yashtarik al-Ikhwan Fil-Intikhabat" (Why the Ikhwan take part in the elections). *Malaf Liwa' al-Islam* (Cairo), n.d.

Barut, M. *Yathrib al-Jadidah: al-Harakat al-Islamiyah ar-Rahinah* (New Yathrib: The current Islamic movements). London: Riad el-Rayyes Books, 1994.

Beinin J. and J. Stork, eds. *Political Islam: Essays from Middle East Reports.* London: Tauris, 1997.

Belhaj, A. *Ghayat al-Murad Fi Qadaya al-Jihad.* N.p: FIS Publication, 1994.

Bennabi, M. *Al-Qadaya al-Kubra* (The grand issues). Beirut: Dar al-Fikr, 1991.

Berlin, I. "Two Concepts of Liberty." In *Four Essays on Liberty.* Oxford: Oxford University Press, 1969.

el-Bishri, T. "Ahkam al-Wilayah al-'Ammah Li-Ghayr al-Muslimin." In *Ash-Shar'iyah as-Siyasiyah Fil-Islam.* Edited by Azzam Tamimi. London: Liberty for Muslim World Publications, 1997.

Bobbio, N. *Democracy and Dictatorship.* Oxford: Polity Press, 1997.

——. *The Future of Democracy.* Oxford: Polity Press, 1987.

Burgat F. and W. Dowell. *The Islamic Movement in North Africa.* Austin, Tex.: University of Texas Press, 1993.

Burgat, F. "Bilateral Radicalization." In *Power-Sharing Islam?* Edited by A. Tamimi. London: Liberty for Muslim World Publications, 1993.

——. 'How Can a Muslim Live in This Era?" in *Political Islam, Essays from Middle East Reports,* edited by Joel Beinin and Joe Stork, Tauris, London 1997.

Chehabi, H. *Iranian Politics and Religious Modernism: The Liberation Movement of Iran Under the Shah and Khomeyni.* Ithaca, N.Y.: Cornell University Press, 1990.

Cohen, J., and A. Arato. *Civil Society and Political Theory.* 3rd ed. Cambridge, Mass.: MIT Press, 1994.

Dahir, M. "Al-Mujtama' al-Madani Waddawlah Filmashriq al-'Arabi." In *Al-Mujtama' al-Madani Fil-Watan al-'Arabi.* Beirut: Markaz Dirasat al-Wahda al-'Arabiyah (Arab Unity Studies Centre), 1992.

ad-Dajani, A. "Tatawur Mafahim ad-Dimuqratiyah Fil-Fikr al-'Arabi al-Hadith" (The development of the concepts of democracy in the modern Arab thought). In *Azmat ad-Dimuqratiyah Fil-Watan al-'Arabi* (The crisis of democracy in the Arab homeland). Beirut: Markaz Dirasat al-Wahda al-'Arabiyah (Arab Unity Studies Centre), 1984, p. 115.

Dhawahiri, A. *Al-Hasad al-Murr: al-Ikhawn al-Muslimum Fi Sittin 'Aman* (The bitter harvest: The Muslim brotherhood in sixty years). No place or date given; published between 1991 and 1992.

Ad-Darwish, Q. *Hiwarat* (Dialogue). London: Khalil Media Service, 1992.

Davis, J. *Between Jihad and Salaam: Profiles in Islam.* New York: St. Martin's Press, 1997.

Davutoglu, A. "The Clash of Interests: An Explanation of the World [Dis]order," *Intellectual Discourses,* vol. 2, no. 2 (1994).

Diamond, L., and M. Platter, eds. *The Global Resurgence of Democracy.* 2nd ed. Baltimore: Johns Hopkins University Press, 1996.

Dunn, M. "The al-Nahda Movement in Tunisia: From Renaissance to Revolution." In *Islamism and Secularism in North Africa.* Edited by John Rudy. London: Macmillan, 1994.

Elgindy, K. "The Rhetoric of Rachid Ghannouchi." In *Arab Studies Journal,* Spring 1995.

Eliade, Mircea, ed. *Encyclopedia of Religion.* New York: Macmillan, 1987.

Elias, N. "Violence and Civilization: The State Monopoly of Physical Violence and Its Infringment." In *Civil Society and the State.* Edited by J. Keane. London: Verso, 1988.

Elmessiri, A. "Ma'alim al-Khitab al-Islami al-Jadid" (Features of the new Islamic discourse). In *Ash-Shar'yiah as-Siyasiyah Fil-Islam* (Political legitimacy in Islam). Edited by Azzam Tamimi. London: Liberty for Muslim World Publications, 1997.

——. *Tafkik al-Khitab al-'Ilmani* (Deconstructing the secular discourse). 4 vols. forthcoming, Cairo: Dar Ash-Shuruq, Summer 2001.

——. "Towards a More Comprehensive and Explanatory Paradigm of Secularism." Paper presented at the Collapse of Secularism Symposium, Centre for the Study of Democracy, University of Westminster, London, 10–11 June 1994.

Enayat, H. *Modern Islamic Political Thought*. London: Macmillan, 1982.

Encyclopedia Britannica, CD edition.

Esposito, J. *Islam and Politics*. 3rd ed. Syracuse, N.Y.: Syracuse University Press, 1991.

——. *Islam: The Straight Path*, New York: Oxford University Press, 1991.

——. *The Islamic Threat: Myth or Reality*. Oxford: Oxford University Press, 1995.

Esposito, J., ed. *The Oxford Encyclopedia of the Modern Islamic World*. New York: Oxford University Press, 1995.

Esposito, J., and J. Piscatori. "Democratization and Islam." In *The Middle East Journal* 45, no. 3.

Esposito, J., and J. Voll. *Islam and Democracy*. Oxford: Oxford University Press, 1996.

Al-Fasi, A. *Maqasid Ash-Shari'ah Al-Islamiyah Wa-Makarimuha*, Rabat, Ar-Rislah, Publications, 1979.

The Fontana Dictionary of Modern Thought. London: Fontano Press, 1988.

Ford, R., R. Jenkings, and A. Leathley. "Ministers 'in plot to expel dissident.'" *The Times* (London), 6 January 1996.

Fowler R., and J. Orenstein. *An Introduction to Political Theory*. New York: HarperCollins, 1992.

Fregosi, R. "From the Secular to the Politico-Religious." *Contemporary European Affairs* 2, no. 4 (1989).

Fukuyama, F. *The End of History and the Last Man*. New York: The Free Press, 1992.

Gellner, E. *Conditions of Liberty, Civil Society, and its Rivals*. London: Hamish Hamilton, 1994.

——. "The Enemies of Civil Society." Lecture at the London School of Economics, 19 June 1995.

——. "Ethnicity, Culture, Class, and Power." In *Ethnic Diversity and Conflict in Eastern Europe*. Edited by P. F. Surgar. Santa Barbara and Oxford: ABC-Clio, 1980.

——. "Marxism and Islam: Failure and Success." In *Power-Sharing Islam?* Edited by A. Tamimi. London: Liberty for Muslims World Publications, 1993.

Giddens, A. *The Consequences of Modernity*. Cambridge: Polity Press, 1990.

——. *Modernity and Self-Identity: Self and Society in the Late Modern Age*. Cambridge: Polity Press, 1991.

——. *The Nation-State and Violence*. Cambridge: Polity Press, 1985.

Guibernau, M. *Nationalisms, the Nation-State, and Nationalism in the Twentieth Century*. Cambridge: Polity Press, 1996.

Habermas, J. *The Philosophical Discourse of Modernity*. Translated by F. Lawrence. Oxford: Policy Press, 1987.

Hamdi, M. "An Analysis of the History and Discourse of the Tunisian Islamic Movement al-Nahda: A Case Study of the Politicization of Islam." Ph.D. diss., School of Oriental and African Studies, University of London, July 1996.

——. *Ashwaq al-Hurriyah: Qissat al-Haraka al-Islamiya Fi-Tunis* (Longings for freedom: The story of the Islamic movement in Tunisia). Kuwait: Dar al-Qalam, 1989.

——. "Islam and Liberal Democracy: The Limits of the Western Model." *The Journal of Democracy* 7, no. 2 (April 1996), pp. 81–85.

——. "Malamıh at-Tamayuz Fi-Tafkır al-Ghannouchi Wafı at-Tajruba al-Islamiyah at-Tunisiyah" (Distinctive features of Ghannouchi's thought and of the Tunisian Islamic experiment). In *Mınal-Fikr al-Islami Fı-Tunıs*. Vol. 1. Kuwaıt: Dar-al-Qalam, 1992.

——. "Press Statement." *Al-Quds Al-Arabı* (London), 13 May 1992.

Hampsher-Monk, I. *A History of Modern Political Thought: Major Political Thinkers from Hobbes to Marx*. Oxford: Blackwell, 1992.

Hasan, A. *Jamal ad-Dın al-Afghanı*. Cairo: Wahba, 1982.

Hasan, M. "Radd Ifira'at 'Ala al-Imam Ash-Shatibi" (Refuting false allegations attributed to Imam Ash-Shatibi). *Al-Wa'y* (Beırut), August 1994, pp. 21–30.

Hassan, B. "Toward Human Rights Enforcement in the Arab World: A Comprehensive Strategy." In *Islam and Justice*. New York: Lawyers Committee for Human Rights, January 1997.

Hastings, James, ed. *Encyclopedia of Religion and Ethıcs*. Edinburgh: T. & T. Clark, 1971.

Hawwa, S. *Al-Islam*, 4 vols. Syria: Dar as-Salam Publications, n.d.

——. *Jund-U-Llah Takhtitan*. Beirut: Dar Ammar, 1988.

Held, D. "Democracy: Past, Present, and Possible Future." *Alternatives* 18, no. 3 (summer 1993).

Hermassi, E. "The Islamicist Movement and November 7." In *Tunısıa: The Political Economy of Reform*. Edited by I. William Zartman. London: Lynne Rienner, 1991.

Heywood, A. *Political Ideologıes: An Introduction*. London: Macmillan, 1992.

al-Hilali, Muhammad Taqıy-ud-Din, and Muhammad Muhsin Khan. *Al-qur'an al-karim: The Interpretation of the Meanıngs of the Noble Qur'an ın the English Language*. Riyadh: Maktaba Dar-us-Salam, 1994.

Hicks, N. *Promise Unfulfilled: Human Rıghts ın Tunısia Sınce 1987*. New York: The Lawyers Committee for Human Rights, October 1993.

Hiro, D. *Islamic Fundamentalısm*. London: Paladın, 1989.

Hobbes, T. *Leviathan*. London: Penguin Classics, 1985.

Hoffman, M. *Islam Is the Alternative*. Reading: Garnet, 1993.

Honk, Z. *God's Sun Shınes on the West*. Beirut: Dar El-Jil, 1993.

Honderıch T. (ed), *The Oxford Companıon to Phılosophy*. Oxford: Oxford University Press, 1995.

Hourani, A. *Arabic Thought ın the Liberal Age 1798–1939*. Cambridge: Cambrıdge University Press, 1991.

Hunke, S. *Shams-Ul-'Arab Tasta' 'Alal-Gharb* (the original title in German ıs *Allahs sonne uber dem Abendland unser Arabısches erbe*). Beirut: Dar-ul-Jil, 1993.

Huntington, S. "The Clash of Civilizations." *Foreıgn Affairs* (summer 1993).

——. *The Clash of Cıvılızatıons and the Remaking of World Order*. New York: Simon and Schuster, 1996.

Huwaidi, F. *Al-Islam Wad-Dımuqratiyah* (Islam and democracy). Cairo: al-Ahram Translation and Publishing Centre, 1993.

——. *Iran Minad-Dakhil* (Iran from within). 4th ed. Cairo: al-Ahram Translation and Publishing Centre, 1991.

Hizb-ut-Tahrir. *Ad-Dımuqratıyah Nızam Kufr* (Democracy is a system of unbelief). No date or place given.

Ibn al-'Arabi. *Al-'Awasim Min-al-Qawasim*. Cairo: al-Maktaba as-Salafiyah, 1968.

A. Ibn Hazm. *Al-Fasl Fıl-Mılal Wal-Ahwa' Wan-Nıhal*. Cairo: Al. Mısriyah, 1964.

Ibn Hisham, *As-Sirah an-Nabawıyah*. Beirut: Dar-al-Fikr, n.d.

Ibn Kathir, *Al-Bidayah Wan-Nıhayah* (The beginning and the end), 7 vols., 3rd ed. Beirut: Maktabat-ul-Ma'arif, 1980.

Ibrahım, Ezzeddin, and Denys Johnson-Davies, trans. *An-Nawawi's Forty Hadiths*. Lebanon: Dar al-Koran al-Kareem, 1976.

al-Ibrahımi, A. "Algeria Now: Crises and Mutations in Gestations." Public lecture, SOAS, London, 2 June 1994.

Imami, A. *Tanzimat Al-Irhab Fil-'Alam Al-Islami: Unmudhaj Al-Nahda* (Terrorist organizations in the Islamic world: the model of Ennahda). Tunis: Al-Dar al-Tunisi lil-l-nashr, 1992.

Ismail, S. "Al-Mujtama' al-Madani Wad-Dawlah." In *Al-Mujtama' al-Madani Fil-Watan al-'Arabi*. Beirut: Markaz Dirasat al-Wahda al-'Arabiyah (Arab Unity Studies Centre), 1992.

Jaber, K. *The Arab Ba'ath Socialist Party*. Syracuse, N.Y.: Syracuse University Press, 1966.

Jad'an, F. *Usus at-Taqaddum 'Inda Mufakkiri al-Islam* (Progress foundations as perceived by Islamic thinkers). 3rd ed. Amman: Dar Ash-Shuruq, 1988.

Jones, L. "Portrait of Rachid al-Ghannouchi." *Middle East Report*, Jul.-Aug. 1988.

Jordan, W. *The State: Authority and Autonomy*. Oxford: Oxford University Press, 1985.

al-Kawakibi, A. *Umm-Ul-Qura* (Mother of villages). Beirut: Dar Ash-Shuruq al-Arabi, 1991.

———. *Taba'i' al-Istibdad* (Traits of despotism). Algiers: Mofam Publications, 1988.

Kawtharani, W. "Al-Mujtama' al-Madani Waddawlah Fit-Tarikh al-'Arabi" (Civil society and the state in Arab history). In *Al-Mujtama' al-Madani Fil-Watan al-'Arabi*. Beirut: Markaz Dirasat al-Wahda al-'Arabiyah (Arab Unity Studies Centre), 1992.

Keane, J. "Despotism and Democracy." In *Civil Society and the State: New European Perspectives*. Edited by J. Keane. London: Verso, 1988.

———. "Introudction: Democracy and the Decline of the Left," in N. Bobbio, *Democracy and Dictatorship*. Oxford: Polity Press, 1997.

———. *The Media and Democracy*. Cambridge: Polity Press, 1991.

———. "Nations, Nationalism, and the European Citizen." In *CSD Perspectives*. London: University of Westminster, Autumn 1993.

———. "Power-Sharing Islam?." In *Power-Sharing Islam?* Edited by A. Tamimi. London: Liberty for Muslim World Publications, 1993.

———. *Reflections on Violence*. London: Verso, 1996.

———. "Secularism." Public lecture at the Muslim Students Society's Annual Winter Conference, Manchester, England January 1995.

Kedourie, E. *Politics in the Middle East*. Oxford: Oxford University Press, 1992.

Khaldoun, I. *Al-Muqaddimah*. Beirut: Dar al-Hilal, 1983.

Khalil, I. *Dirasa Fis-Sirah*. Beirut: ar-Risalah Publications, 1978.

al-Kilani, M. *Al-Harakat al-Islamiyah fi al-Urdun wa Filastin* (The Islamic movements in Jordan and Palestine). Beirut: Mu'assasat ar-Risalah, 1991.

Kramer, G. "Does the Arab-Muslim World Constitute an Exception to the Global Process of Transformation?" Paper at Conference on Legitimacy and Governance: Transformation of Societies and Political Systems in the Middle East and North Africa, Paris, 11–13 July 1995.

Lawrence, B. *Defenders of God: The Fundamentalist Revolt against the Modern Age*. New York: Harper and Row, 1989.

Linz J., and A. Stepan. *Problems of Democratic Transition and Consolidation*. Baltimore: Johns Hopkins University Press, 1996.

The Longman Illustrated Encyclopedia of World History, Ivy Leaf, 1991.

Machiavelli, N. *The Prince*. Oxford and New York: Oxford University Press, 1984.

Macpherson, C. *The Life and Times of Liberal Democracy*. Oxford: Oxford University Press, 1977.

Magnuson, D. "Islamic Reform in Contemporary Tunisia: Unity and Diversity." In *Tunisia: The Political Economy of Reform*. Edited by I. William Zartman. London: Lynne Rienner, 1991.

Manzoor, P. "Desacralizing Secularism." In *Islam and Secularism in the Middle East*. Edited by A. Tamimi and J. Esposito. London: Hurst, 2000.

Marx, K., and F. Engels. *The Communist Manifesto*. Oxford and New York: Oxford University Press, 1992.

Mawdudi, A. *Al-Islam Fi Muwajahat at-Tahaddiyat al-Mu'asirah* (Islam in the face of contemporary challenges). Translated by Khalil al-Hamidi. Kuwiat: Dar al-Qalam, 1971.

———. Al-Islam Wal-Jahiliyah (Islam and barbarity). 2nd ed. Dar at-Turath al-Arabi, 1980.
———. Islamic Law and Constitution. Lahore, Pakistan: Islamic Publications Ltd.
———. Waqi' al-Muslimin Wasabeel Annuhud Bihim (Muslim reality and the way to renaissance). 3rd ed. Beirut: ar-Rislah Publications, 1978.
Mawlawi, F. "Al-Musharaka Fil-Hukm" (Participation in government). Unpublished paper, summer 1996.
Al-Mawsu'ah al-'Arabiyah al-Muyassarah (The concise Arab encyclopedia). Cairo: Dar Al-Sha'b, 1965.
McLellan, D. Karl Marx: A Biography. London: Papermac, 1995.
Micaub, C., L. Brown, and C. More. Tunis: The Politics of Modernization. London: Pall Mall Press, 1964.
al-Mili, M. Al-'Ilmaniyah Aw Falsafat Mawt al-Insan (Secularism or the philosophy of the death of man). Carthage: The Tunisian Press, 1986.
Mill, J. On Liberty and Other Essays. Oxford: Oxford University Press, 1991.
Miller, David, ed. The Blackwell Encyclopaedia of Political Thought. Oxford: Blackwell, 1991.
Miller, David, ed. Liberty. Oxford: Oxford University Press, 1991.
Miller, J. "The Challenge of Radical Islam." Foreign Affairs (spring 1993).
Moten, R. "Democratic and Shura-Based Systems: A Comparative Analysis." Encounters (England) 3, no. 1 (March 1997).
an-Nawawi, Riyad as-Salihin. Beirut: Dar ibn Hazm, 1989.
Nuhic, M. "Press, Radio, and Television Propaganda in Preparation of Genocide." Paper presented at the International Congress for the Documentation of the Genocide in Bosnia-Herzegovina, Bonn, 31 August–4 September 1995.
Offe, C. "The Future of Democracy." Paper presented at the CSD weekly seminar, University of Westminster, 11 October 1994.
Osman, M. Min Usul al-Fikr as-Siyasi (Of the fundamentals of Islamic political thought). Beirut: ar-Risalah, 1984.
Outhwaite, W., and T. Bottmore, eds. Blackwell Dictionary of 20th Century Social Thought. Oxford: Blackwell, 1995.
Paine, T. The Rights of Man. London: Everyman, 1993.
Pipes, D. "An Islamic Internationale?" Forward, 22 July 1994.
———. "Islam's Intramural Struggle." The National Interest, no. 35 (spring 1994).
al-Qaradawi, Y. Awlawiyat al-Harakah al-Islamiyah Fil-Marhala al-Qadimah (Islamic movement's priorities in the upcoming era). 2nd ed. Cairo: Maktabat Wahbah, 1991.
———. Al-Hal al-Islami: Farida-Tun Wa-Darurah (The Islamic solution: An obligation and a necessity). 3rd ed. Cairo: Maktabat Wahbah, 1977.
———. Al-Hulul al-Mustawradah Wa-Kayfa Janat 'Ala Ummatina (Imported solutions and how they harmed our Ummah). 15th ed. Beirut: Mu'assasat ar-Risalah, 1989.
———. Al-Islam Wal-'Almaniyah, Wajhan Liwajh (Islam and secularism, face to face). 2nd ed. Beirut: Mu'assasat ar-Risalah, 1990.
Al-qur'an al-karim: The Holy Qur'an, English Translation of the Meanings and Commentary, Medina: King Fahd Holy Quran Printing Complex, 1990.
El-Kray El-Qusantini, 'At-Thawbit wat-Tajdid fil-Fikr al-Islahi Ghadat Khuruj Al-Mihwar Min Tunis' in Actes du Ivè Séminaire sur l'Histoire du Mouvement National La Tunisie de 1939 à 1945. Tunis: Ministère de l'Education, 1989.
Qutb, M. Madhahib Fikriyah Mu'asirah (Contemporary intellectual trends). Cairo: Dar Ash-Shruq, n.d.
Qutb, S. Islam: The Religion of the Future. Kuwait: International Islamic Federation of Student Organizations (IIFSO), 1992.
———. Ma'alim Fit-Tariq (Milestones). 8th edition. Beirut: Dar Ash-Shuruq Publications, 1980.

———. *Milestones*. (English translation of *Ma'alim Fit-Tariq*.) New Delhi: Naushaba Publications, 1991.

———. *Tafsir Surat Ash-Shura* (Interpretation of Qur'anic Chapter # 42). Cairo: Dar Ash-Shuruq, 1983.

Ali Abd Ar-Raziq, *Al-Islam Wa Usul Al-Hukm* (Islam and the fundamentals of government). Cairo: Misr Press, 1925.

Rashid Rida, M. *Al-Khalifah* (The caliphate). Cairo: az-Zahra Publications, 1988.

Richards, A., and J. Waterbury. *A Political Economy of the Middle East*. Boulder, Colo.: Westview Press, 1990.

Robertson, David, ed. *The Penguin Dictionary of Politics*. London: Penguin Books, 1985.

Sadiki, L. *Authoritarianism, Islamism and the Search for Arab Democracy* (Ph.D. diss., Australian National University, Canberra, 1996).

as-Sawi, S. *At-Ta'addudiyah Fid-Dawlah al-Islamiyah* (Pluralism in the Islamic state). 2nd edition. Cairo: Dar al-I'lam ad-Dawli, 1993.

as-Sayid, Sabiq. *Fiqh as-Sunnah*. Beirut: Dar al-Fikr, 1977.

Schmitter, P., and T. Karl, "What Democracy is . . . and Is Not" in *The Global Resurgence of Democracy*. 2nd ed. Edited by L Diamond and M. Plattner. Baltimore and London: John Hopkins University Press, 1996.

Schmitter, P. "Is it Safe for Transitologists and Consolidologists to Travel to the Middle East and North Africa?" Paper presented at the Conference on Legitimacy and Governance: Transformation of Societies and Political Systems in the Middle East and North Africa, Paris, 11–13 July 1995.

Schumpeter, J. *Capitalism, Socialism, and Democracy*, New York: Harper & Row, 1942.

Scruton, Roger. *Dictionary of Political Thought*. London: Pan Books, 1983.

Shafiq, M. "Al-Istratijiyah al-Amrikiyah Wa-Athar an-Nidham al-'Alami al-Jadid 'Alal-'Alam al-'Arabi" (The American strategy and the impact of the new world order on the Arab world). *Qira'at Siysiyah* (Tampa), winter 1992.

———. "Hal Al-Hadtha Mutaha Aslan?" (Is modernity readily available/), *Al-Mujtama'*, 3 March 1998.

Abu Ishaq Ash-Shatibi, *Al-Muwafaqat fi Usul Ash-Shari'ah* (Analogies in the foundations of Shari'ah). Beirut: Dar Al-Kutub Al-'ilmiyah, n.d.

ash-Shawi, T. *Fiqh Ash-Shura Wal-Istisharah* (The jurisprudence of Shura and consultation). Cairo: al-Wafa' Publications, 1992.

Shively, W. *Power and Choice*. 3rd ed. n.p.: McGraw-Hill, 1993.

as-Siba'i, M. *As-Sirah an-Nabawiyah, Durus Wa 'Ibar*. Beirut: al-Maktab al-Islami, 1972.

Siedentop, L. *Tocqueville*. Oxford: Oxford University Press, 1994.

Sivan, E. *Radical Islam Medieval Theology and Modern Politics*. New Haven: Yale University Press, 1985.

as-Suyuti. *Tarikh al-Khulafa'* (History of the caliphs). Cairo: al-Fajjalah Press, 1969.

at-Tabari. *Tarikh ar-Rusul Wal-Muluk* (History of messengers and kings). Cairo: Dar al-Ma'arif, 1961.

Taha, A. *Malamih al-Fikr as-Siyasi 'Inda Rachid al-Ghannouchi* (Features of Rachid Ghannouchi's political thought). Master's thesis, Lebanese University, 1996.

Abdelhadi Abu Talib, *Al-Marji' Fil-Qanun Ad-Dusturi Wal-Mu'assasat As-Siyasiyah* (Reference of Constitutional Law and Political Institutions), Casablanca: Dar Al-Kitab, 1980.

Tamimi, A. "Political Violence in the Arab World." *CSD Bulletin* 1, no. 2 (January 1994).

———. "Rachid al-Ghannouchi: Jur'atun Fit-Tarh 'Ala Nahjit-Tajdid" (Rachid Ghannouchi: A daring discourse in pursuit of revival). *Assabeel* (Amman), 21 October 1996.

Tamimi, A., ed. *Ash-Shar'iyah as-Siyasiyah Fil-Islam* (Political legitimacy in Islam). London: Liberty for Muslim World Publications, 1997.

Taylor, C. "What's Wrong with Negative Liberty?" In *Philosophical Papers*. Vol. 2, Chap. 7. Cambridge: Cambridge University Press, 1985.

Thomson, D. *Political Ideas*. London: Penguin Books, 1966.

Touraine, A. *Critique of Modernity*. Oxford: Blackwell, 1995.

——. *What Is Democracy?* Translated by David Macey. Boulder, Colo.: Westview Press, 1997.

at-Tunisi, K. *Aqwam al-Masalik Fi Ma'rifati Ahwal al-Mamalik*. Tunis: Al-Dar Al-Tunisiyah, 1972.

at-Turabi, H. *Ash-Shura Wad-Dimuqratiyah* (Shura and democracy). Casablanca: al-Furqan Publications, 1993.

Turner, B. *Status*. Milton Keynes: Open University Press, 1988.

Vatikiotis, P. *Islam and the State*. London and New York: Routledge, 1991.

Ali Abdulwahid Wafi, *Huquq Al-Insan Fil-Islam* (Human Rights in Islam), Cairo: Dar Nahdat Misr, 1967.

Nur-ud-Din al-'Waididi, "Taqdim Kitab Al-Hurriyat Al-'Ammah Fid-Dawlah Al-Islamiyah," *Al Insam* (Paris) 3, no. 13 (December 1994).

Weber, M. *The Protestant Ethic and the Spirit of Capitalism*. New York: Routledge, 1996.

Wright, R. "Islam and Liberal Democracy: Two Visions of Reformation." *The Journal of Democracy* 7, no. 2 (April 1996).

al-Yahya, S. *Al-Harakat al-'Askariyah Lir-Rasul al-A'zam Fi Kaffatayy al-Mizan* (The military campaigns of the Great Prophet in the balance). Beirut: ad-Dar al-'Arabiyah Lilmawsu'at, 1983.

Husni Abul-Yazid, ed., *Misr Bayna Ad-Dawlah Ad-Diniyah Wal-Madaniyah* [Egypt between the Civil and Religious State], Cairo: Al-dar al-masriya Publishing House, 1992.

Zaehner, R. D., ed. *The Hutchinson Encyclopedia of Living Faiths*. 4th ed. 1994.

Zaghal, A. "Al-Istratijiyah al-Jadidah Liharakat al-Ittijah al-Islami: Munawara Am Ta'bir 'Ani-Th-Thaqafa as-Siyasiyah at-Tunisiyah." In *Ad-Din Fil-Mujtama' al-'Arabi* (Religion in the Arab society). Beirut: Markaz Dirasat al-Wahda al-'Arabiyah (Arab Unity Studies Centre), 1990.

Zaidan, A. *Ahkam Ahl Adh-Dhimmah Wal-Musta'manin* (Rules applicable to dhimmis and those granted asylum). Beirut: Ar-Risalah, 1976.

M. az-Zamzami, *Tunis al-Islam al-Jarih* (Tunisia: The wounded Islam), Bonn: n.p., 1994.

Zartman, I. W. "The Challenge of Democratic Alternatives in the Maghrib" in *Islamism and Secularism in North Africa*. Edited by J. Ruedy. London: Macmillan, 1994.

Zartman, I., ed. *Tunisia: The Political Economy of Reform*. London: Lynne Rienner, 1991.

Zghal, A. "Al-Mujtama' al-Madani Was-Sira' Min-Ajl al-Haymana al-Aydilujiyah Fil-Maghrib al-'Arabi." In *Al-Mujtama' al-Madani Fil-Watan al-'Arabi*. Beirut: Markaz Dirasat al-Wahda al-'Arabiyah (Arab Unity Studies Centre), 1992.

——. "The New Strategy of the Movement of the Islamic Way: Manipulation or Expression of Political Culture?" In *Tunisa: The Political Economy of Reform*. Edited by I. William Zartman. London: Lynne Rienner, 1991.

Index

Habannaka, Sheikh, 21
Haddad, at-Tahir al-, 44, 64
Haddad, Nicola, 112
Haddad, Yvonne, 178
Haiti, 178
hajj, 49, 65, 192
hakimiyah, 44, 131, 185-187
Hamdi, Mohamed Elhachmi, 209-213
Hamidullah, Muhammad, 27
Hamma, 3,6,7
Hanafi, Hasan, 44
Harakat al-Ittijah al-Islami. See MTI
Hasan, Mahmud Abdulkarim, 184
Hasan, Son of Ali, 193
Hassan, Bahey Eddin, 204, 205
Havel, Vaclav, 132
Hawwa, Said, 77
Hazm, ibn, 61
hedonism, 72
Hegel, 87, 128, 145
Heidegger, Martin, 132
Hemingway, Ernest, 8
Herzog, Chaim, 173
hijab, 114
Hijaz, 97
Hirmasi, Abdelbaqi al-, 50
Hizb-ut-Tahrir, 21, 23, 183, 197, 200
Hobbes, Thomas, 74, 141
Holaku, 161
Holyoak, George Jacob, 108, 109
Hugo, Victor, 8
human rights, 106, 118, 121, 124, 132, 139,
  147, 151, 153, 167, 170, 180, 181, 199,
  201, 215, 219; global movement of, 205;
  Universal Declaration of, 97
Human Rights Watch, 201
humanism, 108, 207
Huntington, Samuel, 172
Husri, Sati' al-, 20-21
Hussein, Saddam, 166, 177, 178, 213
Hussein, Sheif of Mecca, 164

Ibrahimi, Abdelhamid al-, 120
ijma', 80, 103, 185, 194
ijtihad, 41, 48, 49, 58, 59, 61, 80, 83, 84,
  99, 100, 132, 138, 140,169, 183, 188-
  189, 191, 197; activation of, 198; *faraghat*
  (spaces) for, 187
Ikhwan. See Muslim Brotherhood
Ilyas, Maulana Muhammad, 24

imamah, 101
imperialism, 15, 156, 186; cultural, 184
India, 160
individualism, 128, 130, 144, 149
industrialism, 116, 117
Indonesia, 205
industrialization, 145, 150, 167
Inland Revenue, 147
intégrisme scientiste, 167
Iqbal, Muhammad, 22, 76
Iran, 55, 102, 158, 174, 201, 204, 205, 206,
  211; Islamic Republic of, 156
Iranian revolution, 46, 53-56, 59, 64, 156,
  158, 171
Iraq, 56, 105, 164, 188, 190, 192, 193, 199,
  205, 206, 213
Irgun, Zionist terrorist group of, 6
Islamic civilization, 28
Islamic movement, 36, 38, 41, 45, 50, 53,
  57, 60, 64, 69, 88, 90, 201, 211, 215;
  and civil society, 126, 129
Islamic Salvation Front. See FIS
Islamic Tendency Movement. See MTI
Islamic Thought Seminars, 31
Islamism, 19, 50, 63, 209
Islamophobia, 172
Israel, 6, 24, 27, 119, 142, 143, 162, 168,
  173- 176, 177, 179, 180, 185, 213
Istanbul, 198
Italy, 102, 122, 151, 156

Ja'fari school, 55
Ja'fariyah, 27
jabriyah, al-, 41
jahiliyah, 44, 46, 163, 185-186, 197
Japan, 129
Jerusalem, 18, 21, 177, 180
Jewish, Defense League, 171; question, 176;
  tribes, 95
Jews, 95, 134, 143, 171, 179
jihad, 18, 42, 141, 161, 202
Jihad, Egyptian, 182
jihadis, 190, 197, 199, 200
Jobar, Michael, 121
Jones, Linda, 202
Jordan, 105, 106
Judaism, 171, 179
judiciary, 82, 83; independence of, 102,153,
  157, 195
jurisprudence, Muslim. See *fiqh*